Pvt. Ltd.

***Dedication***

*"We dedicate this book to our families".*

# Digital Forensic

## *Current Trends and Practices*

**Ruchira Naskar**
**Venkata Udaya Sameer**
**Rahul Dixit**
**Jamimamul Bakas**

**2019**

**Studium Press (India) Pvt. Ltd.**

# Digital Forensic
## *Current Trends and Practices*



ISBN: 978-93-85046-48-3

*Published by*:

**Studium Press (India) Pvt. Ltd.**
*4735/22, 2nd Floor, Prakash Deep Building*
*(Near Delhi Medical Association)*
*Ansari Road, Darya Ganj, New Delhi-110 002*
*Tel.: + 91-11-43240200-15 (15 lines); Fax: 91-11-43240215*
*E-mail: pubdir@studiumpress.in*

*Printed at India*

# About the Authors

## Dr. Ruchira Naskar

**Dr. Ruchira Naskar** is an Assistant Professor in the Department of Computer Science and Engineering, National Institute of Technology, Rourkela, India. She received a Ph.D. in Computer Science and Engineering from Indian Institute of Technology, Kharagpur, India. Major areas of her research interest are Multimedia Security and Image Processing. She has over 40 publications in international peer—reviewed journals and conferences of repute, and has one Indian patent filed, and one Indian copyright granted on her contributions in the area of Multimedia Security.

## Mr. Venkata Udaya Sameer

**Mr. Venkata Udaya Sameer** received his Bachelor in Technology (B.Tech.) degree in Computer Science and Engineering from Jawaharlal Nehru Technological University, Kakinada in 2009. He worked as Senior Software Engineer with Infosys Technologies for over 2.5 years. He received a degree in Master of Technology (M.Tech.) from International Institute of Information Technology, Bhubaneswar in 2014. He is currently pursuing a Ph.D. in Computer Science and Technology from National Institute of Technology, Rourkela. He has published in international peer reviewed journals and conferences of high repute and has one Indian copyright granted to his contributions in digital forensics. His research interests include digital forensics, multimedia security, cyber security and information security.

## Rahul Dixit

**Rahul Dixit** is Ph.D. scholar in the department of Computer Science & Engineering at National Institute of Technology, Rourkela, India. He has recently joined the Department of Computer Communication and Engineering, at Manipal University, Jaipur, India as an Assistant Professor. Major areas of his research interest include Digital Forensics and Multimedia Security. His work in the domain of Digital Forensics has been published in peer-reviewed journals and conferences of international repute.

## Jamimamul Bakas

**Jamimamul Bakas** is a Ph.D. scholar in the Department of Computer Science and Engineering, National Institute of Technology, Rourkela, India. His primary area of research interest is Digital Multimedia Forensics. His Ph.D. research is funded by the Board of Research in Nuclear Sciences (BRNS), Department of Atomic Energy, Govt. of India.

# Preface

The rapid increase in rate of cyber crime in today's digital era, has given rise to huge requirement of appropriate preventive security measures.The techniques that have been in use since past decades, such as digital rights management schemes as watermarking, or steganography, or cryptography in general, always involve some form of data pre-processing, in other words, some pre-cautionary measures on the user's part. However, given the large volumes of multimedia data transmitted and shared over the internet in the present day, it is not always feasible to assume that every user would have taken such a-priori precautions (such as always using a digital camera, specially equipped with specialized security chip or software, for capturing images), anticipating any forth-coming cyber security hazard. Moreover, given the fact that digital images and videos are largely being considered as prime evidences towards several events in court rooms or by the media and broadcast industries, protection of their security and integrity become a critical challenge today, especially without any above form of precautions taken.

Here comes the role of Digital Forensics, which is a rapidly evolving branch of science and technology, where cyber crime investigation and detection is completely based on data post-processing. Digital Forensics majorly deals with collection, evaluation and investigation of digital evidences remnant in cyber crime scenarios, which are often helpful clues to the forensic analyst to track the criminal or source of crime.

In this book we mainly address digital forensics for images and videos, since these form the crucial part of digital evidences produced in court-of-law in the present day. The first problem that we focus on in this book, is digital image source identification. We discuss about blind forensic techniques to identify source of a contentious image. The available solutions are either machine learning classification based, or based on camera fingerprinting. The second important problem taken up in this book is that of doctored image detection, Specifically, we talk about the problem of region duplication detection, whereby a part of a natural image is copied by an intelligent adversary, and pasted somewhere else in the image, so as to obscure or repeat significant image objects. Detection of this form of attack become more challenging due to the fact that this attack does not modify the natural image statistical properties. The third problem addressed involves forensics related to compressed multimedia. For example, JPEG images and MPEG videos. This form of multimedia is the most widely adopted one today, due to optimal space storage requirement. However, the challenge here is that, due to the compression effects, the existing forensic solution fails to detect any form of modification or tampering in these forms of data. Recent researches propose to utilize nothing other that compression artefacts in such images and videos, to detect tampering. Specifically, re-compression artefacts are used in this case, for JPEG/MPEG forgery detection. Finally, in this book, we write about counter-forensic attacks, which are attacks against existing forensic techniques. We study about counter-forensic attacks here, with an aim to find out how to strengthen the stat-of-the-art in digital forensics further.

The chapter-wise organization of the book is provided below:

*Chapter-1: Why Digital Forensics:* This chapter introduces the readers to the basics of Digital Forensics and its requirement in the present day in addition to already existing security protocols provided by cryptography. *Chapter-2: Most Common Forensic Problems Today:* In this chapter we state about the most important present day challenges to be addressed in the domain of Digital Forensics. These are the problems which are elaborated upon, throughout the remainder of this book.

*Chapter-3: Forensic Source Camera Identification- Challenges, Solutions and State-of-the-Art*: In this chapter, the source camera identification is introduced and the current state-of-the-art is presented briefly. The current research problems and possible solutions are also presented. The open problems include unknown models detection, combating counter forensics, and identifying the exact camera device. *Chapter-4*: *Features based Source Camera Identification*: In this chapter, the state-of-the-art machine learning based solutions to identify the source camera of an image are studied. The different feature sets such as Image Quality Metrics (IQM), Higher Wavelet Statistics (HOWS), Binary Similarity Measures (BSM), Image texture features, Co-occurrence features are studied in detail. Various classification methodologies such as using a Support Vector Machine (SVM) to using an ensemble of classifiers is discussed in this chapter.

*Chapter-5*: *PRNU Correlation based Forensic Techniques for Source Camera Identification*: In this chapter, the fingerprint based source camera identification approach is discussed. The Photo Response Non-Uniformity (PRNU) noise is treated as a unique trait to identify underlying camera source of an image. In this chapter we discuss the state-of-the-art forensic techniques that exploit PRNU fingerprints for blind image source identification. *Chapter-6: Unknown Model Detection in Source Camera Identification*: The problem that this chapter discusses is to identify unknown camera models in forensic source identification problem. Various state-of-the-art techniques such as Binary SVM, Decision Boundary Carving, K-unknown model detection, etc. are discussed in this chapter.

*Chapter-7: Recent Development: Deep Learning based Source Camera Identification*: In this chapter we, identify the recent developments in source camera identification which use deep learning as the basis of operation. *Chapter-8: Introduction to Region Duplication Attack or Copy-Move Forgery in Digital Images*: In this chapter, we introduce the problem of copy-move forgery or region supplication detection in images and discuss about the solutions in general.

*Chapter-9: Region Duplication Attack and its Forensic Solutions – State-of-the-Art Research Practices*: This chapter presents a detailed overview of existing solutions to region duplication detection. We categorize the available solution hence. *Chapter-10: Image Block Matching based Region Duplication Detection*: Image block matching forms one class of solutions to region duplication detection. In this chapter we elaborate on the operating principle of block-matching based region duplication detection.

*Chapter-11: Addressing Post-Processing Attacks in Copy-Move Forgery Detection*: Region duplication detection becomes more challenging, given the presence of additional post-processing attacks, such as edge blurring in images. In this chapter we provide a solution to such problem of post-processing detection in copy-move forgery.

*Chapter-12: Combining Geometric and Post-Processing Attacks in Copy-Move Forgery:* This chapter presents a solution to identify a combination of multiple post-processing attacks (like noise addition, edge blurring, brightness adjustment) and geometric attacks (like rotation, rescale), in copy-move forgery.

*Chapter-13: Region Duplication Detection Using Image Key-points*: In this chapter, we present the second class of digital forensic solution to region duplication detection, that is, image keypoint matching based region duplication detection. Such techniques in general are more computationally efficient as compared to block matching technqiues. *Chapter-14: Double Compression based Forgery Detection in Images and Videos:* In this chapter we introduce the readers to forensic problems specific to compressed multimedia such as JPEG images and MPEG videos. We also present two state-of-the-art schemes for forgery detection in JPEG and MPEG in this chapter.

*Chapter-15: Intra and Inter Frame Video Forgery Detection: State-of-the-Art Problems and Solutions*: We identify the different forensic problems associated with video forgery detection in this chapter, and provide state-of-the-art solutions to those. *Chapter-16: Present Day Counter Forensic Challenges:* This chapter introduces the readers to the present day counter forensics challenges which need to be addressed immediately. Specifically, we elaborate on different counter-forensic attacks that have been devised till date.

*Chapter-17: Deep Learning based Counter Forensics*: In this chapter, we provide a recently proposed deep learning based solution to perform blind source identification with counter-forensic images, hence to limit the adverse effect of counter-forensics.

---

## ACKNOWLEDGEMENT

The authors would like to thank the Department of Computer Science and Engineering, National Institute of Technology (NIT), Rourkela, for providing sufficient access to resources for writing this book, and carrying out related research for it. The authors are thankful to all members of *Digital Forensic Laboratory,* Department of Computer Science and Engineering, NIT Rourkela, for their support and encouragement throughout this journey.

# Table of Contents

# 1
# Why Digital Forensics?

## 1. INTRODUCTION

In today's digital world, every common man's regular life encompasses huge volume of multimedia data transmission and exchange, across the globe. This, on one hand, has borne massive benefits for the human race in terms of person-to-person communication as well as network communications, especially to access data remotely and avail remote services such as online disease diagnosis and treatment. However, on the other hand, it has given rise to huge perils whereby sensitive and secure data have fallen into the risks of losing integrity-confidentiality, and moreover, risk the possibility of being exploited at the hands of adversaries and criminals. This, many times leads to massive loss of human rights, emphasizing enhancement of rate of cyber-crimes, and getting innocents falsely charged and accused.

In this case, it becomes a critical question as how to verify integrity and authenticity of digital multimedia, and how to preserve their integrity. This becomes even a greater requirement in sensitive legal and media applications, where majority of the prime evidences towards a cyber crime or a general crime scene, is constituted by digital images, videos and audios. Such as CCTV footages often produced in the court-of-law as legal evidences. Even the media and broadcast industries operate based on such clues obtained/collected, which is capable to impact large masses. Before considering such multimedia data as sources of evidence towards any event, it is an absolute requirement that the credibility and trust-worthiness of such data be verified and proven. It has now become a child's play to tamper with such multimedia data. A number of efficient yet low-cost image, video and audio editing software and tools are available widely today. This helps adversaries to easily modify multimedia files. Artificially generated videos, computer generated (artificial) images (CGI), and edited audio (speed/volume/pitch edited) are some of the examples to the above. The adverse effects range from video and audio piracy, to more serious issues of child pornography and terrorism attacks, all of which can be implemented based on artificially generated or tampered images, audio and video.

Hence, we need efficient security mechanisms in place, which would be capable enough to address all present day security issues, as discussed above. Given the large volumes of multimedia data transmitted on a regular day-to-day basis in the present day, scalability is also an added concern. The traditional security mechanisms mainly target to prevent/detect such attacks and resist our system against such vulnerabilities, based on some form of data pre-processing. Here lies the major difference between forensic investigation and traditional security measures. Forensic investigations are solely based on post-processing of data, without involvement of any form of pre-processing or precautionary measures.

In the following we provide two real life scenarios where traditional security measures would be helpful:

- Let us consider the case of digital rights protection of a video. A video which is recorded by a specially equipped recorder or camcorder, where a specialized software or hardware chip is used to equip the device, will be resistant to video piracy or illegal copy. This is conventionally made possible by insertion of device specific fingerprints, watermarks or hash into the media.
- Another example is preservation of data confidentiality. In this, using special encryption and decryption oracles, the user is able to preserve the confidentiality of data, which of course requires a-priori key negotiation or exchange between the users.

Now, with such traditional security measures as watermarking, steganography or cryptography in general, problem arises in cases where the users involved did not have the opportunity to adopt any precautionary measure. Since all traditional security measures are based on data pre-processing, which in other words is nothing but precautions adopted by the user(s), in such scenarios the traditional security mechanisms are bound to fail. For example, the device involved was not equipped any specialized security software or hardware chip. Once an event took place and got over, it is now the task of a *forensic analyst* to investigate the scenario, and come up with correct conclusions regarding the event. Such as the sources of image/video/audio forgery, the source device which captured the file (without considering the device header or fingerprint, which might be easily tampered or replaced), the owner of the device, and so on. Such forensic applications majorly relate to cyber crime scenarios.

In this introductory chapter, we aim to provide a basic knowledge about what exactly digital forensics encompasses, why is it required in addition to the traditional security measures in today's date, how is this branch of research different from the traditional ones, and finally an overview of requirements of present day forensics techniques, given the boom of online social networking today.

Rest of the chapter is organized as follows. In Section 2, we compare between traditional security measures and the much newer digital forensic branch of security, and hence establish the requirement of both. In Section 3, we discuss about the role of digital forensics in online social networking. We conclude the chapter in Section 4.

## 2. TRADITIONAL SECURITY MEASURES *VIS-À-VIS* DIGITAL FORENSICS, THE FIELD IN MULTIMEDIA SECURITY

The last couple of decades have seen rapid growth of research interest in the fields of *Digital Content Protection* and *Digital Rights Management*, due to rapid increase of cyber-crime rate. The most widely used practices in this direction encompass digital techniques such as *Watermarking* and *Steganography*. In this section we discuss the major difference and benefit of digital forensic techniques, over such traditional digital content protection measures.

In *Digital Watermarking* techniques, the data to be protected (*cover data*) undergoes some form of pre-processing such as embedding, compression (lossless or lossy) etc., which later help to detect malicious third party interventions. The *watermark* is a piece of information that is kept embedded into the cover data and is used to provide security to the cover data. For example, the watermark may be authentication information such as hash computed over the cover data, which is subsequently extracted and matched for detecting modification attacks or tampering activities. The major purposes of digital watermarking are digital rights management, secure media distribution and authentication.

On the other hand, *Steganography* refers to the act of hiding data into digital media without drawing any suspicion from an observer (either manual or automated).. The major purpose of Steganography is to protect sensitive data against eavesdropping while transmission over an insecure channel. This is achieved by embedding the sensitive data into a *stego-file* while transmission. It is assumed that no active attack is carried out on the stego-file while transmission. Steganography is sometimes discussed in the same breath as cryptography; however, they are essentially different arts. Cryptography scrambles a message, so an uninvited reader is unable to understand it. On the other hand, steganography is about secrecy, so a potential eavesdropper won't even have a reason to suspect there's a hidden message to be read, or if he does search for it, would be unable to recover it.

All such techniques belong to the class of *non-blind* cyber security measures. *Non-blind* security measures are those which mandatorily need some external information in addition to the data to be secured; and such external information is obtained by preprocessing the data in some form or the other. For example, the watermark (or hash) in Digital Watermarking is a form of pre-computed external data. However, such external data pre-computation is not possible in every situation. Also in Steganography, the cover-image into which the sensitive image is hidden, may be viewed as additional information. Securing multimedia data by Digital Watermarking or Steganography can only be enforced by means of special software, embedded into the devices forming the image or video. Considering that digital images and videos act as major evidences in court of law worldwide, it now becomes mandatory that all image and video capturing devices be designed to have special security capabilities such as encryption, watermarking and data embedding. However, these added capabilities usually increase the cost of such devices, which adversely affects the business of the camera manufacturing companies. This, along with ever-increasing cyber crime rates, has lead to the search of *blind* security measures with the expectation to reduce the need for pre-computing any additional information.

Digital forensics is a developing research field which aims at *blind digital forgery detection.* Digital forensic techniques provide security and protection to multimedia data in those situations where the user has neither any apriori information about that data to be secured, nor has carried out any computation on the data prior to forgery detection. Such techniques do not need any external information, apart from the data to be secured. The goal of digital forensics is cyber forgery detection without any requirement of preprocessing the data to be secured. Hence such techniques belong to the class of *blind* security measures for digital content protection. Block diagrams demonstrating the operation of digital forensic techniques, and traditional digital content protection measures, have been presented in Fig. 1.

## 3. THE ROLE OF DIGITAL FORENSICS IN THE DOMAIN OF ONLINE SOCIAL NETWORKING (OSN)

Given the above, a major security concern in today's digital world, is to protect the integrity of digital multimedia data, especially in cases where they are shared/transmitted in huge numbers on a regular basis, over social networking sites. Especially with the vast evolution of Online Social Networks in the present day, the above problem has been aggravated. A major dimension of today's digital era is constituted of Online Social Network (OSN) usage. Today, every common man's day-to-day life involves vast amount of information sharing and transmission over the internet, *via* OSNs, out of which the principle component is image and video sharing. Vast number of images are uploaded and downloaded on a regular basis on every social networking websites, especially the ones popular to the common mass such as Facebook, Twitter, Instagram and Whatsapp. Each OSN has its own proprietary compression features, which are applied to the images before they are uploaded, stored or transmitted. In presence of such inherent image compression features of the OSNs, the existing forensic techniques for forged image or video detection, fail. So, this has given rise to the requirement of specialized security protocols applicable to OSN forensics.

The state-of-the-art digital forensic techniques, however, are not suitable to work with images downloaded from online social networks. This is because, online social networks impart specific image artefacts, due to proprietary image compression requirements for storage and transmission, which prevents accurate forensic source investigations.

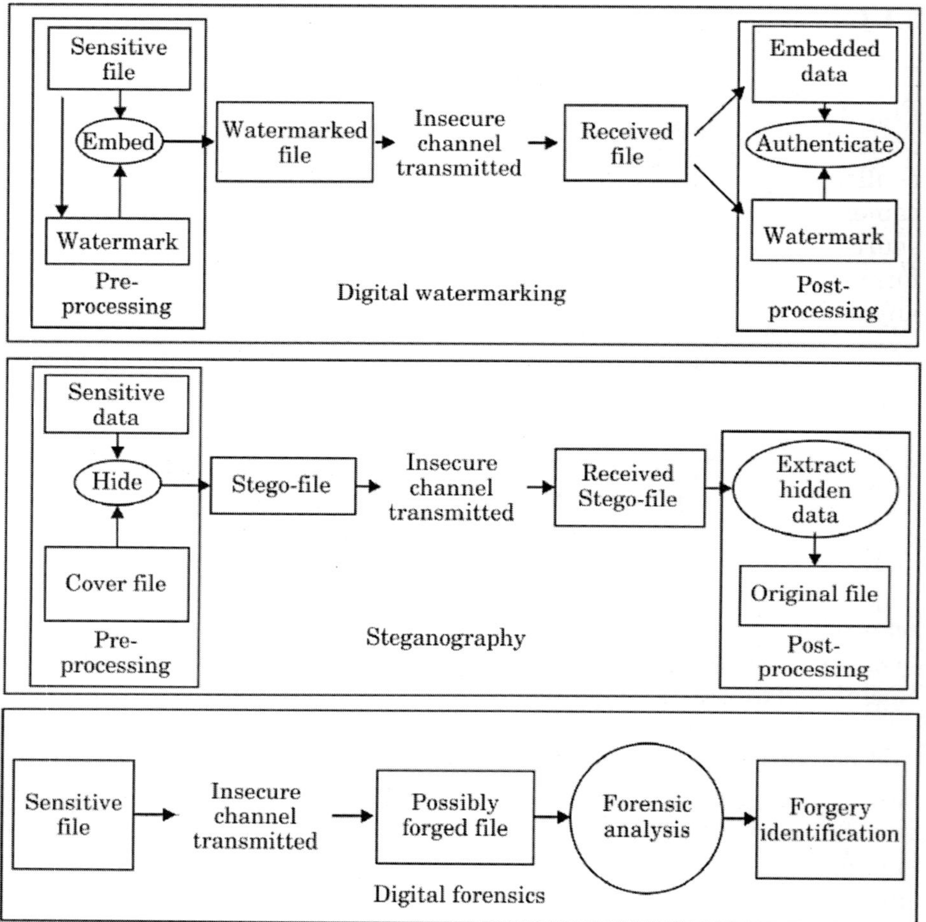


**Fig. 1:** Block diagrams representing the operation of traditional security measures *vis-à-vis* modern day digital forensic techniques, completely based on post-processing investigation. (Top) Digital Watermarking, (middle) Steganography; and (bottom) blind Digital Forensic technique.

Moreover, each social network has its own compression standards, which are never made public due to ethical issues. This makes forensic investigation tasks even more difficult for the forensic analysts. In present day and age, where there is abundant use of social networks for image transmission, it is high time that forensic investigation with images downloaded from social networks, be efficiently addressed.

In this section, we present a case study to demonstrate the impact of social networks on image forensics.

## 3.1 Case Study

The forensic problem taken up in this case study has been depicted in Fig. 2(A), where we depict the common forensic problem of *source camera identification.* (All common present-day forensic problems and challenges will be discussed in the next chapter). The forensic source camera identification problem relates to investigation and detection of source of a contentious multimedia file, which did not undergo any form of pre-processing. That is, the forensic analyst does not possess any device specific watermark/hash/fingerprint to let correct image-to-source mapping.

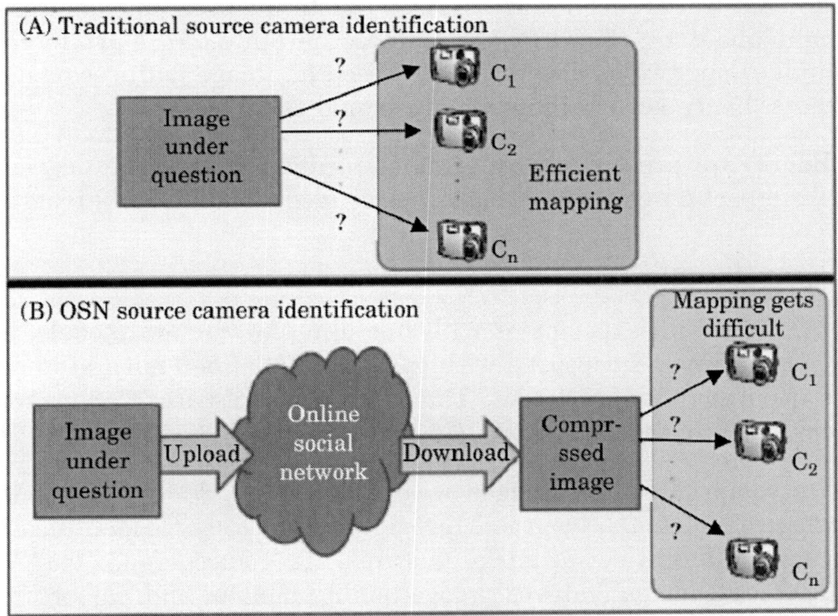


**Fig. 2:** Traditional forensic source camera identification *vs.* Source camera identification with OSNs

In this example, we have shown image source identification. The task of the forensic analyst here is to map a given image to its correct source device of original, from out of a closed set of *n* possibilities, completely based on post-processing of the given image. In general this problem of forensic source is identification, operate in either one of two ways:

(a) Either by modelling the problem as a machine learning classification model, where *features* from a large set of training samples generated with all possible devices of origin, are collected, and a machine is trained to predict the correct source with those.

(b) Or by noise residue based source identification, where the image *noise residue* is used to map it back to its source, by correlating this noise content with the sensor pattern noise of the cameras.

Fig. 2(B) depicts the impact of Online Social Networks (OSNs) on the above problem. When the above problem is addressed with images downloaded from OSNs, the efficiency of the forensic investigation drastically drops. In this case, the forensic analysis fails because the image's natural properties are harmed due to the inherent compressed brought about by the OSN. And since the state-of-the-art forensic techniques operate as above, that is based on image features or noise contents, hence such techniques are bound to fail here.

Below, we present an experiment to demonstrate the degree of OSN's impact on existing forensic source identification techniques.

### 3.2 Experiment

We performed an experiment with *five* different camera models, and 100 natural images captured with each. A total of 500 natural images were used in this experiment. The camera models are: *Canon A640, Nikon D200, Nikon D70, Sony H50* and *Sony T77*.

We compressed the images with different JPEG quality factors ranging from 50 to 90. Then we performed forensic source identification with four different set of image features, *viz.* co-occurrence features, residual local image features, image quality metrics and higher order wavelet statistical features, and image noise residual. (All these feature sets belong to the state-of-the, which have proven to be efficient in forensic source camera identification. We discuss more on these image features and their extraction in Chapters 4 and 5 later).

Finally, we measured the accuracy of source prediction with the compressed images. The results are presented in Table 1 below, which shows that even with compression ratio 90, the source prediction accuracy drops considerably.

Since every OSN (like Facebook, Whatsapp, Instagram etc.) enforces a considerable degree of compression on the images uploaded to it, the above example and its results gives us an estimate of the effect of such compression, enforced by OSNs, on prevalent forensic source identification techniques.

**Table 1:** Forensic source identification accuracy drop with JPEG compressed images. Results presented in terms of detection accuracy (%)

| | ***Compression Ratio*** | | |
|---|---|---|---|
| ***Image Features*** | ***90*** | ***75*** | ***50*** |
| Co-occurrence features | 62.7% | 60.8% | 57.9% |
| Residual local features | 63.1% | 61.8% | 59.6% |
| Image noise residual | 75.3% | 74.6% | 74.2% |
| Image quality metrics and higher order wavelet statistical features | 78.5% | 77.4% | 76.2% |

This again proves the requirement of specialized digital forensic techniques capable of operating in an OSN environment, that is with highly compressed digital images and videos.

## 4. CONCLUSIONS

In this chapter, we have introduced the readers to the basics of digital forensics, and related present day challenges. We have highlighted the main difference in operation of such techniques, as compared to the traditional security measures. Finally, we presented a case study with an experiment to demonstrate how present-day Online Social Networks adversely impact the accuracy of such forensic techniques; hence paving the path for devising even more efficient forensic technology, with would be capable enough for such social networking environments. In the next chapter, we shall introduce the readers to the most common forms of digital forensic problems in the present day.

# 2

# Most Common Forensic Problems Today

## 1. INTRODUCTION

In the last chapter we have introduced digital forensics, the field of research and its requirement in the present day. We have seen a case study which establishes the further developmental requirements in this domain, given the recent advancements and rapid use of Online Social Networks (OSNs), which have now become the main platform for sharing and exchange of multimedia files.

In the case study we encountered a very common present day digital forensic problem of blind source camera identification. This is the problem of mapping a specific multimedia file, often in relation to cyber-crime investigation, back to its correct source. Digital forensic approach to solve such problem is *blind* in the sense that all investigations and subsequent decisions here, are based on complete post-processing based forensic analysis. The existing solution to the problem of blind forensic source detection, are mainly two-way: First, feature based machine learning classification approach; and second, noise pattern based correlation approach.

The above problem is one out of many forensic problems which need attention in the present day. In this chapter discuss all those problems and the solutions to those which are available, or possible.

One of the most predominant among the present day forensic problems is the problem of *blind source identification* of images and

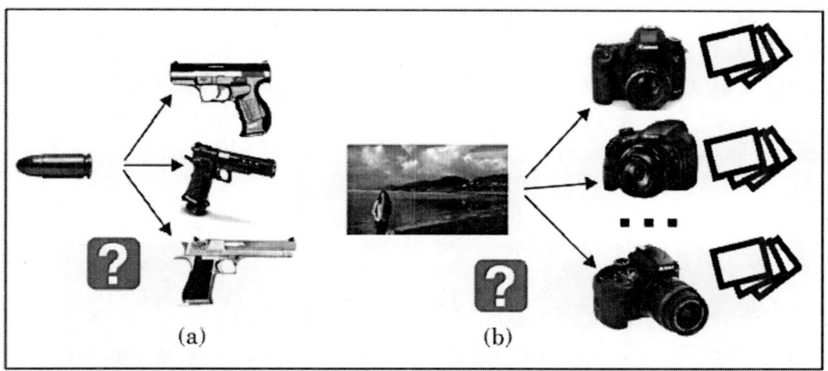


**Fig. 1:** The forensic source identification problem: An analogy.

videos, which has been briefly introduced above and depicted in Fig. 1. Fig. 1 presents an analogy between the legal scenario of tracing a criminal his revolver's bullet marks left behind at the crime scene, and the forensic investigative case of tracing the source of an image from the artefacts left behind by the capturing device. Just like a bullet leaves behind bullet scratches/marks, which may later on be used as clues to trace its source, similarly, a digital device leaves behind some artefacts into an image/video while capturing its, which is later on studied and investigate by the forensic analyst to trace the source of the image/video.

The second problem involves detection of computer generated images (CGI). This basically involves differentiation between artificial images and natural images. It is not sufficient to merely detect an image/ video to be tampered or artificially modified, but also it is equally necessary in sensitive application domain to identify the region of the tampering or forgery. This might be some portions of the image, or some frames in a video, or selective regions within some frames of a video. Artificial modification of images are brought about by selecting some image regions and copying it onto the same image, at a different location. This is done with the malicious intention to obscure or regenerate significant objects within an image. This form of attack is called *copy-move forgery* or *region duplication attack,* which is shown in Fig. 2 . Fig. 2 depicts that a part of the bush shown in the original image is copied and pasted at a different location to obscure the truck object, hence generating a forged image. It appears in the forged image that at the scene only a jeep was present, and there was no truck. This, when done with a malicious intention, would easily mislead any legal investigation. The other form of attack to generate artificial images is *splicing* or *image compositing*. Hereby, portions from two different (natural) images are combined to produce an illusion of a third natural image.

**Fig. 2:** Example of region duplication attack in digital images. (Left) Original image (Right) Forged image.

The third most important problem in the area of digital multimedia forensics is detection of forgery specific to compressed domain multimedia. For example, JPEG and MPEG are the most widely adopted image and video formats today. Almost all present day digital devices capture and store multimedia files in such lossy compressed formats. Now, due to the effect of compression, the state-of-the-art forensic solutions to detect image/video forgeries, fail. (This has also been proven by a case study in Chapter 1 of this book). Hence, a new problem arises which involves detection of tampering in compressed domain multimedia files.

There have been number of researches towards identification of forgeries in JPEG and MPEG files. Most of the existing techniques exploit the compression artefacts of such files. Such techniques are based on the finding that, when a compressed image or video is tampered with, the compression artefacts get affected. Specifically, it generates a *re-compression artefact*. That is, the manipulated portions of the image/video get doubly compressed, giving rise to non-uniformity of compression ratios within a single image/video. These re-compression artefacts are what are exploited in forensic investigation of this form of forgery. Hence, such techniques are combinedly called *re-compression based forgery detection* mechanisms. In Fig. 3, we show an example of tampering in a JPEG image which can be detected by re-compression based forensic techniques. This figure shows a JPEG attack, where the central region of the JPEG gets resaved at a different compression ratio, after manipulation.Hence, in the original image (Fig. 3(a)), the quality factor is QF1; the central portion which undergoes the attack now assumes a second quality factor QF2 (shown in Fig. 3(b)), and the forged image assumes two different quality factors QF1, QF2 (shown in Fig. 3(c)).

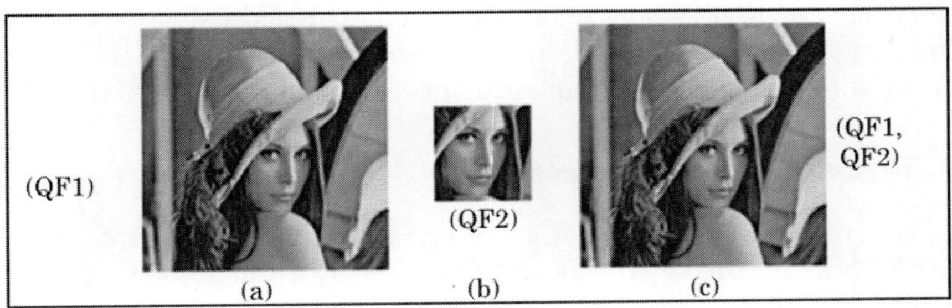


**Fig. 3:** Example of multi-compression based JPEG attack.

The fourth challenge in present day digital forensic research domain is that of combating *counter forensics*. Counter forensics is the art and science of preventing forensic measures. This can be viewed as an attack to forensic technology, just like the branch of *cryptanalysis* is aimed to defeat cryptography. A number of counter forensic attacks against the existing forensic techniques have come up very recently. This is now a rapidly evolving and expanding domain. Hence, it is no more sufficient to have efficient forensic investigation techniques in place. But, alongside we also need to make those safe, secure and resistant against these forms of counter forensic attacks.

In this chapter we elaborate on the above problems, and provide an insight nto their possible solutions.

The rest of the chapter is organized as follows. In Section 2, we elaborate on the problem of forensic source identification, along with probable solutions to the problem. In Section 3, we present the problem of doctored image detection in forensics. In Section 4, we discuss about re-compression based JPEG forgery detection. We conclude this chapter in Section 5.

## 2. IMAGE SOURCE IDENTIFICATION

The origin of an image many times forms important evidence in the court of law. Image source identification deals with recognizing the device which is responsible for formation and storage of the image under question. In cases where an intruder tries to forge the image source, it may be useful for the forensic analyzer to indicate device or class of device captured the image, or at least which did not. The area of forensic research, discussed in this section, is dedicated for this kind of investigation and analysis. First, we shall briefly discuss the various components of a present-day image capturing device: the digital camera.

### 2.1. Digital Camera Components

The two major components of an image capturing device are the *lens* and the *sensor*. Below we discuss their roles in image formation and storage, in a digital camera:

**A.** ***Taking Lens:*** Forms an image of the scene (in front of the camera) on the surface of the sensor. The taking lens is responsible for bending and curving the path of incident radiation, so as to make it reach the sensor.

**B.** ***Sensor:*** Converts incident radiation into photocharges, which are subsequently digitized and stored as raw image data. Basic imaging element of a sensor is a "pixel" and a sensor is made up of a rectilinear grid of pixels. The sensor is responsible for sensing a sampled version of the image formed. A good sensor forms generates photocharges at precise locations in the image and also prevents subsequent random dispersion of these charges, until they are read out. After capturing the incident radiation in form of photocharges in a digital camera sensor, what remains is to acquire the color information about the image. This is done by *color filters.*

**C.** ***CFA:*** *Color filters* are nothing but (single or multiple) thin layer(s) of different colorants, laid on the surface of the camera sensor. An array of pixel sized color filters, arranged over the sensor surface, enables detection of full color information of an image, using only a single sensor. This array is called *CFA* or *Color Filter Array*.

Since a color image can be fully digitally represented by three components, for *e.g.* RGB (Red Green Blue), precise capture of full color information of an image requires a set of at least three sensors at each pixel location. However this specification would highly increase the cost and complexity of manufacturing the device. Hence in conventional digital cameras, at each pixel location is designed to sample only one color. Hence the cost and complexity are reduced by the use of single color filter at each pixel location; the missing colors are interpolated from the neighboring pixel locations. CFA interpolation is often termed as *Demosaicing*. The Bayer patter, shown in Fig. 4, is one such example of arrangement strategy for color filters over a sensor CFA. The Bayer pattern uses 50% green filters and 25% filters to sense each of red and blue color, taking into account the fact that the HVS is more sensitive to the green component of a an RGB image. In this pattern, at each pixel location, one color is precisely recorded and other two colors are interpolated from the neighboring pixels.

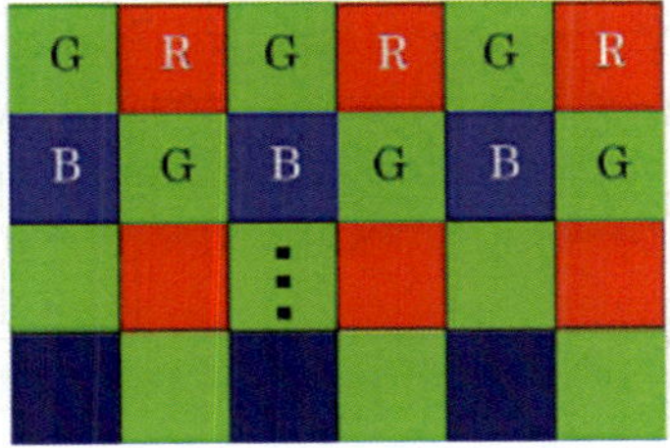


**Fig. 4:** Bayer pattern

After collection of color information of an image is over and the interpolated image is available, some further image enhancement steps, such as sensor noise reduction, color correction, edge enhancement etc. are carried out before the finished image is finally produced in the camera.

Information about the image and its source may be obtained from image metadata, such as the file header or EXIF (Exchangeable image file format). Such metadata include information such as camera make and model (but not the specific camera identity), manufacturer details, image size, date and time of image capture, compression ratio in JPEG images, etc. However, such information contained in the file header is highly vulnerable to modification attacks. Hence we need blind forensic techniques to throw some light on the origin of an image. Next, we shall present the state-of-the-art digital forensic techniques, proposed for image source investigation.

Blind forensic techniques exploit the different traces left behind in an image, as a result of various processing steps, while its formation and storage by a particular device. Those traces or artefacts are formed in an image in either one of two steps:

(a) *Image Acquisition:* Image Acquisition artefacts are nothing but either the distortions generated by the camera lens while capturing a scene, or the sensor noise produced during color information acquisition (and interpolation) by the CFA.

(b) *Image Storage:* Image storage artefacts are those patterns which are generated in an image while processing it for storage in a standard format. Such processing activities includes noise removal, image enhancement etc.

The image artefacts described above, function as means of distinguishing between different camera models, depending on their components such as the camera lens. Those artefacts may also provide specific device related information, utilizing the traces produced by the sensor.

## 2.2. Source Identification Based on Lens Aberration

The primary feature for distinguishing one camera model from another, is the camera lens. Model specific (photosensitive or geometric) properties of a lens cause some distortions to be created in its captured images. This kind of image distortions are collectively called *lens aberration.*

One example on lens aberration is *chromatic lens aberration*, which provides an efficient measure to identify digital forgery an image. *Chromatic lens aberration* refers to the lens imperfection that causes a point of incident light to form an image on an imprecise sensor location. The shift in position of the point of light (formed on the sensor surface), varies with the wavelength of incident radiation, due to difference in *angle of refraction.* Due to this fact, in an image, there must be some specific alignment between the locations at which the sensor receives lights from different color channels. However, if an adversary transplants some external data into an image, this color channel specific location alignment, is found to be different in the transplanted image region, compared to its neighborhood. This feature can be exploited to identify forged images. Another lens feature used to identify image source device is *radial aberration. Radial aberration* is the geometric distortion produced by a lens which makes the straight lines in a scene to appear curved, in the image capture. The deviation of image (curved) lines from the original (straight) lines formed by a particular lens may be used as a camera fingerprint. Radial aberration artifacts can be efficiently used as image source device identifier as well. However, this feature cannot distinguish between distinct exemplars belonging to the same camera model, hence using identical lens.

## 2.3. Source Identification Based on Sensor Noise and Processing Artefacts

As discussed previously the sensor of camera converts incident radiation into photo-electric charges, which are subsequently converted to digital values and later stored into the memory. Before storage, the image undergoes other processing steps such as white balancing, gamma correction, noise reduction, image enhancement and JPEG compression. These processing steps induce some sort of unique pattern or fingerprint on the image, which may be used as sensor identifier by a forensic analyzer. Various digital forensic researchers have modeled the artifacts produced by the sensor and the subsequent processing steps, to identify the image origin. For example, some authors have modeled the camera sensor noise and processing artifacts, by analyzing a set of images formed by the camera. The noise model may be represented as:

$$I' = IK + N \tag{1}$$

where $I$ is the distortion-free image, $I'$ is the observed image having sensor noise and processing artifacts, K is the sensor-generated noise pattern called *Photo Response Non Uniformity* (*PRNU*), and N is the noise contribution of other processing steps.

The above model (Eq. 1) estimates the noise of an image for a specific camera. This estimate may be used for authenticating an image, claimed to be originating from a particular camera. Noise in an image, actually originating from the camera, will have high correlation with the estimated value; whereas low correlation indicates forgery, the where observed noise value largely deviates from the estimated value.

During the *demosaicing* phase of image acquisition, characteristic artefacts are left on the image in form of specific pattern, which may serve the purpose of digital fingerprint or signature of the capturing device. *Demosaicing* involves interpolation of a particular (missing) color component, at a particular pixel location, from its neighboring pixels. For example, in Fig. 4 pixel at location (2,4) has the G (green) color component information only. The R (red) component at pixel location (2,4) is computed by interpolation of R values of pixels (1,4) and (3,4). Similarly, its B (Blue) component is computed by interpolation of B values at (2,3) and (2,5). Every demosaicing algorithm leaves behind a specific pattern on the final complete color image. This pattern represents nothing but a specific correlation among the precise and interpolated values, at various locations for a particular color channel. Such demosaicing algorithm based image artefacts have often served as indicators to the image source device in various digital forensic techniques.

### 2.4. Image Storage Based

The final step of image formation is image storage. The image storage stage also provides cues to identify image source device. In this chapter we shall discuss the standard JPEG image format. JPEG is used to compress an image so that it occupies less space in the memory. The JPEG standard applies DCT to each $8 \times 8$ image block and quantizes the DCT coefficients by a factor $q$. The quantized DCT coefficients are what actually represent the compressed JPEG image. However, JPEG is a *lossy compression* technique where some information is permanently lost in the process. The complete (original) image data cannot be retrieved by decompressing the JPEG image. JPEG compression produces permanent, camera-specific patterns or artifacts in the stored image, which are exploited by many forensic researchers as unique image source identifier.

Image *thumbnails* are also used by some forensic analyzers as finger prints to identify the device. A thumbnail is a low-resolution representation of a complete image. It is mainly used for simultaneous preview of multiple images, stored in a device. Thumbnail formation encompasses various image processing steps such as JPEG compression, cropping, down-sampling and filtering, which generate device-specific artefacts in the thumbnails.

## 3. DOCTORED IMAGE FORENSICS

Natural images refer to images of natural events or scenes. Many digital forensic methods exploit the statistical characteristics, inherently present in natural images (for *e.g.,* very high pixel-value correlation) to identify forged or unnatural images. Image editing software is usually the major mean of producing such unnatural images, which the attackers generate with a target to deceive the viewer. In this section we present "visual descriptors", as means to differentiate between natural and unnatural (or computer-generated) images.

*Visual descriptors* are the characteristic features of a digital image that describes its visual appearance. In natural images, visual descriptors are used to quantify the visual stimulus that the image produces in the *Human Visual System* (*HVS*). One example of visual descriptors to identify natural images, is *color properties* of the image. The other visual descriptor used is *texture*. *Gabor Texture Descriptor* have been found to be particularly helpful here. The intensity of edges in an image, also serve as visual descriptors to differentiate between natural and computer-generated images. *Regularity in color composition* is another statistical feature inherent in natural images that can be exploited for identification of forged computer-generated images.

Examples of other natural image statistics used in digital image forensics are shadow texture, surface roughness or smoothness, power spectrum of image etc. Wavelet domain coefficients and various moments of the wavelet distribution, such as mean and variance, are also used by some researchers as natural image statistics in digital forensics.

### 3.1. Image Forensics for Copy-move Forgery or Region Duplication Attack

In copy-move forgery, one portion of an image is copied and moved to another region of the same image (as discussed in introduction), with the intention to obscure the latter from the viewer. Copy-move attack is more prevalent in images having uniform texture or patterns, for *e.g.* sand, grass, water etc. There must be repetition of one or more regions in a copy-move forged image. This kind of repetition is termed as "cloning", and digital forensic techniques to identify copy-move forgery are based on identification of such repetitions or "cloning" activities in an image.

One of the earliest digital forensic techniques for copy-move attack, proposed by Fridrich *et al.,* in[1] is based on the principle of cloning identification. In [1], the authors search for two image regions, having exactly identical pixel values. However standard images consisting of thousands of pixels, it is computationally quite infeasible to carry out a brute-force search to find such identical (image region) pairs. To make the searching efficient, the authors divide the entire image into fixed-sized blocks and then sort the blocks lexicographically. Post-sorting, extraction of identical image blocks from this sorted list is trivial. Note that in this case, there may be more than one pairs of identical blocks.

While transplanting an image block onto some other region of the image, many times the adversary needs to resize the block, to match the dimension of the region to obscure. One such forgery approach has been presented in[2]. Here, the attacker resizes the image by up-sampling or down-sampling the image signal. This kind of forgery is detected by searching for signal correlation among different image blocks. When a block is down-sampled by a factor of two, every alternate sample in the original block may be found in the re-sampled block. Alternatively, when a block is up-sampled by a factor of two, every sample in the original block may be found in the new block, along with alternate samples in the new block being linear combination of its neighbors. Re-sampling image blocks by any integer factor induces such periodic correlations among original and forged image blocks. Re-sampling (by an integer factor) induces such periodic correlations among original and forged image blocks. Such correlation among signal samples, a phenomenon not prevalent in natural images[2], is exploited in digital forensics to detect transplantation of re-sampled image blocks.

The image blocks which are transplanted may also be geometrically transformed by the attacker in many situations, *e.g.* an image block may be rotated by some angle by the attacker before it is transplanted. In such case, duplicate image regions may be detected by matching SIFT (Scale-invariant feature transform) keypoints of the regions. Such forensic approaches to diagnose copy-move forgery having geometrically transformed image blocks, have been proposed in[3,4].

### 3.2. Forgery Involving Multiple Images

A forged image formed by compositing multiple (different) images cannot be identified by the forensic analysis techniques applicable to single image forgery, such as cloning detection or detection of image regions re-sampling or transformation. However, there exist some differences in statistical features between the composed image regions, coming from distinct images. Those statistical differences are often helpful for digital forensic investigators to identify forgeries involving multiple images.

Detection of forgeries involving multiple images may be done by analysis of patterns, left within the image by the capturing device. Different cameras leave different unique patterns or fingerprints on the images they capture. When a composed image is analyzed based on such characteristic of the camera sensor, it gives clues regarding different regions of the image being captured by different devices.

## 4. RE-COMPRESSION BASED FORGERY DETECTION IN JPEG

As mentioned previously, in most present-day digital camera the standard format for image storage is JPEG (Joint Photographic Experts Group). This standard is used due to the fact that JPEG format provides the best compression, hence optimal space requirement for image storage. The statistical as well as perceptual redundancy in natural images, are efficiently exploited in JPEG compression. Moreover, the JPEG format has an adaptive compression scheme that allows saving in varying levels of compression. However, every time we compress an image some space is saved but at the same time some information loss occurs. Also when the image is reconstructed from its JPEG compressed version, it contains degradations compared to the original image. Although the loss of information is disadvantageous while image forgery detection, various JPEG features are advantageous for identification of alteration or modification of JPEG images.

In the technique proposed by[5], the phenomenon of multiple JPEG compressions in an image is exploited. Let us consider a modification attack carried out on a JPEG image. To deliver such tampering, the attacker first opens the image in an image editing software, manipulates some regions of the image, and finally resaves the image back in JPEG format. In this entire process, some regions of the image get compressed more than once. Hence, compression of the forged part is different from the rest of the image. This difference in compression provides evidence of image manipulation and is useful in the detection of forgery.

*JPEG ghost classification*[6] is a forensic analysis technique that enables detection of multiple JPEG compressions in an image. Multiple JPEG compressions limited to specific image regions are also detectable by investigation of JPEG ghosts. JPEG ghosts differentiate between the different compression ratio in the image while compressing the image more than once. A JPEG ghost is uncovered by comparing original and resaved versions of an image. The technique of JPEG image forgery detection through analysis of JPEG ghosts is beneficial in situations where some parts of the image is forged and it is very difficult to visually identify the tampering. Digital forensic techniques for JPEG forgery detection, based on analysis of JPEG ghosts are proposed in[5,6].

The procedure followed in standard JPEG compression[7] is as follows:

1. The image is divided into small blocks (of size 8 x 8 pixels).
2. The YCbCr color space is considered and chrominance components Cb, Cr are sub-sampled by a factor of two. This step exploits the fact that the chrominance components of a color image produce lower sensitivity in the HVS, compared to what the luminance component Y produces.
3. The 8 x 8 image blocks are transformed to frequency domain by application of 2D DCT (*2-Dimensional Discrete Cosine Transform*).
4. Now the set of DCT coefficients, $c$, is quantized by a factor $q$ to produce the set of quantized values $c'$. This is represented by:

$$c' = round(c / q) \tag{1}$$

where the function *round*() maps every real number (belonging to the set of DCT coefficients) to its nearest integer.

Now, the procedure of JPEG image tampering detection by investigating JPEG ghosts may be broadly divided into the following steps:

1. Let the image be successively quantized by factors *q1* and *q2*. Let the initial set of DCT coefficients be represented by *c*, which produces the quantized set *c'* after quantization by *q1*, and *c"* be the second quantized set produced by quantizing *c'* by *q2*, *i.e.*,

$$c \rightarrow q1 \rightarrow c' \rightarrow q2 \rightarrow c'' \qquad (2)$$

2. Now we consider the sum of squared differences between the elements of *c* and *c"*, as a function of *q2* (where *q1* is a constant).This function may be represented as:

$$f(q2) = \sum_i \left(c_i - c''_i\right)^2 \qquad (3)$$

3. We find that this function (shown in Eq. 3) increases with increasing *q2*. We also find that function attains a global minimum at *q2* = *q1*.

Now let us investigate the characteristics of the above function in case of a forged image which undergoes an additional step of illegal quantization.

1. Let the set of initial DCT coefficients be *c*. Consider that the forger has quantized *c* multiple times to yield *c'*. We look at the optimal case of two-step quantization on c:

$$c \rightarrow q0 \rightarrow q1 \rightarrow c' \qquad (4)$$

   Now, *c'* is quantized (as before) by factor *q2* to yield *c"*:

$$c' \rightarrow q2 \rightarrow c'' \qquad (5)$$

   The entire process may be represented as:

$$c \rightarrow q0 \rightarrow q1 \rightarrow c' \rightarrow q2 \rightarrow c'' \qquad (6)$$

2. Now, if we investigate the function $f(q2) = \sum_i \left(c_i - c''_i\right)^2$, (where *q1* is constant), we shall again find a minima at *q2* = *q1*.

3. Additionally, since the coefficients *c* were initially quantized by *q0*, we also find another minimum at *q2* = *q0*. However this second minimum is not necessarily global. This second minima is referred to as the *JPEG ghost*. Multiple such ghosts may be found in a forged JPEG image which has been quantized more number of times. These JPEG ghosts indicate quantization, after each image manipulation.

Fig. 5 demonstrates the formation of a JPEG ghost. In Fig. 5 the sum of differences $\sum(c_i - c''_i)^2$ has been plot against *q2* € [0,30]. The values of *q0* and *q1* are constant.

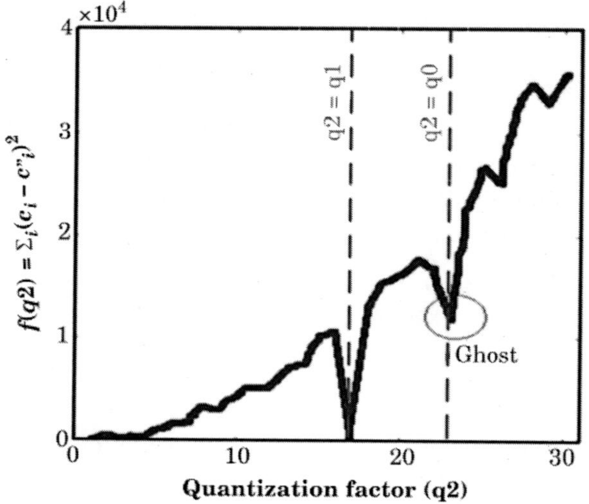


**Fig. 5:** Formation of JPEG ghosts in multiply compressed JPEG images.

## 5. CONCLUSIONS

In this chapter we have elaborated on the present day digital forensic problems, including source identification, doctored image detection and compressed multimedia forensics. We have presented the preliminary solutions to those problems, as adopted by forensic analysts world-wide, hence to give the readers an idea about how to proceed with solving those security problems through digital forensic technology. However, a number of challenges remain unaddressed in this domain as of today. This is a very rapidly evolving field of research, which is gaining immense importance day-by-day. We expect that this book will open up this interesting field to many beginners and would provide proper guidance to them to progress in this field.

All the above problems and their variants along with respective solutions are what constitutes this entire book. In Part II of this book we have five chapters on forensic source camera identification. In Part III of the book, we present six chapters on region duplication detection through digital forensics. Part IV discuss bout digital forensics for compressed multimedia. In Part V of this book, we present state-of-the-art counter forensic attacks and their impact on forensic techniques.

# 3

# Source Camera Identification: Challenges, Solutions and State-of-the-Art

## 1. INTRODUCTION

Images play a major role in domains such as the legal industry, by acting as the primary sources of evidence towards any event in the court of law. Under such circumstances, it becomes crucial to verify the authenticity of images before their usage. Traditional techniques for protection and verification of the integrity of digital images, such as *digital watermarking* and *steganography*, fall under the purview of *active protection mechanisms*. Such techniques rely on data pre-processing in some form or the other, such as watermark computation, data embedding etc. On the contrary, the rapidly evolving domain of digital forensics provides image security and authentication measures which are completely post—processing based, hence called *passive* techniques. *Image forensics* in particular deals majorly with two problems namely Copy Move Forgery detection which is identifying forgeries in images, Source Camera Identification which is identifying the source camera which has captured the image under question.

In Source Camera Identification (SCI) the problem is to map a suspect's camera to an illegal image repository like child–pornography, to settle copy–right cases, to ascertain the validity and authenticity of whistle-blower information and many other sensitive scenarios. To identify the source camera of an image, the Meta Data which stores the camera information in an image, in the image headers, can be well-exploited. However, wide availability of efficient image editing tools today; it would take minimal effort to modify such headers. Thus such pre-processed information added to the images cannot be trusted or treated as reliable. This makes the forensic expert to completely rely on post--processed information to evaluate the authenticity of images. The image processing pipeline in any digital camera adds information particular to the imaging sensor, due to the hardware and software artefacts.

As the source camera identification techniques are used to provide legal evidences, the false alarm rate in this problem domain has to be kept minimal, given its sensitive context. With more than 99% accuracy achieved by recent researchers in source camera identification, there lie a number of critical open challenges which would hinder the practical usage of such techniques in most real--life contexts.

One practical challenge is the presence of unknown models. The forensic expert can have access to only a finite number of camera models and if the test image is not from one of them, then it may be falsely mapped to one of the known models. Another major challenge is the presence of counter forensics. The counter forensics is like a nemesis to digital forensics that constantly tries to defeat the existing techniques by applying some transformation to the test image. The biggest enemy to source camera identification is the effect of compression. The many social networking websites apply their own proprietary compressions to store images and in the process disrupt the state-of-the-art source identification.

Before studying all the above mentioned practical challenges to source camera identification, it requires to understand the basic principles/methods using which an image can be attributed to its source camera. In next chapter, we present an overview of the state-of-the-art research practices in source camera identification.

In the next three subsections, we present the present-day open challenges of source camera identification, one-by-one. In Section 2, we present an overview about unknown models detection, a brief description about counter forensics in Section 3, and finally about exact device linking in Section 4. We present an overview of the recent state-of-the-art in Section 5. Finally we conclude the chapter in Section 6.

## 2. UNKNOWN MODELS DETECTION

*Unknown model detection* is a very common problem associated with source camera identification. In machine learning applications it is known as an *open set challenge* which poses a serious threat. In a machine learning classification there are two phases, training and testing. In the training phase the model gets built and trained, in the testing phase the model is evaluated. In a closed set scenario, the classes, whether in the training or testing phase are known to the system a-priori, *i.e.* the classes form a closed set. In closed set scenario, if the training is accomplished with $X_1, X_2, \ldots, X_n$ classes, testing is also done with the same n classes. In an open set scenario, the testing data is not known to the system before hand, *i.e.* if the model is build using $X_1, X_2, \ldots X_n$ classes, the testing may happen with $X_1, X_2, \ldots, X_n, X_{n+1}, X_{n+2}, \ldots, X_{n+k}$ classes. This has a serious impact on the classification efficiency of the model. What goes on is: all samples belonging to the unknown classes, are mapped as one or more of the known classes, thus increasing false positives and reducing classification accuracy drastically.

In source camera identification, the open set challenge is persistent. As shown in Fig. 1, in a traditional source camera identification model, let the training set consist of images from three camera models $C_1, C_2$ *and* $C_3$, and the test set consist of images from five camera models $C_1, C_2, C_3, C_4$ *and* $C_5$. Such a condition arises when a forensic analyst has access to $C_1, C_2, C_3$, but not $C_4, C_5$, however he is presented with samples from all five classes $C_1, \ldots C_5$, to detect their sources. Here, the classes $C_4$ *and* $C_5$ are unknown to the forensic model. In conventional scenario, samples/images from $C_4, C_5$ are mapped to $\{C_1, C_2, C_3\}$, which is highly undesirable. Not only with the machine learning systems, but also with fingerprint based methods, the presence of unknown camera models directly hampers the source identification accuracy.

To handle the presence of unknown models in the above context, in an ideal source camera identification model, the primary processing should be the separation between known and unknown test samples/ images. As shown in Fig. 1, we need a module to separate images from known and unknown devices first. Next, both these sets are separately dealt with. Images from known sources are handled by conventional techniques, whereas those from unknown devices are taken care of by unsupervised techniques such as clustering. In literature, few researches

(Sameer *et al.*[8], Gloe *et al.*[9], Huang *et al.*[10], and Filipe *et al.*[11]) have recently addressed this issue. In such sensitive contexts as image forensics, where a false positive might lead to an innocent being found guilty, it is of paramount importance to overcome this challenge.

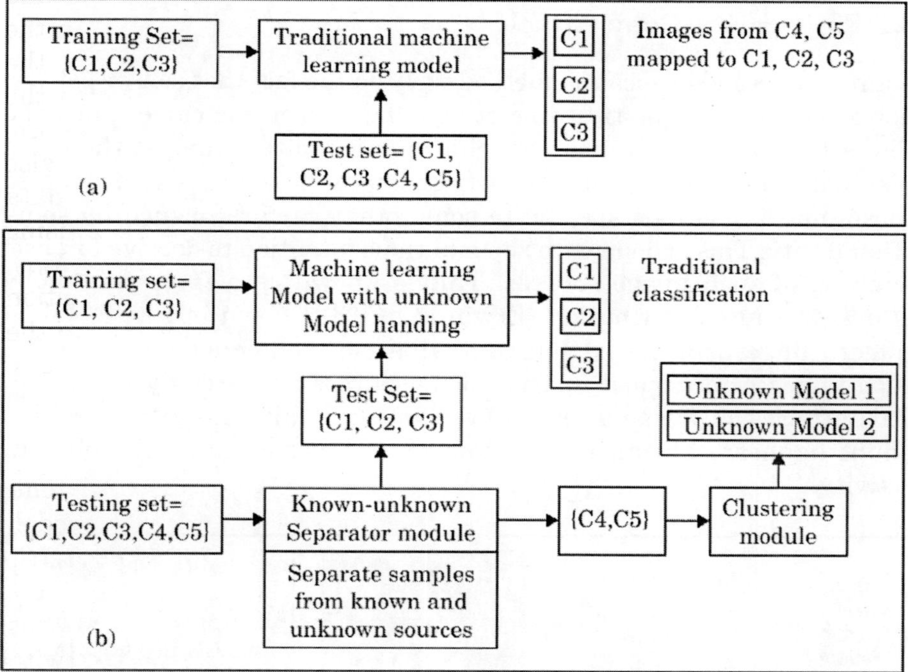


**Fig. 1:** Unknown models detection in source camera identification: (a) Traditional model; (b) Ideal model.

## 3. COUNTER FORENSICS

It is utmost important for activists, human rights defenders and whistle-blowers to stay anonymous while providing sensitive information through images/videos. Image anonymization is an area of science which deals in this context majorly with making users anonymous by countering the source attribution methods.

Source attribution strategies are not only used by the legal industry and in the court—of—law, but also by people who want to track whistle-blowers or activists, hence making their safety compromised. In the recent years there have been significant researches (Ahmet *et al.*[12]

and Erwin *et al.*[13]) to counter source camera attribution techniques and to render them useless. Such works majorly involve image anonymity and serve as counter forensic mechanisms. In the following we present some efficient strategies to suppress source attribution.

### 3.1 Fingerprint Copy Attack

Source camera identification methods rely on the fact that sensor pattern noise acts as a unique trait to distinguish between the camera models. The attacker (one who tries to achieve anonymity) removes the noise residuals in the images he is distributing or uploading, and adds to those, noise residuals specific to some other camera, owned by some other entity. This is done with the malicious intention to deceive forensic analysis of such image sources. This is known as a *fingerprint copy attack* on source attribution (Erwin *et al.*[13]), shown in Fig. 2. When camera fingerprint based source attribution techniques operate upon such finger print copied images, their sources are wrongly identified. This attack can frame a victim by planting a fake fingerprint, which might implicate an innocent person to be involved in some unlawful activity.

**Fig. 2:** Fingerprint copy attack in source Camera Identification

Due to the *fingerprint copy attack,* the number of *false positives* and *false negatives* increase in a multi-class classification scenario. The characteristics of the source camera get disturbed due to the copied fingerprint, and hence the source detection fails.

### 3.2 Seam Carving Attack

Another major attack on PRNU based source camera identification methods is *seam carving*, shown in Fig. 3. Seam carving is a content aware image resizing process where connected pixels that have least variation with neighbours, known as *seams*, are removed. Seams are horizontal or vertical pixel rows in an image. Generally a dynamic programming method is employed to find the seams with minimum total energy. The seam removed image, is a downsized image, in which the remaining pixels in horizontal or vertical directions are shifted to fill the gaps. There is no way to get any information about the location or the number of seams removed from an image. The loss of information that happens due to seam carving makes the noise residual of the image dilute. Also, due to the fact that the seam carved images cannot be reversed back to their original forms, the PRNU obtained from a seam carved image will not correlate well with that of its source camera. Seam carving has been identified as a major attack on source attribution methods by Ahmet *et al.*[14].

**Fig. 3:** Seam carving attack on source attribution

Though seam carving primarily targets the PRNU based source camera identification methods, it indirectly impacts the feature based methods too. Efficient feature sets such as, IQM, HOWS, fundamentally extract the sensor noise characteristics in spatial as well as wavelet domains. Thus, seam carving poses a threat to the machine learning based source camera identification techniques, in addition to the fingerprint based ones.

### 3.3 Adaptive PRNU Removal Attack

The next major way of suppressing PRNU content in an image is through Adaptive PRNU Denoising (APD) methods (Ahmet *et al.* [12]). *Denoising* is nothing but removing the noise content of an image, and adaptive PRNU denoising anonymizes an image by suppressing its noise residual. With a right denoising filter, the PRNU residual of an image can be efficiently removed. Denoising can be done in spatial as well as transform domains, where transform domain denoising has proved to be superior. If PRNU content of an image is removed, the noise correlation based source identification methods discussed earlier (which try to correlate PRNU of test images with the sensor pattern noise of cameras), will fail to yield correct results. All the above discussed counter forensic techniques, attack source camera identification by targeting the PRNU content in an image. To fight these counter forensic strategies, ideally the forensic research community has to evolve to perform source identification, even with images having undergone counter forensic transformations. This may be done through appropriate anti—counter forensic techniques development, or in the worst case through a bypassing mechanism which would help to identify if an image has undergone counter—forensic transformations, and hence to reject it.

As APD methods try to remove the PRNU content in an image, the sensor characteristics, which are used to identify the source camera also get disturbed, similar to fingerprint copy. They also make the source detection difficult by increasing the false positives and false negatives in a multi-class classification scenario, thus affecting the credibility of the entire source camera identification system.

## 4. EXACT DEVICE LINKING: THE NEXT MAJOR CHALLENGE

A very recently identified practical challenge in source camera identification is *exact device linking*. The challenge can be formulated as follows. While investigating the source of an image, there can be three possible cases of identification:

- Was this image captured by Camera Make $X$ or $Y$? (Example, Canon or Nikon?)
- Was this image captured by Camera Model $X_A$ or $X_B$? (Example, CanonD70 or CanonA640?)
- Was this image captured by Device $X_{A,1}$ or $X_{A,2}$? (Example, Device 1 of CanonD70 or Device 2 of CanonD70?)

The source camera identification procedures work efficiently when the test images come from different makes like Canon, Nikon, and Sony etc. This is because a camera make will have a unique sensor system and a unique image processing system, which vary from manufacturer to manufacturer. Intra--make camera classifications fair considerably well because the conventional source identification techniques, (whether machine learning based or fingerprint based), are designed a way so as to understand the intricate details of source sensors and image formation. Hence, the first two cases stated above can be efficiently addressed.

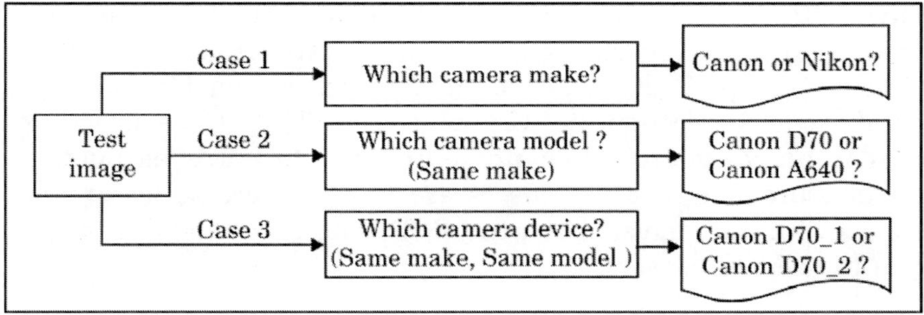


**Fig. 4:** Exact device linking in source camera identification

However, in exact device linking, where the camera makes and models are the same for multiple test images, yet they are captured *via* distinct devices (Fig. 4), the conventional source identification techniques fail due to obvious reasons. This scenario can be particularly seen in settling copy--right cases.

In such a case, if there is an image I under question, and it is to be found who among two or more persons is the legal owner of the image, all with different cameras, but of same make and model, has captured I, with the existing techniques the identification confidence would not be high and it would clearly hinder investigations in settling copy--right cases.

## 5. BACKGROUND ON STATE-OF-THE-ART RESEARCH PRACTICES IN FORENSIC SOURCE CAMERA INDENTIFICATION

Source Camera Identification (SCI) is an important problem of interest in the domain of digital forensics. Source Camera Identification is performed by studying various intrinsic properties of images, imparted by the underlying camera sensor.

There are various stages to form a digital image from a natural scene in a digital camera as shown in Fig. 5. Each camera manufacturer is unique in using different image processing techniques to finally form the digital image. The light first enters through the camera lens and passes through different filters and the colour filter array to reach the sensor. The colour filter array is used to reduce the cost by having only one sensor to detect all three colour channels. The camera sensor converts the light into electrons which would ultimately be mapped to colour intensities at each pixel. There are two types of camera sensors, namely, Charge Coupled Device (CCD) sensor and Complementary Metal-Oxide Semiconductor (CMOS) sensor. The CCD sensors create high quality images, low noise images but are expensive to manufacture. The CMOS sensors are low cost, create lesser quality images with more noise. Also, the CCD sensors consume more power than the CMOS sensors.

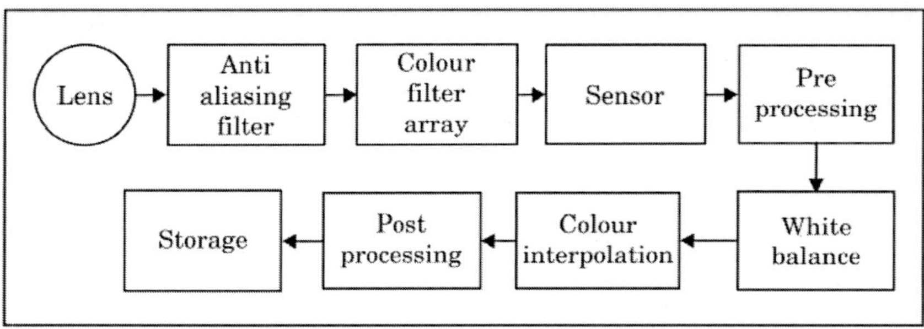


**Fig. 5:** Image processing pipeline

Every camera manufacturer does a lot of in-camera processing to further improve the image quality from the raw image produced by the camera sensor. Some of the important processings that happen are dark correction, gain non-uniformity correction, optics correction etc. Processings like dark correction try to remove the noise (especially dark noise) acquired by the sensor, the other processings might cause small noise to get deposited at some pixel positions. White balance operation is to correct the colours in the image to make it more natural. It is nothing the process of maintaining a uniform colour temperature in the image. Colour Interpolation is performed after the white balancing wherein all the three colour intensities are interpolated from the neighbour pixels. The interpolation is necessary because at each pixel only one colour is measured from the CFA array. The post processing operations usually enhance the final output image through noise removal, edge enhancement, colour artefact removal etc.

Different camera manufacturers have their own set of tools and techniques in each stage of image processing pipeline to capture an image. At each device level also there are many imperfections in the manufacturing stage. These unique artefacts are used by the researchers to perform source camera identification.

Though the meta data information about the source of an image is stored in the image headers, it is not greatly reliable. The meta information contains data about the make and model of the camera, date and time of the image capture and other information related to image capture such as focal length, shutter speed etc. However, with the evolution of many image editing tools/software, the reliability of meta data is at stake. The image meta data can be easily edited or can be removed altogether. The meta data can also get corrupted when the image format is changed. The meta data also is corrupted with the evolution of social networking websites, due to several image processings involved for uploading, transferring and various compressions for storing images. In this scenario, identifying the source of a given image without depending on the meta data information is particularly important with respect to a forensic investigation.

There are broadly two ways of achieving camera model identification, *viz.*, fingerprint based techniques and features based machine learning techniques. The noise residual in an image is considered as the source camera fingerprint.

## 6. CONCLUSIONS

In digital forensics scenario, source camera identification is a very important research area to identify the source camera of a query image. Source camera identification is introduced in this chapter and various current challenges are presented. The challenges presented are such as unknown models detection, combating counter forensics, identifying the exact device of the source images etc.

# 4

# Feature Based Source Camera Identification

## 1. INTRODUCTION

The problem of camera model identification came to the fore majorly with the works of Lukas *et al.*[1] and Kharrazi *et al.*[15]. The former work started exploring camera fingerprinting techniques, where a unique trait of a camera model (in this case Photo Response Non Uniformity (PRNU) noise), is used to attribute an image to its source camera. The latter work deals with the problem of camera model identification by extracting various image features and using machine learning techniques to classify the given images into their source classes. Since then, a number of researchers around the world followed similar approaches, based on either machine learning or camera fingerprinting principles, for image source identification. We first discuss about the machine learning based techniques, followed by camera fingerprinting techniques in chapter 4.

We briefly explain various techniques using different feature sets used in the literature. We are not able to cover each and every feature set in the literature but we put together most prominent feature sets. All of these feature sets are used for performing a machine learning classification. The majority of the literature used Support Vector Machine (SVM) as the machine learning classifier due to its ability to perform accurate classification.

In the following sections, we briefly introduce various feature extraction techniques for source camera identification. In Section 2, we present the widely-adopted IQM and HOWS image metrics. In Section 3, we discuss on the BSM image metrics. In Section 4 and Section 5, we present the extended color feature set and frequency domain features, respectively. In Section 6 we present the co-occurrence image features, followed by the higher order wavelet statistics on PRNU noise in Section 7 and Discrete Cosine Transform Residue (DCTR) features in Section 8. Finally we present some prevalent image texture features in Section 9. We conclude the chapter in Section 10.

## 2. IMAGE QUALITY METRICS AND HIGHER ORDER WAVELET STATISTICS

Kharrazi *et al.*[15] conducted one of the primitive works in feature based camera model identification. They proposed features which capture the camera processing left on the image irrespective of the image content. The feature set broadly contains three types of features namely (1) Image Quality Metrics (IQM), (2) Non Image Quality Metrics (Non-IQM), (3) Higher Order Wavelet Statistics (HOWS).

If $C_k(i,j)$ represents the multispectral component of an image at pixel position (i,j) and band k. C(i,j) represents the multispectral pixel vectors at position (i,j). $\hat{C}$ represents the distorted version of an image. $M_i$ represents the $i^{th}$ IQM measure. R, C, K represents the number of rows, column and bands in an image respectively.

### 2.1. IQM Metrics

The Image Quality Metrics capture the quality metrics of the image based on the variation between the filtered and original image. Four types of filters are used namely, additional noise, Gaussian blur, additional JPEG compression, and additional SPIHT compression.

1. Mean Absolute Error (MAE)
2. Mean Square Error (MSE)
3. Czekanowski Distance
4. Cross-Correlation Measure
5. Normalized Cross-Correlation Measure
6. Statistics of angles between pixel vectors of 2 of images
7. Spectral Magnitude

8. Spectral Phase Distortion
9. HVS measure
10. Laplacian Mean Square Error (LMSE)

### 2.2 Non IQM Metrics

The Non IQM metrics capture the colour processing of the image by the underlying sensor. The measures are as given below:

11. Average Pixel Value Mean
12. RGB Pairwise Correlation
13. RGB Pairwise Energy Ratio
14. Neighbour Distribution Centre of Mass

### 2.3 Higher Order Wavelet Statistics (HOWS)

Each colour band of the image is decomposed into using wavelet transformations and the following statistical measures are calculated:

15. Mean
16. Variance
17. Skewness
18. Kurtosis

## 3. BINARY SIMILARITY MEASURES

Celiktutan *et al.* [16] used Binary Similarity Measures (BSM) in addition to Image Quality Metrics and Higher Order Wavelet Statistics. The BSM are also known as the famous Ojala moments. These are 512 bin histograms that are calculated in a 3 x 3 neighbourhood. The histograms are computed as:

$$S = \sum_{i=0}^{7} x_i 2^i \qquad (1)$$

The BSM features are extracted from a pair of adjacent bit planes within a colour channel, and from a pair of corresponding bit planes across the colour channels. The pairs are formed of bit planes as R3—R4 (*i.e.* between 3rd bit plane of Red and 4th bit plane of Red), R4—

R5, R5—R6, R6—R7, R7—R8, G3—G4, G4—G5, G5—G6, G6—G7, G7—G8, B3—B4, B4—B5, B5—B6, B6—B7, B7—B8, R3—G3, R4—G4, R5—G5, R6—G6, R7—G7, R8—G8, G3—B3, G4—B4, G5—B5, G6—B6, G7—B7 and G8—B8. In this formation of bit plane pairs, the similarity between the binary texture statistics of adjacent bit planes, in both spatio—quantal (adjacent bit planes within colour channel) and spatio—chromatic (across colour channels) directions are computed. The spatio—quantal direction consists of 5 pairs of adjacent bit planes within the colour channels, and totally 15 pairs while considering red, green and blue channels. The spatio—chromatic direction consists of 12 pairs of corresponding bit planes across the colour channels (Red—Green and Green—Blue).

## 4. EXTENDED COLOR FEATURE SET

Thomas Gloe[9] conducted a thorough investigation into camera model identification using the existing feature sets at that time. He used an extended version of Image Quality Metrics and Higher Wavelet Statistics. The extended feature sets includes features from colour processing. Lateral Chromatic Aberration features are also included and experimented with. The extended feature set consisted of 6 additional colour features that were computed from the white-point corrected image, and the difference of the original version and the white-point corrected version of an image.

## 5. FEATURES IN FREQUENCY DOMAIN

Tsai *et al.*[17] used colour features, quality features, and image characteristics in frequency domain. The colour features are computed in each of the three colour channels. Statistical features are computed such as mean, pair correlation, and pair energy ratio etc. The image quality metrics are used as the quality features. The colour features and quality features are computed in spatial domain. The other image characteristics are computed in frequency domain. Wavelet transformation is used to convert the image to frequency domain. Daubechies filter is used for the transformation. In the frequency domain, different wavelet statistics such as mean, variance, skewness, and kurtosis are computed. Using the hybrid of all these features give rise to a larger feature set. Various feature selection algorithms are used such as Plus-m-minus-r, Sequential forward feature selection, Sequential backward floating search etc. to find feature subsets. All these feature subsets are used separately to perform classification using a support vector machine. Ultimately decision fusion techniques such as count based aggregation and rank based aggregation are used to arrive at the final classification.

## 6. CO-OCCURRENCE FEATURES

Marra *et al.*[18] proposed local residual based features for camera model identification. Co-occurrences of histograms are extracted from the quantised residuals of images. These features are used in a machine learning setup to train a support vector machine classifier.

A third order linear filer is defined as the following:

$$r_{i,j} = x_{i,j-1} - 3x_{i,j} + 3x_{i,j+1} - x_{i,j+2} \tag{2}$$

where '$x$' indicates the original image, '$r$' indicates the residual image. The image residual is then quantised using a quantization step 'q'. Then the co-occurrences are computed along the direction of rows as well as columns as follows:

$$C_1(k_0, k_1, k_2, k_3) = \sum_{i,j} I(r_{i,j} = k_0, r_{i,j+1} = k_1, r_{i,j+2} = k_2, r_{i,j+3} = k_3)) \tag{3}$$

$$C_2(k_0, k_1, k_2, k_3) = \sum I(r_{i,j} = k_0, r_{i,j+1} = k_1, r_{i,j+2} = k_2, r_{i,j+3} = k_3)) \tag{4}$$

Where,

$$I(A) = \begin{cases} 1 & A = True \\ 0 & otherwise \end{cases} \tag{5}$$

## 7. HIGHER ORDER WAVELET STATISTICS ON PRNU NOISE

Akshatha *et al.*[19] proposed a feature extraction strategy by using the higher order wavelet statistics and the Photo Response Non-Uniformity (PRNU) noise. The first step is to extract the PRNU noise from the training images. It is performed by subtracting the denoised image from the original image to get the noise residual. The higher order wavelet statistics are then extracted on the noise residuals as well as the original images. The collection of features is then fed to train a SVM classifier and used to perform camera model identification as shown in Fig.1.

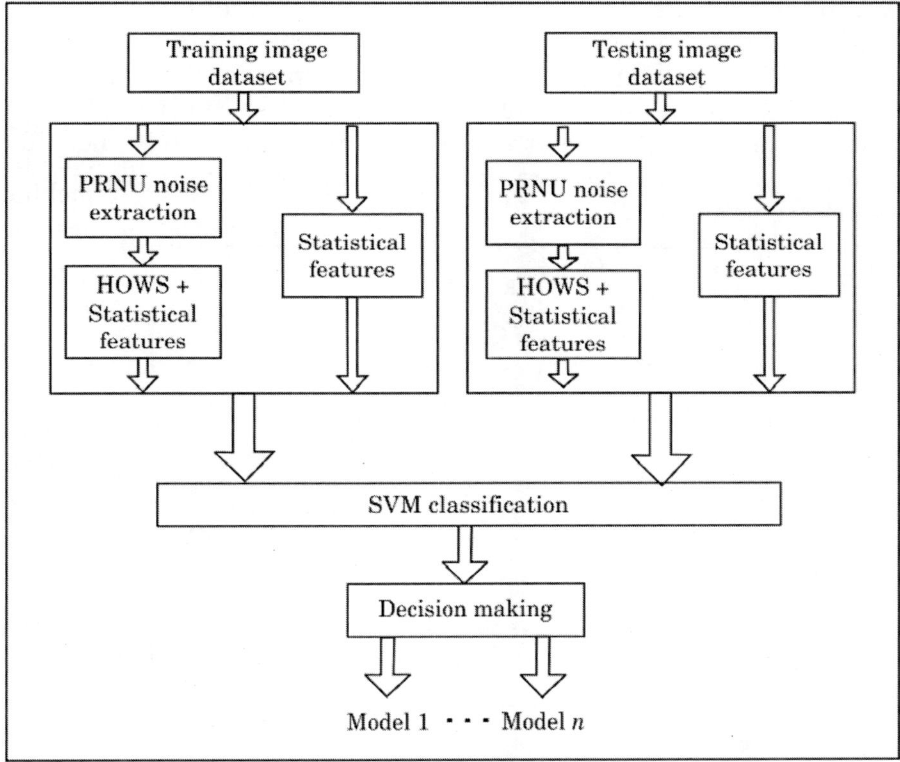


**Fig. 1:** Feature extraction and classification procedure

## 8. DISCRETE COSINE TRANSFORM RESIDUE (DCTR) FEATURES

Discrete Cosine Transform Residue (DCTR) features[20] are used to perform camera source identification. The DCTR features are computed as shown in the following section:

The JPEG image is decompressed to spatial domain and the DCT basis patterns of size 8 x 8 are generated as:

$$B^{k,l} = \left(B^{k,l}_{m,n}\right), 0 \le m,n \le 7 \tag{6}$$

$$B^{k,l}_{m,n} = \frac{w_k w_l}{4} \cos\frac{\pi k(2m+1)}{16} \cos\frac{\pi l(2n+1)}{16} \tag{7}$$

The decompressed image is convolved with 64 DCT basis patterns. The filtered image is sub-sampled by a step size of 8 to get 64 sub images as shown in Fig. 2. For each sub image, histogram feature is extracted. For each filtered image, sixty-four separate (T+1) dimensional histogram feature sets could be obtained when the threshold for histogram is set to T. Then, these histogram features can be merged to form one histogram feature set with dimension 25 × (T+1) using symmetry properties.

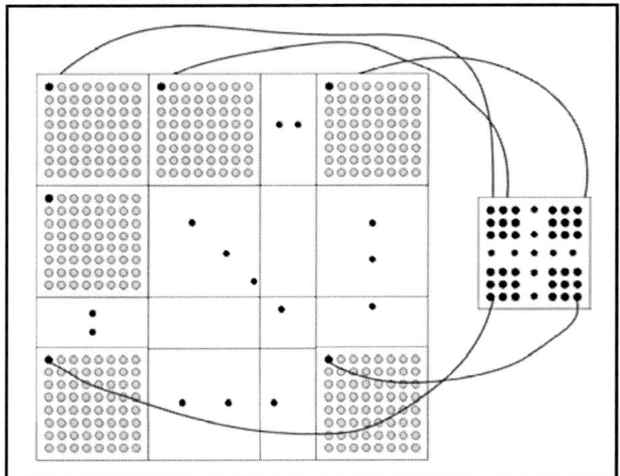

**Fig. 2:** Sub sampling procedure in DCTR feature extraction

The procedural flowchart is shown in Fig. 3. DCTR features are extracted from the training images, then the features dimensions are reduced using Principal Component Analysis (PCA). The reduced feature set is given to many weak learners using random forest classifier and a decision fusion technique is applied to finally predict the class label.

## 9. IMAGE TEXTURE FEATURES

Xu *et al.*[21] identified image texture to be a very successful feature descriptor in performing source camera identification. They postulated that the image texture is one such feature which is consistent across the entire set of images taken by a given camera model. Local Binary Patterns (LBP) and Local Phase Quantization (LPQ) are treated to be the most useful image texture features.

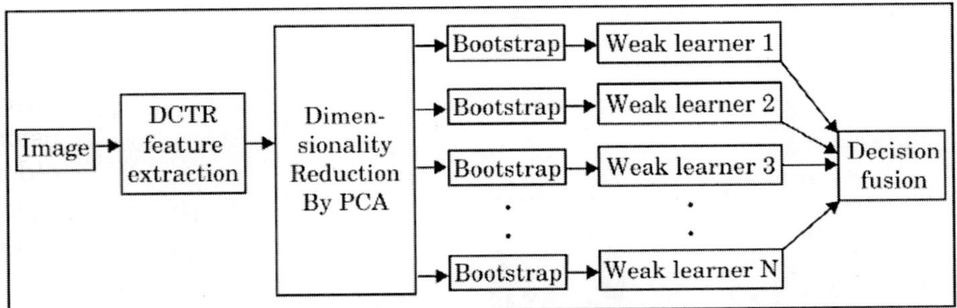


**Fig. 3:** Procedural flowcart

LBP is a highly descriptive texture operator. It records the occurrences of patterns in the neighbourhood of each pixel. In a pixel's neighbourhood defined by (N,R), where N is the number of neighbours and R is the radius of its (circular) neighbourhood, the LBP operator is defined as follows:

$$LBP_{NR} = \sum_{i=0}^{N} s(g_i - g_c)x\, 2^i \tag{8}$$

where $g_c$ is the grayscale value of the central pixel (pixel under consideration) belonging to the neighbourhood defined by R, and $g_i$ is grayscale value of the $i^{th}$ neighbour of $g_c$. s(x) assumes a value of 0 when x is less than 0, and 1 otherwise.

The LPQ features are computed in frequency domain. A 2—dimensional Discrete Fourier Transform (DFT) is computed over a rectangular neighborhood ($N_x$) of area M x M pixels, defined as follows:

$$F(u,x) = \sum_{y\, \in N_x} f(x-y)x\, e^{-i2\pi u^T y} \tag{9}$$

where u represents the frequency of 2—dimensional DFT, x is the central pixel of image f, f(x) represents the grayscale value of the $x^{th}$

pixel in f, and y represents each pixel in the neighbourhood of x (neighbourhood represented as $N_x$, x being the central pixel of $N_x$).

Four frequency positions are used for LPQ (Fig. 4), those are: $u_1=[a,0]^T$, $u_2=[0,a]^T$, $u_3=[a,a]^T$, $u_4=[a,-a]^T$, where a represents the scalar frequency with a positive phase. Then, for each pixel x:

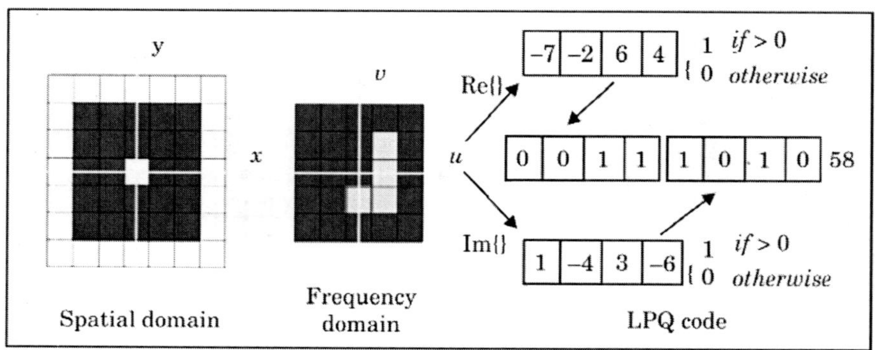


**Fig. 4:** LPQ operator

$$F_x = [\,F(u_1,x), F(u_2,x), F(u_3,x), F(u_4,x)] \tag{10}$$

$$G_x = [RealPart(F_x), ImaginaryPart(F_x)] \tag{11}$$

A scalar quantization step is applied to each element $g_j$ in $G_x$. Each element $g_j$ is coded as 0 or 1, as follows:

$$q_j = \begin{cases} 1, & if\ g_j \geq 0 \\ 0, & otherwise \end{cases} \tag{12}$$

Each binary 8-bit coefficient of $g_j$ is converted into its equivalent integer form as:

$$LPQ(x) = \sum_{i=1}^{8} q_i 2^{i-1} \tag{13}$$

Finally, a frequency histogram of LPQ(x) (over all pixel positions), gives the desired LPQ features of the image.

The LBP and LPQ features are then extracted in three stages as shown in Fig. 5. First, on the original image, second, on the residual noise residual, and third, on the contourlet decomposition. Finally, a SVM classifier is used to perform source camera identification.

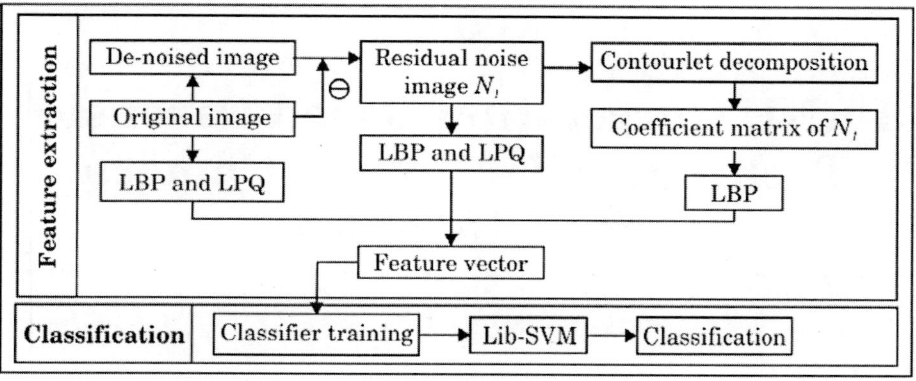


**Fig. 5:** The feature extraction process

## 10. CONCLUSIONS

To identify the source camera of a query image, the problem can be setup as a machine learning classification scenario. Various image features are extracted and a machine learning classifier is used to perform the source camera classification. In this chapter, various image features and various classification strategies are studied by various researchers. In source camera identification domain, all of the above discussed features have proved to be successful in identifying the source camera of a query image. The future research in this direction is to develop features which could map the exact camera device more accurately than the existing techniques.

# 5

# PRNU Correlation Based Forensic Techniques for Source Camera Identification

## 1. INTRODUCTION

Source camera identification has been solved following two primary approaches. First, using camera fingerprints, and second, through machine learning based model. In the camera fingerprinting based techniques, Photo Response Non Uniformity (PRNU) noise, a unique fingerprint formed on the camera's sensor while an image is captured, acts as the primary attribute to map an image to its source. Every camera manufacturer uses different sensors for different devices. The photo-electronic conversion of incident light to digital form, generates a noise at each pixel location of the sensor, hence producing a noise pattern, completely unique to the underlying sensor and thus the camera device.

There are two main components of noise in a sensor, they are: fixed pattern noise (FPN) and photo-response nonuniformity noise (PRNU). The first component *i.e.* the fixed pattern noise is generated when the camera is idle and is caused by the free electrons in the sensor. It is also known as dark current because the noise is generated even in the absence of any light. But the lead component of any sensor noise is the PRNU noise which is caused by the sensor manufacturer defects. Although PRNU is the component of the sensor pattern noise (SPN), the concepts of SPN and PRNU in some of the papers are interchangeable. We use the PRNU as the most camera specific component of the SPN.

The source attribution from the PRNU of an image can be performed as follows. Basically the whole process boils down to correlating the noise residual in a test image (*i.e.* the PRNU of the test image) to the camera fingerprint (*i.e.* the SPN). The noise residual can be extracted by using a denoising filter to remove noise from the image and collecting the noise. Sensor Pattern Noise is nothing but the average noise residuals of many images (normally minimum 50 images) from a camera. A correlation mechanism such as Normalized Cross Correlation (NCC) or a Peak-to-Correlation-Energy ratio (PCE) to decide the source camera. The correlation between the PRNU of test image and its original source will be high, and it will be low for other cameras.

The rest of this chapter is organized as follows. In Section 2, we discuss forensic source camera identification from camera sensor pattern noise (SPN). In Section 3, a large scale test of sensor fingerprint camera identification has been presented. In Section 4, we present and discuss an improved source camera identification technique using a simplified total variation based noise removal algorithm. In Section 5, a compressed fingerprint matching based camera identification has been discussed. In Section 6, a sensor fingerprint identification technique based on composite fingerprints and group testing is discussed. A technique to pre-process reference sensor pattern noise *via* spectrum equalization has been presented in Section 7. In Section 8, a sensor pattern noise estimation technique based on improved locally adaptive DCT filtering and weighted averaging has been described. In Section 9, we discuss on improving PRNU compression. Finally, we conclude in Section 10.

## 2. DIGITAL CAMERA IDENTIFICATION FROM SENSOR PATTERN NOISE

### 2.1 Introduction

Lukas *et al.*[1] first proposed that the noise pattern in an image is a unique fingerprint mechanism to identify the source of an image. They postulated this theory and proved with sufficient experiments to validate it.

To verify if an image $I$ is taken by a given camera $C$, first the sensor pattern noise ($\rho$) in $C$ is determined and then the noise residual of $I$ denoted by $n$, is correlated with the sensor pattern noise.

The camera manufacturing imperfections and the sensor noise are the main components of the fingerprint used in identifying the camera device. For example, at one pixel location, though the actual light intensity at the scene is '$x$', some additional noise is recorded in the camera device due to many causes. The final recorded value may become '$x + \varepsilon$'. The noise '$\varepsilon$', is due to two types of noises, one is called as shot noise and the other type of noise is pattern noise. The shot noise is completely due to the scene component. The pattern noise stays the same across multiple images of the same scene.

The types of pattern noise are shown in Fig. 1. There are two components of the pattern noise, one, is *fixed pattern noise (FPN)* and the other is *photo response non uniformity (PRNU).* The fixed pattern noise is a component which is caused by the excitement of a few dark electrons inside the camera sensor. This noise is removed by many digital cameras with dark noise correction using dark frames.

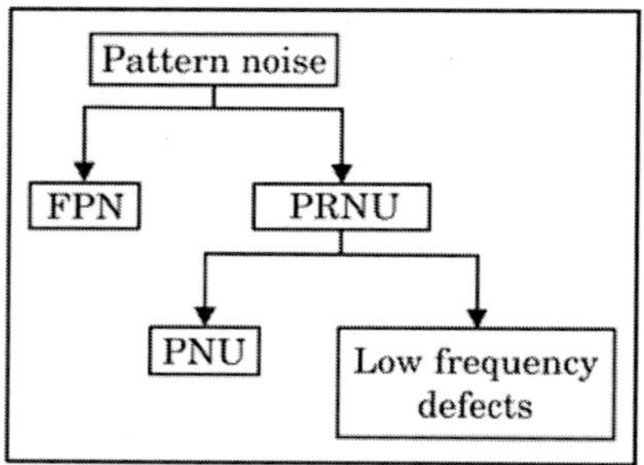


**Fig. 1:** Types of pattern noise

The other main component, *photo response non uniformity (PRNU),* is a noise added due to the reaction of every pixel location to the entered light. Different pixels react differently to light, the sensor imperfections due to manufacturing defects is the major cause of PRNU noise. The PRNU is composed of two types of noises; one is Photo Non Uniformity (PNU) and some low frequency components. The low frequency components can be easily removed by applying a denoising filter.

The mathematical model of the image acquisition process is explained in the following equation.

$$y_{ij} = f_{ij}(x_{ij} + \eta_{ij}) + c_{ij} + \varepsilon_{ij} \quad (1)$$

Here, $x_{ij}$ is the number of photons received at $ij^{th}$ pixel location where i represent the row number, j represents the column number. 'η' is the shot noise, 'c' is the dark current, 'ε' is the additive random noise.

## 2.2 Noise Residual Extraction

The noise residual in an image is obtained by subtracting the image from the denoised image, as shown in Fig. 2. The choice of the denoising filter plays an important role and the authors used a wavelet based filter for best results. The sensor pattern noise of a camera is approximated by taking multiple images and averaging the noise residuals.

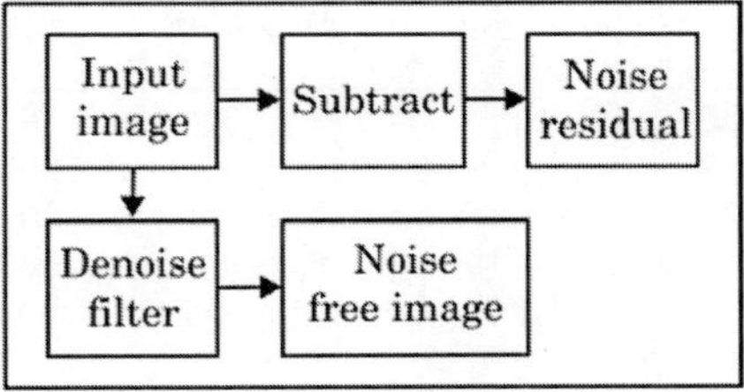


**Fig. 2:** Noise residual extraction

$$NCC(n, \rho) = \frac{(n - \bar{n}).(\rho - \bar{\rho})}{||n - \bar{n}||\ ||\rho - \bar{\rho}||} \tag{2}$$

The bar above represents mean operation. The distribution of different NCC values is determined by collecting many NCC values. The distribution contains the NCC values between images and their original source cameras as well as other cameras. By observing both the distributions and using a Neyman Pearson testing[1] approach, a threshold value for each camera is determined. Now, when the NCC is calculated for a test image, it is checked against the tested camera's threshold to either attribute or reject it as a source.

The individual threshold for each camera in experiments is shown in Fig. 3. In order to determine the threshold values of each camera, the False Acceptance Rate (FAR) needs to be fixed at a pre-determined value. In this work, the authors used a FAR of $10^{-3}$. The FAR is kept at such a low rate because of the sensitive nature of the source camera identification's application. A wrong prediction in source camera identification might imply that an innocent person be criminalized.

Decision threshold *t* and FRR for all 9 digital cameras for far = $10^{-3}$

| Processing camera | None | | Gamma 0.7 | | Gamma 1.4 | |
|---|---|---|---|---|---|---|
| | *t* | FRR | *t* | FRR | *t* | FRR |
| Nikon | 0.0449 | $4.68\times10^{-3}$ | 0.0443 | $1.09\times10^{-2}$ | 0.0435 | $6.33\times10^{-3}$ |
| C765–1 | 0.0170 | $3.79\times10^{-4}$ | 0.0163 | $3.88\times10^{-4}$ | 0.0172 | $3.85\times10^{-4}$ |
| C765–2 | 0.0080 | $5.75\times10^{-11}$ | 0.0076 | $2.57\times10^{-11}$ | 0.0081 | $2.83\times10^{-10}$ |
| G2 | 0.0297 | $2.31\times10^{-4}$ | 0.0271 | $3.23\times10^{-4}$ | 0.0313 | $4.78\times10^{-5}$ |
| S40 | 0.0322 | $1.42\times10^{-4}$ | 0.0298 | $1.64\times10^{-4}$ | 0.0343 | $1.02\times10^{-4}$ |
| Sigma | 0.0063 | $2.73\times10^{-4}$ | 0.0060 | $2.93\times10^{-4}$ | 0.0064 | $2.76\times10^{-4}$ |
| Kodak | 0.0097 | $1.17\times10^{-11}$ | 0.0096 | $1.08\times10^{-8}$ | 0.0094 | $3.73\times10^{-13}$ |
| C3030 | 0.0209 | $1.87\times10^{-3}$ | 0.0216 | $1.58\times10^{-3}$ | 0.0195 | $2.67\times10^{-3}$ |
| A10 | 0.0166 | $7.59\times10^{-5}$ | 0.0162 | $4.71\times10^{-5}$ | 0.0160 | $2.93\times10^{-4}$ |
| **Processing camera** | **JPEG 90** | | **JPEG 70** | | **JPEG 50** | |
| | *t* | FRR | *t* | FRR | *t* | FRR |
| Nikon | 0.0225 | $3.71\times10^{-3}$ | 0.0231 | $5.83\times10^{-2}$ | 0.0210 | $1.63\times10^{-1}$ |
| C765–1 | 0.0122 | $5.36\times10^{-6}$ | 0.0064 | $1.55\times10^{-6}$ | 0.0060 | $1.17\times10^{-4}$ |
| C765–2 | 0.0061 | 0 | 0.0065 | $9.63\times10^{-14}$ | 0.0065 | $2.14\times10^{-6}$ |
| G2 | 0.0097 | $8.99\times10^{-11}$ | 0.0079 | $4.85\times10^{-11}$ | 0.0076 | $5.13\times10^{-4}$ |
| S40 | 0.0133 | $9.96\times10^{-11}$ | 0.0085 | $4.41\times10^{-14}$ | 0.0083 | $9.48\times10^{-5}$ |
| Sigma | 0.0050 | $3.44\times10^{-6}$ | 0.0055 | $9.16\times10^{-6}$ | 0.0059 | $6.57\times10^{-5}$ |
| Kodak | 0.0107 | $2.27\times10^{-9}$ | 0.0127 | $4.53\times10^{-4}$ | 0.0131 | $4.65\times10^{-3}$ |

**Fig. 3:** Decision threshold for each camera

Under the FAR of $10^{-3}$, the individual thresholds of various cameras and corresponding False Rejection Rate (FRR) are shown in Fig. 3. Also, the experiments are repeated for various gamma correction values of 0.7 and 1.4. The results show that the FRR values are very low even at a small FAR value of $10^{-3}$. The FRR for gamma corrected images is also maintained low and hence proves the robustness of the approach.

The disadvantage of using NCC as correlation measure is that it needs a full sized image for correlation. It cannot work for images that are scaled or cropped. This is overcome by Goljan *et al.*[22] who proposed a PCE based correlation metric which scales well to scaling and cropping.

## 3. LARGE SCALE TEST OF SENSOR FINGERPRINT CAMERA IDENTIFICATION

Goljan *et al.,*[22] performed a large scale of sensor fingerprint based camera identification and concluded that the Peak-to-Correlation-

Energy ratio (PCE) correlation is a better test statistic the normalized cross correlation. The procedure is briefly discussed in the following:

To extract the camera's fingerprint, also called the Sensor Pattern Noise (SPN), the PRNU noise of many images taken by the camera is averaged. The forensic expert having physical access to a finite number of cameras extracts the sensor pattern noises of each camera and stores those. To map an unknown test image to one of those finite cameras, PRNU of the image is extracted and a correlation based mechanism is employed against the available sensor pattern noises. Depending on the correlation values, the forensic expert can determine the possible source of the image.

A digital camera imaging output can be written as:

$$P_x = P_0 + (P_0 F + \phi_1 \qquad (3)$$

where $P_x$ is the image output, $P_0$ is the amount of incident light, F is the PRNU factor and $\phi_1$ is the collection of other noises such as dark current, shot noise etc. The Noise Residual or the PRNU component of a single ($i^{th}$) image $I_i$ can be calculated as:

$$PRNU_i = P_x^i - DF(P_x^i) \qquad (4)$$

where, the original image $P_x^i$ is passed through a *Denoising Filter* (DF). The denoised image is then subtracted from the original image to generate the noise residual $PRNU_i$. The Sensor Pattern Noise (SPN) of a camera model $C_j$ can then be calculated as:

$$SPN(C_j)= \frac{\sum_{i=1}^{n} PRNU_i \cdot P_x^i}{\sum_{i=1}^{n} (P_x^i)^2} \qquad (5)$$

where n is the number of images used to calculate the camera fingerprint.

The similarity between an image PRNU and a camera SPN is computed in terms of Peak-to-Correlation-Energy ratio (PCE) (Goljan *et al.,* 2009) as:

$$PCE\ (I_i, C_j)= \frac{\mathrm{b}_{peak}^2 \cdot (|r|-|\varepsilon|)}{\sum_{r \neq s} \mathrm{b}_r^2} \qquad (6)$$

where, þ represents the normalized cross correlation between $PRNU_i$ and $SPN(C_j)$, $þ_{peak}$ is the largest cross correlation value specific to $(I_i,C_j)$, r represents the set of all cross correlation values for $(I_i,C_j)$ and ε represents a small area near the cross correlation peak which is removed in order to calculate the PCE ratio, $þ_r$ represents the cross correlation values corresponding to the entries in r, but not belonging to ε.

After finding the PCE values for each physically available camera, hypothesis testing theory is followed to find the threshold PCE value for each camera. The test image's PCE value is then checked against the thresholds to find out its possible source.

The superiority of using PCE as the test statistic is show-cased by conducting a large scale experiment using flickr images. The dataset which was collected from publicly available flickr images consists of the following information:

- Total number of camera models= 150
- Total number of individual cameras = 6896
- Total number of images = 1,052,700

The experiment starts by obtaining the camera fingerprint from 50 randomly selected images and the PCE correlation values for each of test image with the camera fingerprints are calculated. The experimental results show that at a fixed false acceptance rate (FAR) of $2.4 \times 10^{-5}$, the false rejection rate is 0.0238. This shows the effectiveness of using PCE as the correlation metric over NCC.

## 4. IMPROVING SOURCE CAMERA IDENTIFICATION USING A SIMPLIFIED TOTAL VARIATION BASED NOISE REMOVAL ALGORITHM

### 4.1. Introduction

In the traditional Photo Response Non-Uniformity based source camera identification techniques, the camera identification is performed by extracting sensor pattern noise of the cameras and correlating with the noise residual of the test image. Usually a wavelet based filter is used for the noise residual extraction. When the test images are of large number in nature, then the time taken to extract the noise residual is important, otherwise it would take considerably large time to process the source camera identification. In this work, the authors [23] proposed a technique to speed up the noise residual extraction process. A total variance based noise removal algorithm is proposed instead of the wavelet based filter to compute the noise residual faster.

## 4.2 Total Variance Based Noise Removal Algorithm

The denoised image is obtained by minimizing the total variation norm of the estimated solution. The process of total variance is simplified in this work to make it time efficient. Let $u_0(x,y)$ be the intensity of the image at pixel location denoted by (x,y) in an image of 'n' rows and 'm' columns. Let an additional noise of n(x,y) is at the location (x,y). Then the ideal noise free image is denoted as :

$$u(x,y) = u_0(x,y) - n(x,y) \tag{7}$$

Here, the additive noise n(x,y) is a zero mean noise, *i.e.* E(n(x,y)) = 0. The constrained minimization is given in the following:

$$\min TV[u] = \min \int_{\omega} |\nabla u| dxdy \tag{8}$$

The constraints to solve the minimization are as follows:

$$\int_{\omega} u dxdy = \int_{\omega} u_0 dxdy \tag{9}$$

$$\int_{\omega} \frac{1}{2}(u - u_0)^2 dxdy = \sigma^2 \tag{10}$$

Solving the minimization problem and the constraints leads to finding the noise free image and further estimate the noise residual of the image.

The total variance based noise residual estimation reduces the time complexity involved in finding the noise residual. The introduction of a new parameter with respect introduces a little complexity. When time is of the essence, one could experiment using the total variance based filter to identify the noise residual in the image.

## 5. COMPRESSED FINGERPRINT MATCHING AND CAMERA IDENTIFICATION *VIA* RANDOM PROJECTIONS

### 5.1 Introduction

In this work, an interesting problem with respect to the sensor fingerprint based source camera identification is addressed *i.e.* to address storage requirements of the sensor fingerprints to reduce space complexity. To store and transmit camera fingerprints over a network of limited bandwidth, the size of the fingerprint needs to be compressed to be able to transmit faster. Random projections technique is applied to camera fingerprints and the scalability of the whole process is studied in this paper. This has been depicted in Fig. 4.

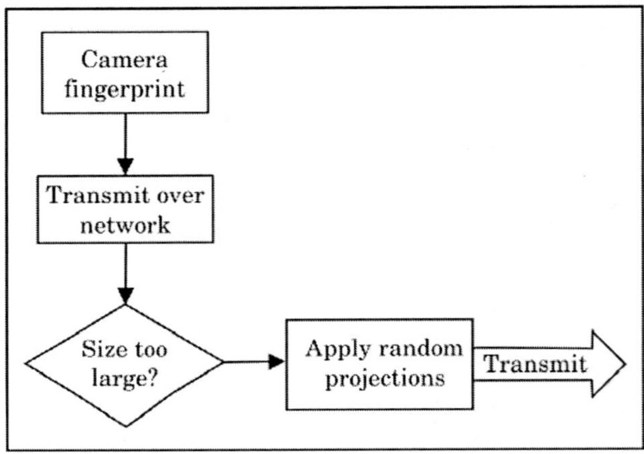


**Fig. 4:** Random projections

### 5.2 Random Projections

The principle used in random projections states that a small set of points in a high dimensional space can be embedded into a lower dimensional space approximately preserving the distances between the points, and by recent results showing that random linear projections can provide such embeddings with high probability. In the case of PRNU fingerprints, it is easy to show that preserving the distance between two fingerprints is equivalent to preserving the angle between them.

The introduction of random projections in PRNU based finger printing technique makes the storage and transmission easy and space efficient.

# 6. SENSOR FINGERPRINT IDENTIFICATION THROUGH COMPOSITE FINGERPRINTS AND GROUP TESTING

## 6.1 Introduction

Bayram *et al.,*[24] addressed a very important issue with respect to PRNU based source camera identification *i.e.* to make the one-to-many mapping of image fingerprint to camera fingerprints efficient. To perform image attribution to a camera, one has to match the image noise residual against a large number of camera fingerprints. This process is time consuming and sometimes is not suited for real time applications.

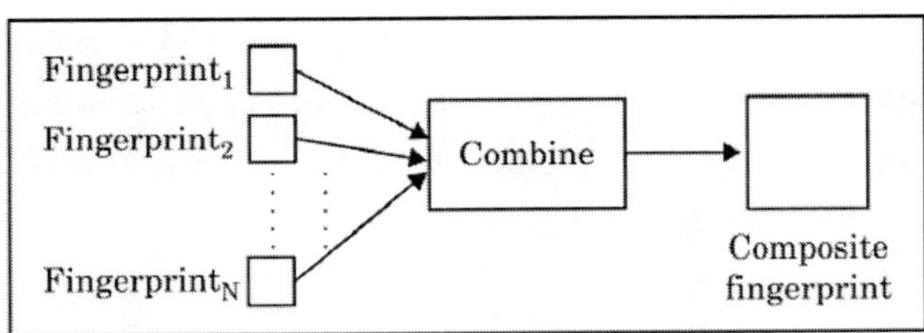


**Fig. 5:** Composite fingerprints

A group testing approach which was inspired from the group blood testing strategy is used to enhance the process of one-to-many matchings. In this process, a composite fingerprint from many fingerprints is used for matching (shown in Fig. 5). A binary search tree strategy is used to find the exact camera model by eliminating the other models.

As is shown in Fig. 6, a binary search tree methodology for composite fingerprint matching is depicted. As an example, eight camera fingerprints are considered from $Fp_1$, $Fp_2$, ... $Fp_8$. The fingerprints are combined from leafs to the root. The matching starts from the root and ultimately is traversed to the leaf node which gives the identity of the source camera.

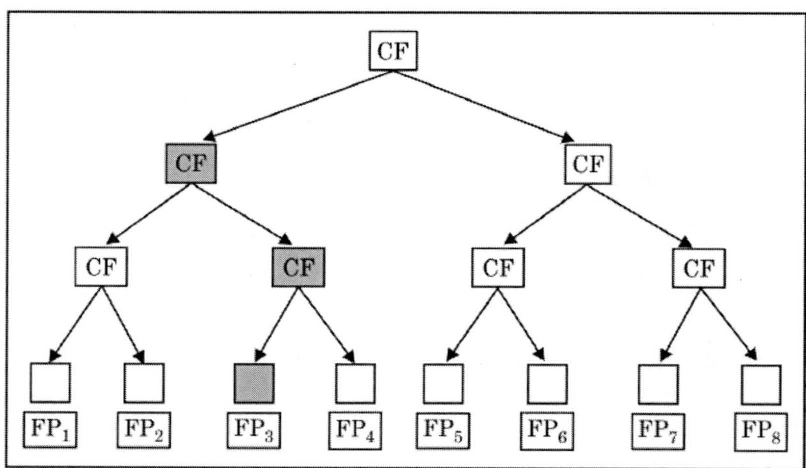


**Fig. 6:** Binary search tree method for composite fingerprint matching

## 6.2 Search Strategies

There are two types of search strategies studied in this work.

1. ***Hypothesis test based search:*** A hypothesis test is performed at each stage to decide if to proceed to the next stage or not. The matching is proceeded to the next stage only if all the nodes in the same level reject the null hypothesis *i.e.* none of the composite fingerprints could yield a match.
2. ***Comparison based tree search:*** The comparison based tree search is a combination of binary search method and the hypothesis test based method of search. Here, at each node the correlation statistics with the composite fingerprint are used to decide if to proceed to the leaf level or not.

## 6.3 Experimental Results

The group testing methodology is evaluated against short digest technique which is a fingerprint compression technique. The experimental results are shown in Table 1. The results are shown for a total 2048 images from Dresden image dataset.

The composite tree method with hypothesis test based search (HBS) is shown to work superior to short digest, and CBS search methods. The processing time as well as the I/O times is found to be the least for composite tree method with hypothesis test based search method.

**Table 1:** Results comparison

| *Method* | *Fingerprint Estimate Length* | *# of corelations* | *Load time* | *Processing time* | *Total time* |
|---|---|---|---|---|---|
| Short digest | 5120 | 2048 | 0.9439 | 0.8475 | 1.7914 |
| Composite Tree method with HBS | 1048576 | 17.84 | 0.5901 | 0.4839 | 1.074 |
| Composite Tree method with CBS | 1048576 | 30 | 0.9989 | 0.8703 | 1.8692 |

## 7. PRE-PROCESSING REFERENCE SENSOR PATTERN NOISE *VIA* SPECTRUM EQUALIZATION

### 7.1 Introduction

The PRNU based fingerprint technique is a very successful technique to identify the source of the image. In this, the fingerprint of the camera in the form of sensor pattern noise is matched against the noise residual of a query image. One of the major problem is the presence of extra artefacts in the image which hinder the camera identification. Lin *et al.*[25] in this paper, have proposed a spectrum equalization technique for pre-processing the reference pattern noise.

The magnitude spectrum of the noise residual is equalized to remove any external interference. The peaks in the local characteristics are removed so as to remove the interfering periodic artefacts.

### 7.2 Spectrum Equalization

One major problem with the sensor pattern noise is that it is not a periodic signal. For the matching between the sensor noise pattern and the noise residual to be effective, it makes sense to make the sensor pattern noise flat and free from any contamination from the scene details. In the process of forming the sensor pattern noise, it is computed from the zero mean, wavelet based filter[1]. This makes the horizontal and vertical DC components to be totally removed, but still there are some peaks in the high frequency components.

The spectrum equalization is the process of ensuring the local flatness of the sensor pattern noise instead of the global flatness. The intention is to remove the additional artefacts in the sensor pattern noise to make the matching more effective. The additional artefacts targeted to be removed are:

- Colour Filter Array (CFA) Interpolation Artifacts
- JPEG Blocky Artifacts
- Diagonal Artifacts

---

**Alg. 1: *Spectrum Peak Detection***

---

*Input:* R: Original reference SPN of U X V pixels;
w: Size of a local neighbourhood;
$T_1$, $T_2$: Two thresholds for peak detection , $T_1 < T_2$
*Output:* P: U X V binary map of detected peak locations;

---

Calculate the magnitude spectrum D=DFT (R);
$P_1 = P_2 = 0$
$M_1 = M_2 = 0$
*count*=0
Repeat
For u=1 to U do
For v=1 to V do

$$M_1(u,v) = \frac{\sum_{(k,l)\in N_w} D(k,l)P_1(k,l)}{\sum_{(k,l)\in N_w} P_1(k,l)}$$

$$M_2(u,v) = \frac{\sum_{(k,l)\in N_w} D(k,l)P_2(k,l)}{\sum_{(k,l)\in N_w} P_2(k,l)}$$

End for
End for

$$P_1 = \mathcal{L}\left(\frac{|D|}{|M_1|} \geq T_1\right)$$

$$P_2 = \mathcal{L}\left(\frac{|D|}{|M_2|} \geq T_2\right)$$

*count* = *count* +*1*
Until *count* > *2*
Create a U XV binary matrix B;
$P = P_1$ & B | $P_2$
Return P;

---

### 7.3 Spectrum Equalization Algorithm

The spectrum equalization algorithm works in two phases: First, to detect the peaks in the spectrum Second, to remove/suppress the peaks

- ***Spectrum peak detection:*** The procedure of spectrum peak detection is shown in Alg. 1. The input to the procedure is the original camera reference pattern (SPN) of size U x V. A local neighbourhood of size w is chosen. Two thresholds are also used for peak detection given as input. The expected output is the binary map of detected peak locations.

  The first step is to convert the reference pattern noise into Discrete Fourier Transformation. The whole idea is to calculate a ratio of the total spectrum to the local mean of the spectrum and then check it against a pre-selected threshold to identify a peak. The local mean calculation is shown in steps 8, 9 in Alg. 1. The ratios comparison is shown in steps 12, and 13.
- ***Spectrum peak suppression:*** The spectrum peak suppression is shown in Alg. 2. The input is the original reference pattern of the camera and the binary map of detected peak locations. The expected output is the spectrum equalized reference pattern (SPN) of the camera. The main step is to replace the peaks of the spectrum with the local mean intensities of the spectrum as shown in step 4 of Alg. 6. This is performed in the DFT space and once the peaks are suppressed, the inverse DFT will produce the desired output.

The spectrum equalization is a very important pre-processing step for calculating the sensor pattern noise to eliminate any contamination from the scene details. The other correlation metrics such as PCE[22], CCN[26] are also used to suppress the scene content in the sensor pattern noise but the involvement of query noise residual makes the contamination still possible in those cases.

## 8. SENSOR PATTERN NOISE ESTIMATION BASED ON IMPROVED LOCALLY ADAPTIVE DCT FILTERING AND WEIGHTED AVERAGING FOR SOURCE CAMERA IDENTIFICATION AND VERIFICATION

### 8.1 Introduction

The photo response non uniformity (PRNU) based source camera identification techniques are successful in performing the identification

**Alg. 2: *Spectrum Peak Suppression***

*Input:* R: Original reference SPN of U X V pixels;
P: U X V detected peak locations
W: Size of a local neighborhood
*Output:* $R_{SEA}$: U X V spectrum equalized reference SPN;

D=DFT (R)
For u=1 to U do
For v=1 to V do

$$L(u,v) = \frac{\sum_{(k,l)\in N_w} D(k,l)P(k,l)}{\sum_{(k,l)\in N_w} P(k,l)}$$

End for
End for

$$R_{SEA} = \text{IDFT}\left(\frac{LD}{|D|}\right)$$

Return $R_{SEA}$ ;

as well as verification of the source of an image under scrutiny. The identification and verification processes differ slightly. In case of source camera identification, the question that is answered is, "which camera out of these finite cameras has captured this image?". In the case of verification, "is this image captured by this camera?" is answered. In the former process, the output from the framework is to give the camera ID of the suspect image, in the latter case, the output is a binary Accept/Reject depending on the verification process.

The existing literature is abundant on establishing PRNU as the unique fingerprint trait to identify the source of a query image. The major hindrance to PRNU based identification is the contamination of noise residuals due to scene details. The sensor pattern noise of a camera is estimated by averaging the noise residuals of many images taken by ensuring the scene content remain same. But there is no such control on the noise residual of the query image. The query image could have been captured in various lighting conditions, with/without proper focus, and may also contain some blur.

The process of PRNU based source camera identification process basically consists of three stages.

- Filtering stage
- Estimation stage
- Identification stage

In the filtering stage, a denoising filter such as a wavelet based filter[1] is used to extract the noise residuals for sensor pattern noise calculation, as well as the noise residual calculation of the query image. In the estimation stage, the sensor pattern noise is estimated by averaging the noise residuals. In the identification stage, a correlation mechanism such as Normalized Cross Correlation (NCC)[1], and Peak-to-Energy-Ratio correlation (PCE)[22] are used to finally identify the source camera.

In this work, by Lawgaly *et al.*[26] the source camera identification of PRNU based detection is enhanced in many ways to combat the scene contamination problem. The authors focussed on enhancing each of the three stages as discussed earlier.

## 8.2 Proposed Workflow

The workflow proposed by Lawgaly *et al.*[26] is shown in Fig. 7. As is the norm with any PRNU based source identification methodology, there are two modules in the process. One, PRNU extraction module, and the other is the PRNU matching module. Unlike the other techniques, each color channel of the image are used in the PRNU calculation. A Locally Adaptive DCT (LADCT) filter is used for PRNU extraction. A weighted averaging operator is used for adding all the noise residuals of same color channels. The noise residuals of the color channels are concatenated and stored in the PRNU database. The same procedure is followed for the query image, and a circular cross correlation (CCN) similarity measure is used to match the PRNU.

The authors proposed three alternate enhancements in each of the three stages discussed earlier:

- A Locally Adaptive DCT (LADCT) filter to extract the noise residual
- A weighted averaging mechanism to add the noise residuals of each channel
- Use of a circular cross correlation (CCN) similarity measure for PRNU matching

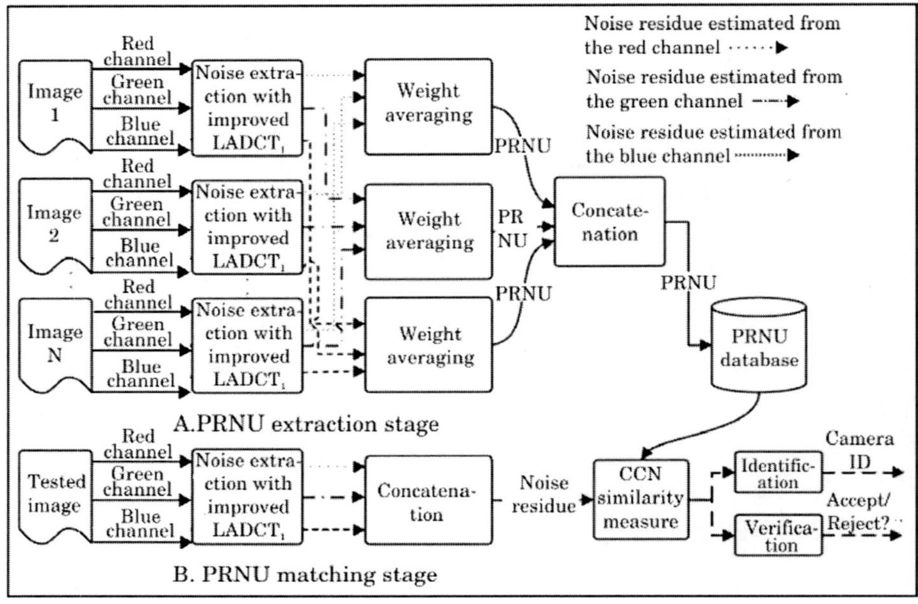


**Fig. 7:** The process model

### 8.2.1 *Locally Adaptive DCT (LADCT) Filter*

The working of Locally Adaptive DCT filter is shown in the following:

1. First, the image is divided into $u$ x $v$ blocks.
2. For every block 'b', which starts at the pixel location (m,l), Discrete Cosine Transform coefficients are calculated as:

$$B(p,q) = c(p)c(q)\text{x} \sum_{m=0}^{u-1} \sum_{l=0}^{u-1} b(m,l) \cos\frac{(2m+1)p\pi}{2u} \cos\frac{(2l+1)p\pi}{2u} \tag{11}$$

Here,

$$c(i) = \begin{cases} \dfrac{\sqrt{2}}{\sqrt{u}} & if\ 1 < i < u, \text{i} = 0 \\ \dfrac{1}{\sqrt{u}} & \end{cases} \tag{12}$$

3. For every block b, a threshold is calculated as follows:

$$T = k\,\alpha\,\hat{b} \tag{13}$$

Where, $\hat{b}$, is the local mean of the block, *a* is the standard deviation.

4. Using the threshold in step 3, each DCT block of step 2 is recomputed.

$$\hat{B}(p,q) = \begin{cases} B(p,q), & if\ (B(p,q) > T \\ 0 & otherwise \end{cases} \tag{14}$$

5. Inverse DCT on $\hat{B}$ gives the locally adaptive DCT filter applied image.

### 8.2.2 *Weighted Averaging*

A weighted averaging operation is performed to aggregate the noise residuals of multiple noise residuals of various images. The operation is performed as follows:

$$PRNU(j) = \sum_{i=1}^{N} w_i r_i(j) \tag{15}$$

Where, '$w_i$' represents the weight associated with $i^{th}$ image, and '$r_i$' is the noise residual. The weight is calculated as follows:

$$w_i = \frac{1}{\sigma_i^2}\left(\frac{1}{\sum_{k=1}^{N}\frac{1}{\sigma_k^2}}\right) \tag{16}$$

Here, $\sigma$ is the noise variance.

The proposed LADCT filter is efficient in suppressing the scene contamination. Also, the proposed weighted averaging operating is effective in improving the source detection accuracy.

## 9. IMPROVING PRNU COMPRESSION THROUGH PRE-PROCESSING, QUANTIZATION AND CODING

### 9.1 Introduction

A major problem in PRNU based fingerprint techniques in a large scale search scenario is the storage requirement. A normal image compression technique is not suitable for storing and transmitting a PRNU noise residual. This is especially important in searching for an image noise residual in a database of sensor pattern noises.

In Fig. 8, the proposed query matching is depicted. First, the fingerprint estimation is performed followed by the fingerprint compression for storage. The noise residual of the query image is also compressed and transmitted. A decoding module is placed to extract the camera fingerprints and the noise residual and matched using the conventional correlation based strategies.

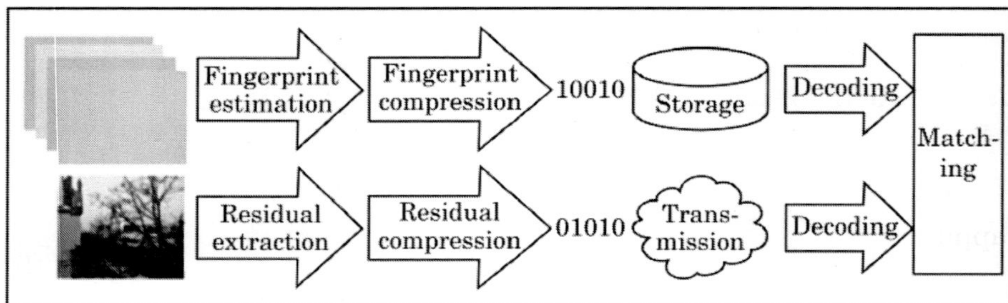


**Fig. 8:** Query pipeline

The compression technique is depicted in Fig. 9. The camera fingerprint is first decimated by a factor (d) to obtain the decimated fingerprint. Random projections are used to create a lower dimensional fingerprint. A dead zone quantization is used to quantize the fingerprint and then an encoding mechanism (entropy coding) is used to encode the camera fingerprint.

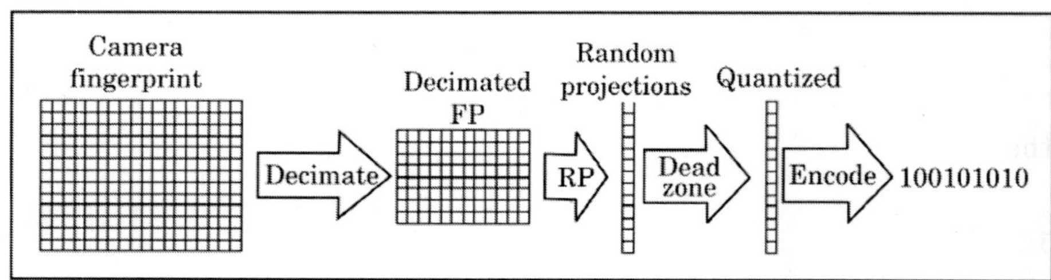


**Fig. 9:** Compression pipeline

## 9.2 Decimation

The first step in compression is the decimation step. Using a traditional compression mechanism such as JPEG introduces further complications in the matching procedure. Hence, to reduce the dimensionality of the camera fingerprint a decimation step is used. The decimation step is through a cubic interpolation mechanism, which is defined as follows:

$$h_c(x) = \begin{cases} 1.5|x|^3 - 2.5\,|x|^2 + 1 & if\ |x| < 2 \\ -0.5|x|^3 + 2.5|x|^2 - 4|x| + 2 & if\ 1 < |x| < 3 \\ 0 & otherwise \end{cases} \quad (17)$$

The decimation by a factor d, is carried out as follows:

$$a_d(i) = \sum_{j=0}^{L-1} h_c(j - i.d).a(j), \qquad \forall\, i \in \{0, \ldots N\} \quad (18)$$

Here, L is the length of the vector $a$ for which decimation is to be applied, $d$ is the decimation factor.

## 9.3 Dead Zone Quantization

Another major step in the compression procedure is the dead zone quantization which is applied to the random projections[27] of the decimated fingerprint. In the dead zone quantization, for the i$^{th}$ element of the random projection, the following formula leads to the quantization:

$$r^{\delta}(i) = \begin{cases} +1 & if\ r^*(i) > \delta\sigma \\ 0 & if - \delta\sigma \leq r^*(i) \leq \delta\sigma \\ -1 & if\ r^*(i) < -\delta\sigma \end{cases} \quad (19)$$

Where, $r^*$ is the random projection of the camera fingerprint, $\sigma$ is the standard deviation of $r^*$.

## 10. CONCLUSIONS

In this chapter, various fingerprint based techniques are studied for source camera identification. The most prominent and successful fingerprinting technique is based on the use of Photo Response Non-Uniformity (PRNU) noise. The other techniques are built upon the foundations of PRNU as the camera fingerprint. Different correlation techniques such as NCC and PCE are also studied.

# 6

# Recent Development: Deep Learning Based Source Camera Identification

## 1. INTRODUCTION

It is inevitable that the technology that caught everyone's eye and imagination *i.e.,* deep learning, finds its way into source camera identification. In the traditional machine learning methodologies, the primary thing to do would be to identify appropriate feature sets for performing a desired operation (classification in this scenario). On the other hand, with the evolution of deep learning techniques, feature engineering has become obsolete. There is no need to hand craft a feature set to perform classification but the raw data itself acts as the input.

In fact, deep learning has been present from a long time. It is in a way an extension of the neural network architectures which have been present for a long time. With the recent advent of powerful GPUs (Graphical Processor Unit), the ability to add more layers in a neural network also grew. Once the research started gaining momentum, new principles and strategies are developed to make the deep neural networks more powerful than ever. This gave rise to the branch of science which we call today as deep learning. In recent times, deep learning is highly successful in many applications such as character recognition, object classification, character text generation, image caption generation and many other computer vision related applications.

As discussed in earlier chapters, the source camera identification can be performed in two ways. One, using the photo response non-uniformity (PRNU) noise of the test image and correlating it to the sensor pattern noise of the suspecting camera (Discussed in Chapter 4). In the second family of source camera identification techniques, machine learning is used to perform classification using various sets of features. Here, each camera is considered as a class and each image is considered as a sample. To map a test image to a camera, the trained machine learning model is used and the test image is used as the test sample to predict the class label which in this case is the camera.

It is not possible every time to accurately identify the correct feature set for a particular classification task. There is also no guarantee that the identified feature sets are the optimum sets. The deep learning neural networks have the ability to learn from data and perform classification. This makes the deep learning networks to be more robust to any type of data and learn new features every time the data changes.

There are many feature based source camera identification techniques as discussed in chapter 3, and in recent times deep learning is also used to perform source camera identification. In this chapter, we will study these strategies and compare the pros and cons with the feature based counterparts.

In the following section, we present the basics of neural networks and then proceed to discuss about different deep learning contributions in source camera identification.

### 1.1 Basics of Neural Networks

Neural networks were designed as an inspiration from human brain and to mimic the working of human brain through a computer.

- ***Neurons:*** The basic building blocks of a human brain are neurons. A neuron receives input from various dendrites, and then processes the information to generate an output signal to be passed to other neurons which then carry out the same task. Similar to this, a neuron in an artificial neural network is defined as the basic structure, shown in Fig. 1 and Fig. 2. It processes the information it receives from various inputs and processes the information to produce an output which is to be passed to next neuron or to be given as the final output.

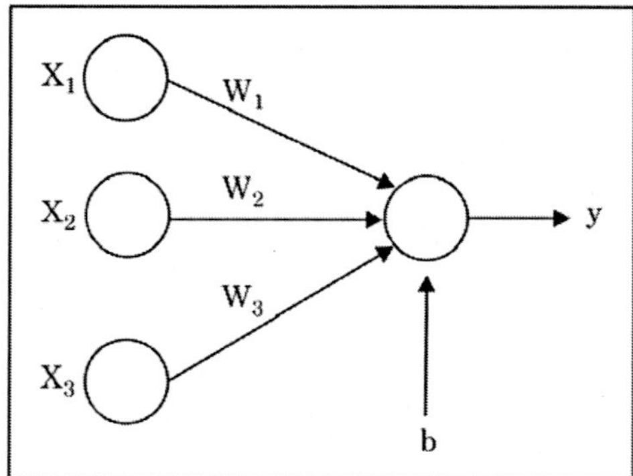


**Fig. 1:** Neuron in a neural network

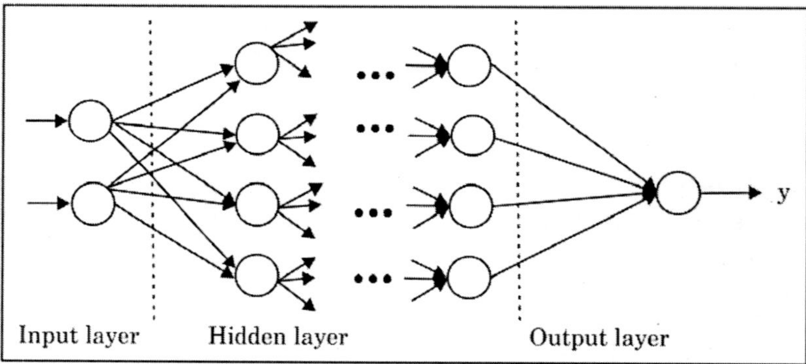


**Fig. 2:** A sample neural network

- ***Weights:*** A weight which is a real value is used to optimize the output produced by a neuron. The input passed to each neuron will have an associated weight which controls the importance of the input. The higher the weight, it denotes that the particular input is more important to that neuron.
- ***Bias:*** A bias component is also added to the summation of weighed input at a neuron. The main advantage of using a bias is to properly fit the data according to the output. The output of the central neuron would be $y = X_1W_1 + X_2W_2 + X_3W_3 + b$, where each X represents the input signal, b represents the bias.
- ***Activation Function*:** The simple output generated by a neuron as shown above is a linear term. Activation function is a

transformation function used to change the linear output of a neuron to nonlinear form. There are many commonly used activation functions available such as sigmoid, tanh, log, cosine, Rectified linear units, softmax etc.

- ***Hidden Layers:*** The Input layer is the layer of neurons in an artificial neural network that receives the inputs data. The output layer as the name suggests, produces the output from the neural network. The main processing for the machine learning task is performed by the hidden layers. It is named as hidden because the neural processing is not visible outside.
- ***Forward Propagation:*** The artificial neural network is defined with a set of input, hidden, and output layers. Each neural connection has an associated weight which is randomly initialized. In the phase known as forward propagation, the input data are passed through each neuron and the associated weights are multiplied. Activation functions are used at each neuron to introduce non linearity.
- ***Cost Function:*** The cost associated with an artificial neural network is nothing but the difference between the actual value and the predicted value. Ideally, this cost should be zero or close to zero. The main objective of a neural network is to minimize the cost function and enhance its predictive power.
- ***Gradient Descent:*** It is an optimization algorithm used to find the best weights of the network that minimizes the cost.
- ***Back Propagation:*** The most important tasks involved in a neural network is the ability to back propagate the error. The error is nothing but the cost at the output layer which is the difference between actual value and predicted value. When the network is initialized with random weights, and the cost is calculated at the output layer, it would be very high. The cost is sent backwards from the output layer and at each layer, the weights are updated to minimize the cost. This is repeated, until there is no change in cost or there is no change in the network weights.
- ***Batches:*** A very important concept that is used in deep learning along with back propagation is batches. The entire input is not sent at once, to the neural network but sent in chunks of batches. This helps the network to generalize and also helps load the entire dataset into memory easily.

- ***Epochs:*** The number iterations to send the entire input in forward propagation and backward propagation is known as a unit epoch. The number epochs plays a major role in the learning processing along with other parameters.

## 1.2 Convolutional Neural Network

The convolutional neural networks are a type of recently evolving deep neural networks that generally are applied to images. All the researchers in source camera identification used convolutional neural network to perform the classification. In the following, we briefly explain various concepts involved in a convolutional neural network (CNN).

- ***Convolution:*** The primary operation involved in a convolutional neural network is the convolution operation. The convolution operation on a signal S, using a window W, is defined as follows:

$$C(t) = \int S(x)W(t-x)dx \tag{1}$$

  On a two dimensional signal, such as an image I, of dimension m X n, using a kernel K, the convolution operation is carried out as follows:

$$C(i,j) = \sum_{m}\sum_{n} I(m,n)K(i-m,j-n) \tag{2}$$

- ***Activation and Pooling:*** A CNN performs three primitive operational steps while doing a classification. It starts with a convolution operation using a specific kernel, then uses an activation function in the detector stage for feature extraction, and finally enhances the output further, through a pooling layer. An activation function takes the output of the previous layer which is nothing but a weighted data and produces a non-linear transformation of the data. Rectified Linear Units (ReLU) are used extensively in deep learning to achieve non-linearity.

In the pooling layer, the output of the previous layer at a particular position is replaced with the summary statistics of its neighbourhood. The popular pooling mechanisms adopted are, max pooling (which replaces the value with the maximum element in the predefined neighbourhood), average pooling (which replaces the average value of the predefined neighbourhood), $L^2$ norm of neighbourhood (which replaces the value with square root of sum of squares of the activations in the neighbourhood).

- ***Optimizer:*** The most important module involved in a neural network is the performance evaluation of the learning task at hand, to measure how well the network is able to optimize the cost function J(ϴ) (where s is the parameter space of the architecture). The function of the optimizer in a CNN is to find the optimal set of s values, *i.e.*, the set which would optimize cost function J(ϴ). The types of optimizers used commonly in deep learning are, Stochastic Gradient Descent, RMS Prop, Adam, AdaDelta etc.

Rest of this chapter is organized as follows. In Section 2, we introduce the readers to Deep CNN based Camera Model Identification. In Section 3, we present a discussion on the first steps towards Camera Model Identification with CNNs. An augmented convolutional feature map for robust CNN-based camera model identification has been presented in Section 4. Residual Neural Network based Camera Model Identification has been introduced in Section 5. In Section 6, we discuss about the vulnerability of Deep Learning to adversarial attacks with regard to Camera Model Identification. Finally we conclude in Section 7.

## 2. CAMERA MODEL IDENTIFICATION WITH THE USE OF DEEP CONVOLUTIONAL NEURAL NETWORKS

Deep Learning is first used with respect to source camera identification by Amel *et al.*[28], where Camera Model Identification is performed using deep convolutional neural networks. Camera model identification is one of the sub problems in source camera identification, where the camera brand is identified from the test image. The source camera identification is a broad problem which deals with identifying the particular camera device irrespective of the brand and camera model.

A deep convolutional neural network is developed by Amel *et al.*[28] which uses a CNN at the core to perform camera model identification as a classification problem. The input images are passed through a high pass filter and the resultant denoised images are used as an input to the network.

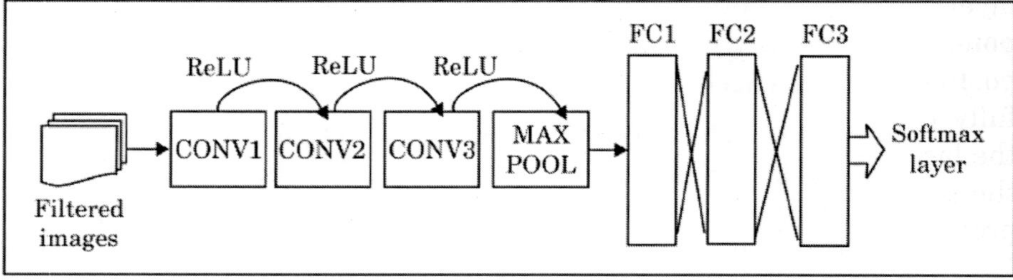


**Fig. 3:** The Deep CNN Architecture of Amel *et al.*,

## 2.1 Pre-processing

In this work, the authors experimented with two types of filters. The first filter used was a high pass filter which is used on an Image I as follows:

$$A = I * \frac{1}{12}(B) \tag{3}$$

$$B = \begin{pmatrix} -1 & 2 & -2 & 2 & -1 \\ 2 & -6 & 8 & -6 & 2 \\ -2 & 8 & 12 & 8 & 2 \\ 2 & -6 & 8 & -6 & 2 \\ -1 & 2 & 2 & 2 & -1 \end{pmatrix} \tag{4}$$

When an Image I is passed through the above filter, it produces an image with less noise and less interference from edges, texture. The other filter experimented with was a wavelet based denoising filter. All the training and test images are passed through these high pass filters as a pre-processing step.

## 2.2 Network

The deep convolutional network is as shown in Fig. 3. Three convolution layers ($CONV_1$, $CONV_2$, $CONV_3$) each followed by a ReLU activation and then a max pool layer which is followed by three fully connected layers ($FC_1$, $FC_2$, $FC_3$) and ultimately a softmax layer to predict the class label. The first convolutional layer uses 64 kernels of size 3 x 3 and a stride of size 2. The second convolution layer also uses a 3 x 3 kernel size and produces a 64 x 64 feature map. The third convolution layer uses 32 kernels of size 3 x 3 and a stride of size 2. To introduce non-linearity, Rectified Linear Unit (ReLU) functions are used. The pooling layer used was a max pool layer with size 3 x 3. The first two fully connected layers have 256 and 4096 neurons respectively and the last fully connected layer is given to softmax function which predicts the probability of each class label and labels the class with maximum predicted probability.

### 2.3 Dataset

The dataset used in this experiment was the benchmarked image forensic dataset known as "The Dresden Image Database"[29]. Total 33 camera models are used where 27 are from the Dresden dataset and the other 6 models are proprietary. The list of camera models is shown in Table 1. The images are further divided into 256 x 256 blocks to increase the dataset. 80% of the data is used for training and the rest 20% is used for testing.

### 2.4 Experiment 1

In the first experiment, the first 12 camera models from Table 1 are used in the experiment. Both the high pass filters mentioned earlier are used for evaluation. The classification accuracy with the high pass filter is 98% and with the wavelet based filter is 95.1%.

### 2.5 Experiment 2

In the next experiment, the first 14 camera models from Table 1 are used. With the high pass filter as preprocessing, the classification accuracy is 97.09% and with the wavelet based filter is 93.23%. The two camera models additional from experiment 1 are Sony DSC H50 and Sony DSC W170. The decrease in accuracy from experiment 1 to experiment is attributed to the addition of two camera models from the same manufacturer.

### 2.6 Experiment 3

In this experiment, all 33 camera models listed in Table 1 are used. The classification accuracy reported is 91.9% with the high pass filter and much lower when wavelet based filter is used. The results are compared with AlexNet [30] and GoogleNet [31]. However, the GoogleNet

**Table 1:** List of camera models used in experiment

| *Sl. no.* | *Camera brand* | *Model* | *Resolution* | *Number of Images* |
|---|---|---|---|---|
| 1 | AGFA | DC-733s | 3072×2304 | 30349 |
| 2 | AGFA | DC-830i | 3264×2448 | 39204 |
| 3 | AGFA | Sensor 530s | 4032×3024 | 55585 |
| 4 | CANON | Ixus 55 | 2592×1944 | 15680 |
| 5 | FUJIFILM | Fine Pix J50 | 3264×2448 | 22680 |
| 6 | KODAK | M1063 | 3664×2748 | 64960 |
| 7 | NIKON | D200 Lens A/B | 3872×2592 | 55800 |
| 8 | OLYMPUS | M1050SW | 3648×2736 | 28560 |
| 9 | PANASONIC | DMC-FZ50 | 3648×2736 | 37100 |
| 10 | PRAKTICA | DCZ 5.9 | 2560×1920 | 14630 |
| 11 | SAMSUNG | L74 wide | 3072×2304 | 24948 |
| 12 | SAMSUNG | NV15 | 3648×2736 | 30380 |
| 13 | SONY | DSC-H50 | 3456×2592 | 36920 |
| 14 | SONY | DSC-W170 | 3648×2736 | 28700 |
| 15 | AGFA | DC-504 | 4032×3024 | 10074 |
| 16 | AGFA | Sensor 505-x | 2592×1944 | 12040 |
| 17 | CANON | EOS-1200D | 3648×2736 | 26780 |
| 18 | CANON | Power Shot SD790 IS | 3648×2736 | 30016 |
| 19 | CANON | Ixus70 | 3072×2304 | 20196 |
| 20 | CANON | Power Shot A640 | 3648×2736 | 26320 |
| 21 | CANON | EOS7D | 3648×2736 | 9360 |
| 22 | CASIO | EX-Z150 | 3264×2448 | 19548 |
| 23 | NIKON | Cool Pix S710 | 4352×3264 | 37944 |
| 24 | NIKON | D70 | 3008×2000 | 13860 |
| 25 | NIKON | D70s | 3008×2000 | 13706 |
| 26 | NIKON | D200 | 3648×2736 | 34500 |
| 27 | PENTAX | Optio A40 | 4000×3000 | 27885 |
| 28 | PENTAX | Optio W60 | 3648×2736 | 26880 |
| 29 | RICOH | GX100 | 3648×2736 | 26880 |
| 30 | ROLLEI | RCP-7325XS | 3072×2304 | 21384 |
| 31 | SONY | DSC-HX50 | 3648×2736 | 15960 |
| 32 | SONY | DSCHX60V | 3648×2736 | 44400 |
| 33 | SONY | T77 | 3648×2736 | 25340 |

architecture proved to be more accurate than the other neural networks with a classification accuracy of more than 98% in all the cases.

The authors used a three layer convolutional neural network with max pool layer and three fully connected layers to perform camera model identification on 33 camera models. A preprocessing step was selected as passing the images through a high pass filter to remove interferences from edges and texture. The experimental results are compared with AlexNet and GoogleNet and the latter is proved to be a better classifier than the other networks. Fine-tuning of the network parameters might improve the classification accuracy of the proposed architecture.

## 3. FIRST STEPS TOWARDS CAMERA MODEL INDENTIFICATION WITH CONVOLUTIONAL NEURAL NETWORKS

Luca Bondi *et al.*[32] proposed a CNN based deep learning methodology to perform camera model identification. They used 18 camera models from the Dresden image dataset[29] as shown in Table 2.

**Table 2:** List of cameras used in experiments by Luca *et al.*,

| *Sl. no* | *Camera brand* | *Model* | *Resolution* |
|---|---|---|---|
| 1 | CANON | Ixus70 | 3072×2304 |
| 2 | CASIO | EX-Z150 | 3264×2448 |
| 3 | FUJIFILM | FinePix J50 | 3264×2448 |
| 4 | KODAK | M1063 | 3664×2748 |
| 5 | NIKON | CoolPixS710 | 4352×3264 |
| 6 | NIKON | D70 | 3008×2000 |
| 7 | NIKON | D200 | 3648×2736 |
| 8 | OLYMPUS | M1050SW | 3648×2736 |
| 9 | PANASONIC | DMC-FZ50 | 3648×2736 |
| 10 | PENTAX | OptioA40 | 4000×3000 |
| 11 | PRAKTICA | DCZ 5.9 | 2560×1920 |
| 12 | RICOH | GX100 | 3648×2736 |
| 13 | ROLLEI | RCP-7325XS | 3072×2304 |
| 14 | SAMSUNG | L74wide | 3072×2304 |
| 15 | SAMSUNG | NV15 | 3648×2736 |
| 16 | SONY | DSC-HX50 | 3648×2736 |
| 17 | SONY | DSCHX60V | 3648×2736 |
| 18 | SONY | T77 | 3648×2736 |

### 3.1 Brief Procedure

In this work, the authors proposed a CNN based feature extractor which is used by a Support Vector Machine (SVM) to perform classification as shown in Fig. 4. An image is divided into 64 x 64 patches to increase the training dataset. Each patch is given the same class label as that of the parent image. A CNN training module is placed to learn the features about each class of images and a 128 element feature vector is formed at the final later. This feature vector is used by a SVM training module in a One-*vs*-All manner and classification is performed using majority voting principle.

The CNN training module is shown in Fig. 5. The image patches are passed through the first convolutional layer (CNN1) where 32 filters of size 4 x 4 x 3 are used and a stride of size 1 is used. It is followed by a Max Pooling layer (MP1) to connect to the next convolution layer (CNN2). Here, 48 filters of size 5 x 5 x 32 are used and a stride of size 1 is followed. It is then passed through a Max Pool layer (MP2) and to be connected to the next convolution layer (CNN3) which has 64 kernels of size 5 x 5 x 48 and stride of 1. It is followed by a Max Pool layer (MP3) and then a fourth convolution layer (CNN4) with 128

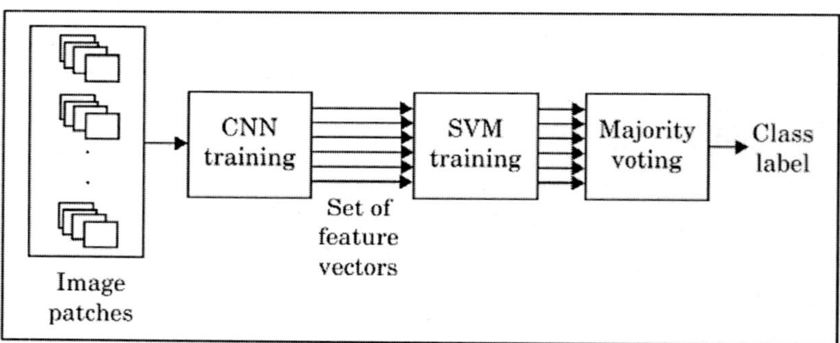


**Fig. 4:** Overall architecture of Luca *et al.*[32]

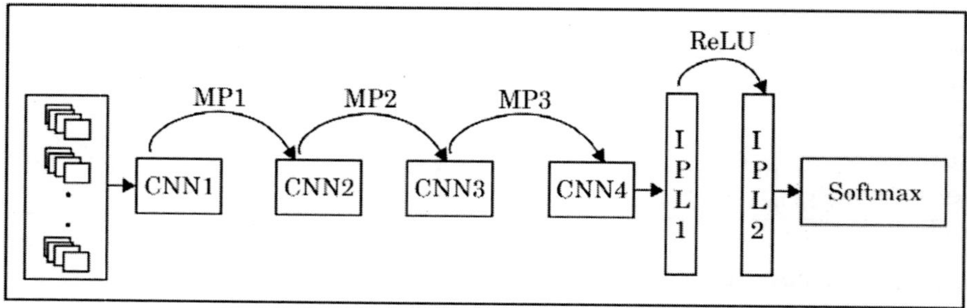


**Fig. 5:** The CNN architecture. (CNN: Convolutional layer, MP: Max Pool layer, IPL: Inner Product layer)

filters of size 5 x 5 x 64 and stride of 1. All the three Max Pool layersuse kernel of size 2 and stride of size 2. The fourth convolution layer is followed by two inner product layers with a ReLU activation in between them. The final inner product layer produces a feature vector of size 128 x N where N is the number of training classes and it is followed by a softmax layer for calculation of the loss.

Stochastic Gradient Descent (SGD) is used as the optimizer. To better use the memory resources, batch processing is used with a batch size of 128. The momentum term is used as 0.9 and learning rate of 0.015. A decay factor of 7.5 x $10^{-3}$is used to optimize the network.

### 3.2 Experimental Results

The authors have used 18 camera models from the Dresden image dataset. A total of 13,000 images are used for experiments. The training, testing and validation data are used for a fair evaluation. The training, testing and validation data is split in such a way that there is no overlap of images, nor the scene. This was done to ensure that the underlying deep learning network is not learning about the image scenes but about the source of the images. First, the model is evaluated without using the majority voting, which resulted in a classification accuracy of 93%. The final evaluation is performed using the 64 x 64 image patches and compared with state-of-the-art methods in Chen *et al.*[33] and Marra *et al.*[18]. The results show that the deep learning based method proposed by the authors outperformed the others significantly when 64 x 64 image patches are used. When a whole image is used, then the methodology of Chen *et al.*[33] outperforms the rest.

The authors proposed a deep convolutional network to perform camera model identification. The authors were able to achieve a considerable performance even with image sizes of 64 x 64 which would be highly helpful in scenarios with lower image sizes. Further study is needed to extend this work to perform source camera identification and also to check the robustness with geometrically modified images.

In the next section, we study another research by Marra *et al.*[34] which focuses on the vulnerability of the successful deep learning methods in case of adversarial attacks for camera model identification.

## 4. AUGMENTED CONVOLUTIONAL FEATURE MAPS FOR ROBUST CNN-BASED CAMERA MODEL IDENTIFICATON

### 4.1 Introduction

Deep learning is used as the classification methodology in many Camera Model Identification researchers. The main challenges in deep learning based camera model identification as well as in traditional camera model identification are the presence of resampling and recompression. The resampling and recompression are currently not addressed successfully in earlier research. These problems are especially problematic in current day and age of social networks. Each social network resamples and/or recompresses an image uploaded. The authors used augmented convolutional feature maps to make the CNN based camera model identification robust to resampling and compression.

The robustness of deep learning based techniques is a major problem to address. In all the previous deep learning based camera model identification approaches, the deep learning network learns linear features from the input images. In this work, the authors studied if the addition of non-linear residual features would address the robustness with respect to resampling and recompression. The authors used median filter residual (MFR) as the non-linear feature descriptors in addition to the CNN based network, hence the name augmented convolutional feature maps.

In this approach, both a constrained convolutional layer and a nonlinear residual feature extractor such as the MFR are used in parallel. The feature maps produced by both of these layers are then concatenated and higher level associations between these feature maps are learned by subsequent convolutional layers.

### 4.2 Augmented Convolutional Network

The original images are input to a constrained convolutional neural network along with the Median Filter Residuals in parallel to form the augmented convolutional network.

#### *Median Filter Residual extraction*

For an image I, for an $(i,j)^{th}$ pixel, the median filter residual is defined as follows:

$$MFR(i,j) = I(i,j) - med3(i,j) \tag{5}$$

where, *med3* is the median filter being applied to that pixel location of (i,j). The number 3 represents the kernel size of the median filter. Applying the above procedure for all the pixel locations, the output is in the form of an image with each pixel representing the median filter residual.

### *Constrained Convolutional Neural Network*

In a normal convolutional neural network, the image features are learned based on the image content. But this is not recommended in applications that do not need to depend on the image content, such as digital forensics. The constrained convolutional neural networks are a modification to the existing convolutional networks which are modified to accommodate all types of image content. In these types of networks, a constraint is placed to on the convolution layer. The constraints used in the work are given as follows:

$$W\mathrm{k}(0{,}0) = -1 \tag{6}$$

$$\sum_{m,n\neq 0} wk(m,n) = 1 \tag{7}$$

Training proceeds by updating the filter weights at each iteration using the stochastic gradient descent algorithm during the back-propagation step, then projecting the updated filter weights back into the feasible set by reinforcing the constraints.

## 4.3 The Network Architecture

The network architecture is as shown in Fig. 6. The network details are given as follows:

- The input layer is of size 256 x 256 x 2, the last dimension consists of MFR images as well as the original images.
- The MFR images are passed through an identity convolution layer of size 5 x 5 x 1 and with a stride of 1.
- The original images are passed through a constrained convolution layer with size 5 x 5 x 1 and a stride of 1.

- The above two parallel streams are concatenated using a CFMA layer.
- A convolution layer is followed with kernel size of 7 x 7 x 4/7 x 7 x 3, with number of filters as 96. A stride of size 2 is used.
- A batch normalization and a TanH activation is followed.
- A max pooling layer is used with 3 x 3 size kernel and a stride of 2.
- A convolution layer of size 5 x 5 x 96, stride of size 1, and 64 number of kernels is used.
- A batch normalization and a TanH activation is followed.
- A max pooling layer is used with 3 x 3 size kernel and a stride of 2.
- A convolution layer of size 5 x 5 x 64, stride of size 1, and 64 number of kernels is used.
- A batch normalization and a TanH activation is followed.
- A max pooling layer is used with 3 x 3 size kernel and a stride of 2.
- A convolution layer of size 1 x 1 x 64, stride of size 1, and 128 number of kernels is used.
- A batch normalization and a TanH activation is followed.
- An average pooling layer is used with 3 x 3 size kernel and a stride of 2.
- Fully connected layer with 200 neurons is followed.
- An activation function with TanH activation is used.
- Fully connected layer with 200 neurons is followed.
- An activation function with TanH activation is used.
- Extremely Randomized Trees classifier is followed for performing camera model identification.

A *stochastic gradient descent* optimizer is used with the following parameters:

Momentum = 0.9, decay = 5 x $10^{-4}$ , a learning rate of $10^{-3}$ that decreases by a factor of 0.5 for every 4 epochs. A total of 44 epochs are used, and with a batch size of 64.

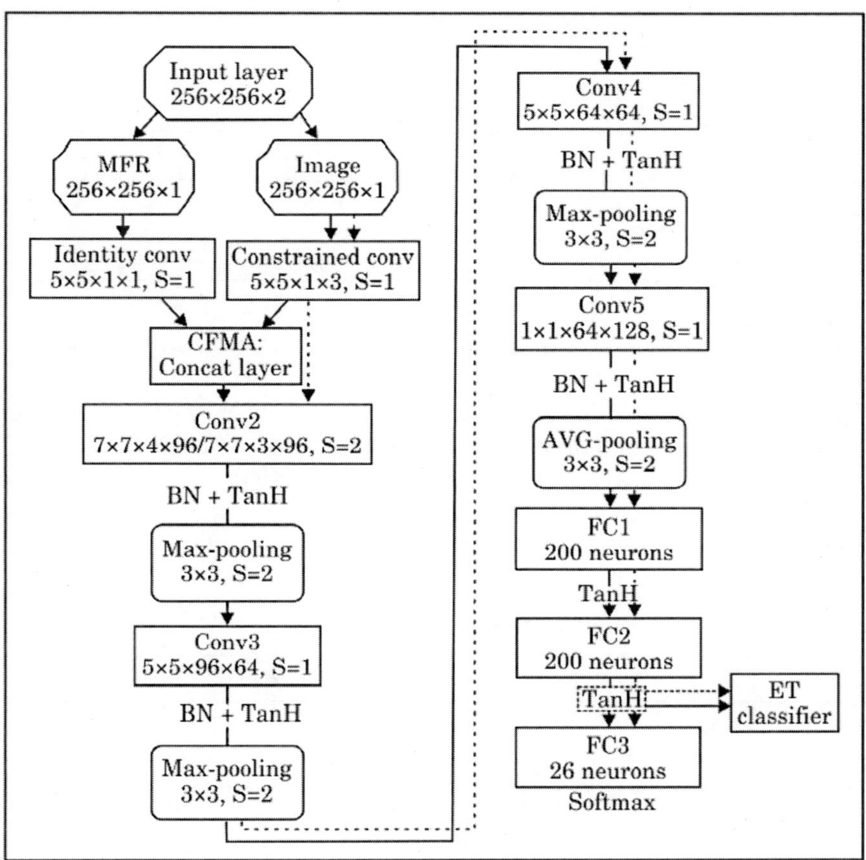


**Fig. 6:** Network architecture

## 4.4 Experimental Results

A total of 15,000 images from the Dresden image dataset are used for experiments. 256 x 256 patches are extracted from each image and are used in training. The central patches are extracted from the green channel. The experiments concentrated on establishing the robustness of the camera model identification in resampling and recompression. A total of seven databases are created in many scenarios such as resampling and recompression. Three forms of resampling are experimented which are with downscaling of 90% and 50% as well as upscaling by 120%. These three are again compressed with a quality factor of 90 using JPEG compression. The effects of JPEG compression alone with a QF = 90 is also studied.

**Table 3:** Original images

| *Method* | *Original* |
|---|---|
| ACFM based CNN | 98.26% |
| Non ACFM based CNN | 98.24% |
| HPF based CNN | 97.52% |

The performance of the augmented convolutional neural network with respect to the other deep learning based neural networks is shown in Tables 4, 5, 6 and 7. The performance in case of only original images presence is shown in Table 3. The augmented based CNN works the best with a classification accuracy of 98.26%. The non ACFM based CNN has an accuracy of 98.24% and the HPF based CNN has an accuracy of 97.52%.

**Table 4:** JPEG compression with quality factor 90

| *Method* | *JPEG QF=90* |
|---|---|
| ACFM based CNN | 97.26% |
| Non ACFM based CNN | 97.23% |
| HPF based CNN | 96.00% |

The experimental results in case of jpeg compression with a quality factor of 90 is shown in Table 4. The ACFM based CNN outperforms the rest with a classification accuracy of 97.26%. The non ACFM based CNN has a classification accuracy of 97.23%. The HPF based CNN has an accuracy of 96%.

The classification accuracy for images with resampling is shown in Table 5. The classification accuracy of ACFM based CNN with an upscaling of 120% is 97.14%, with a downscaling of 90% is 95.93%, with downscaling of 50% is 90.75%.

The classification accuracy of images with both resampling and recompression is shown in Table 6. The non ACFM based CNN works slightly better than the ACFM based CNN.

**Table 5:** Resampling without compression

| | *Resampling* | | |
|---|---|---|---|
| ***Methods*** | 120% | 90% | 50% |
| ACFM based CNN | 97.14% | 95.93% | 90.75% |
| Non ACFM based CNN | 96.75% | 95.76% | 87.70% |
| HPF based CNN | 95.94% | 95.68% | 87.54% |

**Table 6:** Resampling with compression

| | **Resampling + JPEG (QF=90)** | | |
|---|---|---|---|
| ***Methods*** | 120% | 90% | 50% |
| ACFM based CNN | 93.86% | 91.42% | 79.31% |
| Non ACFM based CNN | 94.94% | 91.89% | 75.68% |
| HPF based CNN | 90.45% | 83.96% | 67.16% |

# 5. CAMERA MODEL IDENTIFICATION WITH RESIDUAL NEURAL NETWORK

## 5.1 Introduction

Many of the deep learning networks in the domain of source camera identification are focussed only on performing the camera model identification. The authors in this work performed a complete analysis on using Residual Neural Network (ResNet) to identify the source camera of a given image. Three different experiments are performed, the first to identify the camera brand, second to identify the camera model, and finally third to perform the exact device identification.

The deep learning network used is known as the Residual Neural Network (ResNet). In this network, both low level features as well as the high level features are learned by the network simultaneously. The presence of blocks in the network known as *residuals*, helps in learning deep interpretation about the input data.

## 5.2 Network Architecture

In the resent architecture shown in Fig.7, the following layers are used:

- The input image is passed through a convolution layer with kernel size of 7 x 7, 64 filters are used. The stride size is 2.

- Max pool layer is followed with a kernel size of 3 x 3, and stride of 2.
- The first residual block begins that is repeated 3 times which has the following structure,
  - Convolution layer with 1 x 1 kernel, and 64 number of filters
  - Convolution layer with 3 x 3 kernel, and 64 number of filters
  - Convolution layer with 1 x 1 kernel, and 256 number of filters
- The second residual block begins that is repeated 4 times which has the following structure,
  - Convolution layer with 1 x 1 kernel, and 128 number of filters
  - Convolution layer with 3 x 3 kernel, and 128 number of filters
  - Convolution layer with 1 x 1 kernel, and 512 number of filters
- The third residual block begins that is repeated 6 times which has the following structure,
  - Convolution layer with 1 x 1 kernel, and 256 number of filters
  - Convolution layer with 3 x 3 kernel, and 256 number of filters
  - Convolution layer with 1 x 1 kernel, and 1024 number of filters
- The final residual block begins that is repeated 3 times which has the following structure,
  - Convolution layer with 1 x 1 kernel, and 256 number of filters
  - Convolution layer with 3 x 3 kernel, and 256 number of filters
  - Convolution layer with 1 x 1 kernel, and 1024 number of filters
- The average pooling layer is followed to get an output feature map is produced which is then passed through a softmax layer to predict the class label.

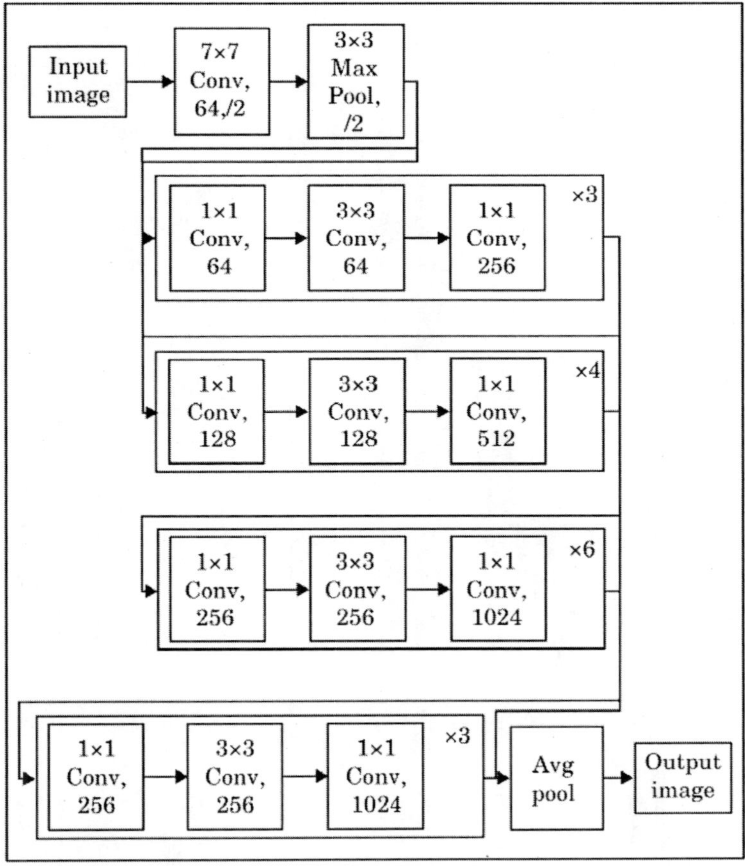


**Fig. 7:** ResNet architecture

### 5.3 Experimental Results

There are four different experiments conducted on images downloaded from the Dresden image dataset.

- *Experiment 1:* First, camera brand identification is performed. Here, 13 different camera brands are used from Dresden dataset. The experimental results are shown in Fig.8. The classification accuracy is 99.12% by the resnet.
- *Experiment 2:* In this experiment, camera model identification is performed. Here, 27 camera models from Dresden dataset are

| | Agfa DC-830i | Canon Ixus70 | Fujifilm Finepix J50 | Kodak M1063 | Nikon coolpix 3710 | Olympus MJU 1050SW | Panasonic DMC-FZ50 | Pentax optioA40 | Praktica DCZ5.9 | Ricoh Gx100 | Rollei RCP-7325XS | Samsung L74 wide | Sony DSC-W170 |
|---|---|---|---|---|---|---|---|---|---|---|---|---|---|
| Agfa DC-830i | 0.93 | 0.02 | 0.00 | 0.00 | 0.00 | 0.01 | 0.00 | 0.00 | 0.02 | 0.00 | 0.00 | 0.02 | 0.00 |
| Canon Ixus70 | 0.00 | 1.00 | 0.00 | 0.00 | 0.00 | 0.00 | 0.00 | 0.00 | 0.00 | 0.00 | 0.00 | 0.00 | 0.00 |
| Fujifilm Finepix J50 | 0.00 | 0.00 | 0.99 | 0.00 | 0.00 | 0.00 | 0.00 | 0.00 | 0.00 | 0.00 | 0.00 | 0.00 | 0.01 |
| Kodak M1063 | 0.00 | 0.00 | 0.00 | 0.99 | 0.00 | 0.00 | 0.00 | 0.00 | 0.00 | 0.00 | 0.00 | 0.00 | 0.00 |
| Nikon coolpix 3710 | 0.00 | 0.00 | 0.00 | 0.00 | 1.00 | 0.00 | 0.00 | 0.00 | 0.00 | 0.00 | 0.00 | 0.00 | 0.00 |
| Olympus MJU 1050SW | 0.00 | 0.00 | 0.00 | 0.00 | 0.00 | 1.00 | 0.00 | 0.00 | 0.00 | 0.00 | 0.00 | 0.00 | 0.00 |
| Panasonic DMC-FZ50 | 0.00 | 0.00 | 0.00 | 0.00 | 0.00 | 0.00 | 1.00 | 0.00 | 0.00 | 0.00 | 0.00 | 0.00 | 0.00 |
| Pentax optioA40 | 0.00 | 0.00 | 0.00 | 0.00 | 0.00 | 0.00 | 0.00 | 1.00 | 0.00 | 0.00 | 0.00 | 0.00 | 0.00 |
| Praktica DCZ5.9 | 0.00 | 0.00 | 0.00 | 0.00 | 0.00 | 0.00 | 0.00 | 0.00 | 0.98 | 0.00 | 0.00 | 0.01 | 0.00 |
| Ricoh Gx100 | 0.00 | 0.00 | 0.00 | 0.00 | 0.00 | 0.00 | 0.00 | 0.00 | 0.00 | 1.00 | 0.00 | 0.00 | 0.00 |
| Rollei RCP-7325XS | 0.00 | 0.01 | 0.01 | 0.00 | 0.00 | 0.00 | 0.00 | 0.00 | 0.00 | 0.00 | 0.98 | 0.01 | 0.00 |
| Samsung L74 wide | 0.00 | 0.00 | 0.00 | 0.00 | 0.00 | 0.00 | 0.00 | 0.00 | 0.00 | 0.00 | 0.00 | 0.98 | 0.00 |
| Sony DSC-W170 | 0.00 | 0.00 | 0.01 | 0.00 | 0.00 | 0.00 | 0.00 | 0.00 | 0.00 | 0.00 | 0.00 | 0.00 | 0.98 |

**Fig. 8:** The confusion matrix of identification with 13 different camera brands

| | AgfaDC-504 | AgfaDC-733s | AgfaDC-830i | Afga sensor 505x | Afga sensor 530s | Canon ixus55 | Canon ixus70 | Canon powers shotA640 | Casio EX-Z150 | Fujifilm FinePix 150 | Kodak M1063 | Nikon coolpix S710 | Nikon 200 | Nikon D70 | Nikon D70S | Olympus mju 1050SW | Panasonic DMC-FZ50 | Pentax optioA40 | Pentax optio W60D | Praktica DCZ5.9 | Ricoh Gx100 | Rollei RCP-7325XS | Samsung L74 wide | Samsung Nv15 | Sony DSC-H50 | Sony DSC-T77 | Sony DSC-W170 |
|---|---|---|---|---|---|---|---|---|---|---|---|---|---|---|---|---|---|---|---|---|---|---|---|---|---|---|---|
| AgfaDC-504 | -0.98 | 0.00 | 0.00 | 0.00 | 0.00 | 0.00 | 0.00 | 0.00 | 0.02 | 0.00 | 0.00 | 0.00 | 0.00 | 0.00 | 0.00 | 0.00 | 0.00 | 0.00 | 0.00 | 0.00 | 0.00 | 0.00 | 0.00 | 0.00 | 0.00 | 0.00 | 0.00 |
| AgfaDC-733s | -0.00 | 0.90 | 0.03 | 0.00 | 0.00 | 0.00 | 0.00 | 0.00 | 0.00 | 0.00 | 0.00 | 0.04 | 0.00 | 0.00 | 0.00 | 0.00 | 0.00 | 0.00 | 0.00 | 0.00 | 0.00 | 0.01 | 0.03 | 0.00 | 0.00 | 0.00 | 0.00 |
| AgfaDC-830i | -0.00 | 0.02 | 0.95 | 0.00 | 0.00 | 0.00 | 0.01 | 0.00 | 0.00 | 0.00 | 0.00 | 0.00 | 0.00 | 0.00 | 0.00 | 0.01 | 0.00 | 0.00 | 0.00 | 0.00 | 0.00 | 0.00 | 0.00 | 0.00 | 0.00 | 0.00 | 0.00 |
| Afga sensor 505x | -0.00 | 0.00 | 0.00 | 1.00 | 0.00 | 0.00 | 0.00 | 0.00 | 0.00 | 0.00 | 0.00 | 0.00 | 0.00 | 0.00 | 0.00 | 0.00 | 0.00 | 0.00 | 0.00 | 0.00 | 0.00 | 0.00 | 0.00 | 0.00 | 0.00 | 0.00 | 0.00 |
| Afga sensor 530s | -0.02 | 0.00 | 0.00 | 0.00 | 0.94 | 0.00 | 0.00 | 0.00 | 0.00 | 0.00 | 0.00 | 0.00 | 0.00 | 0.00 | 0.00 | 0.01 | 0.00 | 0.00 | 0.00 | 0.00 | 0.00 | 0.00 | 0.00 | 0.03 | 0.00 | 0.00 | 0.00 |
| Canon ixus55 | -0.00 | 0.00 | 0.00 | 0.00 | 0.00 | 0.56 | 0.38 | 0.00 | 0.00 | 0.00 | 0.00 | 0.00 | 0.00 | 0.00 | 0.00 | 0.00 | 0.00 | 0.00 | 0.00 | 0.00 | 0.00 | 0.00 | 0.03 | 0.01 | 0.00 | 0.01 | 0.00 |
| Canon ixus70 | -0.00 | 0.00 | 0.00 | 0.00 | 0.00 | 0.06 | 0.87 | 0.00 | 0.00 | 0.00 | 0.00 | 0.00 | 0.00 | 0.00 | 0.00 | 0.00 | 0.00 | 0.00 | 0.00 | 0.00 | 0.00 | 0.01 | 0.00 | 0.05 | 0.01 | 0.00 | 0.00 |
| Canon powers shotA640 | -0.00 | 0.00 | 0.00 | 0.00 | 0.00 | 0.02 | 0.02 | 0.93 | 0.00 | 0.00 | 0.00 | 0.00 | 0.00 | 0.00 | 0.00 | 0.00 | 0.02 | 0.00 | 0.00 | 0.00 | 0.00 | 0.00 | 0.00 | 0.00 | 0.00 | 0.00 | 0.00 |
| Casio EX-Z150 | -0.00 | 0.00 | 0.00 | 0.00 | 0.00 | 0.00 | 0.00 | 0.00 | 1.00 | 0.00 | 0.00 | 0.00 | 0.00 | 0.00 | 0.00 | 0.00 | 0.00 | 0.00 | 0.00 | 0.00 | 0.00 | 0.00 | 0.00 | 0.00 | 0.00 | 0.00 | 0.00 |
| Fujifilm FinePix 150 | -0.00 | 0.00 | 0.00 | 0.00 | 0.00 | 0.00 | 0.00 | 0.00 | 0.00 | 1.00 | 0.00 | 0.00 | 0.00 | 0.00 | 0.00 | 0.00 | 0.00 | 0.00 | 0.00 | 0.00 | 0.00 | 0.00 | 0.00 | 0.00 | 0.00 | 0.00 | 0.00 |
| Kodak M1063 | -0.00 | 0.00 | 0.00 | 0.00 | 0.00 | 0.00 | 0.00 | 0.00 | 0.00 | 0.00 | 1.00 | 0.00 | 0.00 | 0.00 | 0.00 | 0.00 | 0.00 | 0.00 | 0.00 | 0.00 | 0.00 | 0.00 | 0.00 | 0.00 | 0.00 | 0.00 | 0.00 |
| Nikon coolpix S710 | -0.00 | 0.00 | 0.00 | 0.00 | 0.00 | 0.00 | 0.00 | 0.00 | 0.00 | 0.00 | 0.00 | 1.00 | 0.00 | 0.00 | 0.00 | 0.00 | 0.00 | 0.00 | 0.00 | 0.00 | 0.00 | 0.00 | 0.00 | 0.00 | 0.00 | 0.00 | 0.00 |
| Nikon 200 | -0.00 | 0.00 | 0.00 | 0.00 | 0.00 | 0.00 | 0.00 | 0.00 | 0.00 | 0.00 | 0.00 | 0.01 | 0.96 | 0.00 | 0.03 | 0.00 | 0.00 | 0.00 | 0.00 | 0.00 | 0.00 | 0.00 | 0.00 | 0.00 | 0.00 | 0.00 | 0.00 |
| Nikon D70 | -0.00 | 0.00 | 0.00 | 0.00 | 0.00 | 0.00 | 0.00 | 0.00 | 0.00 | 0.00 | 0.00 | 0.00 | 0.04 | 0.58 | 0.39 | 0.00 | 0.00 | 0.00 | 0.00 | 0.00 | 0.00 | 0.00 | 0.00 | 0.00 | 0.00 | 0.00 | 0.00 |
| Nikon D70S | -0.00 | 0.00 | 0.00 | 0,00 | 0.00 | 0.00 | 0.00 | 0.00 | 0.00 | 0.00 | 0.00 | 0.00 | 0.02 | 0.42 | 0.56 | 0.00 | 0.00 | 0.00 | 0.00 | 0.00 | 0.00 | 0.00 | 0.00 | 0.00 | 0.00 | 0.00 | 0.00 |
| Olympus mju 1050SW | -0.00 | 0.00 | 0.00 | 0.00 | 0.00 | 0.00 | 0.01 | 0.00 | 0.00 | 0.00 | 0.00 | 0.00 | 0.00 | 0.00 | 0.00 | 0.96 | 0.96 | 0.00 | 0.00 | 0.00 | 0.00 | 0.00 | 0.00 | 0.00 | 0.00 | 0.00 | 0.00 |
| Panasonic DMC-FZ50 | -0.00 | 0.00 | 0.00 | 0.00 | 0.00 | 0.00 | 0.00 | 0.00 | 0.00 | 0.01 | 0.01 | 0.00 | 0.00 | 0.00 | 0.00 | 0.00 | 0.99 | 0.00 | 0.00 | 0.00 | 0.00 | 0.00 | 0.00 | 0.00 | 0.00 | 0.00 | 0.00 |
| Pentax optioA40 | -0.00 | 0.00 | 0.00 | 0.00 | 0.00 | 0.00 | 0.00 | 0.00 | 0.00 | 0.00 | 0.00 | 0.00 | 0.00 | 0.00 | 0.00 | 0.00 | 0.00 | 0.99 | 0.00 | 0.00 | 0.01 | 0.00 | 0.00 | 0.00 | 0.00 | 0.00 | 0.00 |
| Pentax optio W60D | -0.00 | 0.00 | 0.00 | 0.00 | 0.00 | 0.00 | 0.00 | 0.00 | 0.00 | 0.02 | 0.02 | 0.00 | 0.00 | 0.00 | 0.00 | 0.00 | 0.00 | 0.00 | 0.97 | 0.00 | 0.00 | 0.00 | 0.02 | 0.00 | 0.00 | 0.00 | 0.00 |
| Praktica DCZ5.9 | -0.00 | 0.00 | 0.00 | 0.00 | 0.00 | 0.00 | 0.00 | 0.00 | 0.00 | 0.00 | 0.00 | 0.00 | 0.00 | 0.00 | 0.00 | 0.00 | 0.00 | 0.00 | 0.00 | 0.98 | 0.00 | 0.02 | 0.00 | 0.00 | 0.00 | 0.00 | 0.00 |
| Ricoh Gx100 | -0.00 | 0.00 | 0.00 | 0.00 | 0.00 | 0.00 | 0.00 | 0.00 | 0.00 | 0.00 | 0.00 | 0.00 | 0.00 | 0.00 | 0.00 | 0.00 | 0.00 | 0.00 | 0.00 | 0.00 | 1.00 | 0.00 | 0.00 | 0.00 | 0.00 | 0.00 | 0.00 |
| Rollei RCP-7325XS | -0.00 | 0.00 | 0.00 | 0.00 | 0.00 | 0.00 | 0.00 | 0.00 | 0.00 | 0.00 | 0.00 | 0.00 | 0.00 | 0.00 | 0.00 | 0.00 | 0.00 | 0.00 | 0.00 | 0.04 | 0.00 | 0.94 | 0.00 | 0.02 | 0.00 | 0.00 | 0.00 |
| Samsung L74 wide | -0.00 | 0.01 | 0.00 | 0.00 | 0.00 | 0.00 | 0.00 | 0.00 | 0.00 | 0.00 | 0.00 | 0.01 | 0.00 | 0.00 | 0.00 | 0.00 | 0.00 | 0.00 | 0.00 | 0.01 | 0.00 | 0.00 | 0.97 | 0.01 | 0.90 | 0.90 | 0.00 |
| Samsung Nv15 | -0.00 | 0.01 | 0.00 | 0.00 | 0.00 | 0.00 | 0.00 | 0.00 | 0.00 | 0.00 | 0.01 | 0.00 | 0.00 | 0.00 | 0.00 | 0.00 | 0.00 | 0.00 | 0.00 | 0.00 | 0.00 | 0.02 | 0.01 | 0.96 | 0.00 | 0.00 | 0.00 |
| Sony DSC-H50 | -0.00 | 0.00 | 0.00 | 0.00 | 0.00 | 0.00 | 0.00 | 0.00 | 0.00 | 0.01 | 0.00 | 0.00 | 0.00 | 0.00 | 0.00 | 0.00 | 0.01 | 0.00 | 0.00 | 0.00 | 0.00 | 0.00 | 0.00 | 0.00 | 0.96 | 0.01 | 0.01 |
| Sony DSC-T77 | -0.00 | 0.00 | 0.00 | 0.00 | 0.00 | 0.00 | 0.00 | 0.00 | 0.00 | 0.01 | 0.00 | 0.00 | 0.00 | 0.00 | 0.00 | 0.00 | 0.00 | 0.00 | 0.00 | 0.00 | 0.00 | 0.00 | 0.00 | 0.00 | 0.00 | 0.92 | 0.04 |
| Sony DSC-W170 | -0.00 | 0.00 | 0.00 | 0.00 | 0.00 | 0.00 | 0.00 | 0.00 | 0.00 | 0.02 | 0.00 | 0.00 | 0.00 | 0.00 | 0.00 | 0.00 | 0.00 | 0.00 | 0.00 | 0.00 | 0.00 | 0.00 | 0.00 | 0.00 | 0.10 | 0.02 | 0.35 |

**Fig. 9:** The confusion matrix of identification with 27 different camera models

used. There are different camera brands involved and also different camera makes are involved. The classification accuracy is 94.73% by the ResNet architecture. The confusion matrix is shown in Fig. 9.

- *Experiment 3:* Exact device linking is performed in experiment 3. The three camera devices of same make and model are used from Fujifilm FinepixJ50. The classification accuracy is 45.81%.
- *Experiment 4:* In experiment 4, mobile devices are also involved. The classification accuracy is 97.73%. The confusion matrix is shown in Fig. 10.

The overall comparative results are shown in Table 7. A simple CNN architecture, much successful AlexNet and GoogleNet are used for comparison.

**Table 7:** Experimental results

| *Method* | *EXP1* | *EXP2* | *EXP3* | *EXP4* |
|---|---|---|---|---|
| CNN | – | 94.1% | 29.8% | – |
| AlexNet | 62.21% | 45.41% | 16.19% | 61.06% |
| GoogleNet | 96.31% | 87.25% | 35.09% | 92.81% |
| ResNet | 99.12% | 94.73% | 45.81% | 97.73% |

## 6. ON THE VULNERABILITY OF DEEP LEARNING TO ADVERSARIAL ATTACKS FOR CAMERA MODEL INDENTIFICATION

### 6.1 Introduction

In this work, the authors study the vulnerability of deep learning based camera model identification. With a rise in current deep learning practices across all domains, it is imperative that a vulnerability assessment is performed. As discussed in the previous sections, a few deep learning based camera model identification techniques[28,32] are proposed. In this section, the vulnerability of deep learning based techniques in camera model identification is discussed.

The primary concern with the current deep learning solutions[28,32] is the image patch size. In an experimental setup, the image patch sizes are maintained according the best available GPU architecture. In reality, the image patch sizes are much larger. The original test

| | AgfaDC-830i | Canon ixus70 | Fujifilm FinePix 150 | I phone6 | Kodak M1063 | Meizu- Pro6 | Nikon coolpix S710 | Olympus mju 1050SW | Panasonic DMC-FZ50 | Pentax optioA40 | Praktica DCZ5.9 | Ricoh Gx100 | Rollei RCP-7325XS | Samsung GTI9300 | Samsung L74 wide | Smartisan-U1 | Sony DSC-W170 | VIVO X7 | XIAOMI-MI5 |
|---|---|---|---|---|---|---|---|---|---|---|---|---|---|---|---|---|---|---|---|
| AgfaDC-830i | 0.96 | 0.00 | 0.00 | 0.00 | 0.00 | 0.00 | 0.00 | 0.00 | 0.00 | 0.00 | 0.00 | 0.00 | 0.00 | 0.00 | 0.00 | 0.00 | 0.00 | 0.00 | 0.00 |
| Canon ixus70 | 0.00 | 0.96 | 0.00 | 0.00 | 0.00 | 0.00 | 0.00 | 0.00 | 0.00 | 0.00 | 0.00 | 0.00 | 0.00 | 0.00 | 0.00 | 0.00 | 0.00 | 0.00 | 0.00 |
| Fujifilm FinePix 150 | 0.00 | 0.00 | 0.96 | 0.00 | 0.00 | 0.00 | 0.00 | 0.00 | 0.00 | 0.00 | 0.00 | 0.00 | 0.00 | 0.00 | 0.00 | 0.00 | 0.00 | 0.00 | 0.00 |
| I phone6 | 0.00 | 0.00 | 0.00 | 0.92 | 0.00 | 0.00 | 0.00 | 0.00 | 0.00 | 0.00 | 0.00 | 0.00 | 0.00 | 0.00 | 0.00 | 0.00 | 0.00 | 0.05 | 0.04 |
| Kodak M1063 | 0.00 | 0.00 | 0.00 | 0.00 | 1.00 | 0.00 | 0.00 | 0.00 | 0.00 | 0.00 | 0.00 | 0.00 | 0.00 | 0.00 | 0.00 | 0.00 | 0.00 | 0.00 | 0.00 |
| Meizu- Pro6 | 0.00 | 0.00 | 0.00 | 0.02 | 0.00 | 0.89 | 0.00 | 0.00 | 0.00 | 0.00 | 0.00 | 0.00 | 0.00 | 0.00 | 0.00 | 0.06 | 0.00 | 0.04 | 0.00 |
| Nikon coolpix S710 | 0.00 | 0.00 | 0.00 | 0.00 | 0.00 | 0.00 | 1.00 | 0.00 | 0.00 | 0.00 | 0.00 | 0.00 | 0.00 | 0.00 | 0.00 | 0.00 | 0.00 | 0.00 | 0.00 |
| Olympus mju 1050SW | 0.00 | 0.00 | 0.00 | 0.00 | 0.00 | 0.00 | 0.00 | 0.95 | 0.00 | 0.00 | 0.00 | 0.00 | 0.00 | 0.00 | 0.02 | 0.00 | 0.00 | 0.00 | 0.00 |
| Panasonic DMC-FZ50 | 0.00 | 0.00 | 0.00 | 0.00 | 0.00 | 0.00 | 0.00 | 0.00 | 1.00 | 0.00 | 0.00 | 0.00 | 0.00 | 0.00 | 0.00 | 0.00 | 0.00 | 0.00 | 0.00 |
| Pentax optioA40 | 0.00 | 0.00 | 0.00 | 0.00 | 0.00 | 0.00 | 0.00 | 0.00 | 0.00 | 0.99 | 0.00 | 0.01 | 0.00 | 0.00 | 0.00 | 0.00 | 0.00 | 0.00 | 0.00 |
| Praktica DCZ5.9 | 0.00 | 0.00 | 0.00 | 0.00 | 0.00 | 0.00 | 0.00 | 0.00 | 0.00 | 0.00 | 0.99 | 0.00 | 0.01 | 0.00 | 0.00 | 0.00 | 0.00 | 0.00 | 0.00 |
| Ricoh Gx100 | 0.00 | 0.00 | 0.00 | 0.00 | 0.00 | 0.00 | 0.00 | 0.00 | 0.00 | 0.00 | 0.00 | 1.00 | 0.00 | 0.00 | 0.00 | 0.00 | 0.00 | 0.00 | 0.00 |
| Rollei RCP-7325XS | 0.00 | 0.00 | 0.00 | 0.00 | 0.00 | 0.00 | 0.00 | 0.00 | 0.00 | 0.00 | 0.01 | 0.00 | 0.99 | 0.00 | 0.00 | 0.00 | 0.00 | 0.00 | 0.00 |
| Samsung GTI9300 | 0.00 | 0.00 | 0.00 | 0.00 | 0.00 | 0.00 | 0.00 | 0.00 | 0.00 | 0.00 | 0.00 | 0.00 | 0.00 | 0.84 | 0.00 | 0.11 | 0.00 | 0.03 | 0.00 |
| Samsung L74 wide | 0.00 | 0.00 | 0.00 | 0.00 | 0.00 | 0.00 | 0.00 | 0.00 | 0.00 | 0.00 | 0.02 | 0.00 | 0.02 | 0.00 | 0.96 | 0.00 | 0.00 | 0.00 | 0.00 |
| Smartisan-U1 | 0.01 | 0.00 | 0.00 | 0.00 | 0.01 | 0.01 | 0.00 | 0.00 | 0.00 | 0.00 | 0.00 | 0.00 | 0.00 | 0.04 | 0.00 | 0.86 | 0.00 | 0.07 | 0.00 |
| Sony DSC-W170 | 0.00 | 0.00 | 0.02 | 0.00 | 0.01 | 0.00 | 0.00 | 0.00 | 0.00 | 0.00 | 0.00 | 0.00 | 0.00 | 0.00 | 0.00 | 0.00 | 0.97 | 0.00 | 0.00 |
| VIVO X7 | 0.00 | 0.00 | 0.00 | 0.00 | 0.00 | 0.00 | 0.09 | 0.02 | 0.00 | 0.00 | 0.00 | 0.00 | 0.00 | 0.02 | 0.00 | 0.02 | 0.00 | 0.84 | 0.00 |
| XIAOMI-MI5 | 0.00 | 0.00 | 0.00 | 0.00 | 0.00 | 0.00 | 0.00 | 0.01 | 0.00 | 0.00 | 0.00 | 0.00 | 0.00 | 0.00 | 0.00 | 0.00 | 0.00 | 0.04 | 0.94 |

**Fig. 10:** The confusion matrix of identification with 13 different camera brands and 6 different telephone brands.

image would have a much larger size compared to the image sizes used for training the deep learning network.

The attack model is shown in Fig. 11. As shown, if the target image is divided many image patches, and the adversarial method is applied on each patch and then combined together. The stitched up image can be saved using a lossless mechanism such as Portable Network Graphics (PNG) or using a lossy mechanism such as JPEG. The lossy compression is usually employed when transmitted using any social network.

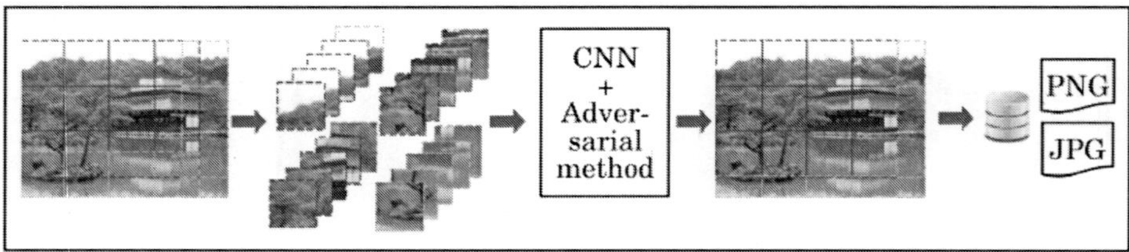


**Fig. 11:** Patchwise attack model

Assuming that the underlying classification network is known, the attack protocol is as follows:

- The entire adversarial image is generated patchwise
- A number of patches are extracted from random positions and classified by the network
- A Maximum likelihood decision is made to fuse results from all patches.

In another group of experiments, the attacker has no knowledge of the underlying deep learning network used for camera model identification. In this scenario, the attack is performed on a known model A and then transferred to an unknown model B. This scenario is depicted in Fig. 12. And also, a defender strategy is also depicted where the defender can use the adversarial samples to train the classification network.

### 6.2 Experimental Results

The experiments are conducted on the publicly available VISION dataset. The dataset consists of 35 devices coming from 30 different camera models. 150 JPEG images from each device are selected. For training, 100 random patches from each image are used to enhance the training samples.

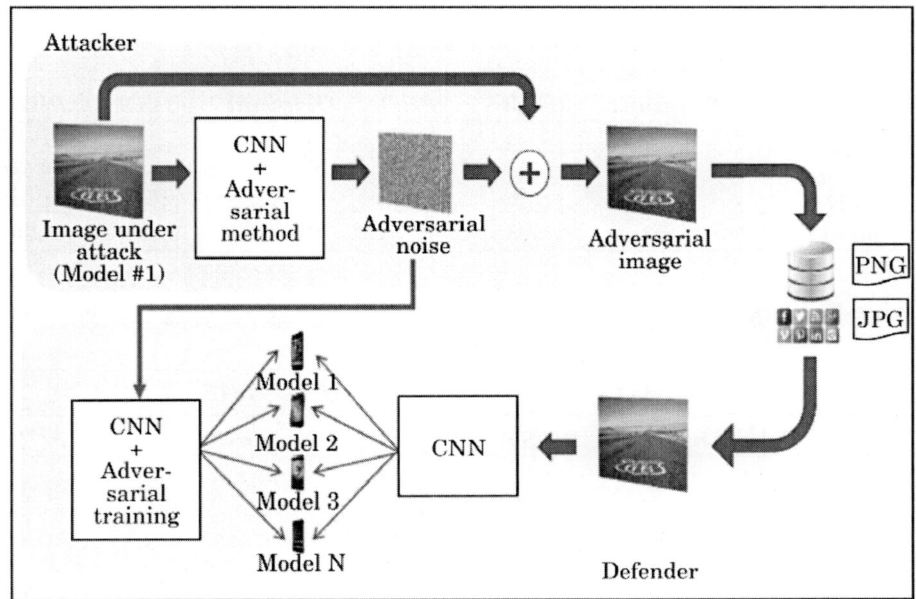


**Fig. 12:** The complete workflow

The adversarial samples are generated using the cleverhans software available for public use. There are two techniques used to generate the adversarial samples. The first technique is the Fast Gradient Sign Method (FGSM) and the other technique is the Projected Gradient Descent (PGD).

The classification accuracies of the various deep learning architectures against the original image samples and adversarial samples is shown in Table 8. It can be observed that the classification accuracy with the original image samples is atleast above 95% in case of lossless coding schemes. The Shallow CNN shows an accuracy of 95.06%, DenseNet40 has 97.8%, DenseNet121 gives 99.1%, and the XceptionNet gives an accuracy of 99.3%. With the adversarial samples, the classification accuracy drops significantly in case of lossless coding.

In case of lossy coding, JPEG with a quality factor of 75, the XceptionNet performs best with an accuracy of 91.36% in case of original samples. When the adversarial images are involved, the classification accuracy drops significantly. The best classification accuracy is observed for the case of PGD samples and with XceptionNet at 85.27%.

**Table 8:** Classification accuracies of original *vs.* adversarial image samples

| | ***Lossless Coding*** | | | ***JPEG Q=75*** | | |
|---|---|---|---|---|---|---|
| | ***Original*** | ***FGSM*** | ***PGD*** | ***Original*** | ***FGSM*** | ***PGD*** |
| Shallow CNN | 95.06 | 12.18 | 23.68 | 32.87 | 25.17 | 29.93 |
| Dense Net 40 | 97.80 | 7.47 | 5.63 | 76.78 | 72.99 | 72.76 |
| Dense Net 121 | 99.10 | 16.09 | 6.78 | 85.06 | 71.03 | 75.29 |
| Xception Net | 99.3 | 14.73 | 11.39 | 91.36 | 77.68 | 85.27 |

**Table 9:** Classification Accuracies of Original *vs.* Adversarial image samples, in case of adversarial training

| | ***Lossless Coding*** | | | ***JPEG Q=75*** | | |
|---|---|---|---|---|---|---|
| | ***Original*** | ***FGSM*** | ***PGD*** | ***Original*** | ***FGSM*** | ***PGD*** |
| Shallow CNN + AT | 95.86 | 95.52 | 92.53 | 84.60 | 77.93 | 80.92 |
| Dense Net 40 + AT | 89.66 | 98.85 | 91.26 | 72.87 | 72.30 | 72.18 |
| Dense Net 121 + AT | 89.20 | 85.98 | 82.41 | 96.55 | 96.32 | 95.98 |
| Xception Net + AT | 98.85 | 98.97 | 98.62 | 97.82 | 96.44 | 97.59 |

To counter the presence of the adversarial samples, the defender can train their deep learning networks with the adversarial samples. The classification results are shown in Table 9, with each deep learning network having the adversarial samples in the training. The results show an improvement over the previous experiment in every network.

## 7. CONCLUSIONS

Deep learning is a recently evolving and powerful classification technology. Various researchers in source camera identification also used deep learning as a classification methodology to identify the source camera of a query image. In this chapter, various recent deep learning architectures for source camera identification are discussed. As a future research direction, the robustness of source camera identification using deep learning needs to be studied with respect to various image modifications such as compression, geometric transformations such as rotation and scaling.

# 7

# Identifying Unknown Models in Source Camera Identification

## 1. INTRODUCTION

A major hindrance to source camera identification is the presence of unknown camera models. In a source identification setup, there are a finite number of camera models used by the forensic analyst for pre-processing. The pre-processing in a machine learning based source identification technique is to train the machine learning classifier on images from each camera model. The pre-processing in a fingerprint-based source identification technique is finding the sensor pattern noise of each camera model.

Rest of this chapter consist of the followings. In Section 2 and Section 3, we present the Unknown Model Detection Problem in forensic Source Camera Identification, in Machine Learning and Feature based Learning Approaches. In Section 4, we present the solutions to the Unknown Model problem. We conclude the chapter in Section 5.

## 2. PROBLEM OF UNKNOWN MODELS IN MACHINE LEARNING BASED SOURCE CAMERA IDENTIFICATION

In case of a machine learning setup for source camera identification, the training of the classifier model is done in a closed set. Let there be '*N*' camera models ($C_1$, $C_2$... $C_N$) at hand with the forensic analyst. The training is performed by taking enough number of images from each camera model and extracting the appropriate features such as either IQM, HOWS, BSM etc. (discussed in chapter 4) and feeding the feature matrix to the classifier. When the test image $I_T$ comes from a camera models $C_U$ which was not part of the camera models used for training the machine learning classifier, then the machine learning classifier will try to map $I_T$ to one of the camera models used in training. This is shown in Fig. 1, where there are three camera models C1, C2, and C3 used in the training whereas the test images are originating from camera models C1, C2, C3, C4, C5, C6, and C7. Though the classifier can perform source identification when the test images are from either C1, C2, and C3, the class labels of images which originated from C4, C5, C6, and C7 (which are unknown to the classifier), are labelled either with C1, or C2, or C3. In the Fig. shown (Fig. 1), the known camera models to the system are C1, C2, and C3. The unknown camera models are C4, C5, C6, and C7.

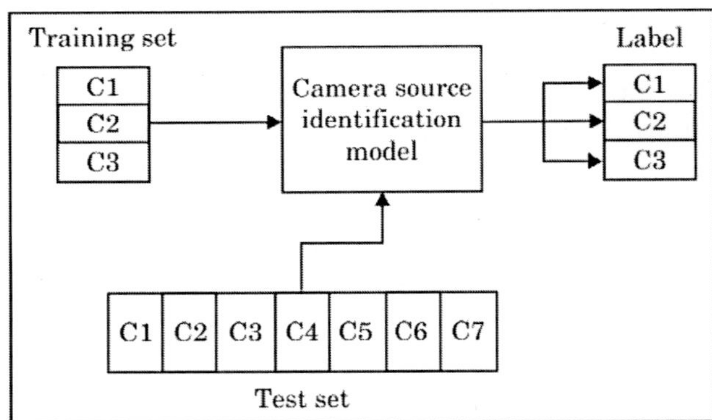


**Fig. 1:** Unknown models in machine learning based source camera identification

## 3. PROBLEM OF UNKNOWN MODELS IN FINGERPRINT BASED SOURCE CAMERA IDENTIFICATION

In a fingerprint based setup for source identification, the procedure is to find the correlation between the noise residual of the test image against the sensor pattern noises of the existing cameras which is depicted in Fig. 2. It involves two stages, pre-processing is performed in stage1 and the actual source attribution is performed in stage 2. The pre-processing stage is nothing but finding the sensor pattern noises of each camera model available to the forensic analyst. This again comes from a closed set of camera models $C_1$, $C_2$...$C_N$. The sensor patterns for each camera model are stored as $SPN_1$, $SPN_2 \ldots SPN_N$.

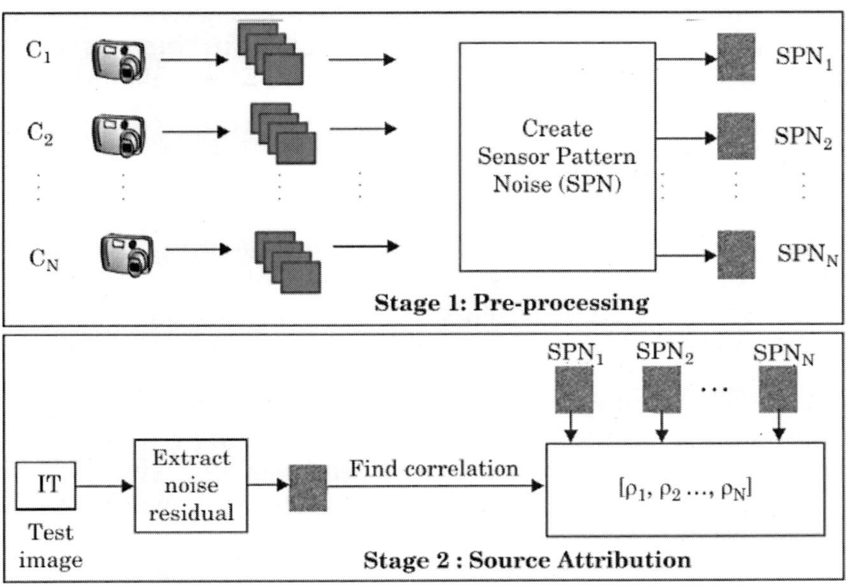


**Fig. 2:** Fingerprint based source attribution

In the next stage *i.e.* source attribution stage, the noise residual of the test image is extracted and correlated with the sensor pattern noises. The correlation mechanisms followed can be either Normalized Cross Correlation (NCC), or Peak-to-Correlation-Energy ratio (PCE) as discussed in chapter 4. The correlation with the source camera will usually be a HIGH value, whereas the correlations with other cameras will be LOW. The correlations $\rho_1, \rho_2 \ldots \rho_N$ are tested against a threshold value (discussed in chapter 4) to find the source camera. If a particular $\rho_i$ is greater than the pre-selected threshold then the camera model $C_I$ is treated to be the source camera.

When the test image is actually originated from camera $C_U$, which is not part of $C_1, C_2 \ldots C_N$, and then the correlation of noise residual of the test image against all the sensor pattern noises will be LOW. And hence, the source attribution for the test image is not possible.

## 4. SOLUTIONS TO UNKNOWN MODELS DETECTION IN SOURCE CAMERA IDENTIFICATION

In literature, this important problem in source camera identification is addressed only by a few researchers. In this section, we present briefly the approaches used to identify the unknown camera models.

### 4.1 Binary SVM for Unknown Model Detection

Though not very successful, Gloe[9] tried to address the open set problem *i.e.* unknown models problem in source camera identification for the first time. He has followed a machine learning approach by using the extended colour features set (discussed in chapter 4).

A one class support vector machine (SVM) classifier is used to identify if an image from the class or not. It required generating a classifier for each camera model and hence not very suitable in real world applications. Also, a binary support vector machine (SVM) classifier is used to distinguish the known models *vs* unknown models, but the accuracy in separating is very limited. It decreased as the number of unknown models increased.

In a one class SVM methodology, each camera model is trained with an associated classifier. If there are N camera models known to the forensic analyst, then there will be N one class SVM classifiers designed to only identify images coming from those models.

The binary SVM classification is made possible by making all the combinations of known and unknown models simulated with the camera models at hand. A two class SVM is designed for every combination to identify the known and unknown camera models. When the results of all the combinations of binary SVMs are combined through a majority voting principle, the ultimate classification can be made.

In this work, the principles of one class SVM and binary SVM are discussed and the results of binary SVM on the Dresden dataset are shown in Table. The experiment is conducted by varying the unknown camera models from 2, 5, 10, 15 and 18 in the Dresden dataset.

**Table 1:** Experimental results of binary SVM

| ***Number of unknown models*** | ***Known Recall (01)*** | ***Unknown Precision (01)*** | ***Source Detecion Accuracy (%)*** |
|---|---|---|---|
| 2 | 0.83 | 0.6 | 86.1 |
| 5 | 0.78 | 0.51 | 78.4 |
| 10 | 0.6 | 0.81 | 70.3 |
| 15 | 0.48 | 0.83 | 49.8 |
| 18 | 0.29 | 0.84 | 41.6 |

### 4.2 Decision Boundary Carving (DBC) for Unknown Model Detection

Costa *et al.*[11] proposed a boundary carving technique to identify unknown camera models. They proposed correlation based features on 9 regions of interest of a pair of images from a camera model. The regions of interest in an image are considered as follows: the centre portion of the image, top right corner, top left corner, bottom left corner, bottom right corner, and the four peripheries at the centre portion.

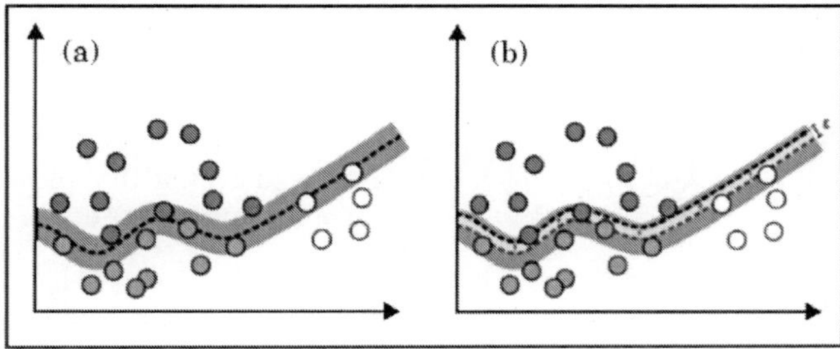


**Fig. 3:** (a) Normal SVM hyperplane (b) Decision boundary carving using SVM

Correlations are calculated between a pair of images at all the above 9 regions of interest. The correlations are calculated in Red, Green, and Blue channels of the image, giving rise to 27 feature vectors. A decision boundary carving principle is designed using a SVM classifier to identify the unknown camera models. In an SVM classifier, a hyperplane is calculated to separate the positive and negative classes. But if the unknown classes are also present, then it makes it difficult to operate the classifier. In the decision boundary carving technique, the decision boundary at the hyperplane is carved to mitigate the loss incurred due to the unknown models.

**Algorithm 1: *Decision Boundary Carving***

| | |
|---|---|
| Input : $\mathcal{P}$, $N$ - | ▷ Set of elements of the positive class of interest and the known negative class (es) ,respectively ε |
| Output: Decision hyperplane parameters $\vec{w}$ and $b$, and the open set threshold | ▷ Calculating the SVM hyperplance parameters |
| | |
| $(\vec{w}, b) \leftarrow$ SVM- Training ( $\mathcal{P}$ ,$N$ ); | |
| C ← Classification ($\vec{w}, b, \mathcal{P}, N$); | ▷ Obtaining the decision scores |
| Min ← lowest – decision – score (C ); | |
| Max ← Highest – decision – score (C ) | |
| $\mathcal{D} \leftarrow +\infty$ | ▷ Setting the initial data error to a maximum value |
| For ε′← min to max do | ▷ ε′ spans possible scores in C (increasing of $10^{-4}$ herein |
| $(A^+, A^-) \leftarrow 0$ | |
| For all $x^+ \in \mathcal{P}$ do | |
| $A^+ \leftarrow A^+ + \theta(x^+, \varepsilon')$ | |
| End for | |
| For all $x^- \in \kappa$ do | |
| $A^- \leftarrow : A^- + \omega(x^+, \varepsilon')$: | ▷ True negative for this particular position of the hyperplane |
| End for | |
| $A_x \leftarrow \frac{1}{2}\left(\frac{A^+}{p}\ \frac{A^-}{N}\right)$: | ▷ Normalized averaged accuracy |
| $\mathcal{D}' \leftarrow \frac{1}{Ax}$, | |
| If $\mathcal{D}' < \mathcal{D}$ then | |
| $\mathcal{D} \leftarrow \mathcal{D}'$ | |
| $\varepsilon \leftarrow \varepsilon'$ | |
| End if | |
| End for | |
| Return ($\vec{w}$, $b$, ε) | |

The decision boundary carving methodology is depicted in Fig. 3 where the orange points represent the positive class, the green points show the negative class, and the white points show the samples from unknown class. In a traditional SVM classifier, as shown in Fig. 3 (a), the classifier finds a margin between the classes as a hyperplane. Still, some points of unknown classes fall into one of the known classes which in turn impact the classification accuracy. In a decision boundary carving (DBC) methodology, as depicted in Fig. 3(b), the decision boundary between the known classes is further carved to keep the unknown samples away from the boundary.

The detailed procedure of Decision Boundary Carving is shown Algorithm 1. The input to the procedure is a set of elements of the positive class and the known negative classes. The algorithm then first calculates the SVM hyperplane parameters. The normalized average accuracy is used to carve the decision boundary.

The experimental results are shown in Table 2 for the DBC method. Images from Dresden dataset are used and the unknown camera models are varied from 2, 5, 10, 15, and 18 from 20 camera models. The known models recall, unknown images precision, and the source detection accuracy are detailed in Table 2.

**Table 2:** Experimental results of DBC

| ***Number of unknown models*** | ***Known Recall (01)*** | ***Unknown Precision (01)*** | ***Source Detecion Accuracy (%)*** |
|---|---|---|---|
| 2 | 0.9 | 0.28 | 80 |
| 5 | 0.82 | 0.41 | 75 |
| 10 | 0.67 | 0.62 | 68 |
| 15 | 0.57 | 0.73 | 60 |
| 18 | 0.32 | 0.8 | 51 |

Though, this technique is promising and performed better than the previous binary SVM technique, it is not very successful when the number of unknown camera models are more.

### 4.3 Source Camera Identification with unknown models (SCIU)

Huang *et al.*[10] addressed the unknown model camera model identification using a K-Nearest Neighbour approach. From an unlabelled training set, the unknown samples are first identified using the KNN method. Further, a self-training method is used to enhance the training strategy of identifying all the unknown models. Ultimately a (N+1) class classification is performed where N is the number of camera models, and all the unknown images are categorised as one class. As shown in Fig. 3, if there are three known classes of cameras C1,C2, and C3 and four unknown camera models (C4, C5, C6, and C7), the methodology by Huang *et al.,* maps all the unknown models into one single class named as UC (unknown class).

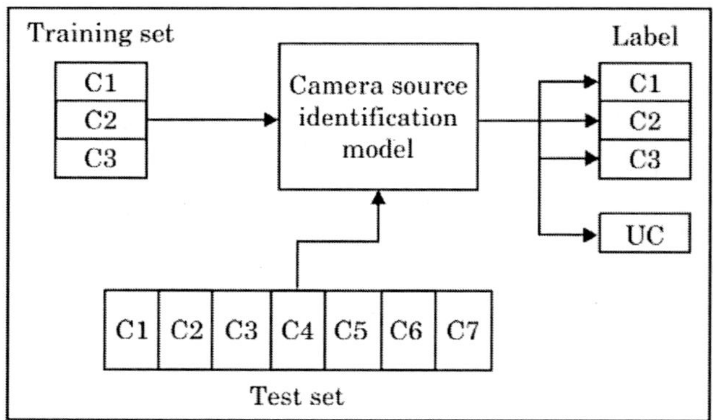


**Fig. 4:** Unknown model identification in Huang *et al.,* scheme

In this work, the authors have used the IQM and HOWS features for consideration. To identify the unknown models, a KNN based approach is employed. The idea is to find K-nearest neighbours of test image in the labelled training set. The labelled training set contains images only from the known camera models and hence if the test image is from one of the known cameras, then there will be at least a few nearest neighbours in the feature space. Otherwise, if the test image is from an unknown model, there will not be any nearest neighbours in the feature space. Those images for which the number of nearest neighbours is close to zero (0 or 1) are treated to be originated from unknown camera models and are separated.

The detailed workflow is shown in Fig. 5. From the labelled training dataset, unknown images are identified using the KNN based unknown detection principle. Parameter optimization is applied to find the optimum parameters of the KNN principle. The trained model is used to detect the unknown images from the test image dataset.

The KNN based unknown model detection is explained using the procedure shown in Algorithm 2. The input is the labelled training dataset, unlabelled training dataset and the optimization parameter *k*. The output from the procedure is the set of unknown images. IQM and HOWS features proposed in the paper by Kharrazi *et al.*[15] are used for image representation. For each image in the combined training set of known and unknown images, K nearest samples of the image sample are identified. If the intersection of the set of images identified by KNN and the set of known images is NULL, then that image sample is treated to be from an unknown model. This process is repeated for all the images in the dataset to identify the unknown images.

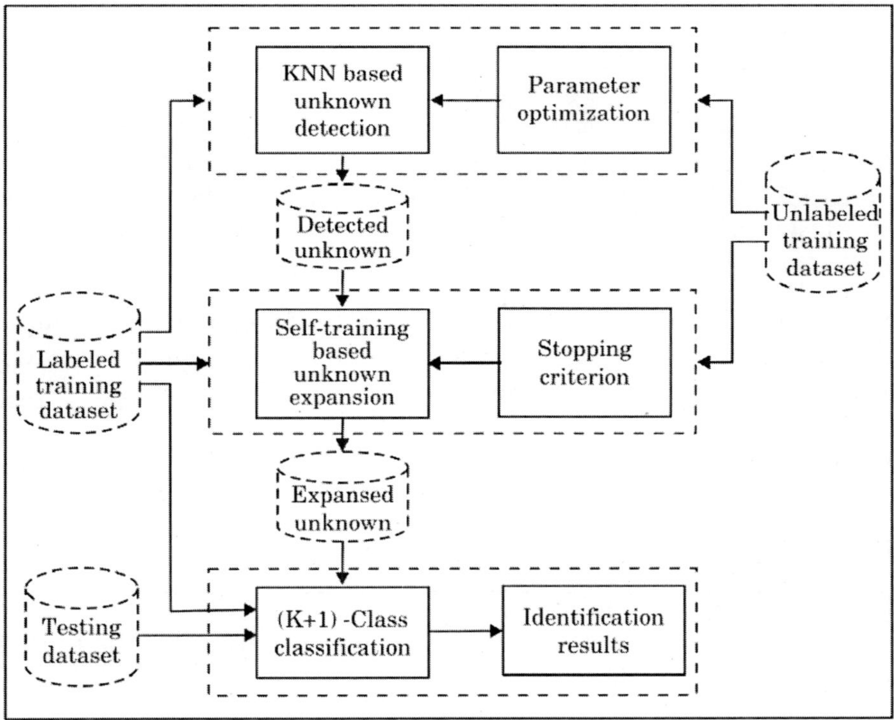


**Fig. 5:** The SCIU work flow

The parameter optimization for KNN based unknown model detection performed. The main parameter to be optimized is the value of K. It is identified by varying 'K' from 1 to $K_{max}$ and identifying the particular 'K' value at which the False Positive Rate (FPR) is less than an acceptable threshold.

**Alg. 2: *KNN Based Unknown Model Detection***

*Input:* Labelled training dataset P, Unlabelled training dataset Q, Parameter 'k'
*Output:* Image set of unknown models: U

```
U ← Ø
T ← P ∪ Q
Foreach Image I ϵ Q do
N^I ← KNN (I, T, k)
If N^I ∩ P == Ø
U ← U {I}
End
End
Return U
```

The experimental results are as shown in Table 3. Images from Dresden dataset are used and the unknown camera models are varied from 2, 5, 10, 15, and 18 from 20 camera models. The known models recall, unknown images precision, and the source detection accuracy are detailed in Table 3.

The results show that the SCIU method proposed by Huang *et al.*[10] is superior to the earlier techniques are offer a simplistic solution in identifying the unknown images.

**Table 3:** Experimental results of SCIU

| *Number of unknown models* | *Known Recall (01)* | *Unknown Precision (01)* | *Source Detecion Accuracy (%)* |
|---|---|---|---|
| 2 | 0.91 | 0.84 | 90.5 |
| 5 | 0.89 | 0.8 | 89.1 |
| 10 | 0.85 | 0.91 | 88.9 |
| 15 | 0.81 | 0.92 | 87.6 |
| 18 | 0.78 | 0.93 | 91 |

## 4.4 K-Unknown Model Detection in Camera Model Identification

In previous literature, the problem of unknown models detection is addressed in two stages. In the first stage, the unknown images are separated from the known images. In the second stage, the separated known images are used for performing the source camera identification. All the separated unknown images are treated to be a single class. The problem with this approach is that there is no way to know about the number of unknown models involved. It helps the forensic expert in a great way if the number unknown models are also known. Clustering the unknown models helps the forensic expert to minimise further computations in finding out their possible sources. Each cluster has to be involved in the computation separately, than clubbed together.

In our work[8], we proposed a scheme which improves the known-unknown separation and also performs an accurate clustering on the unknown images. The proposed workflow is as shown in Fig. 6. If there are three known models {C1, C2, and C3} and four unknown models {C4, C5, C6, and C7}, the proposed model separates the known-unknown models and also performs a clustering to map C4 to UC1, C5 to UC2, C6 to UC3, and C7 to UC7 (UC represents unknown class).

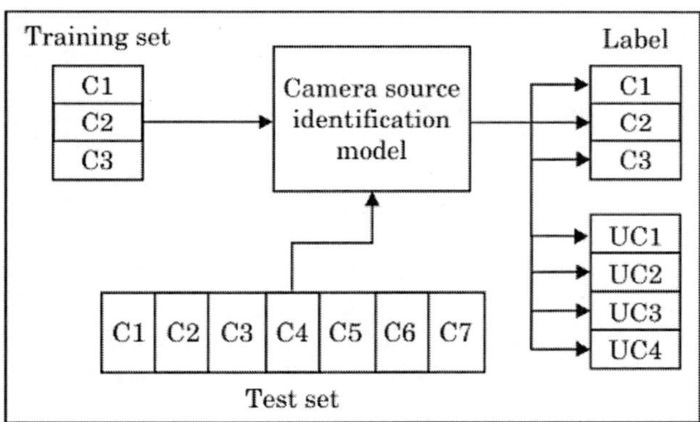


**Fig .6:** Unknown model clustering in Sameer *et al.*[8] scheme

The proposed scheme is shown in detail in Fig. 7. It comprises three modules. The first module is to separate the known and unknown images, the second module is to perform a blind clustering of unknown images; the third module is to classify the known images.

### 4.4.1 *Module 1: Known-Unknown Separation*

The first task is to separate the unknown images from the known images in a blind source identification environment. In the procedure 1 shown here, the separation of unknown images from known images is based on an observation that the PCE value of unknown images with known cameras is LOW and for the known images there will be at least one HIGH value of PCE with known cameras.

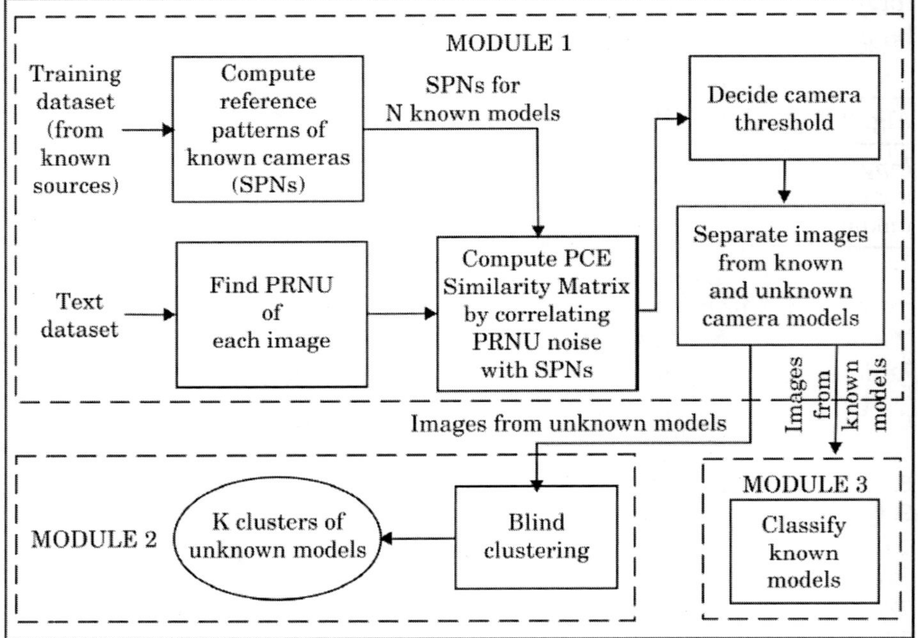


**Fig. 7:** The detailed scheme of Sameer *et al.*[8]

The detailed algorithm is shown in Alg. 3: SEPARATE _KNOWN _UNKNOWN. The input to the procedure is a set of training images $I_{train}$ from known camera models. A set of test images $I_{test}$ is passed from both known and unknown camera models to validate the separation procedure. The output from the procedure would be a set of images from known models ($S_K$) and a set from unknown models ($S_U$). The procedure starts with calculating the sensor pattern noise (SPN) of each known camera model. Then, PCE correlation between each sensor pattern noise and each image from $I_{test}$ is calculated.

In the PCE matrix, a column represents the known camera's SPN and the row represents an image from the test set. A k-means clustering is employed on the PCE matrix for each column with a k value of 2. The clusters formed are those with HIGH PCE value and LOW PCE values. Then the PCE matrix is binarized to have a value of 1 for HIGH value, 0 for LOW value of PCE. The matrix is then traversed row wise to find if any samples are present with all 0 values. Those images with all 0 values are treated to be the images from the unknown models. This is based on the fact that the PCE value would be HIGH for images belonging to known camera models. And hence there will be atleast one HIGH value for images from known camera models.

---

**Alg. 3: *Separate_Known_Unknown***

*Input:* Training image set ($I_{Train}$) from known models; Test image set ($I_{Test}$) from known and unknown models *Output:* Set of images from known models $S_K$, set of unknown models $S_U$

$S_K \leftarrow \emptyset$<br>
$S_U \leftarrow \emptyset$<br>
Foreach known camera model $C_j$ do<br>
$SPN_j \leftarrow SPN\ (C_j)$<br>
Foreach image $I_i \in I_{Test}$<br>
Foreach known camera model $C_j$<br>
$M(i,j) \leftarrow PCE\ (I_i, C_j)$<br>
Foreach known camera model $C_j$<br>
[ClusterHj, ClusterLj] = 2_means_clustering (M (:,j))<br>
$Threshold_j \leftarrow$ mean(min(ClusterHj), max (clu-ster Lj))<br>
Foreach image $I_i \in I_{Test}$<br>
$S_U \leftarrow S_U \cup I_i$<br>
Foreach known camera model $C_j$<br>
If M(i,j) > threshold<br>
$S_K \leftarrow S_K \cup I_i$<br>
$S_U \leftarrow S_U \setminus I_i$<br>
Return $S_K, S_U$

---

### 4.4.2 *Module 2: Clustering Unknown Images*

The second module is to cluster the unknown images that are separated in the module 1. Fig. 8 shows the step by step procedure of the clustering process. The key is to find connected components in the PCE correlation space, iteratively. The detailed procedure is as shown in Alg. 4: Cluster_Unknown_Models. The input to the procedure is the set of images from unknown sources. The output is a set of clusters where each cluster composes images from the same camera source.

A PCE similarity matrix is computed between all the unknown images. Here, each row and column represents a single image to beginwith. An empirical threshold of 50 is used to binarize the matrix.

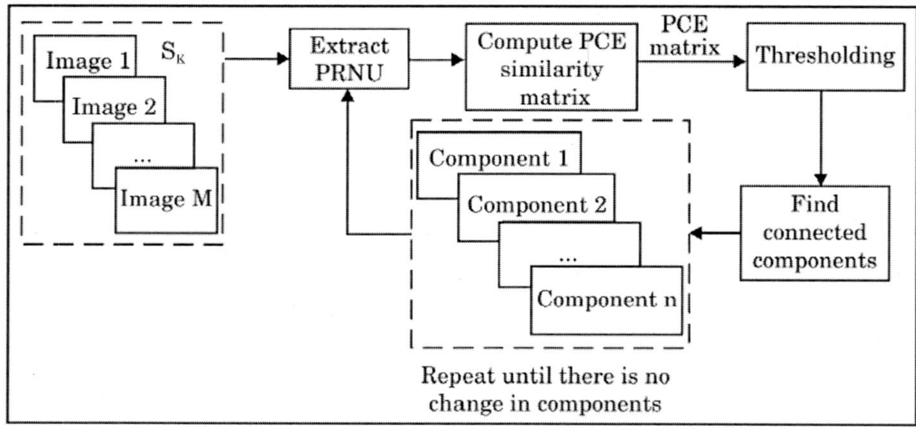


**Fig. 8:** Clustering unknown models

**Alg. 4: *Cluster_Unknown_Models***

*Input:* Set of images from unknown models ($S_U$) *Output:* Clusters of images from unknown models

$G_0 \leftarrow (V_0,E_0)$, $V_0 = \emptyset$, $E_0 = \emptyset$
$G_1 \leftarrow (V_1,E_1)$, $V_1 = S_U$, $E_1 = \emptyset$
i=0
Repeat
$i \leftarrow i+1$
Foreach pair of nodes $(n_p,n_q)$ in $V_i$
If PCE (PRNU $(n_p)$, PRNU$(n_q)$) > $T_i$
$E_i \leftarrow$ Ei *” $(n_p,n_q)$
Conn Clusters$^{(i)} \leftarrow$ Connected Components $(G_i)$
$G_{(i+1)} \leftarrow (V_{(i+1)}, E_{(i+1)})$
$V_{(i+1)} \leftarrow$ Conn Clusters $^{(i)}$
$E_{(i+1)} \leftarrow \emptyset$
Until $G_i = G_{i-1}$
Return Conn Clusters $^{(i)}$

A connected component algorithm from graph theory is employed to find connected components. Ideally, the connected components should contain the set of images from the same source. In the next iteration, the same process is repeated with a single change *i.e.* the PCE matrix is computed between the components. This process is repeated until there are no changes in the components formed.

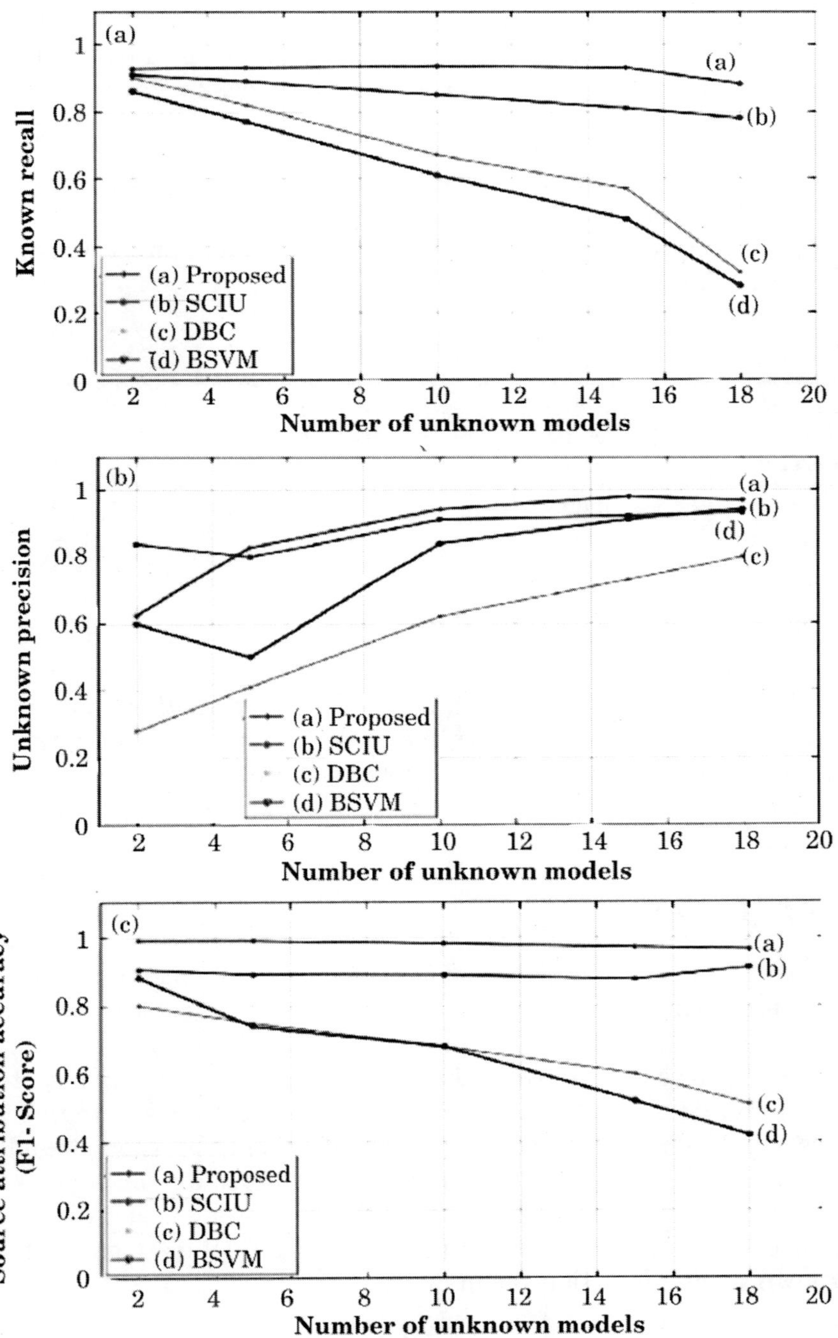


**Fig. 9:** Results comparison

The next module is to perform the source attribution on the known images. In this work, the source attribution is performed in the conservative way, using the PCE correlation measure proposed in[22].

The experimental results are shown in Table 4. Images from Dresden dataset are used and the unknown camera models are varied as 2,5,10,15, and 18 from 20 camera models. The known models recall, unknown images precision, and the source detection accuracy are detailed in Table 4.

**Table 4:** Experimental Results of Sameer *et al.*[8]

| *Number of unknown models* | *Known Recall (01)* | *Unknown precision (01)* | *Source Detecion Accuracy (%)* |
|---|---|---|---|
| 2 | 0.92 | 0.63 | 98.9 |
| 5 | 0.93 | 0.83 | 98.9 |
| 10 | 0.935 | 0.94 | 98.1 |
| 15 | 0.9304 | 0.98 | 97.0 |
| 18 | 0.882 | 0.97 | 96.4 |

All the unknown model techniques discussed in this chapter are compared with each other in Fig. 9 in terms of known recall, unknown precision, and source detection accuracy. It can be clearly seen that the technique proposed by Sameer *et al.*[8] works better than the other techniques.

## 5. CONCLUSIONS

The open set scenario is a current research topic in a machine learning setup for classification. The unknown images are serious threat to any source camera identification technology. It is high-time to identify unknown images and separate them from the source detection system. In this chapter, several unknown model detection strategies are discussed. The earlier works such as binary SVM, Decision Boundary Carving (DBC), K-NN based unknown model detection, are discussed. A recent K-Unknown models detection with clustering is also discussed. The future research direction in this area is to further strengthen the unknown model detection techniques.

# 8

# Introduction to Region Duplication Attack or Copy-Move Forgery in Digital Images

## 1. INTRODUCTION

Digital Forensics[35,36] is a branch of Computer Science deals with the investigation, verification and recovery of digital data and evidences found in digital devices such as computers, digital cameras or video recorders. Digital images and videos act as the major sources of evidence towards any event or crime, specifically in the legal industry as well as media and broadcast industries. Such industries are the major application domains of digital image forensics[35,36,37]. The present day wide availability of a large number of low–cost multimedia file processing tools, techniques and software, having numerous advanced features, has made editing and manipulation of multimedia data extremely easy. All types of unauthorized modification or tampering of digital multi- media data pose as threats to their integrity. With the vast availability of digital image processing tools and techniques today, and the alarming number of digital images used in televisions, newspapers, posters, magazines and websites, the integrity of legal evidences used in the court of law, or the media and broadcast industries, is indeed at stake.

With high rise in cyber-crime rate in the present day, protecting the integrity and authenticity of digital multimedia data is extremely crucial. Security and protection of digital multimedia data require digital devices to be equipped with special software and hardware facilities.

For example, special software modules or hardware chips for watermark embedding. However, such techniques increase the cost of the devices manifolds, hence limiting their usage. The class of blind cyber–crime detection techniques do not require any *a-priori* information to be embedded into digital multimedia data, hence eliminates the need of embedding the digital devices with special hardware or software components.

The forensic approach to cyber-crime detection has gained a lot of research interest in the recent years. Research in digital forensics is majorly focused towards identifying and detecting clues about cyber attacks [38] on digital data. In terms of digital images, copy–move forgery[39,40,41,42,43,44] is one of the most widely prevalent, as well as most well–researched forms of cyber–attacks on digital images. Basic principle behind this form of attack is to copy a portion of an image and paste it onto itself, with an aim to deceive the viewer by duplicating or obscuring significant object(s) in the image. For example, Fig. 1 (a) shows the scenery of a sea–beach with three flying sea–gulls. A copy–move forgery has been carried out on Fig. 1(a), where the image of a sea–gull has been copied from the original scene and pasted onto it. The resultant is shown in Fig. 1 (b). In the forged image it appears as if there are four sea–gulls flying over the sea–beach. Similarly regions of an image may be copy–moved so as to obscure the presence of one or more objects in an image. Specifically, images having regular patterns or textures, such as sea–beach, foliage, sky etc., are more prone to copy–move attacks. The main objectives of this type of attack is to obscure (as shown in Fig. 2 (b) in which a pigeon object is obscured)

(a) Original image (b) Forged image

**Fig. 1:** Typical example of copy-move forgery.

(a) Original image (b) Copy-move forgery (Object obscured) (c) Copy-move forgery (Object repeated)

**Fig. 2:** Objectives of copy-move forgery.

or repeat significant objects (Fig. 2 (c) in which a pigeon object is repeated) in the image.

Different types of copy-move forgery: Copy-Move forgery detection becomes a challenge when accompanied with geometric transform (such as rotation, re-scale or combination of rotation and re-scale) or post-processing on the forged regions, such as brightness adjustment, additive Gaussian noise and blurring of edges, so as to render conventional copy-move forgery detection schemes useless. The different types of copy-move forgeries, may be categorized as follows.

### A. Copy-move forgery with geometric transform

The forgery technique which copies a region and rotates/rescale it before pasting is named as copy-rotate-move (CRM)[45,46] forgery/copy-scale-move (CSM)[46,47]. An example of copy-move forgery with geometric transform *i.e.* rotation/re-scale changes is shown in Fig. 3, where Fig. 3(a) shows the original image having two tanks. In the forged image, one tank is duplicated, and the duplicate region has undergone an additional rotation operation in Fig. 3(b). This makes copy-move forgery detection even more difficult following conventional schemes. In Fig. 3(c), we show an example, where the same forged image is made to undergo a rescale attack.

(a) Original image (b) Copy-move forgery with geometrical attack (Rotation) (c) Copy-move forgery with geometrical attack (Re-scale)

**Fig. 3:** An example of copy-move forgery with geometric attack: (a) the original image, (b) the copy-rotation-move forged image, (c) the copy-scale-move forged image.

(a) Original image (b) Copy-move forgery with post-processing attack (Brightness adjustment)

**Fig . 4:** An example of copy-move forgery with post-processing attack: (a) the original image, (b) the copy-move forged image with brightness adjustment.

### *A. Copy-move forgery with post-processing changes*

This form of image forgery becomes all the more difficult to detect when the adversary performs post processing-based operations [48] such as blurring of edges, brightness adjustment, additive Gaussian noise on the forged regions before duplicating it. For Example: Fig.4 (a) shows the original image. In Fig.4 (b) we show an example, where the same forged image is made to undergo a brightness adjustment attack.

In this chapter, we mainly present an overview of the digital forensic problem of image region duplication detection, and identify the major challenges in this domain. The major challenges of this area of research, and their probable or prevalent solutions are presented and discussed in Section 2. The chapter has been concluded in Section 3.

## 2. MAJOR CHALLENGES OF THE DOMAIN

The major challenges of the research domain related to copy–move forgery investigation and detection using digital forensic techniques, are identified and discussed in this section. Those are mainly 4-folds: *viz.* selection of efficient feature set, efficient feature extraction algorithms for forged image identification, (B) An automatic threshold selection to optimize manual labour, (C) Minimizing False Positive Rate (since this would cause an innocent to be falsely accused), and (D) Detection of geometric and post-processing attacks in this area.

### 2.1 Identification of Efficient Feature Set And Selection of Efficient Feature Extraction Method

We have adopted multiple feature sets including Stationary Wavelet Transform with Singular Value Decomposition, mean value of image blocks, energy coefficients of Dydic Wavelet Transform, and Fourier–Mellin Transform (FMT) with Log Polar mapping. Out of all the feature sets adopted by us, Fourier–Mellin Transform (FMT) proved to be the most efficient feature set. We have implemented Fourier–Mellin Transform[49] by performing a Log Polar mapping [50] followed by Fourier transform [51] for feature extraction. FMT–Logpolar helps us to achieve rotation, re–scale and translation invariance in copy–move forgery detection.

### 2.2 Automatic Selection of Threshold for Block Similarity Decision

A vast majority of existing copy-move forgery detection schemes are based on image pixel block matching. Threshold selection is a crucial step for block-matching based copy–move forgery detection and localization. In this book, we discuss the concept of *automatic threshold fitting* for block similarity matching in images, which is based on a mathematical formulation. This minimizes effort and manual intervention requirement.

### 2.3 Optimization of False Positive Rate in Forensic Region Duplication Detection

Due to inherent presence of homogeneous regions in natural images, generic block based copy–move forgery detection techniques suffer from high false positive rate. In our research, we have proposed a solution for this problem, in form of an *8–connected neighbourhood check* technique, which reduces the rate of false block matching or false positives, encountered during duplicate image region detection. Since the *Hue Saturation Value* (HSV)[48] color space is highly efficient in capturing minor deviations among image pixels, in naturally similar regions of an image, we adopt the HSV color space in our work, which helps us to further optimize the False Positive Rate.

### 2.4 Detection of Geometric and Post-Processing Attacks in Region Duplication

Given the existing state-of-the-art, it is observed that the detection of image region duplication becomes extremely challenging when combined with additional intelligent adversarial attacks. For example, the duplicated image regions being rotated or re–scaled, the edges of the copied regions being blurred, their brightness adjusted, noise added, etc., which largely diminish the performance efficiency of copy-move forgery detection techniques. In this book, we have adopted rotation–invariant, scale–invariant and translation–invariant feature sets, following the footsteps of existing domain experts.

To solve this problem, we adopted a novel *color–based segmentation technique* using *K–means clustering*[52], which succeeded to achieve over 95% invariance to post–processing attacks, along with geometric transform detection. Specifically, we have addressed the following attacks: rotation, re–scale, translation, edge blurring, additive noise, and brightness adjustment.

In this book, these challenges or problems are addressed with introducing the state-of-the-art along with several recent approaches for solving those are also presented in the subsequent chapters.

## 3. CONCLUSIONS

Image forensics is a highly relevant field of study in this day and age of abundant digital content. To verify and validate images is of huge importance especially with images involved as evidences in a court of law. The copy move forgery is a particular problem of interest in this domain. With easily available image editing tools, the integrity of images is at stake, and solving the challenges in copy move forgery detection is the need of the hour. In this chapter, the problem of copy move forgery is established and the current research challenges are presented one by one. The challenge of identifying an efficient feature set which is robust to rescaling and translation is discussed. When a block matching strategy is employed, automatic selection of threshold for block similarity decision is also discussed. Optimizing the false positive rate *i.e.* to improve the accuracy of copy move detection is also discoursed. Also, the presence of a few attacks to copy move forgery detection techniques such as geometric transformations, and a few other post processing operations is also discussed in this chapter. The future research includes overcoming all the above discussed challenges and strengthening the copy move forgery techniques to make further progress in the domain of image forensics. In the next chapters, we present image forensic techniques of detecting copy move forgery using block matching, using image keypoints. Also, we present various ideas and techniques to overcome the geometric attacks in copy move forgery detection.

# 9

# Region Duplication Attack and Its Forensic Solutions-State-of-the-Art Research Practices

## 1. INTRODUCTION

Digital forensics[35] is a developing research field which aims at investigating evidences and clues left behind in digital data as a result of cyber-crime or forgery. Digital forensic techniques provide security and protection to multimedia data in situations, where the user has neither any a priori information about that data to be secured, nor has carried out any pre-computation on the data prior to forgery detection. The investigations are solely based on post-processing of data. Hence, digital forensic techniques belong to the class of *blind* or *passive*[36] security measures for digital content protection. In this chapter, we investigate the forensic techniques currently available in the literature for detection of copy–move forgery in digital images.

The most common forms of modification attacks to digital images include *image retouching*[53] *image splicing*[54] and *copy – move forgery*[54-58]. In *image retouching*, features of an image are altered intelligently, so that the modifications are difficult to be detected. *Image splicing* is the form of digital image forgery where the forger combines regions from multiple images into a single image, so as to form a natural looking *composite* image. However, such modifications are detectable by investigating inconsistencies in natural statistics of the image[59]. In copy–move[60] form of attack on digital images, regions of an image are copied and pasted onto itself, at some different locations, with the malicious intention to obscure or repeat significant objects in the image. For example, Fig. 1 shows an example of a copy–move forgery on an image. The original image has been shown in Fig. 1*a* and *b* as its copy–move forged version, where a lioness object has been copied from the left most position of the original scene and pasted onto itself, at a different location. In the forged image, one can find one additional lioness in the front. Since this form of digital image forgery involves duplication of regions of the same image, the image statistics are not disturbed. This form of forgery does not lead to any significant change in the image characteristics because the texture, noise and colour components do not get altered for the forged region. Rather those statistical features/characteristics remain unaltered over varied regions of the forged image, even after copy–move. Hence, to detect this form of forgery, investigation of image statistical inconsistencies is not particularly helpful. In the recent years, researchers have mainly focused on the identification of region duplication in images in order to detect copy–move forgery. To hinder duplicate regions identification in images, attackers may further modify the duplicated image regions cleverly such as by slight noise addition, blurring, rotation, re-scaling etc. Recently, the problem of identifying geometrically transformed[43,47], blurred and noise-added[44,61] duplicate image regions has attracted considerable research interest as well.

In this chapter, we presently investigate the state-of-the-art copy–move forgery detection techniques for digital images. The operating principles of most of the state-of-the-art copy–move forgery detection

(a) Original image

(b) Forged image
(Duplicated object highlighted)

**Fig. 1:** Copy-move forgery: An example

techniques are 'block-based', *i.e.* based on the identification of duplicate image blocks. Hence, in this chapter, we provide the readers a detailed survey of 'block-based' region duplication techniques for digital images, along with an evaluation, analysis and comparison of their performance efficiencies, through a three- way standard parameterisation platform proposed by us, which would enable the readers to select a particular copy–move forgery detection scheme, according to her requirements and preferences.

Rest of this chapter is organised as follows. In Section 2, we present an overview of related literature. In Section 3, we present detailed survey of the operations of state-of-the-art block-based copy–move forgery detection techniques, and classify them according to their operating principles. In Section 4, we propose a standard parameterisation platform for evaluation and analysis of state-of-the-art copy–move forgery detection techniques. In Section 5, we present the performance evaluation results pertaining to the performance analysis and comparison of different classes of copy–move forgery detection techniques using the proposed parameters. Finally, we conclude in Section 6.

## 2. LITERATURE REVIEW

The past decade has seen considerable growth of research interest in the area of digital image forensics. In this chapter, we deal with a specific class of digital image forgery, the copy–move forgery. One of the pioneer research developments toward copy– move forgery detection in digital images was proposed by Fridrich *et al.*[55]. In[55], Fridrich *et al.,* proposed region duplication detection methods based on the principles of exact block matching, autocorrelation, exhaustive block search and robust match [based on discrete cosine transform (DCT)]. Out of the four different principles, the robust matching method has been proven to be the most efficient and accurate to detect duplicate image regions. However, this method, when applied to images containing large identical textured regions, leads to a lot of false matches. Farid and Popescu[2] proposed an efficient copy–move forgery detection technique based on principal component analysis (PCA). However, this technique does not work equally efficiently for lossy compressed images because of the dimensionality reduction feature of PCA. Kang and Wei[39] proposed a region duplication detection method based on singular value decomposition (SVD), having low computational complexity, yet extremely effective in cases where the duplicate regions are induced with slight noise. Zhang *et al.*[40] proposed an algorithm based on discrete wavelet transform (DWT) for copy–move forgery detection, which again attains a considerably low computational complexity as compared with the other existing schemes. Yang *et al.*[56] applied dyadic wavelet transform (DyWT) on a forged image by decomposing it into four frequency sub-bands, and have used the low-frequency sub-band to divide the image into overlapping pixel blocks. The blocks are then sorted lexicographically according to their Zernike moments. The Euclidean distance between each block pair is computed and the matching pairs are detected using a threshold on the distances. This method produces very less number of false matches, even when image has large flat regions. However, the computation of Zernike moment involves considerable computational complexity. Another duplicate region detection method based on Fourier–Mellin transform was proposed by Bayram *et al.*[57], which prove to be extremely robust against re-scaling, blurring, lossy compression and noise induction into the duplicate regions. A similar approach was followed by Lin *et al.,* in[62], where the forged image is divided into overlapping pixel blocks and seven different characteristic features are extracted from each block. Using lexicographical sorting on the features, the authors find the similar block pairs and finally the matching blocks are detected by applying a threshold on the block-pair similarities.

In the recent years, there have been quite a lot of research developments toward identification of slightly modified duplicate image regions. For example, Ling *et al.*[63] proposed a fast copy– move forgery detection algorithm, which addresses the problem of lossy compressed and noise induction into duplicate image regions. In[58], the scheme proposed by Huang *et al.,* is able to detect copy–move forgery in digital images, containing additive white Gaussian noise[64] as well as distortions caused due to lossy Joint Photographic Experts Group compression[65]. Other noteworthy region duplication detection methods, capable of detecting lossy compressed duplicate image regions, were proposed by Muhammad *et al.*[41] and Li *et al.*[66].

## 3. CLASSIFICATION AND REVIEW OF BLOCK-BASED COPY MOVE FORGERY DETECTION TECHNIQUES

In this section, we provide a detailed review of the operating principles of different categories of state-of-the-art copy–move forgery detection techniques for digital images. As stated in Section 2, majority of the existing copy–move forgery detection techniques operate image pixel block wise. In this chapter, we provide a three-way classification of block-based copy–move forgery detection techniques, on the basis of their operating principles. Subsequently, we provide a detailed review of the operations of each class, by using some representative algorithms selected from each. The three-way classification has been discussed as follows:

**(i) *Dimensionality reduction based techniques***

The operating principle of this class of copy–move forgery detection algorithms is based on the reduction of dimensionality of image features, without losing significant information. The principle of dimensionality reduction helps to achieve a considerably low computational complexity of finding duplicate image regions. State-of-the-art copy–move forgery detection algorithms belonging to this class include the PCA-based algorithm proposed by Farid and Popescu[2], the SVD- based algorithm proposed by Kang and Wei[39] and the PCA- DCT-based algorithm proposed by Sunil *et al.*[67]. We use the above mentioned three representative schemes to describe the operation of this class of copy–move forgery detection, in this chapter.

**(ii) *DCT based techniques***

A number of state-of-the-art copy–move forgery detection schemes are based on DCT. The schemes based on DCT, initially divide the forged image into overlapping blocks, and compute the DCT of each block. The quantised coefficients, containing majority of the image information are found and are exploited to detect the duplicate image blocks. The schemes we use in this chapter to represent the class of DCT-based copy–move forgery detection techniques include those proposed by Fridrich *et al.*[55], Huang *et al.*[58] and Wang *et al.*[68].

**(iii) *Wavelet transform based techniques***

The basic operation of this class of region duplication detection algorithms involves decomposition of a forged image into frequency sub-bands using *wavelet transform*. The frequency sub-bands obtained are approximation, horizontal, vertical and diagonal. All the above sub-bands combined contain the entire image information. The low-frequency approximation sub-band plays the major role in this class of algorithms, to find duplicate image regions, and the diagonal sub-band is used to control the rate of false matches. In this chapter, we describe the operation of this class of copy–move forgery detection in detail, using the following representative state-of-the-art algorithms: DyWT-based algorithm by Muhammad *et al.*[41], DyWT with Zernike moment-based algorithm by Yang *et al.*[56] and complex wavelet transform (CWT)-based algorithm by Wu *et al.*[45].

In the subsequent section, we describe the operations of 2–3 representative algorithms from each of the above classes, in detail. Before that, we present the basic procedure commonly followed by any general image block-based copy–move forgery detection algorithm as follows:

1. Let us consider a forged image of size w × h pixels. The pre-processing step includes conversion of the coloured (possibly forged) image into grey-scale, using the following formula[69]:

$$I = 0.299 \times R + 0.587 \times G + 0.114 \times B \qquad (1)$$

   where $R$, $G$ and $B$ represent the red, green and blue colour channel intensities of the image, and $I$ represents the grey-scale image.

2. The grey-scale image $I$ is uniformly divided into overlapping pixel blocks of fixed size.
3. The next step involves feature extraction from each image block. The set of features to be used is decided by the particular category to which the concerned detection algorithm belongs. Depending on the detection scheme, the image may require to be transformed from spatial to frequency domain, before feature extraction.
4. The feature vectors are sorted lexicographically and subsequently stored into different rows of a matrix.
5. The distances (for example, Euclidean distance[70], Canberra distance[71], Chebyshev distance[72] etc.) of each row of the matrix (representing one feature vector), with its $k$-nearest neighbours, are found.
6. The neighbouring feature vector pairs showing high similarity between them represent duplicate image blocks, which is nothing but the algorithm output.

Out of the neighbouring feature vector pairs, those having the distances between them, higher than an application-specific threshold value (a user-defined value), are ignored. This is considering the fact that in a natural image neighbouring pixel blocks would inherently demonstrate high similarity, and it would be wrong to guess these as maliciously duplicated blocks. Such techniques operate most efficiently when the block size chosen is significantly smaller than the size of forged area.

Next, we present a detailed review of each class of copy–move forgery detection algorithms, as discussed earlier in this section. Following it, a performance analysis and comparison of those different classes have been presented in Section 5.1.

## 3.1 Dimensionality Reduction based Copy–Move Forgery Detection

In this section, we present in detail the operations of three different algorithms belonging to the class of dimensionality reduction- based copy–move forgery detection: the PCA-based algorithm[2], the SVD-based[39] algorithm, and the PCA-DCT-based algorithm[67].

### 3.1.1 *PCA-based copy–move forgery detection*

The PCA- based copy–move forgery detection algorithm divides an image into overlapping blocks. Each block is sorted lexicographically with respect to the pixel intensities. Each sorted block is stored into one row of a matrix. When a w × h image is divided into B × B (overlapping) blocks, the covariance of each such block is computed as:

$$Cm = \sum_{i=1}^{N_{\text{total}}} x_i x_i^T \tag{2}$$

where $x_i$ represents a block for $i$ = 1, 2, 3, ..., $N_{total}$ and $N_{total}$= $(w - B + 1) \times (h - B + 1)$ represent the total number of blocks.

The principal components of $Cm$ are defined by the Eigenvectors $e_j$ *for* $j$ = 1,2,3,...$B$ (of $C_m$) corresponding to the Eigen values $\lambda j$ ( $j$ = 1, 2, ..., $b$ and $\lambda 1 > \lambda 2 > . . . > \lambda B$. Each image block can be linearly represented in terms of the eigenvectors as:

$$x_i = \sum_{j=1}^{B} a_j x_j \tag{3}$$

where $aj = {}_xT_e$ show the new representation for each image block. Each vector $x_i$ is truncated to first $Nt$ terms, $Nt$ being a user-defined parameter, in order to reduce the dimensionality of each block and generate a new $Nt$-dimensional representation of $C_m$, say $C^t{}_m$. The size of $C^t{}_m$ is $Ntotal \times B$.

Following are the steps for detection of duplicate image blocks, utilising $C_m$:

1. Matrix $S$ is obtained by sorting $Cm$ row wise lexico graphically.
2. Let $si$ denote the $i^{th}$ row of matrix $S$. The row $si$ of the matrix $S$ is represented using the tuple $(x_i, y_i)$, such that $(x_i, y_i)$ represents a block's image co-ordinates.
3. A list $L$ is constructed that stores every pair of rows $si$, $sj$ such that $|i - j| < Nn$, where $Nn$ is a user-defined parameter denoting the number of neighbouring rows to be searched.
4. The offset frequency for a pair $(s_i, s_j)$, present in list $L$, is calculated as

$$\begin{array}{l} (x_i - x_j, y_i - y_j) \text{ if } x_i - x_j > 0 \\ (x_j - x_i, y_i - y_j) \text{ if } x_i - x_j < 0 \\ (0, y_i - y_j) \text{ if } x_i = x_j \end{array} \tag{4}$$

5. The offset magnitude for pair $s_i$, $s_j$ in $L$, is calculated as:

$$\sqrt{(x_i - x_j)^2 + (y_i - y_j)^2} \tag{5}$$

6. The pairs having offset frequency less than $N_f$ and offset magnitude less than $N_d$ are discarded. $N_f$ and $N_d$ denote the minimum frequency threshold and the minimum offset threshold, respectively, as chosen by the user empirically.
7. The maliciously duplicated blocks are represented by the remaining pairs of rows contained in $L$.

In Fig. 2, the results of duplicate regions detection, using the above algorithm, has been shown. In Fig. 2*a–c*, we have shown manual forgery of an image, where the size of forgery has been varied as 20, 30 and 40% of the entire image. The copy–move forgery detection results using the above method, for our manually forged images, have been shown in Fig. 2*d–f*.

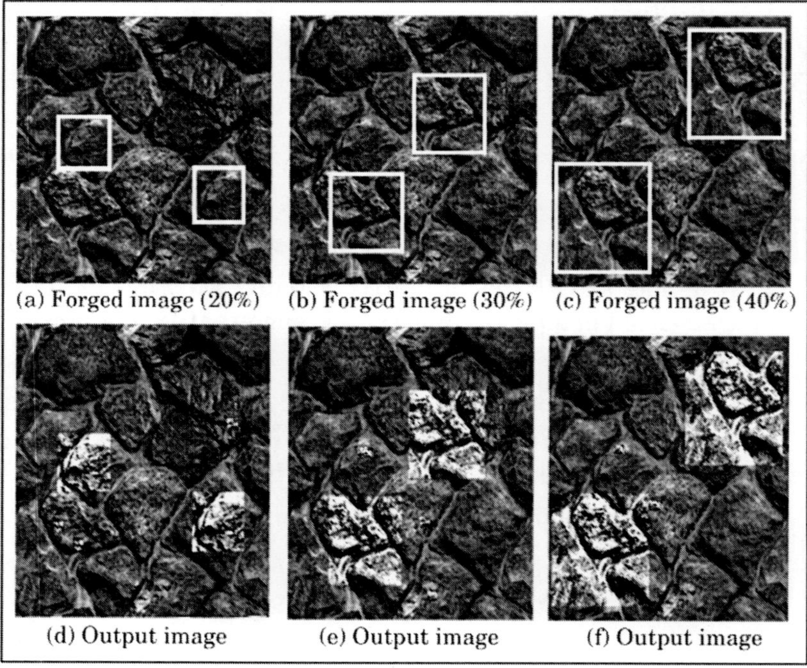


**Fig. 2:** PCA-based copy–move forgery detection (a)–(c); Manually induced forgeries of varying sizes; (d)–(f) Duplicate regions detected

### 3.1.2 *SVD-based copy–move forgery detection*

The SVD is an algebraic transform[73], which finds wide application in several fields such as image and signal processing, pattern analysis, data compression and scientific computing. SVD decomposes one block of an image into three matrices *U*, *S* and *V*, each of which is sufficiently smaller compared with the original image block, yet they preserve the inherent features of the image block. Hence, the process of feature extraction from these matrices becomes computationally lesser intensive and also consumes lesser memory for storage, as compared with the original block. Utilising singular value, the SVD technique accomplishes extraction of unique feature vectors of image blocks, reduces dimension of block features space.

The steps for feature vectors extraction from image blocks[39,74], while reducing the dimensionality of feature space, are as follows:

1. A $w \times h$ image is divided into $(w - B + 1) \times (h - B + 1)$ overlapping blocks, each of size $B \times B$ pixels.
2. Let $A$ be a $B \times B$ matrix representing one block of the image. $A$ is decomposed into its singular value matrices $U$, $S$ and $V$, each of dimension $B \times B$ as:

$$A = USV^{T} \tag{6}$$

where each of $U$, $S$ and $V$ are real number matrices. $S$ is a diagonal singular value matrix of the form:

$$\begin{pmatrix} \sigma_1 & 0 & 0 & \cdots & 0 \\ 0 & \sigma_2 & 0 & \cdots & 0 \\ 0 & 0 & \sigma_3 & \cdots & 0 \\ & & & \vdots & \\ 0 & 0 & 0 & \cdots & \sigma_r \\ 0 & 0 & 0 & \cdots & 0 \end{pmatrix} \tag{7}$$

3. For each image block represented by $A$, the positive diagonal entries in $S$ are sorted in non-increasing order and stored into one row of a matrix, called the *feature vector matrix*. Each row of this matrix represents the features of one block.
4. For each image block represented by $A$, the positive diagonal entries in $S$ are sorted in non-increasing order and stored into one row of a matrix, called the *feature vector matrix*. Each row of this matrix represents the features of one block.
5. The Euclidean distances $D(u, v)$ between two rows, $u$ and $v$, of the feature vector matrix, are computed as:

$$D(u, v) = \sqrt{\sum_{i=1}^{r} (u_i - v_i)^2} \tag{8}$$

where $u = (u_1, u_2, \ldots, u_r)$ and $v = (v_1, v_2, \ldots, v_r)$.
6. All the pairs of rows in the feature vector matrix, whose Euclidean distance is more than the similarity threshold $T_d$, are discarded

as they are considered to be naturally similar blocks of the image. Further verification is performed on the remaining pairs that pass this stage of elimination.

7. For a given pair of image blocks, say $u$ and $v$, with the blocks' image co-ordinates $(i, j)$ and $(k, l)$, respectively, the *Chebyshev distance* between $u$ and $v$ is computed as:

$$Cuv = \max \mid \text{abs}\,(i - k), \text{abs}\,(\text{j} - l) \mid \quad (9)$$

8. If $Cuv \geq Ts$, then blocks $u$ and $v$ are labelled as suspected duplicate blocks, where $Ts$ is chosen as a threshold representing minimum separation between duplicate image regions.

In Fig. 3, the detection of duplicate regions using the above technique is shown. Figs. 3*a–c* represents a test image, manually forged by us, where the forgery size is varied as 20%, 30% and 40% of the entire image. The forgery detection results have been shown in Figs. 3*d–f*.

### 3.1.3 *PCA-DCT-based copy–move forgery detection*

In this algorithm, initially the possibly forged image is divided into fixed-sized overlapping blocks and DCT coefficients of each block are utilised as block features, over which PCA is applied to reduce the dimensionalities of the feature vectors. In detail, the steps of this algorithm can be presented as follows:

1. A $w \times h$ image is divided into $(w - B + 1) \times (h - B + 1)$ overlapping blocks, each of size $B \times B$ pixels.
2. Next, we apply DCT on each image block and store the quantised coefficients for each block into one row of the feature matrix $M$.
3. From every row of the matrix, we consider only the first $\lceil q \times B^2 \rceil$ elements for further processing, where $q \in (0,1)$ (Hence, we work with a $\{(w - B + 1)(h - B + 1)\} \lceil q \times B^2 \rceil$ matrix.).
4. The dimensionality of the feature matrix $M$ is reduced through application of PCA.
5. Next, we apply a lexicographic sorting on the rows of dimensionality reduced $M$. The identical rows are located in the sorted matrix. The duplicate image blocks are none other than those, which corresponding to the identical pairs of rows of $M$.

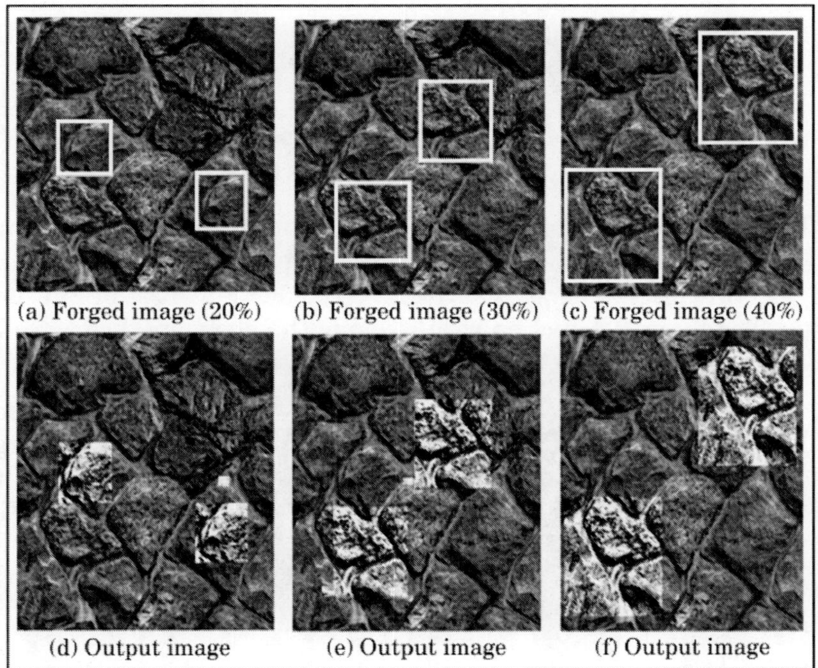


**Fig. 3:** SVD-based copy–move forgery detection (a)–(c); Manually induced forgeries of varying sizes; (d)–(f) Duplicate regions detected.

6. The shift vector or movement vector *M*v for a pair of matching blocks is calculated as:

$$M_V = (mv_1, mv_2) = (i_1 - j_1, i_2 - j_2) \tag{10}$$

   where $(i_1, i_2)$ and $(j_1, j_2)$ are the positions of two matching blocks. The movement vectors “*M*v and +*M*v represent the same movement. Hence, we consider the movement vectors’ absolute values $|M\text{v}|$.

7. A matching vector counter $C$ is used to record the frequency of occurrence of every matching block pair. Initially, all matching vector counters are set to zero. For every pair of matching blocks (vectors or rows of *M*), the counter $C$ is incremented by one. That is, $C(m\text{v}_1, m\text{v}_2) = C(m\text{v}_1, m\text{v}_2) + 1$.

8. The matching vector counter values are computed for all movement vectors $Mv_1$, $Mv_2$, ....

9. At the end of the matching process, the duplicate blocks are identified by the following criteria:

$$C(Mv) > T \tag{11}$$

where $T$ is a user-defined threshold. The block/vector pairs satisfying the above criteria are identified to be duplicates.

In Fig. 4, the results for detection of duplicate image regions using DCT with PCA are shown. Figs. 4*a–c* represents manually forged images, the forgery sizes varying as 20, 30 and 40% of the entire image. The forgery detection results using the above method have been shown in Figs. 4*d–f*.

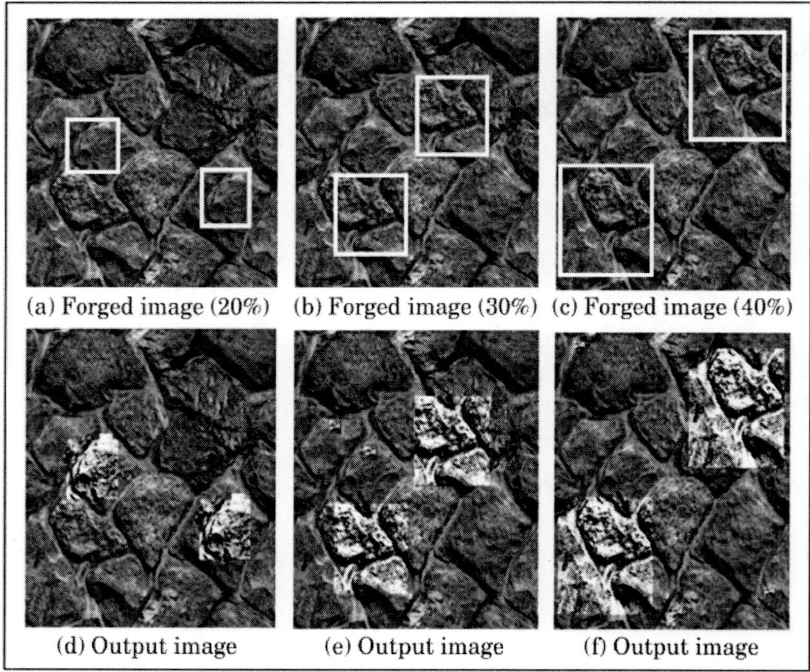


**Fig. 4:** PCA-DCT-based copy–move forgery detection (a)–(c); Manually nduced forgeries of varying sizes; (d)–(f); Duplicate regions detected.

### 3.2 DCT based Copy–Move Forgery Detection

In this section, we describe three representative state-of-the-art DCT-based copy–move forgery detection techniques[55,58,68].

### 3.2.1 *Region duplication detection using DCT*

In this method, initially the input colour image is converted into grey-scale and divided into uniform overlapping blocks. DCT is applied on each block, the quantised DCT coefficients are calculated, and these coefficients are arranged in lexicographic order into one row of a matrix. To find matching block pairs, movement vectors or shift vectors corresponding to every pair of rows, in the matrix, are calculated and subsequently normalised. Now, all the pairs of blocks having their normalised movement vectors greater than a threshold value are found out in order to detect the duplicate regions in the forged image. The basic steps of any DCT-based region duplication detection method are presented as follows:

1. An input image of size $w \times h$ pixels is divided into $(w - B + 1) \times (h - B + 1)$ overlapping blocks, each of size $B \times B$ pixels.
2. DCT is applied on the image blocks sequentially, starting from top left up to bottom right. The quantised DCT coefficients of the individual blocks are stored into the rows of a matrix $M$.
3. Next, we apply a lexicographic sorting on the rows of matrix $M$. Now, the identical rows may be located in the sorted matrix in a time-efficient way. The duplicate image blocks are none other than those, which corresponding to the identical pairs of rows of $M$.
4. The shift vector or movement vector Mv for a pair of matching blocks is calculated as

$$Mv = (mv_1, mv_2) = (i_1 - j_1, i_2 - j_2)) \qquad (12)$$

   where $(i_1, i_2)$ and $(j_1, j_2)$ are the positions of two matching blocks.
5. The movement vectors $- Mv$ and $+ Mv$ represent the same movement. Hence, we consider the movement vector's absolute values $|Mv|$.
6. A matching vector counter $C$ is used to record the frequency of occurrence of a matching block pair. Initially, all matching vector counters are set to zero. For every pair of matching blocks, the counter $C$ is increased by one: $C(mv_1, mv_2) = C(mv_1, mv_2) + 1$.
7. The matching vector counter values are computed for all movement vectors $Mv_1, Mv_2, \ldots$.
8. At the end of the matching process, the duplicate blocks are identified by the following criteria:

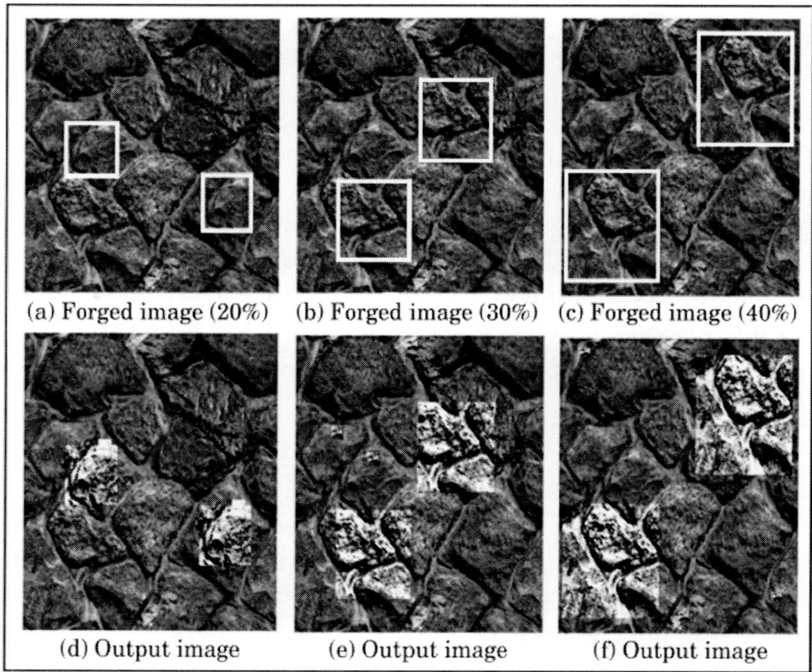

**Fig. 5:** DCT-based copy–move forgery detection (a)–(c); Manually induced forgeries of varying sizes; (d)–(f) Duplicate regions detected

$$C(Mv) > T \tag{13}$$

where $T$ is a user-defined threshold. The block pairs satisfying the above criteria are identified to be duplicates.

In Fig. 5, the results of duplicate region detection using the above technique has been shown. Figs. 5a–c represent a test image forged manually, the size of forgery varying as 20, 30 and 40% of the entire image. The forgery detection results using the above method have been shown in Fig. 5.

### 3.2.2 *Improved region duplication detection using DCT*

In[58], Huang *et al.* have proposed a DCT-based copy–move forgery detection technique, with improved computational complexity and accuracy. In this work, the authors have considered the fact that the top-leftmost coefficients in a DCT block contain the majority of block information. Hence, a factor $q$ $(0 < q < 1)$ is defined and only the first

$[q \times B^2]$ coefficients of each DCT image block are considered for further processing. This has helped the authors to achieve a much lower complexity as well as much higher duplication detection efficiency.

The improved DCT-based region duplication detection algorithm is comprised of the following steps:

1. An input image of size $w \times h$ pixels is divided into $(w - B + 1) \times (h - B + 1)$ overlapping blocks, each of size B × B pixels.
2. Next, we apply DCT on each image block and store the quantised coefficients for each block into one row of a matrix.
3. From every row of the matrix, we select only the first $\lceil q \times B^2 \rceil$ elements, where $q \in (0, 1)$, for further processing.
4. For each block, we repeat steps 2–3. This process generates a matrix $S$ having $(w - B + 1) \times (h - B + 1)$ rows and $\lceil q \times B^2 \rceil$ columns.
5. The matrix $S$ is sorted lexicographically row wise, hence producing matrix *Ssorted*.
6. Let $S_i$ and $S_j$ be two neighbouring rows of the matrix *Ssorted*, where $i$ and $j$ represent their relative positions in Ssorted. If *si* and $S_j$ satisfy the condition $| j - i | < N_f$ then $S_i$ and $S_j$ are said to be similar, where $N_f$ *is* a user-defined threshold parameter.
7. The distance between similar blocks (corresponding to similar *Ssorted* row vectors) is calculated using the following formula:

$$d = \sqrt{(x_i - x_j)^2 + (y_i - y_j)^2} \tag{14}$$

   where $(x_i, y_i)$ and $(x_j, y_j)$ represent the similar blocks' image co-ordinates.
8. The matching block pairs are those for which $d > N_d$, $N_d$ being another user-defined threshold.
9. The shift vector or movement vector $Mv$ for a pair of matching blocks is calculated as:

$$Mv = (mv_1, mv_2) = (i_1 - j_1, i_2 - j_2) \tag{15}$$

   where $(i_1, i_2)$ and $(j_1, j_2)$ are the positions of two matching blocks.
10. The movement vectors $-Mv$ and $+Mv$ represent the same movement. Hence, we consider the movement vectors' absolute values $|Mv|$.

11. A matching vector counter $C$ is used to record the frequency of occurrence of a matching block pair. Initially, all matching vector counters are set to zero. For every pair of matching blocks, the counter $C$ is increased by one: $C(mv_1, mv_2) = C(mv_1, mv_2) + 1$.
12. The matching vector counter values are computed for all movement vectors $Mv_1$, $Mv_2$, ... At the end of the matching process, the duplicate blocks are identified by the following criteria:

$$C(Mv) > T \tag{16}$$

where $T$ is a user-defined threshold. The block pairs satisfying the above criteria are identified to be duplicates.

In Fig. 6, the results for detection of duplicate image regions using improved DCT-based algorithm have been shown. Figs. 6*a–c* show the manually forged images, with forgery sizes: 20%, 30 % and 40% of the entire image. The forgery detection results have been shown in Fig. 6*d–f*.

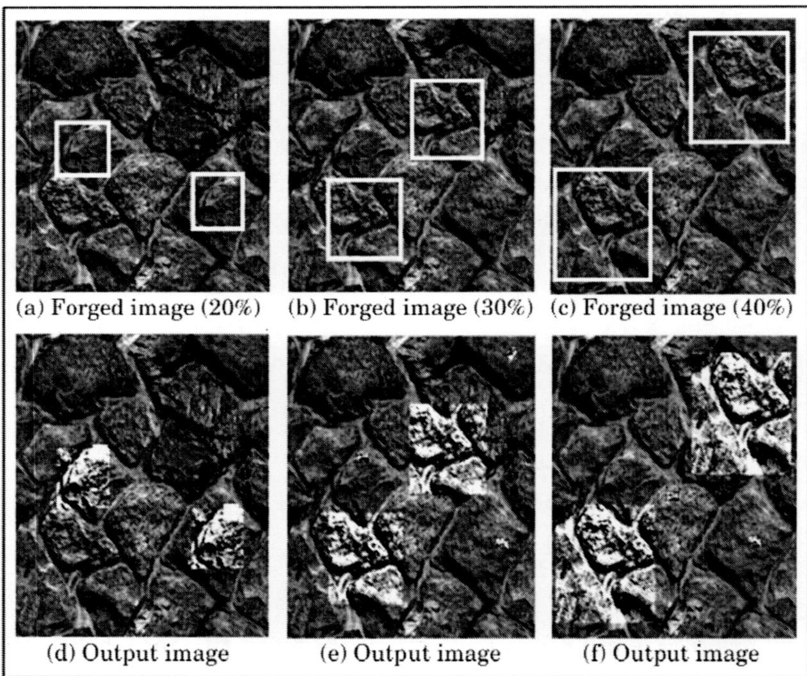


**Fig. 6:** Improved DCT-based copy–move forgery detection (a)–(c); Manually induced forgeries of varying sizes; (d)–(f) Duplicate regions detected

### 3.2.3 *Efficient region duplication detection scheme using DCT*

Wang *et al.*[68] proposed an efficient technique based on DCT to detect duplicate image regions. In this technique, initially, the possibly forged image is divided into fixed-sized overlapping blocks and DCT is applied to each block. The quantised blocks are further divided into fixed-sized non- overlapping sub-blocks. The DCT coefficients mean is computed for each sub-block, and used as block features for duplication detection in this scheme. In detail, the basic steps of this algorithm can be presented as follows:

1. An input image of size $w \times h$ pixels is divided into $(w - 7) \times (h - 7)$ overlapping blocks, each of size $8 \times 8$ pixels.
2. We apply DCT to each image block and obtain the DCT coefficient matrix for each block.
3. Next, for feature extraction, each $8 \times 8$ image block is divided into 16, $2 \times 2$ non-overlapping sub-blocks, and the DCT coefficients mean is calculated for each sub-block. The array of 16 means for each image block serves as the block feature vector, and is stored into a *package*.
4. For matching of duplicate regions, we calculate the pixel mean of each $(i, j)^{th}$ image block as:

$$P_{ij} = \frac{\sum_{x=1}^{8} \cdot \sum_{y=1}^{8} f_{ij}(x,y)}{64} \tag{17}$$

   where $f_{ij}(x, y)$ represents the intensity of the $(x, y)^{th}$ pixel of the $(i, j)^{th}$ image block.
5. *Packages* are produced to store DCT mean feature vectors along with the co-ordinates of the image blocks. Within the intensity range [0, 255] of 8 bit grey-scale images, 64 packages are formed, each of offset 4. Distributions of block feature vectors into packages are done by the following principle. Features and co-ordinates of the $(i, j)^{th}$ image block are put into the $\lfloor \frac{P_{ij}+1}{4} \rfloor^{th}$ package.
6. Similar blocks within the same package are compared by their DCT mean features to determine duplicates.
7. To eliminate false matches, the mutual positions of the block pairs within a package are investigated, through shift vectors. Let two blocks $B_1$ and $B_2$ having co-ordinates $(i_1, i_2)$ and $(j_1, j_2)$,

respectively, belong to the same package. The shift vector or movement vector $M$v for a pair of matching blocks is calculated as:

$$M\text{v} = (m\text{v}_1, m\text{v}_2) = (i_1 - j_1, i_2 - j_2) \tag{18}$$

where $(i_1, i_2)$ and $(j_1, j_2)$ are the positions of two matching blocks.

8. The movement vectors $-M$v and $+M$v represent the same movement. Hence, we consider the movement vectors' absolute values $|M\text{v}|$.
9. A matching vector counter $C$ is used to record the frequency of occurrence of a matching block pair. Initially, all matching vector counters are set to zero. For every pair of matching blocks, the counter C *is* increased by one: $C(m\text{v}_1, m\text{v}_2) = C(m\text{v}_1, m\text{v}_2) + 1$.
10. The matching vector counter values are computed for all movement vectors $M\text{v}_1$, $M\text{v}_2$, ....
11. At the end of the matching process, the duplicate blocks are identified by the following criteria:

$$C(M\text{v}) > T \tag{19}$$

where $T$ is a user-defined threshold. The block pairs satisfying the above criteria are identified to be duplicates.

In Fig. 7, the results for detection of duplicate image regions using the above scheme are shown. Figs. 7*a–c* represents manually forged images, the forgery sizes varying as 20%, 30% and 40% of the entire image. The forgery detection results using the above scheme have been shown in Figs. 7*d–f*.

### 3.3 Wavelet Transform based Copy–Move Forgery Detection

In wavelet transform-based copy–move forgery detection algorithms, in order to extract features from image blocks, we utilise wavelet transformations such as DWT, DyWT etc. Here, the image is decomposed into four sub-bands, namely approximation, horizontal, vertical and diagonal sub-bands. Approximation sub- band contains the maximum amount of information, hence plays the most major role in finding duplicate image regions. The diagonal sub-band, assuming the maximum frequency, contains minimal information and produces false matches during duplication detection. From this class of algorithms,

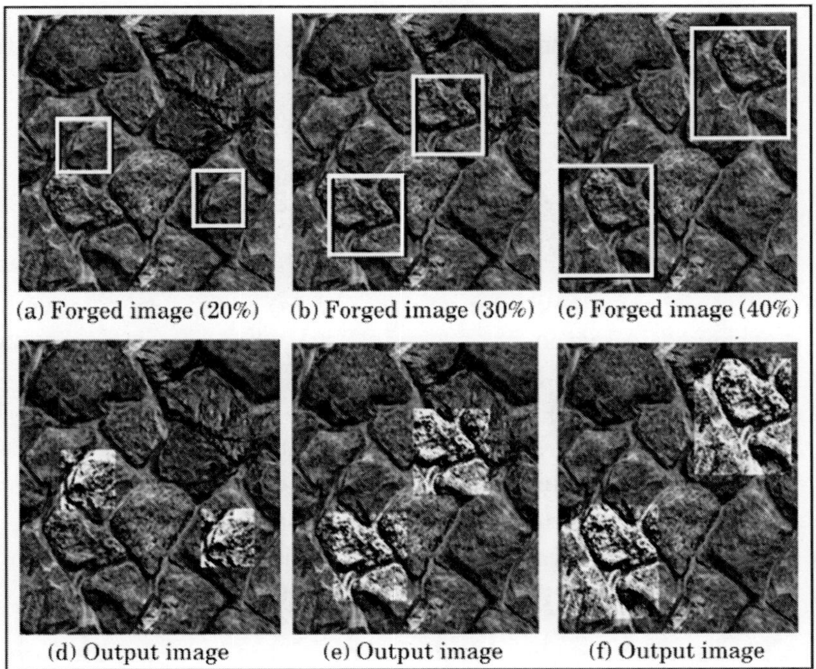


**Fig. 7:** Efficient DCT-based copy–move forgery detection (a)–(c); Manually induced forgeries of varying sizes; (d)–(f) Duplicate regions detected

we have selected three representatives, to be used to describe its operating principle next.

### 3.3.1 *Copy–move forgery detection based on DyWT*

Muhammad *et al.*[41] proposed DyWT-based algorithm to detect duplicate image region. DyWT having shift invariant property helps to achieve considerably high duplication detection accuracy (DA). The operation of this algorithm involves the following steps:

1. The input forged image is decomposed into four sub-bands, *i.e.* approximate, horizontal, vertical and diagonal sub-band by DyWT method.
2. Initially, the approximation sub-band is selected because it has lowest frequency and maximum information content. The approximation sub-band is divided into fixed-sized overlapping blocks.

3. The distance between a pair of blocks, r and s, is calculated using Euclidean formula, as:

$$D(r, s) = \sqrt{\frac{1}{N}\sum_{i=1}^{n}(r_i - s_i)2} \tag{20}$$

$r_i$ and $S_i$ are the corresponding pixels grey-level values in blocks $r$ and $s$, respectively. Let the total number of pixels in a block be $N$.

4. All pairs of blocks, for which $D(r, s) > T_1$ are removed and arranged in increasing order in $list_1$, where $T_1$ is a threshold.
5. Steps 3–4 are repeated for the diagonal sub-band, the highest frequency sub-band, most efficient in representing the dissimilarities in an image. All pairs of blocks, $(r,s)$, for which $D(r,s)$ is less than $T_2$ are discarded and rest are arranged in decreasing order in $list_2$. Here, $T_2$ is another threshold.
6. The block pairs residing at the same location in both the lists ($list_1$ and $list_2$) represent the duplicate image blocks.

In Fig. 8, we have shown the results of duplicate region detection using DyWT-based algorithm. Figs. 8*a–c* represents manually forged images, with forgery sizes varying as 20%, 30% and 40% of the entire image. The forgery detection results using the above method have been shown in Figs. 8*d–f*.

### 3.3.2 *Duplication detection based on DyWT with Zernike moment*

Yang *et al.*[56] proposed a copy–move forgery detection algorithm utilising DyWT along with the *Zernike moment* [56] of an image. In this algorithm, the DyWT sub-bands of an image undergo further decomposition into overlapping blocks; and the Zernike moment of each block is computed and arranged lexicographically into one row of a matrix. The distance between blocks with similar moments is calculated, and the pairs for which the distance is greater than a threshold is output as duplicate block pairs. This algorithm includes the following steps:

1. DyWT is applied on a $w \times h$ input image. We consider the approximation and diagonal sub-bands of the decomposed image for further processing.

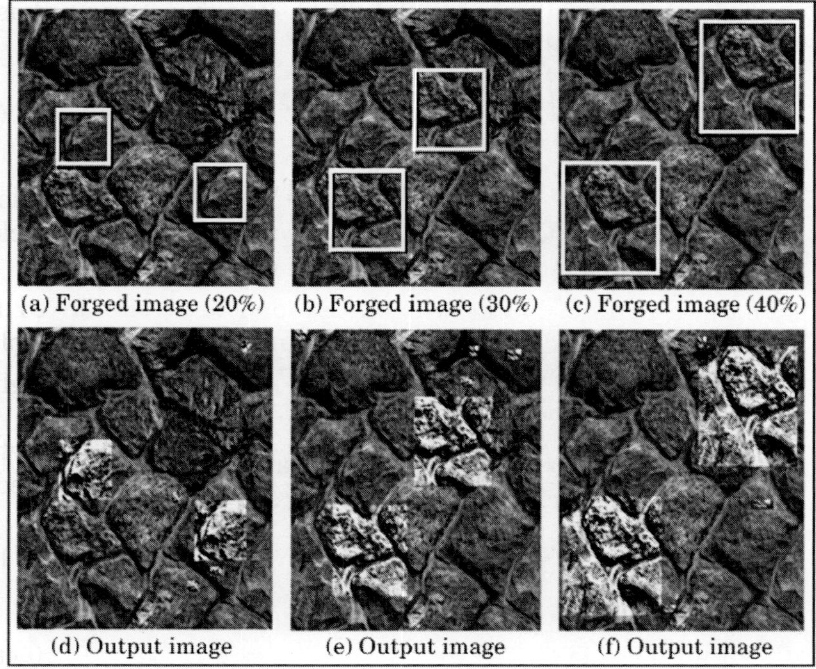


**Fig. 8:** DyWT-based copy–move forgery detection (a)–(c); Manually induced forgeries of varying sizes; (d)–(f) Duplicate regions detected.

2. First, we consider the approximation sub-band and divide it into $(w - B + 1) \times (h - B + 1)$ overlapping blocks, each of size $B \times B$ pixels.
3. Zernike moment of each block is calculated. The Zernike moment[56] of order $n$, with repetition $m$, for a continuous image function $f(x,y)$ that vanishes outside a unit circle, is calculated as follows:

$$A\,(n,m) = \frac{n+1}{\pi} \iint_{x^2+y^2 \leq 1} f(x,y)[Rnm(\rho)\exp(jm\theta)]\,dx\,dy \tag{21}$$

   where $Rnm(\rho)$ represents the Zernike polynomial, $\theta$ represents the angle between $\rho$ and $x$-axis, and $A(n, m)$ is the Zernike moment feature.
4. The Zernike moment of each block, represented by a vector of magnitudes, is stored into one row of a feature matrix $S$.
5. Matrix $S$ is now lexicographically sorted to generate a new feature matrix $S$sorted.

6. Euclidean distance is calculated for each adjacent pair of rows, $s_i$ and $s_i + 1$, of matrix *S*sorted, as:

$$d = \sqrt{\sum_{k=0}^{n}\left(r_i(k) - s_{i+1}(k)\right)^2} \tag{22}$$

where $1 \leq i < (w - B + 1) \times (h - B + 1)$.

7. The block pairs with distance $d < T_1$ (where $T_1$ is a threshold of similarity of moments) are considered to be similar.
8. For those pairs of blocks which are found to be similar by the above step, we find their relative distances in the image, as:

$$d'(Block_i, Block_{i+1}) = \sqrt{(x_i - x_{i+1})^2 + (y_i - y_{i+1})^2} \tag{23}$$

where $(x_i, y_i)$ and $(x_i + 1, y_i + 1)$ represent the image co-ordinates of Block $i$ and Block $i + 1$, respectively.

9. All pairs of blocks for which $d'$ (Block $i$, Block $i + 1$) $> T_2$ ($T_2$ being a threshold) are put into list1.
10. Steps 2–9 are repeated for the diagonal sub-band and the resultant block pairs are put into list2.
11. The block pairs residing at the same location in both the lists (list1 and list2) represent the duplicate image blocks.

In Fig. 9, the results for detection of duplicate image regions using DyWT with Zernike moments are shown. Fig. 9*a–c* represents manually forged images, the forgery sizes varying as 20%, 30% and 40% of the entire image. The forgery detection results using the above method have been shown in Fig. 9*d–f*.

### 3.3.3 *CWT-based copy–move forgery detection*

In this technique, an image is divided into fixed-sized overlapping blocks and feature extraction from each block is done using dual tree CWT (DT-CWT)[75]. The block feature vectors are arranged lexicographically into rows of a feature matrix. The distances between blocks with similar features are calculated, and the pairs of blocks for which the distance is greater than a threshold are output as duplicates.

The CWT-based region duplication detection algorithm is comprised of the following steps:

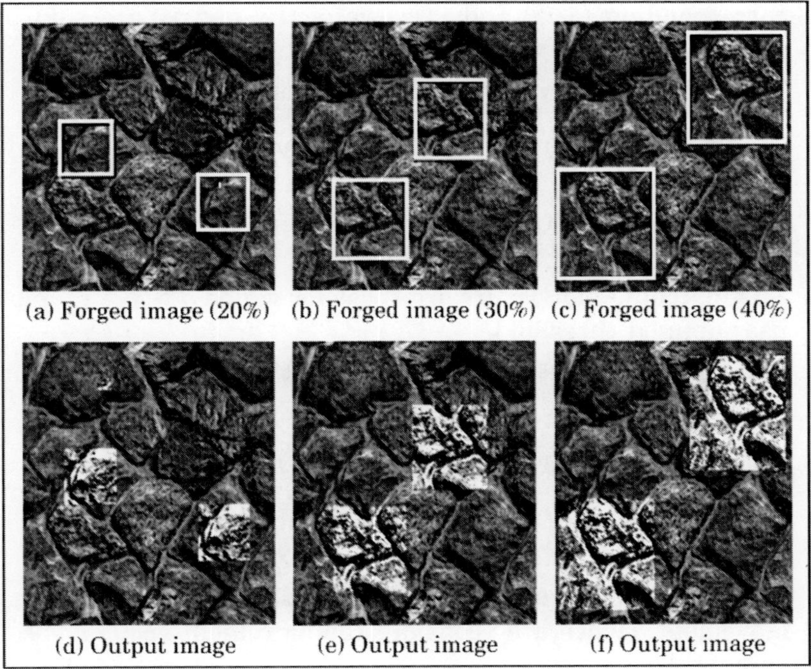


**Fig. 9:** DyWT with Zernike moment-based copy–move forgery detection (a)–(c); Manually induced forgeries of varying sizes; (d)–(f) Duplicate regions detected.

1. An input image of size $w \times h$ pixels is divided into $(w - B + 1) \times (h - B + 1)$ overlapping blocks, each of size $B \times B$ pixels.
2. Next, we decompose the image blocks using DT-CWT and extract their features using Eq. 24, from each sub-band calculated as:

$$E_d^L = \sum_{i=1}^{N} \sum_{j=1}^{N} \| x_d^L(i,j) \| \tag{24}$$

   where each sub-band is $N \times N$ pixels with complex $d$ coefficients $x^L(i, j)$ at level $L$. The extracted features are stored block wise into rows of a feature matrix.
3. The feature matrix is sorted lexicographically row wise, hence producing matrix, a matrix whose every row is sorted.
4. If two rows $i$ and $j$ of the sorted matrix satisfy the condition $| j - i | < T_f$ (where $T_f$ is a user-defined threshold), then blocks

corresponding to $i^{th}$ and $j^{th}$ rows of the matrix are said to be *similar*.

5. The distances between similar blocks are calculated as:

$$d = \sqrt{.}(x_i - x_j)^2 + (y_i - y_j)^2 \tag{25}$$

where $(x_i, y_i)$ and $(x_j, y_j)$ represent the similar blocks' image co-ordinates.

6. The matching block pairs are those for which $d > T_d$, $T_d$ another user-defined threshold.
7. The shift vector or movement vector $M$v for a pair of matching blocks is calculated as:

$$M_V = (mv_1, mv_2) = (i_1 - j_1, i_2 - j_2) \tag{26}$$

where $(i_1, i_2)$ and $(j_1, j_2)$ are the positions of two matching blocks.

8. The movement vectors $-M$v and $+M$v represent the same movement. Hence, we consider the movement vector's absolute values $|M\text{v}|$.
9. A matching vector counter $C$ is used to record the frequency of occurrence of a matching block pair. Initially, all matching vector counters are set to zero. For every pair of matching block, the counter $C$ is increased by one:

$$C\,(mv_1, mv_2) = C(mv_1, mv_2) + 1 \tag{27}$$

10. The matching vector counter values are computed for all movement vectors $M\text{v}_1$, $M\text{v}_2$, ...
11. At the end of the matching process, the duplicate blocks are identified by the following criteria:

$$C(M_V) > T \tag{28}$$

where $T$ is a user-defined threshold. The block pairs satisfying the above criteria are identified to be duplicates.

In Fig. 10, the results for detection of duplication image region using CWT-based algorithm have been shown. Figs. 10*a–c* shows the manually forged images, with forgery sizes: 20, 30 and 40% of the entire image. The forgery detection results have been shown in Figs. 10 *d–f*.

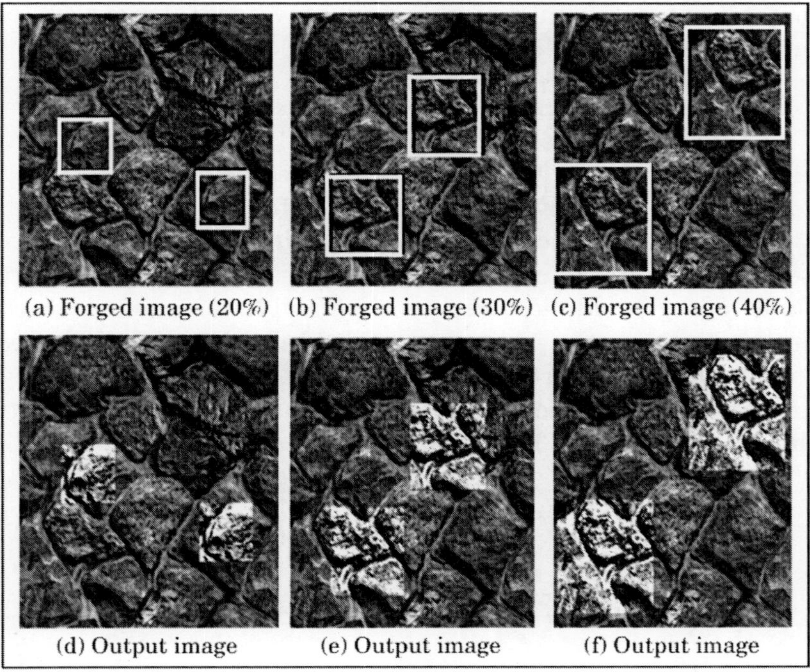


**Fig. 10:** CWT-based copy–move forgery detection (a)–(c); Manually induced forgeries of varying sizes; (d)–(f) Duplicate regions detected.

In the next section, we provide a standard parameterisation platform for evaluation, analysis and comparison of any state-of- the-art block-based copy–move forgery detection technique. Thereafter, we apply the proposed parameters to evaluate and compare the techniques described in this section. The detailed results have been presented in Section 5.1.

## 4. PROPOSED THREE-WAY PARAMETERISATION PLATFORM

In this section, we propose three benchmark parameters – *DA*, *false positive rate* (FPR) and *false negative rate* (FNR) – which would comprise a standard performance evaluation platform for assessing the efficiency of block-based copy–move forgery detection schemes. However, their usage may easily be extended for evaluation of other classes of digital image forgery detection. These parameters will help the users to select a particular forgery detection technique, according to her requirements. Here, we limit our discussion to the applicability of the proposed parameterisation to only block-based copy–move forgery detection algorithms.

The proposed parameters are defined as a function of the forgery size, defined as the area of the duplicated image region in terms of pixels. In the following, we define the proposed parameters – DA, FPR and FNR, one-by-one. For estimating the efficiency of a block-based copy–move forgery detection algorithm, we investigate the variation of those parameters with unit detection block size, where blocks represent the units of region duplication, detection and localisation, as discussed in Section 3. DA is the percentage of total number of forged pixels in an image, which a detection scheme succeeds to identify correctly. We represent DA as a fraction of the total number of pixels, actually duplicated in the image. This is a versatile parameter which is applicable to almost all classes of image forgery detection algorithms, for their performance evaluation. Hence,

$$DA = \frac{Number\ of\ currectly\ detected\ pixels}{Number\ of\ pixels\ actually\ copy-moved} \times 100\ \% \tag{29}$$

FPR is the proportion of absent events that yield positive test outcomes, *i.e.* the conditional probability of a positive test result given an absent event. In the context of image region duplication, FPR measures the area of those image region(s) which is (are) not copy–moved, but still detected to be forged by the forgery detection algorithm. In other words, FPR is defined as the total number of authentic image pixels, falsely detected to be forged and expressed as a fraction of the total number of actually copy–moved pixels in the image. That is,

$$FPR = \frac{Number of\ pixels\ falsely\ detected\ to\ be\ copy-moved}{Number of\ pixels\ actually copy-moved} \times 100\ \% \tag{30}$$

The DyWT-based copy–move forgery detection algorithm discussed in Section 3.3.1, applied on a test image, as shown in Fig. 11*a*, generates a number of false matches. The FP matches in this case, have been shown in Fig. 11*c*, with highlighted regions.

FNR is the proportion of present events that yield negative test outcomes, *i.e.* the conditional probability of a negative test result given the presence of event. In the context of image region duplication, FNR measures the area of those image region(s) which is (are) actually

(a) Original image (b) Forged image (c) Output image

**Fig. 11:** FPs in copy–move forgery detection using DyWT (a) Original image, (b) Forged image, (c) Output image (including FPs) highlighted.

duplicated, but the forgery detection algorithm fails to identify them. In other words, FNR is defined as the total number of actually duplicated image pixels which are overlooked by the detection algorithm, expressed as a fraction of the total number of copy–moved pixels in the image. That is:

$$FNR = \frac{Number\ of\ undetected\ copy - moved\ pixels}{Number\ of\ pixels\ actually\ copy - moved} \times 100\ \% \tag{31}$$

The application of the DyWT based[41] region duplication method on the test image as shown in Fig. 12*a* yields a number of FNs, as is evident from Fig. 12*c*. In Fig. 12*c*, the detected duplicate regions have been darkened in the output image, and within those dark regions, the FNs are clearly visible. Using the parameters introduced above,

(a) Original image (b) Forged image (c) Output image

**Fig. 12:** FNs in copy–move forgery detection using DyWT (a) Original image, (b) Forged image with regions duplicated, (c) Detected duplicate regions darkened.

we present our detailed experimental results for performance analysis and comparison of the different state-of-the- art copy–move forgery detection techniques discussed in Section 3, in the next section.

## 5 PERFORMANCE RESULTS

In this section, we present the performance evaluation results for the block-based copy–move forgery detection algorithms discussed in Section 3. All implementations are performed in MATLAB Image Processing Toolbox. Our test dataset consists of 50 standard image processing test images of size 256 × 256 pixels. We collected those images from Computer Vision Group (CVG), University of Granada (UGR) Image Database[76] and University of Southern California (USC), Signal and Image Processing Institute (SIPI) Image Database[77]. For sake of experiments, we have manually forged our test images. The area of the duplicate region in each test image was varied from 10 to 40% of the entire image. Through our experiments, we have evaluated the performances of the state-of-the-art techniques presented in Section 3, and compared them following the benchmark parameters proposed in Section 4. Finally, we summarise our results so as to provide a complete guidance on pros and cons of the state-of-the- art techniques presented in this chapter in our experiments, we divide our manually forged test images into uniform overlapping blocks of size B × B pixels, where the B is varied from 6 to 36. The performance characteristics of the various techniques presented in Section 3, in terms of DA, have been presented in Fig. 13. The results shown in the plots are the averages taken over all our test images. From Fig. 13, it is evident that for all the algorithms, the DA increases with increasing forgery size. The maximum and average DA of all discussed algorithms are presented in Table 1. Among all the techniques, the CWT-based method exhibits the best DA of 99.59% when the forgery size is 40%. This is due to the inherent properties of CWT exploited in this class of algorithms such as rotation invariance, robustness to noise and multi-level representation, which makes it an extremely efficient method for feature extraction.

Fig. 14 shows the characteristic FPR variation for region duplication detection for all the techniques *versus* unit block size and forgery size. From Fig. 14, it is evident that for all the algorithms, the FPR decreases with increasing the forgery size. However, by wavelet based copy–move forgery detection methods, several identical blocks get falsely

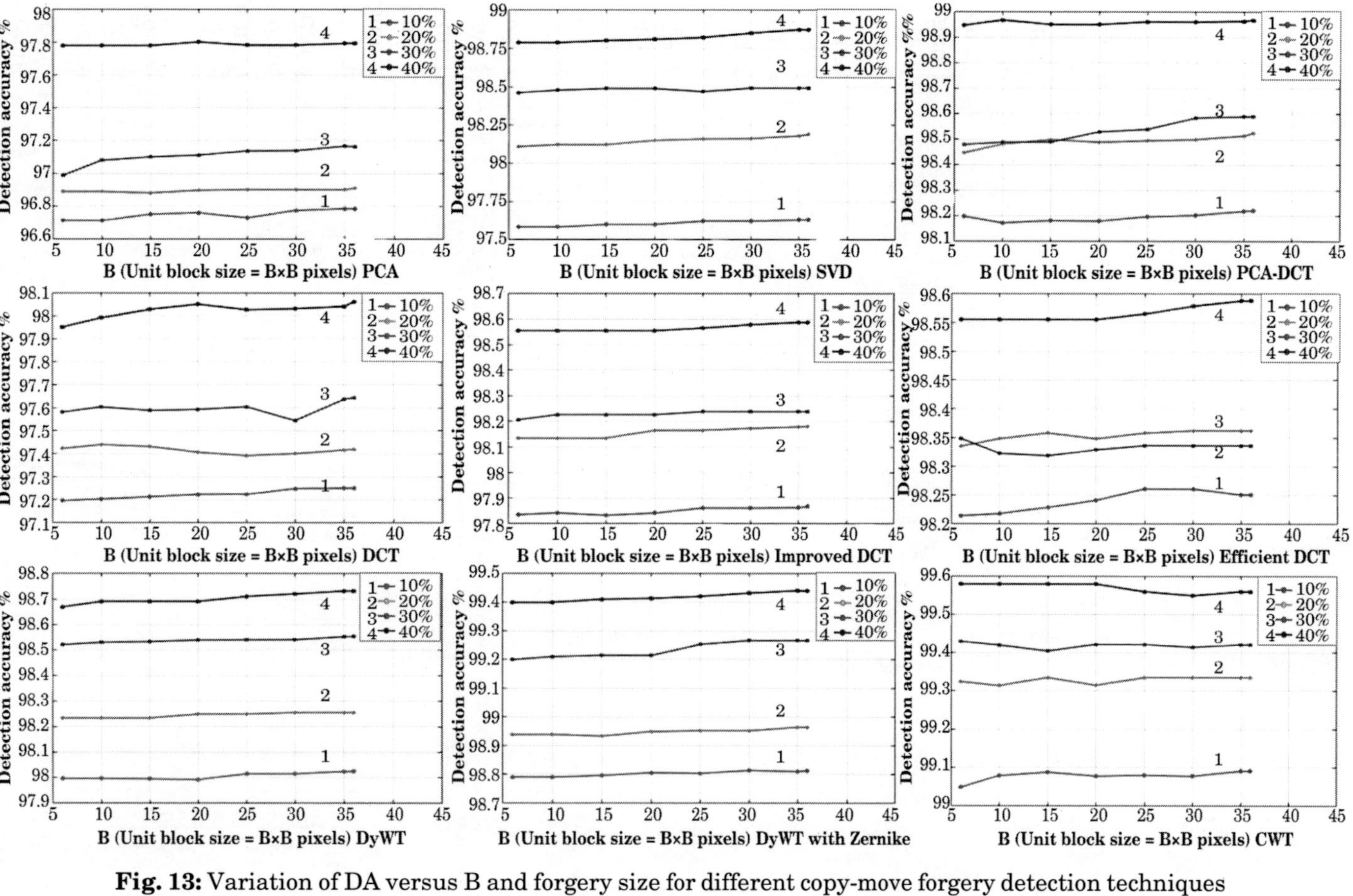


**Fig. 13:** Variation of DA versus B and forgery size for different copy-move forgery detection techniques

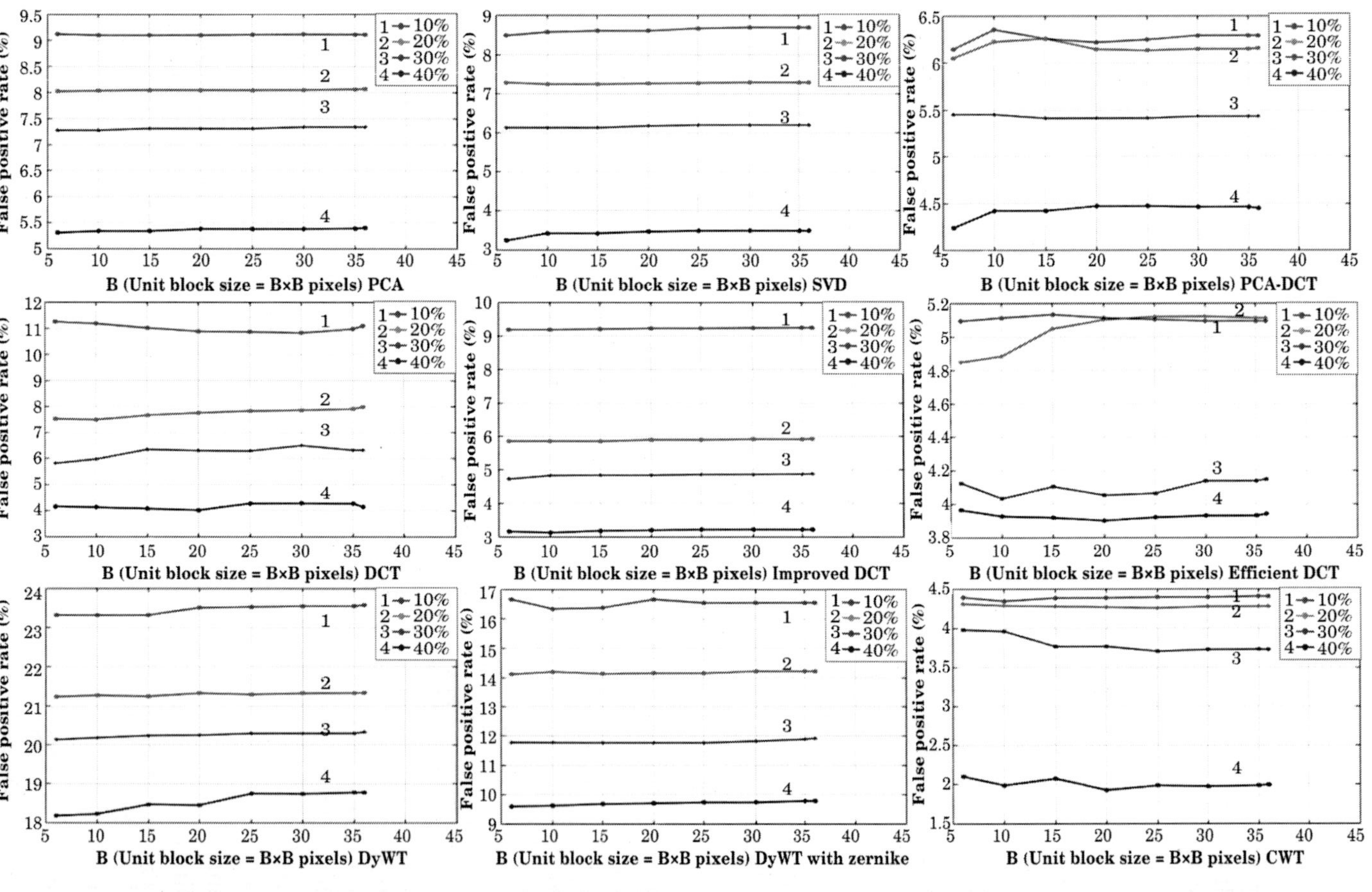


**Fig . 14:** Variation of FPR versus B and forgery size for different copy–move forgery detection techniques

detected at the boundaries of the images; they contribute to the FPs which is not possible to be eliminated completely by adjusting the threshold. In Fig 4, we present the false copy–move forgery detection results, for all the schemes, according to varying forgery sizes. Among all the schemes, the DCT-based techniques demonstrate the lowest rate of FPs.

Similarly, the results for region duplication attacks falsely missed by the state-of-the-art techniques (discussed in Section 3) have been presented in Fig. 15. Fig. 15 shows the plot of FNR versus unit block size and forgery size. From Fig. 15, it is evident that the FN detection rate diminishes with increasing forgery size, for all the techniques. From Fig. 13 and 15, it may be observed that for any copy-move forgery detection technique, its DA and FN forgery detection characteristics are inversely proportional to each other. This is due to the fact that DA is directly computed depending on the number of correctly detected copy– moved pixels, while the FNR is determined by the number of undetected copy–moved pixels, as discussed in Section 4. The computational complexity of any block-based copy–move forgery technique increases as the unit detection block size is reduced. On the other hand, a smaller unit detection block size ensures higher DA. Hence, in such algorithms, it is desirable to obtain a correct trade-off between DA and computational complexity, by selecting an appropriate unit block size. In this regard, our experimental results may help a user to select the most suitable method and unit block size, according to her requirement.

### 5.1 Comprehensive Analysis and Comparison

In this section, we perform a comprehensive comparative analysis of the copy–move forgery detection techniques presented in Section 3. Results of this comprehensive analysis have been presented in a tabular form as Table 1. Our finding in this regard is that the most crucial factor determining the performance accuracy of each algorithm is the image feature that it uses for the purpose of duplication detection. The different image (block) features exploited by different algorithms are presented in the second column of Table 1.

Apart from this, the other major attribute of an algorithm with regard to duplication detection is its block matching criteria. For example, schemes utilising DCT-based features majorly rely on

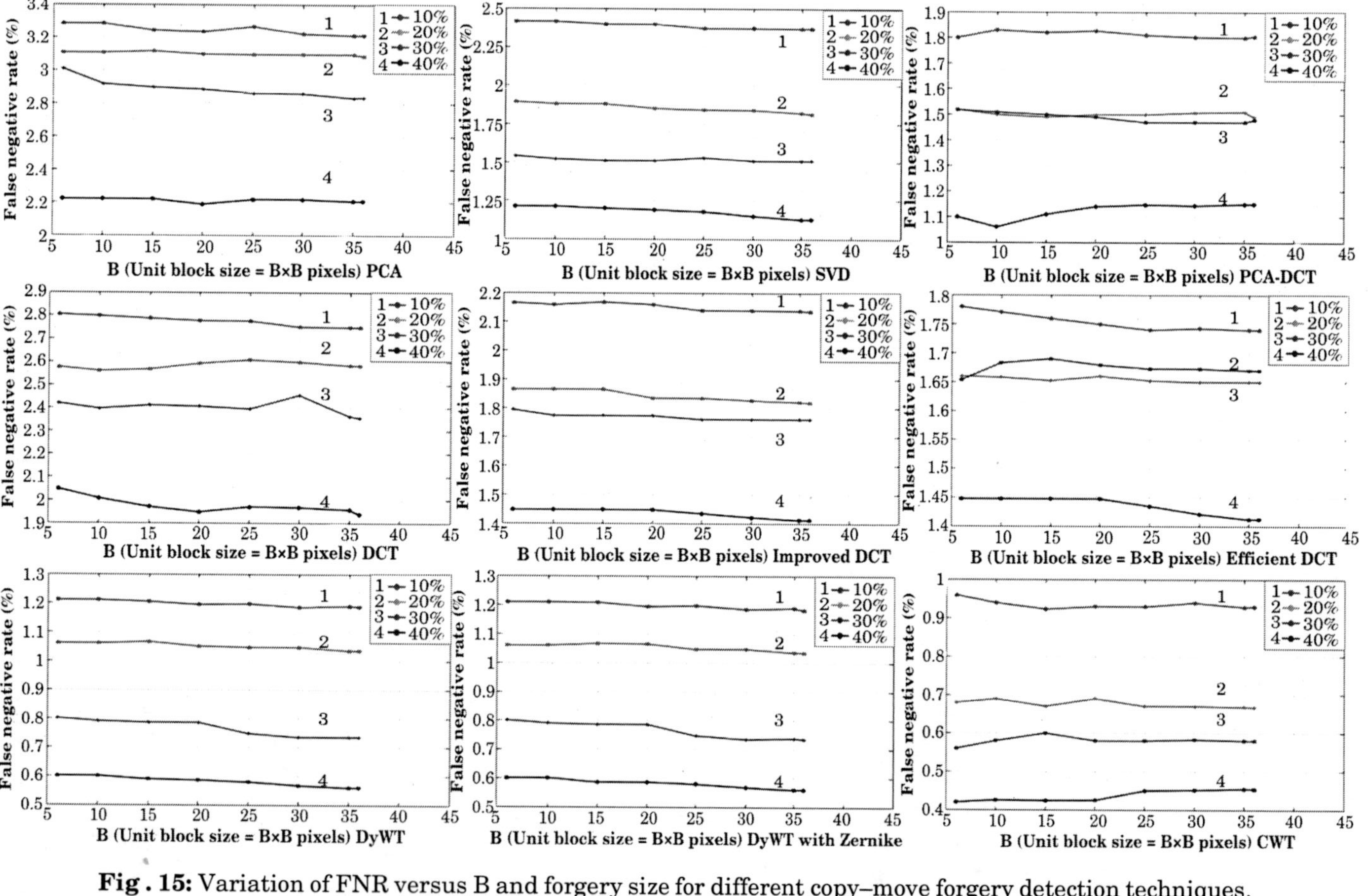


**Fig . 15:** Variation of FNR versus B and forgery size for different copy–move forgery detection techniques.

**Table 1:** Comprehensive comparison of techniques presented in Section 3.

| *Method* | *Features* | *Matching criteria* | *#Threshold* | *Average DA (%)* | *Average FPR (%)* | *Average FNR (%)* | *Multiple detection* |
|---|---|---|---|---|---|---|---|
| PCA | Eigen vectors | Offset frequency | 2 | 97.09 | 7.46 | 2.79 | N |
| SVD | Singular values | Chebyshev distance | 2 | 98.27 | 6.37 | 1.70 | N |
| DCT–PCA | Quantised Coefficients | Movement vector | 1 | 98.54 | 5.56 | 1.46 | N |
| DCT | Quantised Coefficients | Movement vector | 1 | 97.56 | 7.32 | 2.43 | N |
| Improved DCT | Quantised coefficients | Euclidean distance movement vector | 3 | 98.18 | 5.77 | 1.75 | N |
| Efficient DCT | Quantised coefficients | Pixel mean | 2 | 98.37 | 4.51 | 1.62 | Y |
| DyWT | Approximation sub-band energy | Euclidean distance | 2 | 98.38 | 20.81 | 0.89 | Y |
| DyWT-Zernike | Zernike moment | Euclidean distance | 3 | 99.10 | 13.09 | 0.91 | N |
| CWT | Energy of all sub- bands | Euclidean distance, movement vector | 3 | 99.35 | 3.61 | 0.65 | N |

movement vectors between identical block pairs for duplication detection. Similarly, other techniques such as those based on wavelet transform, compute the Euclidean distance between matching block pairs, and perform forgery detection based on those. The block matching criteria adopted by different state-of- the-art techniques are presented along the third column of Table 1.

It is evident from the discussion in Section 3 that the computational-efficiency of all block-based copy–move forgery detection techniques are majorly influenced by the number of block (and sub-block) matching they perform. An estimate of this perspective is given by the number of empirical thresholds adopted by each. The number of empirical/user-defined threshold used in each discussed scheme is presented in the fourth column of Table 1.

The final outcome of this analysis is the overall performance efficiency achieved by the techniques. A summary of this comprehensive performance evaluation of all the schemes, in terms of DA, FPs and FNs, is presented along the 5–7th columns of Table 1. Among all discussed block-based copy–move forgery detection algorithms in Section 3, the wavelet- based algorithms demonstrate highest DA as well as minimum FNR. However, the FPR attained by this class of algorithms is also considerably higher compared with the others. Depending on the problem domain and false acceptance tolerance in a given context, the user will decide the scheme to select. If false acceptance is not a constraint, then the wavelet transform-based techniques may be selected for best forgery DA. However, if the false acceptance is a major concern, as in most conventional forensic problem, then selection of DCT-based schemes may be chosen.

It is evident from Table 1 that the more efficient schemes such as the DyWT-Zernike and CWT-based schemes use the highest number of user-defined thresholds. This helps them achieve comparatively much higher DA, while making them computationally more intensive than the others at the same time. The final criteria used in our comparative analysis of all schemes are the detection of multiple forgeries. According to the authors of those works (in Section 3) and our experimental outcomes, among all discussed block-based copy–move forgery detection algorithms, the efficient DCT-based scheme proposed by Wang *et al.*[68] and the DyWT-based algorithm proposed by Muhammad *et al.*[41], are successful in identifying multiple copy–move forgeries within one image.

## 6. CONCLUSIONS

In the last decade, there have been quite a lot of researches in the direction of image forgery detection. Specifically, the field of copy–move forgery or region duplication detection in images has gained a lot of research interest due to the fact that this form of forgery is one of the most primitive forms of attacks on digital images. However, it is not trivial to detect this form of forgery because the natural statistical properties of the image are not altered here. In this chapter, we provide a detailed review of state-of- the-art copy–move forgery detection algorithms, their implementation, performance evaluation and comparison. In this chapter, we have introduced a set of standard parameters with respect to which we have performed our experiments for the performance evaluation and comparison. The parameters introduced in this chapter encompass three different dimensions of conventional forgery detection operations. The proposed parameterisation would help the users select an appropriate forgery detection algorithm according to his requirements, and the expected forgery type.

# 10

# Image Block Matching Based Region Duplication Detection

## 1. INTRODUCTION

In today's digital world, multimedia act as the primary means of communication, and are regularly transmitted in large numbers over public channels such as the internet. In addition, images and videos act as the primary sources of clue to wards any incident and largely influence judgments related to criminal investigations in the court of law. They are considered as the most valuable evidences to prove the veracity of any incidence. However, with the advent of low–cost image and video editing software and tools, digital images and videos are losing their reliability and trust worthiness, very rapidly[35]. The wide adoption of cheap and easy–to–use image processing software is primarily responsible for the vast increase in image forgery rate into day's cyber world. Hence assuring the integrity and correctness of digital images and videos poses to be a very crucial challenge today.

In this chapter, we deal with copy–move form of image forgery where a region of an image is copied and pasted onto itself, at a different location, with the malicious intention to repeat or obscure significant objects in an image. Here an image object is copied from the original image and pasted on to itself at a different location, to generate the tampered image.

In the recent years, a number of forensic researchers have proposed different techniques for detection of digital image region duplication attack, or copy-move forgery. On the basis of operating principles copy–move forgery detection algorithms can be divided into two classes:

- Algorithms based on Image Block Matching[56-58]
- Algorithms based on Image Key–Points Matching[43,47,60]

In this chapter we present block-matching based image region duplication detection. The block-based methods of region duplication detection in images, are computationally more intensive than the key-point based techniques; however, they perform extremely efficiently even for homogeneous, or smooth textured image regions, unlike the other class. The computational complexity of key–point based method is very low but they do not perform well for smooth or homogeneous regions.

Major Operations of the block based methods can be broadly divided into following key steps:

- Pre–processing
- Feature extraction
- Sorting the feature matrix
- Calculation of similarity
- Block matching

Fig. 1 below presents the common steps for the block based method. On the basis of above key–steps we present the literature survey of block based copy–move forgery detection algorithms.

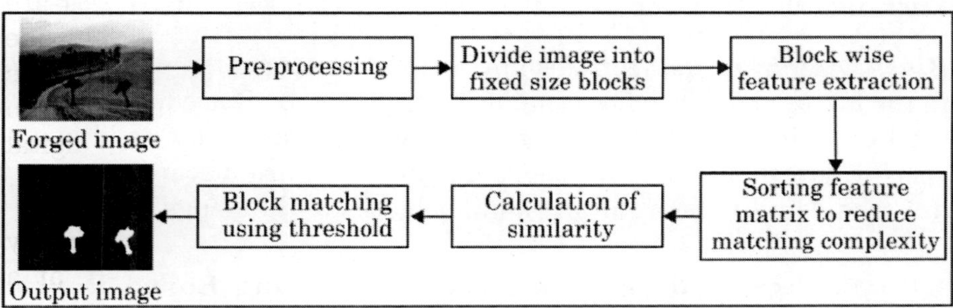


**Fig. 1:** Common steps for block based copy–move forgery detection techniques.

***Pre–processing:*** Pre–processing is the first stage of block based methods. The main object of this step is to prepare the suspected image for feature extraction. This step involves two consequent operations. First color space is converted to grayscale image or YCbCr color space.

Mostly block based algorithms such as[56-58] operate grayscale images while[78,79] operate with YCbCr color space. In the second operation, a grayscale image or YCbCr color space is divided into fixed-sized blocks overlapping blocks[39] or non–overlapping blocks[80,81] or circular blocks[82, 83].

***Feature extraction:*** Feature extraction is the key step of the copy–move forgery detection algorithms. The features are extracted from each blocks and store row–wise into a matrix. If the method is based on Principle Component Analysis (PCA) based[39], Singular Value Decomposition based (SVD)[66,74], Discrete Cosine Transform based (DCT)[58,68] or Wavelet Transform based (DWT)[66] the features are stored in the form of Eigen vectors, singular values, quantized coefficients or energy coefficients of sub–band respectively.

***Sorting the feature matrix:*** The aim of this step is to reduce the time complexity involved in searching matching rows in feature matrix. The traditional state–of–the–art block based copy-move forgery detection algorithm, researcher sort the matrix row wise using any one of method *i.e.,* ascending order[30,41,56,60], radix sort[84,85], k–d tree[86], lexicographical sort[39,55,66], etc. along the row of feature matrix.

***Calculation of similarity:*** Next, in order to measure the similarity between a pair of rows, authors calculate the distance between each pair of blocks using the different similarity metric such as Eucledian[41,58,68], Chebyshev distance[66,74], Canberra metri[88], etc.

***Block matching using threshold adjustment:*** All the pairs of rows in the feature matrix, whose similarity measured by Eucledian[39,56,66,68], Chebyshev distance[66,74], Canberra metric[88] is more than a application–specific threshold value (a user defined value), are discarded as they are considered to be naturally similar blocks of the image.

## 1.1 Background on Image Block Matching Based Region Duplication Detection

In the recent years, forensics researchers have proposed different block based copy–move forgery detection techniques in digital images. First of all, Fridrich *et. al.*[55] proposed region duplication detection based on the principles of exact block matching, autocorrelation, exhaustive block search and robust match (based on Discrete Cosine Transform (DCT)). The robust matching method proves to be most efficient, where the detection is based on matching of quantization DCT coefficients, lexicographically sorted for computation efficiency. However, this method, when applied to images containing large identical textured regions, leads to a lot of false matches. Popescu and Farid [2] presented a computationally efficient block based copy–move forgery detection technique based on Principal Component Analysis (PCA). Here, the inherent dimensionality reduction characteristics of PCA have been used to reduce the number of features to half of that of[55]. Zhang *et. al.*[40], proposed an algorithm based on Discrete Wavelet Transform (DWT), where the image is decomposed in four sub–bands and the low frequency sub–band is used for analysis. The computational complexity of this method is comparatively lower, but the scheme fails to detect forgery present around the center of the image. However, due to dimensionality reduction, the efficiency reduces for lossy compressed or rotated images. Yang *et. al.*[56] applied undecimated shift–invariant Dyadic Wavelet Transform (DyWT) on a forged image by decomposing it into four frequency subbands, and have decomposed low frequency subband into overlapping blocks. The Euclidean distance between each block–pair is computed and the matching pairs are detected using a threshold. This method optimizes the number of false matches, even when image consists of extensive uniform regions. Muhammad *et. al.*[41] proposed another undecimated dyadic wavelet transform (DyWT) based method, by which a forged image is decomposed into sub–bands and sub–bands are divided into overlapping blocks. Similarity between blocks are measured using Euclidean distance with the aim to find a match. This method is capable of detecting lossy compressed duplicate image regions, where both low as well as high frequency components are utilized to get rid of false positives.

The rest of the chapter is organized as follows. In Section 2, we present a state-of-the-art mean and variance based image forgery detection method, based on image block matching, proposed in[88]. The performance of the presented scheme, are presented and discussed in Section 3. Finally, in Section 4 we conclude the chapter.

## 2. A RECENT STATE-OF-THE-ART IMAGE BLOCK MATCHING BASED DIGITAL FORENSIC SOLUTION TO COPY-MOVE FORGERY DETECTION

In this chapter, we discuss image block matching based copy-move forgery detection. As a working example, we present a recent copy–

move forgery detection technique[88], which is based on image block-matching, and utilizes statistical image features, such as mean and variance of the image. Initially, we decompose the possibly forged image into four sub-bands. The LL sub-band (having maximum information) is divided into fixed sized overlapping blocks. The mean of each block is computed and stored into a matrix. Similarities between blocks are computed based on their means, using Euclidean distance, and the most similar block pairs, decided using an empirically chosen threshold, are used to denote the duplicate image regions. The scheme achieves an optimal false positives rate, by utilizing the variance of duplicate image block pairs.

In this section we present a recent image block-matching based copy–move forgery detection technique, proposed in[88]. This technique operates by exploiting statistical image features, mean and variance, and is based on Discrete Wavelet Transform of an image. Fig. 2 shows the flowchart of this technique.

Below, we present the steps involved in the above copy-move forgery detection algorithm, including the detailed feature extraction, similarity calculation and thresholding procedures.

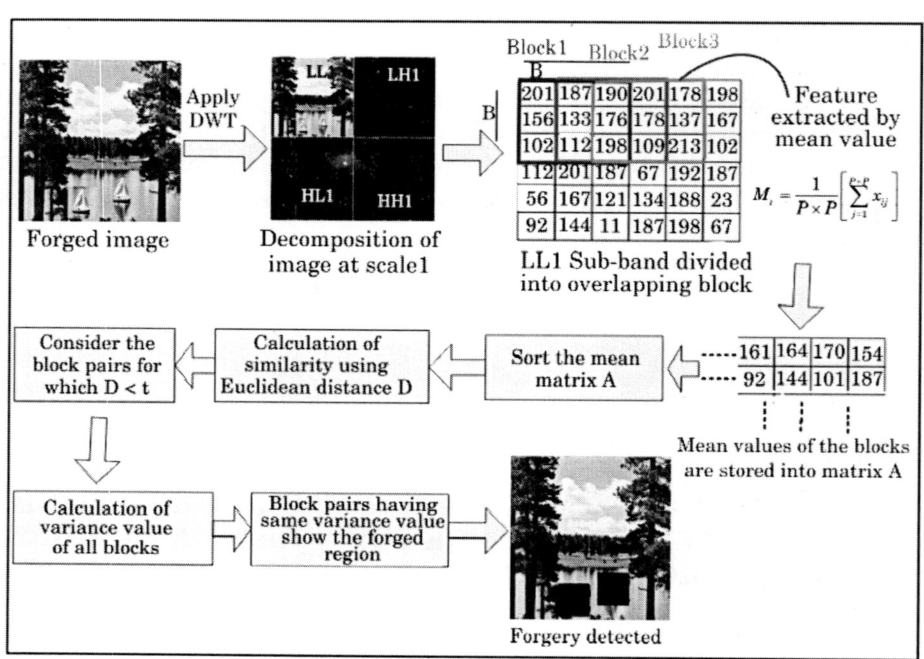


**Fig. 2.** Operational flow chart.

1) Initially we take the forged image of size W × H pixels (say) as an input. If the input image is a color one, we convert it into grayscale according to following equation:

$$I = 0.299 \times Red\ intensity + 0.587 \times Green\ intensity + 0.114 \times Blue\ intensity \quad (1)$$

2) DWT is applied to the forged image to obtain four sub–bands at scale 1, *viz.*, approximation ($LL_1$), horizontal ($LH_1$), vertical ($HL_1$) and diagonal ($HH_1$). $LL_1$ sub–band contains highest similarity as well as maximum information of an image. Hence, we selected LL1 sub–band for further processing..
3) Next, $LL_1$sub-band is divided into overlapping blocks of size P×P pixels.
4) Hence, the total number of overlapping blocks is (W/2–P+1) × (H/2–P+1). The mean value sequence M1, M2.........M((W/2–P+1) × (H/2–P+1)) is calculated from the corresponding blocks B1, B2,...·B (W/2–P+1) × (H/2–P+1), as:

$$M_i = \frac{1}{P \times P} \sum_{j=0}^{P \times P} x_{ij} \quad (2)$$

where $M_i$ is the mean of $LL_1$ approximation coefficients ($x_{ij}$) of block $B_i$. The $M_1$, $M_2$ ... M(W/2–P+1) × (H/2–P+1) values are stored into a (W/2–P+1) × (H/2–P+1) matrix, say A. The rows of matrix A are sorted.

5) For calculation of similarity between blocks, we measure the following Euclidean distance:

$$D(x, y) = \left(\sum_{i=1}^{(H/2-P+1)} (A_{xi} - A_{yi})^2\right)^{1/2} \quad (3)$$

where D(x, y) is the Euclidean distance between a pair of rows of A, $A_x$ and $A_y$, where $A_x$ = ($A_{x1}$, $A_{x2}$, ... Ax(H /2–P +1) and $A_y$ = ($A_{y1}$, $A_{y2}$,....$A_y$ (H/2–P +1)).

6) The block pairs for which D(x,y) < Ts, (where Ts is an empirically selected similarity threshold), are decided to be duplicates.

It was observed that the copy–move forgery detection algorithm presented above produces false block matches or false positives. Here we present a technique for optimization of false matches in the above method. For reduction of false matches, we calculate variance of each block. Variance value is conventionally used to measure the degree of variance of a pixel in an image block, from its neighbors. This has been exploited here to minimize the false matches in the above techniques, as:

7) We consider the block pairs for which D(x, y) <$T_s$ (as computed by steps 1 to 6 above), for false matches reduction.
8) The variance of each such block pair is calculated as:

$$V_i = \frac{1}{P \times P} \sum_{j=1}^{P \times P} .(x_{ij} - M_i) \quad (4)$$

9) Out of all block pairs considered in step 7, now the algorithm decides only those block pairs to be duplicates, which have identical variance values. That is, blocks $B_i$ and $B_k$ are decided to be duplicates if and only if $V_i$=$V_k$.

In Fig. 3, we show the output of the above approach for detection of copy-moved regions for two different images.

We also show in Fig. 3 (b),(e) that the technique leads to some false matches, which are eliminated by application of the false matches' optimization technique (presented above). The final optimized results are shown in Fig. 3 (c),(f).

## 3. PERFORMANCE EVALUATION RESULTS AND DISCUSSION

Here, we present the performance evaluation and assessment results of the scheme presented in Section, to provide an overview to the readers about the performance efficiency of block matching based region duplication detection techniques, in general. Here, the test data set consists of a set of 512 × 512 color as well as grayscale test images, collected from the UGR-CVG[76] and USC SIPI[77] image databases, commonly used for image forensic researches.

The Detection Accuracy (DA) and False Positive Rate (FPR) results of the technique presented in Section 3, are presented in Table 1, columns DA and FPR1, respectively. Column FPR2 indicates the improvement in False Positive Rate obtained after application of the false positive optimization method (presented in Section 3). Results in Table 1 show that as image block size varies from 5 × 5 to 3535, the detection accuracy varies between 98.2972% to 98.5186%, and the FPR

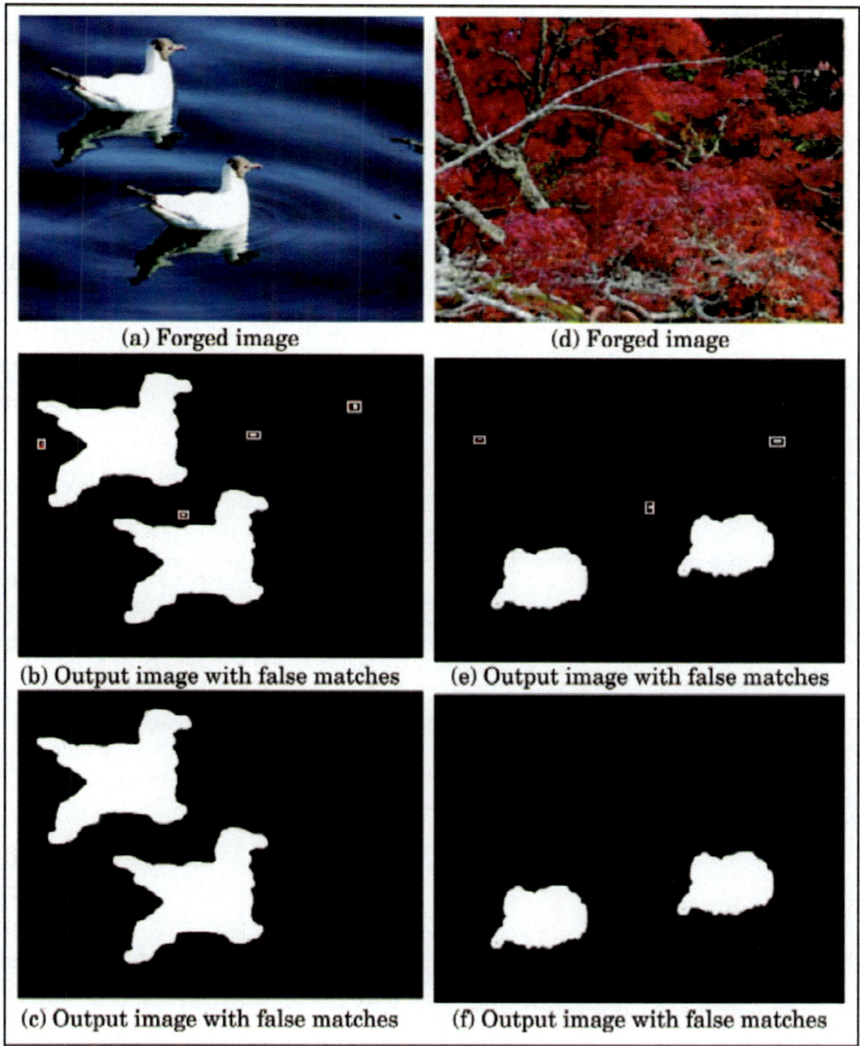


**Fig. 3:** Output of the algorithm. Detected copy-move regions are shown in white. The false matches are highlighted with yellow boxes.

varies between 5.94% to 6.26%. After optimizing the false matches, the False Positive Rate is minimized, which is now in the range of 2.3956% to 2.8134%.

We compare the performance of the method presented in Section 3, with six other state-of-the-art copy-move forgery detection

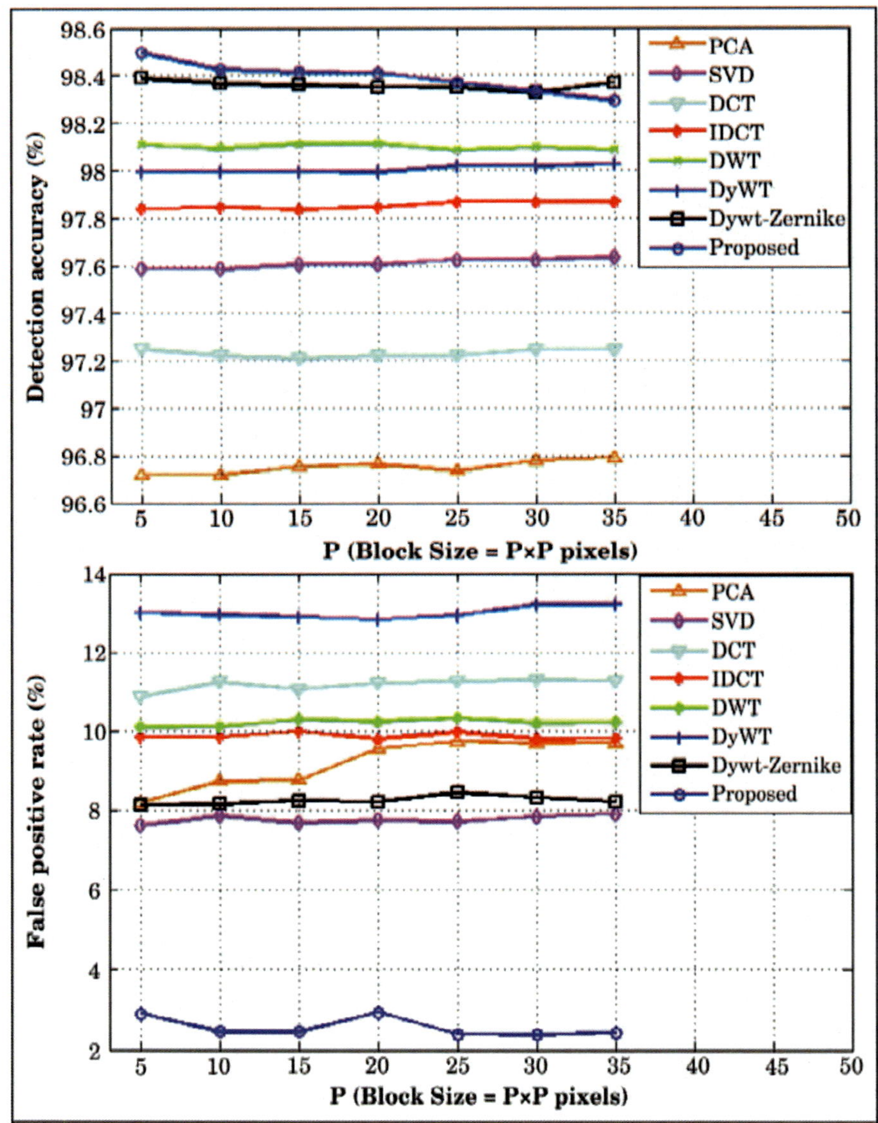


**Figs. 4 & 5:** (Top) Detection accuracy *vs*. P comparison results. (Bottom) False positive rate *vs*. P comparison results.

techniques, which are based on the following principles of operation: (a) Principle Component Analysis (PCA)[2] (b) Discrete Cosine Transform (DCT)[55] (c) Singular Value Decomposition (SVD)[39] (d) Improved

**Table 1:** Detection accuracy and false positive rate results for the copy-move forgery detection technique presented in Section 3.

| ***Block Size (pixels)*** | ***DA (%)*** | ***$FPR_1$ (%)*** | ***$FPR_2$ (%)*** |
|---|---|---|---|
| 5 × 5 | 98.5186 | 6.2592 | 2.7709 |
| 10 × 10 | 98.4263 | 6.1293 | 2.3956 |
| 15 × 15 | 98.4092 | 6.1129 | 2.4251 |
| 20 × 20 | 98.4007 | 6.0382 | 2.8134 |
| 25 × 25 | 98.3770 | 6.0647 | 2.4074 |
| 30 × 30 | 98.3089 | 6.0184 | 2.4692 |
| 35 × 35 | 98.2972 | 5.9374 | 2.6008 |

DCT[58]. (e) Discrete Wavelet Transform (DWT)[66], (f) Dyadic Wavelet Transform (DyWT)[41] and (g) Dyadic Wavelet Transform with Zernike moment[56]. The performance has been compared in terms of DA and FPR, in Fig. 4 and Fig. 5, respectively. Fig 4 and Fig. 5 present the comparison results in terms of detection accuracy *vs.* block size, and false positive rate *vs.* block size plots. From Fig. 4 and Fig. 5, it is evident that the presented method achieves lower false positive rate and higher detection accuracy than the other state–of–the–art techniques

## 5. CONCLUSIONS

In this chapter, we present an overview of image block matching based forensic region duplication detection methods. Also, we present a recent working example here, to present the exact operational steps of such methods clearly to the readers. We also present the evaluation results of this technique, and discuss those. The method operates by dividing an image into fixed size overlapping blocks, in its frequency domain, and considering statistical features, mean and variance, of each individual block. Its performance is evaluated by using detection accuracy and false positive rate. The results show that the performance is optimized, and proves that the technique out-performs the state-of-the-art in terms of detection accuracy and false positive rate.

# 11

# Addressing Post-Processing Attacks in Copy-Move Forgery Detection

## 1. INTRODUCTION

In the last chapter, we learnt about region duplication or copy-move forgery detection methods, based on the principle of image blocks matching. Copy–move forgery or region duplication attack is one of the most primitive as well as prevalent forms of digital image forgeries, where the forger copies region(s) of an image and pastes it onto itself at some other location, with some malicious target, such as to obscure or repeat significant image object(s). The presence of homogeneous texture in an image, such as water, sky, grass, sand etc., makes it all the more vulnerable to this form of attack. The existing techniques may be broadly are classified into block–based algorithms[55,56,57,58] and keypoint–based algorithms[43,47,60,89], depending on their operating principles. Majority of the existing region duplication detection techniques are block–based, *i.e.,* they aim to find pixel blocks that are exact continuous copies of each other in an image. Such methods are effective in detection of copy–move forgery, where an image region is duplicated without any form of alteration to it.

However, such type of forgery detection becomes complicated when the image undergoes some further post-processing modifications, in addition to region duplication. For example, an intelligent adversary *blurs* the edges of the duplicated image region(s), so that block-matching based duplication detection completely fails. Since block-matching algorithms for region duplication detection in images, operate by pixel-block-wise region matching, when the edges of the forged region(s) are blurred, they are not distinguishable from their surroundings, plus block matching fails.

In the recent state-of-the-art, Mahdian and Saic[86] proposed a blur moment invariant method to detect copy–moved image regions, for exposed images that are degraded by blurring or corrupted with added noise. Huang *et al.*[4] developed a method using Scale Invariant Feature Transform (SIFT) for copy–move forgery detection which is scale– and rotation– invariant but fails to be robust to simple noise and blurring, giving a very poor performance for images with small forgery size. Yang *et al.*[56] applied undecimated shift–invariant Dyadic Wavelet Transform (DyWT) on a forged image by decomposing it into four frequency subbands, and has used the low frequency subband to divide the image into overlapping pixel blocks. The Euclidean distance between each block–pair is computed and the matching pairs are detected using a threshold on the distances. This method produces very less number of false matches, even when image consists of extensive uniform regions. Another DyWT based approach, capable of detecting lossy compressed duplicate image regions, where both low as well as high frequency components are utilized to get rid of false positives is proposed by Muhammad *et al.*[41]. Bayram *et al.*[57] proposed a duplicate region detection method based on Fourier Mellin Transform (FMT), which used the notion of Bloom Filters. This method proves to be scale– and rotation–invariant as well as computationally efficient, being able to detect forgery even in highly compressed images. Kang and Wei[39] proposed a region duplication detection method based on Singular Value Decomposition (SVD), having low computational complexity and extremely effective in cases where the duplicate regions are induced with noise. Zhang *et al.*[40] proposed an algorithm based on Discrete Wavelet Transform (DWT) for copy–move forgery detection, which again attains a considerably low computational complexity as compared to the other existing schemes. A sorted neighborhood approach for region duplication detection in images based on DWT and SVD has been proposed by Li *et al.*[66], in which first DWT is applied to the image and then SVD is used to extract the features of the blocks of the low frequency components, leading to dimension reduction of the blocks for achieving lesser computation time.

Most of the above methods suffer from high false positive rate, which reduces their detection accuracy, and are not robust to excessive blurring.

In this chapter, we present a recent state-of-the-art blur–invariant region duplication detection method[90], with optimized false positive rate and improved detection accuracy. The presented method operates block–wise and involves Stationary Wavelet Transform (SWT) to obtain four transform domain subbands of an image (LL, LH, HL, HH). SWT helps in finding the similarities *i.e.* matches and dissimilarities *i.e.* noise, between the blocks of an image, caused due to blurring. The LL and HH subbands are used to find the similar blocks and to detect foreign noise caused due to blurring, if any, respectively. The shift–invariance and undecimated characteristics of SWT, makes this method more efficient compared to other wavelet transform based copy–move forgery detection algorithms. In this method, Singular Value Decomposition (SVD)[74] is used for feature extraction of the overlapping blocks, that the LL and HH subbands are divided into. The blocks here are represented by features extracted using the scaling- and rotation-invariant Singular Value Decomposition of the image. SVD is a low computationally intensive, stable technique which is invariant to translation.

The concepts of automatic threshold fitting has been introduced in this chapter, to optimize manual effort. This chapter also introduces color–based segmentation [52] to the readers, which helps to reduce the huge number of false positives produced when an image contains extensive regions of homogeneous texture. Segmentation also helps here, to reduce the computational complexity by enabling intra segment block matching. Segmentation also helps to avoid unnecessary comparisons between blocks in different segments. The false positive rate is further reduced by using an 8–connected neighborhood checking approach proposed in[91]. Finally, we present experimental results to prove the efficiency of the method in detection of copy-move forgery involving intelligent edge blurring.

The rest of the chapter is organized as follows. A technical background on Stationary Wavelet Transform (SWT) and Singular Value Decomposition (SVD) of an image, are presented in Section 2. Section 3 presents the recent state-of-the-art blur invariant copy–move forgery detection technique[90], and show that it works both when there is no blurring involved (*i.e.* with plain copy-move forgery), as well as when the forged region is blurred intelligently. The performance evaluation results are presented in Section 4. Finally, the concluding remarks are given in Section 5.

## 2. BACKGROUND

### 2.1 Stationary Wavelet Transform (SWT)

Discrete Wavelet Transform (DWT) has been used quite often in the literature by various researchers for image representation in copy–move forgery detection. The major drawback of this representation is that the conservation of translation–invariance, which is a key property in digital image processing, is not achieved by it. In image forensic problems, signal representation (descriptors) must be translation–invariant, as when a pattern undergoes a shift, the descriptors should also be shifted, not altered. For instance, in copy–move forgery, the duplicate regions are not necessarily situated in the same location of two blocks (this has been shown in Fig. 1). When the descriptors are shift–variant, they will result in different representations corresponding to these two blocks, and hence lead to incorrect inference by the forgery detection algorithms. DWT fails to achieve shift–invariance since it includes down–sampling, where during the convolutions in the stage of decomposition only the even–numbered wavelet coefficients are considered, and a constant reduction of size by two in each direction for the next higher scale makes it decimated. This in turn hinders the

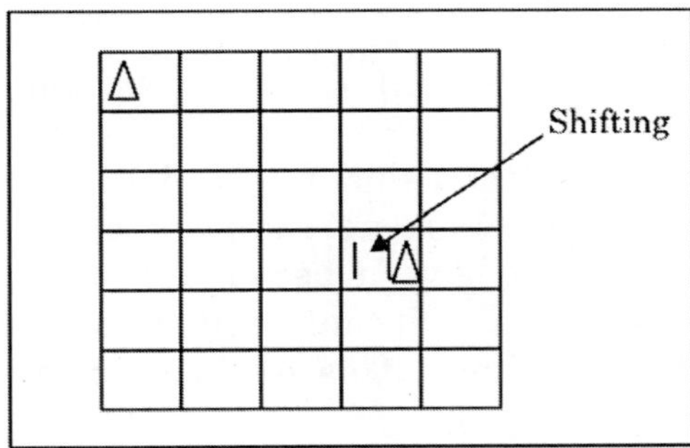


**Fig. 1:** Illustration of the need of translation–invariant descriptors. The highlighted region in the first block is copy–moved to another position in the second block. A translation– invariant descriptor will result in similar features when applied to these two blocks, where as a translation–variant descriptor will produce completely different features.

forgery detection procedure. Even a minute shift in duplicate regions may bring about enormous differences in DWT coefficients at various scales, which may deliver completely different feature vectors for the two duplicate regions, huge variations in the energy distribution at different scales, and finally, huge change in reconstructed waveforms. This is because the critical sampling results in wavelet coefficients that are largely dependent on their locations.

Stationary Wavelet Transform (SWT)[92] plays a vital role to overcome the problem of translation–variance encountered in Discrete Wavelet Transform (DWT). SWT can be applied to the problem of copy–move forgery detection very efficiently, since unlike other wavelet transforms, SWT in essence does not involve down–sampling of signals. Instead, a null placing approach is applied where modification of the filters is carried out at each level, by inserting zero padding. Appropriate low and high pass filters are applied to the signal at each level with no decimation to generate two sequences at the following level, each having the same length as the input sequence. The SWT is a redundant scheme because the output obtained at each level of SWT has equal number of samples as the input. So, for a N–level decomposition a redundancy of N is obtained in the wavelet coefficients. In SWT, every time we perform a wavelet decomposition, up–sampled filters are used. For up–sampling of the filters, an operator$\uparrow$ 2 is introduced which works by alternating a sequence with zeros, *i.e.* if y =$\uparrow$ 2(x) then $y_{2i} = x_i$ and $y_{2i+1} = 0$. Let $g_0[n]$, $h_0[n]$ be the original filters that are used in DWT. Then, the SWT filters for the next level are generated as shown below:

$$g_j + 1[n] = \uparrow 2(g_j)[n],\ h_j + 1[n] = \uparrow 2(h_j)[n] \tag{1}$$

Fig. 2 shows the SWT of a signal (upto 3–levels) and Fig. 3 shows that the filters in each level are up–sampled versions of the previous. SWT has been proven to give a better approximation than other wavelet transforms[92] due to its inherent properties of redundancy, linearity and shift–invariance. This method can be realised using a recursive algorithm.

## 2.2 Singular Value Decomposition (SVD)

Here we present the Singular Value Decomposition method, applicable to an image, represented as a matrix. Let A be a real or complex matrix

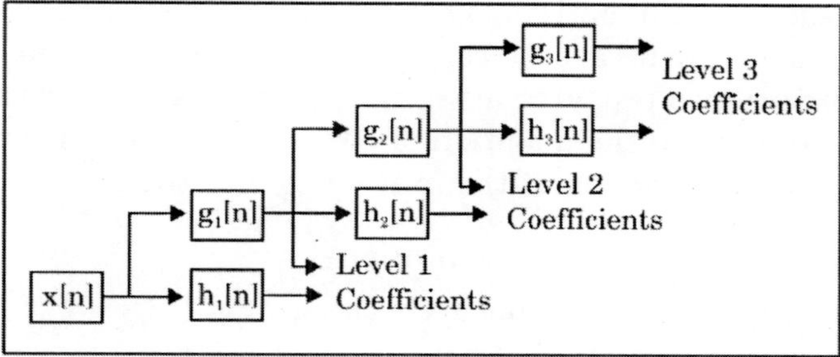


**Fig. 2:** 3–level Stationary Wavelet Transform of a signal.

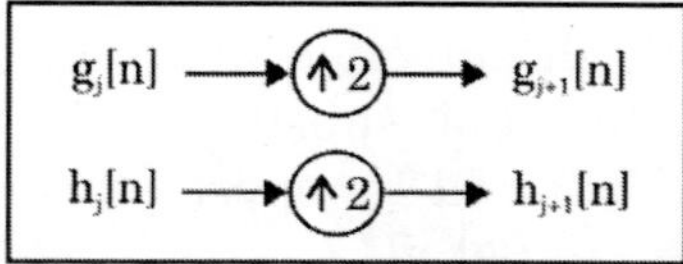


**Fig. 3:** Filter computation from $j^{th}$ to $(j + 1)^{th}$ level.

where $A \in R^{M \times N}$. Its Singular Value Decomposition (SVD) is expressed as the factorization:

$$A = U\,SV^{T} \tag{2}$$

where $U \in R^{M \times M}$ and $V \in R^{N \times N}$ are orthogonal (unitary) matrices and $S \in R^{M \times N}$ is a diagonal matrix.

The major advantages of adopting SVD in digital image forensics are broadly the followings:

1. The dimension of the matrices need not be fixed. The matrix can be square or rectangular.
2. SVD efficiently represents the intrinsic algebraic properties of an image. Singular values reflect the brightness of an image and singular vectors correspond to the geometrical characteristics (size, shape, position of an object etc.) of an image.
3. For reconstruction of an image, only its first singular value is sufficient to be considered, ignoring the rest, without affecting the quality of the reconstructed image.

## 3. ACHIEVING BLUR-INVARIANT REGION DUPLICATION DETECTION BASED ON SWT-SVD

An efficient technique to address post-processing blur attack in region duplication detection of images, has been recently proposed in[90]. This scheme is successful in optimizing the false positives, unlike the other state-of-the-art blur-invariant copy-move forgery detection schemes. This blur-invariance property along with optimized false positive rate is majorly credited to the adoption of SWT-SVD in the above scheme, as well as the introduction of the followings into the scheme:

(A) A color-based image segmentation

(B) 8-connected neighbourhood checking

(C) Automatic threshold fitting

With the introduction of the above, the scheme achieves high blur-invariance, along with high detection accuracy y due to optimization of false positives. In the next subsections, we present the above techniques one-by-one, followed by operation of the main copy-move forgery detection scheme in detail.

### 3.1 Color–based Segmentation Using K–means Clustering

During copy–move forgery detection, when an image is comprised of extensive regular textured regions, such as blue sky, green grass, or scenery with a lot of greenery all around, a sandy desert or beach etc., conventional copy–move forgery detection algorithms tend to produce huge false positive rate. This is due to the fact that in such cases, large parts of the image are naturally similar, and hence lead to incorrect detection results. To solve this problem, we apply color–based segmentation here, so as to eliminate false positives caused due to similarities among different regions of a natural image. By this process, an image is segmented into n segments, according to its colours, and the individual segments are processed independently.

The technique of color–based segmentation using K–means clustering consists of the following broad steps:

1. First the input image is read in form of a RGB matrix. (Input image shown in Fig. 4).
2. Next, the input image is converted from RGB to L*a*b color space. The L*a*b color space is selected since it models the Human Visual System (HVS) extremely efficiently. Also, this color space being a perceptually uniform orthogonal Cartesian coordinate system is appropriate for this problem. The L*a*b space consists of a luminosity layer 'L', a chromaticity layer 'a' that indicates where

**Fig. 4:** Input image in RGB color space

**Fig. 5:** Converted image in L*a*b color space.

a color lies along the red–green axis, and chromaticity layer 'b' that indicates where a color lies along the blue–yellow axis. All of the color information is included in the 'a*' and 'b*' layers. The difference between two colors can be measured using the Euclidean distance metric or Canberra distance metric. The image in L*a*b color space is shown in Fig. 5.

3. Clustering is used to separate groups of objects. According to k–means clustering[52], each object has a location in space. The

**Fig. 6:** Output image labelled by cluster index

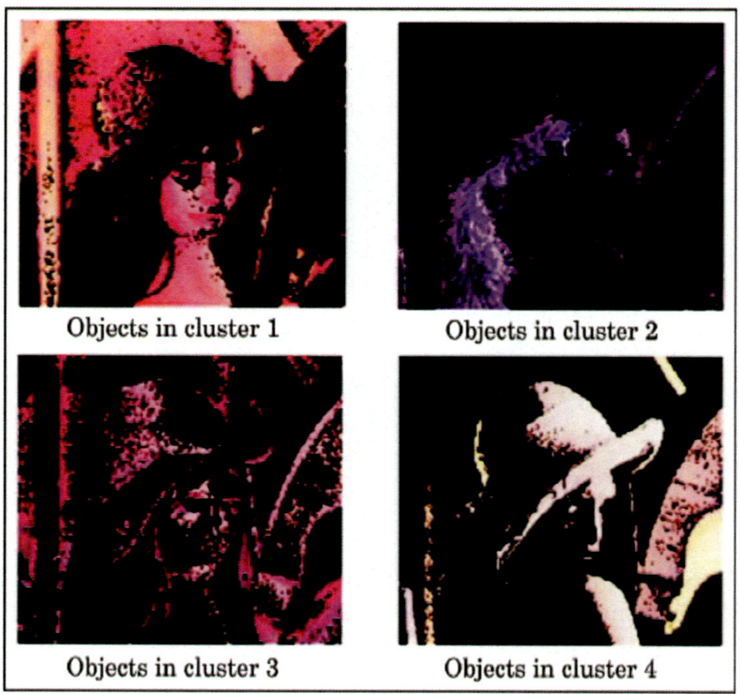


**Fig. 7:** Segments of the input image.

technique creates partitions such that objects that belong to the same cluster are as close to one another as possible, and as far from objects belonging to other clusters as possible. K–means clustering involves following two parameters: the number of clusters that to be partitioned, and a distance metric to quantify the degree of closeness of two objects. Here, objects are nothing but the pixels represented by 'a' and 'b' values. Segmenting the image by color Objects in the image are separated according to color, by the use of pixel labels obtained in the above step, resulting into the segmented image, as shown in Fig. 6, where the image is segmented into four segments or the objects in the image are grouped into four clusters, representing regions with four most distinguishable colors present in the image. (The four segments of the above image are shown in Fig. 7).

### 3.2 8-Connected Neighbourhood Checking

Due to the fact that large parts of the image are naturally similar, we often obtain high false positives in block matching based image region duplication detection. This leads to incorrect forgery detection results. To solve this problem, we adopt an 8-connected neighbourhood checking[93] method here.

By this method, all the image blocks that are detected to be duplicates are marked, and considered. For each marked block, its 8-connected neighbours, *i.e.,* up, down, left, right and the 4 diagonals (as shown in Fig. 8), are checked. The number of neighbours that were also detected as duplicates, are counted. If this count is > x (some empirical value $\geq 1$ and $\leq 7$, say 4), then the original block is kept marked. Else, if the count is $\leq x$, the original block is considered to be a false-positive and hence unmarked. All the residual marked blocks are output as duplicated or forged. This method helps to optimize the number of false positives.

### 3.3 Detection of Copy–Move Forgery

Here, we discuss a copy-move forgery detection method for digital images, based on SWT-SVD, which we gradually improve to obtain blur-invariance too.

A block diagram representing the operational flow of the method is shown in Fig. 9, below:

| | | | | | | | | |
|---|---|---|---|---|---|---|---|---|
| | $N_1^1$ | $N_2^1$ | $N_3^1$ | | | | | |
| | $N_4^1$ | BL1 | $N_5^1$ | | | | | |
| | $N_6^1$ | $N_7^1$ | $N_8^1$ | | | | | |
| | | | | | $N_1^2$ | $N_2^2$ | $N_3^2$ | |
| | | | | | $N_4^2$ | BL2 | $N_5^2$ | |
| | | | | | $N_6^2$ | $N_7^2$ | $N_8^2$ | |
| | | | | | | | | |

**Fig. 8:** 8–connected neighbours of blocks BL1 and BL2.

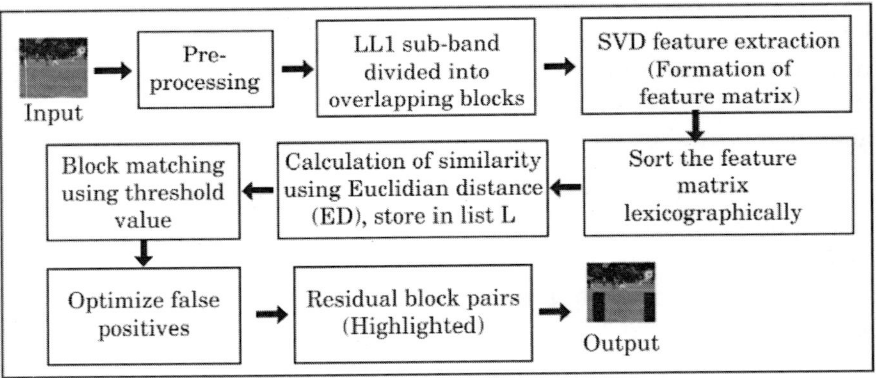


**Fig. 9:** Operational Flowchart: Plain Copy-Move Forgery Detection.

Following are the major steps involved in the above copy–move forgery detection algorithm, based on SWT-SVD:

1. The method operates in gray scale domain. If the possibly forged image is a color one, it is first converted into gray scale. This constitutes the pre–processing step of the algorithm. An image is converted from RGB to grayscale using the following formula:

$$I = 0.299R + 0.587G + 0.114B \tag{3}$$

2. SWT is applied to the input grayscale image (as discussed in Section 3.1) to obtain four subbands, *viz.* approximation (LL),

horizontal (LH), vertical (HL) and diagonal or detail (HH), specifically denoted as LL1, LH1, HL1 and HH1 respectively, at scale 1.

3. The LL1 sub band that gives the smoothed version of the image, say of size M × N pixels, is partitioned into overlapping blocks of size B × B pixels, which is assumed to be smaller than the size of the forged area to be identified, thus giving a total number of (M – B + 1) × (N – B + 1) blocks.
4. Next, SVD is applied to each LL1 block to extract its corresponding singular values feature vector.
5. The feature vectors of the blocks that are stored row–wise in a matrix called the feature matrix resulting in a total number of (M – B + 1) × (N – B + 1) rows, each of which is lexicographically sorted.
6. The Euclidean distances D (u,v) between a pair of rows (blocks), say u and v, where u = $(u_1, u_2, ...u_r)$ and v = $(v_1, v_2, ...v_r)$ are computed, provided blocks u and v are not more distant than a offset threshold, say Tf , that signifies the maximum number of rows to compare, *i.e.* abs[index(u) – index(v)] ≤ Tf . This helps to select only those similar blocks which can be expected to have been copy–moved. The computed Euclidean distance values, along with their corresponding block pairs, are stored in a list L.
7. The list L now consists of all the block–pairs that are to be further processed for detection of forgery. The length of L depends on the size of the image, the block–size, and also the offset threshold Tf, which can be long if the image is big, the block–size is small or $T_f$ is high, thus requiring a method to truncate it consisting of relatively more similar block–pairs than the rest previously present in L. Thus, a similarity threshold $T_d$, that helps to filter out lesser similar blocks from the list L, keeping block pairs having a greater probability to have been duplicated, is fitted. An automatic threshold fitting approach, followed in the algorithm, has been discussed in Section 4.2.
8. All the rows in L whose Euclidean distances are more than the similarity threshold $T_d$ are discarded, as they are considered to be non–duplicated parts of the images. Further verification is performed on the rest of the pairs that pass this stage of elimination, as follows.

9. For a given block pair, say block1 with coordinates (i, j) and block 2 with coordinates (k, l), the offset of coordinates between block 1 and block 2 is given by:

$$C_{12} = \max[\ \mathrm{abs}(i - k), \mathrm{abs}(j - l)\ ] \tag{4}$$

10. Block1 and block2 are labelled as suspected duplicated regions if $C_{12} \geq Ts$ where Ts is the minimum separation between duplicated regions. All such blocks that pass this filter are detected to be duplicated by the method.
11. The final step involves optimization of false positives in the detection method. This is achieved through 8–connected neighbourhood checking[93]. Here, all the blocks that are detected to be duplicates are marked, and considered. For each marked block, its 8–connected neighbours are checked. The number of neighbours that were also detected as duplicates by above steps 1–9, are counted. If this count is > 4, then the original block is kept marked. Else, if the count is ≤ 4, the original block is considered to be a false–positive and hence un- marked.
12. Finally, all the residual marked blocks are output as duplicated or forged. Now the number of false positives has been optimized.

Next we present the detailed threshold fitting technique adopted in the above algorithm.

### 3.4 Automatic Threshold Fitting

The threshold here, can be viewed as a barrier between the authentic and forged regions of the image. Hence, it requires utmost care while being chosen. A perfect fit may be obtained empirically, through selection of various random thresholds (in the valid range), then running the algorithm iteratively for all, and finally selecting the one that produces the most accurate forgery detection results. However, this naive process involves intense computational complexity and constant human interactions. Also, this threshold would vary from image to image; hence this process has to be repeated for every different input image.

Hence, in[90], the authors proposed the concept of an automatic threshold fitting, which we present next.

In the above algorithm (according to step 7, discussed above), it is clear that the threshold value separates the list of block pairs into 2 parts. Empirical studies suggest that the part satisfying the threshold condition is only 0.1 – 0.3% of the entire list. This is the key observation, which has been used in this work to obtain the approximate threshold fit automatically. The list L is sorted in ascending order, and then the threshold value is chosen to be the Euclidean distance of the block pair that is located at the 0.001th position of the sorted list. The threshold is computed as:

$$Td = EDsort_1 \times N \times 0.001; \tag{5}$$

where $EDsort_1$ is the Euclidean distance of the top most block pair in sorted list Lsort, and N is the total number of entities presented in L.

The procedure for threshold calculation in the above algorithm is given below in Algorithm 1 (*Automatic Threshold Fitting*).

**Algorithm 1:** ***Automated Threshold Fitting***

*Input:* List (L) storing euclidean distances of block pairs, N is the length of L;
*Output:* Threshold $T_d$;
$L \leftarrow [ED_1, ED_2, \cdots ED_N]^T$;
$Lsort \leftarrow [EDsort_1, EDsort_2, ...EDsort_N]^T \leftarrow SortAscending(L)$;
for i = 1, 2, .., N do
$Tdi \leftarrow [EDsort_i \times N \times 0.001]$;
End for
$T \leftarrow [Td_1, Td_2, Td_3 \cdots Td_N]$
$Td \leftarrow T_{d1}$; /*Actual threshold */
Return $T_{d1}$;

## 3.5. Next Improvement: Achieving Blur–invariance

Many a times, an intelligent adversary intentionally blurs a region of an image while duplicating it, specifically its edges, so as to ensure that it does not stand out or seem out of place due to the abrupt variations along the edges. This makes the image imperceptible to human eyes, as well as helps to avoid detection of the forgery by conventional copy–move forgery detection algorithms. In this section, we study an enhancement to the algorithm presented in Section 3.3 above, so as to achieve blur–invariance in copy–move forgery detection.

Blurring any part of an image generates a noise in that area, different from the image's original noise, that is the undesired variation of color information or brightness in the image which is random in nature, obtained while taking the image caused due to electronic noise and is different from the manual noise caused during blurring the forged part which can be detected using the diagonal subband (HH) after applying SWT on the image. The diagonal subband allows noise detection. In Fig. 10, we present a block diagram to depict the operational flow of the blur–invariant copy–move forgery detection scheme.

Following are the steps involved in the blur–invariant copy–move forgery detection technique presented here.

1. The method operates in grayscale domain. A possibly forged, color input image is first converted into grayscale using the following formula:

$$I = 0.299R + 0.587G + 0.114B \tag{6}$$

2. SWT is applied to the input grayscale image to obtain four subbands, *viz.* approximation (LL), horizontal (LH), vertical (HL) and diagonal or detail (HH), specifically denoted as LL1, LH1, HL1 and HH1 respectively, at scale 1.
3. Recording blocks dissimilarities. The HH1 subband that captures the details of the image is partitioned into overlapping blocks. In practice, the region undergoing blur is considerably smaller compared to the entire image. Hence, the chosen unit block size should be considerably smaller compared to the image size. However, using extremely small unit blocks (say 2 × 2) hinders the process by increasing the computation time. So a correct trade–of has to be arrived at.
4. Color–based segmentation is performed on the image in the L"a"b color space, using K–means clustering. It is only carried out in the blur case and not the non–blur case beacuse when we have blurring, the other naturally homogeneous textures present in the image exhibit more similarity as compared to the copy–blurred–moved parts but this is not true for the non–blur case as here, the copy–moved parts are exact copies of each other. It may also happen that the threshold we fit accommodates only those false positives and not our real requirement *i.e.* not the

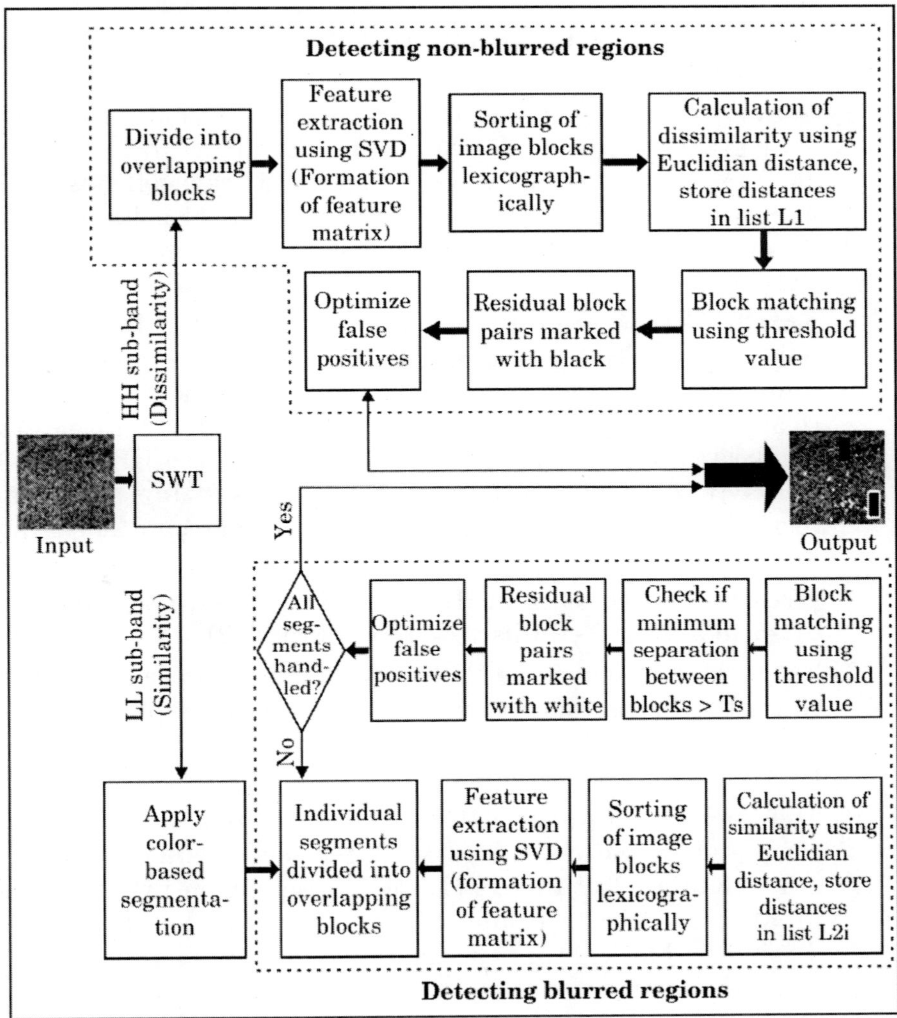


**Fig. 10:** Operational Flowchart: Achieving Blur-Invariance.

forgery part due to blurring and slight changes in the pixel values. To solve this problem, color-based segmentation is applied. The image is segmented into, say n segments according to its colours, and the individual segments are handled independently. The individual segments are divided into overlapping blocks of fixed size and then threshold fitting is carried out on each of them. The threshold is fitted as discussed earlier. However, now it is done for each individual segment, and not the entire image as a whole.

5. Recording blocks similarities. Next, the LL1 subband of the image is divided into overlapping blocks, not for the entire image, but segment–wise. Similar to step 3 above, a trade–off has to be gained while selecting unit block size. It should neither be too small to record similarity accurately, nor too large to belong to the forged region.
6. Note here that, segmentation is required for the LL subband only, not the HH subband. This is because, segmentation is required here to avoid false positives while finding similarity (using LL); specifically, false positives caused due to natural similarities between image regions. However, the HH subband helps in noise detection, and hence used for recording dissimilarities among image regions. So, segmentation is not required here.
7. Features of each block in HH1 and LL1 (for each segment) are extracted using SVD (discussed in Section 3.2).
8. The feature vectors of the blocks, are stored row–wise in a matrix, called the feature matrix, and are sorted lexicographically. This is done for blocks of the entire image (HH1) and of each segment too (LL1).
9. The Euclidean distance between each pair of blocks in HH1 are computed, provided the blocks are not more distant from each other than a offset threshold, say $T_{fh}$, signifying the maximum number of rows to compare. This gives us the set of most dissimilar blocks, that are possibly blurred. The Euclidean distances computed in this step, along with their corresponding block pairs, are stored in a list L1
10. The Euclidean distances for all LL block pairs are computed, provided the blocks are not more distant than the offset threshold, say $T_{f1}$, that signifies the maximum number of rows to compare. This gives us the most similar blocks that are possibly copy–moved. The Euclidean distances computed in this step, along with their corresponding block pairs, are stored in a list L2 i where i = 1, 2, …n and n = total number of segments.
11. Now, a dissimilarity threshold $T_{dh}$ that helps to filter out lesser dissimilar block pairs from list L1, keeping block pairs having

higher probability of being blurred, is fitted using automatic threshold fitting. Similarly, similarity threshold $T_{dli}$ that helps to filter out lesser similar blocks of segment i from the list L2i, keeping block pairs having higher probability of having been duplicated, is fitted.

12. All rows in L1 whose Euclidean distance is less than the dissimilarity threshold $T_{dh}$ are discarded. Similarly, all rows in $L2_i$ whose Euclidean distances is more than the similarity threshold $T_{dli}$ are discarded. Further verification is performed to the rest of the block pairs that pass this stage of elimination.
13. Two blocks, say block1 and block 2 are output as duplicates, if the separation between them is $\geq$ Ts, where Ts is the minimum allowed separation between duplicated regions. This is carried out only for LL1 blocks, not HH1. If two blocks are too close to each other, specifically overlapping, then their feature vectors would also be very similar. Hence, the value of Ts depends on the block–size.
14. All such LL1 blocks, for each segment, that pass the filter at step 12 are marked in black in the output image. The residual block pairs in L2 obtained from step 11, are marked white in the output image.
15. For both the blackened and whitened blocks, the 8–connected neighbour- hood check is carried out to remove the false positives.
16. Finally, the resultant image is displayed with duplicate blocks shown in black, and white blocks indicating the blurred parts.

Note here that, due to the color–based segmentation adopted in the above method, the computational complexity is reduced, since all the blocks are not compared anymore; only intra–segment comparison is performed.

The final output of the above method in terms of copy–move forgery detection, with and without blurring, has been presented in Fig. 11 below. This figure shows a natural image with extensive green (grass) patch, from which a portion has been copy–moved manually. In Fig. 11(a) we have shown the forged image. The copy–move forgery detection results using the above SWT with SVD based method, for the manually forged input image, have been shown in Fig. 11(b)–(d). Fig. 11(b) is the output obtained when there is no blurring at all, Fig. 11(c) is the detection result obtained when the edges of the duplicated region have

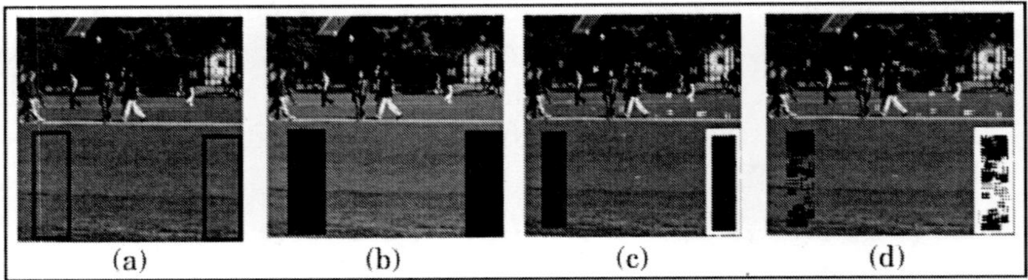


**Fig. 11:** Final Output: (a) Manually forged image (b) Output without blurring (c) Output with blurred edges (d) Output with blurred edges, as well as blurring within the forged area.

been blurred, and Fig. 11(d) is the result obtained when there is blurring along the edges as well as in the inner parts of the forged region.

## 4. PERFORMANCE EVALUATION

In order to evaluate the performance of the method presented above, without blurring, we have varied the unit detection block size, as well as the forgery size, and measured the corresponding detection accuracy results. These results have been presented in Table 1. The test dataset consists of 12 standard texture images of size 256 × 256 pixels, collected from the CVG UGR Image Database[76]. The results in Table 1 are the average results for all the test images. The visual results are also presented below in Fig. 12.

The detection accuracy results of the method when blurring is involved in the forgery have been shown in Table 2 for varying block and forgery sizes. Here, the block sizes for both HH and LL subbands are equal. The results presented in Table 2, represent the average

**Table 1:** Detection accuracy (%) results without blurring.

| ***Block Size*** | ***Forgery Size 10%*** | ***Forgery Size 20%*** | ***Forgery Size 30%*** | ***Forgery Size 40%*** |
|---|---|---|---|---|
| 6 | 98.9923 | 99.1301 | 99.3684 | 99.4101 |
| 10 | 99.0362 | 99.1318 | 99.4109 | 99.4129 |
| 15 | 99.0342 | 99.1303 | 99.4211 | 99.4296 |
| 20 | 99.0367 | 99.1278 | 99.4292 | 99.4301 |
| 25 | 99.0389 | 99.1298 | 99.4312 | 99.4309 |
| 30 | 99.0417 | 99.1303 | 99.4362 | 99.4472 |
| 35 | 99.0472 | 99.1336 | 99.4298 | 99.4492 |
| 36 | 99.0626 | 99.1391 | 99.4366 | 99.4359 |

**Fig. 12:** Forged test images with no blurring and corresponding forgery detection results. (a)–(d) Manually induced forgeries. (e)–(h) Duplicate regions detected.

**Table 2:** Detection accuracy (%) results with blurring.

| ***Block Size*** | ***Forgery Size* 10%** | ***Forgery Size* 20%** | ***Forgery Size* 30%** | ***Forgery Size* 40%** |
|---|---|---|---|---|
| 6 | 95.1628 | 95.2801 | 95.6308 | 95.8927 |
| 10 | 95.2718 | 95.3789 | 95.7692 | 95.9803 |
| 15 | 95.3698 | 95.3709 | 95.6209 | 95.7398 |
| 20 | 95.1623 | 95.2304 | 95.6813 | 95.6507 |
| 25 | 95.0585 | 95.1982 | 95.3709 | 95.6299 |
| 30 | 94.9301 | 95.1403 | 95.3692 | 95.4893 |
| 35 | 95.1509 | 95.1728 | 94.9839 | 95.3878 |
| 36 | 95.1678 | 95.1638 | 95.1803 | 95.2698 |

detection accuracy over all test images. Here the evaluation has been done by combining the results obtained by considering both LL (similarities) and HH (noise) subbands. These results are visually depicted in Fig. 13 as well.

## 4.1 Performance Comparison

We compare the presented method with state–of–the–art in terms of detection accuracy. We have varied the forgery size from 10% to 40%

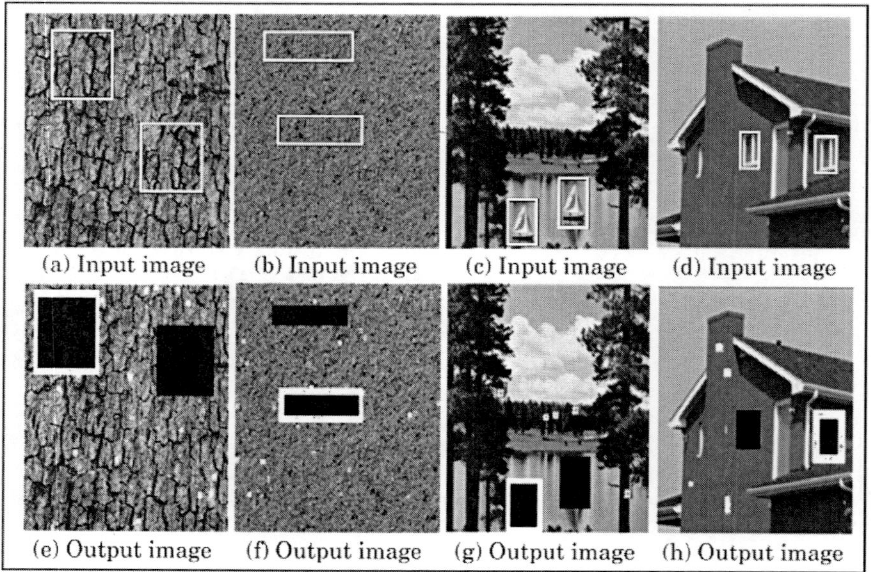


**Fig. 13:** Forged test images with blurring and corresponding forgery detection results. (a)–(d) Manually induced forgeries. (e)–(h) Duplicate regions detected.

in steps of 10%. The results (averaged over the entire test set) have been presented in Table 3, which prove that the technique presented in this chapter is considerably more efficient as compared to the state–of–the–art. We also present the results in form of 2–D plots in Fig. 14.

## 4.2 False Positive Rate Improvement

Next, we present the results pertaining to usefulness of the 8–connected neighbourhood check with respect to reduction of the False Positive Rate (FPR). These results have been presented in Table 4 and Table 5, for forged images without blurring and with blurring, respectively. False Positive Rate is defined as the total number of authentic image pixels, falsely detected to be forged, as:

$$FPR = \frac{Number\ of\ pixels\ falsely\ detected\ to\ be\ copy - moved}{Number\ of\ pixels\ actually\ copy - moved} \times 100\% \quad (7)$$

**Table 3:** Comparative Results

| *Method* | *Forgery Size (%)* | *Detection Accuracy (%) (Highest)* | *Detection Accuracy (%) (Average)* |
|---|---|---|---|
| PCA [2] | 10 | 96.7870 | 96.7588 |
| | 20 | 96.9130 | 96.9095 |
| | 30 | 97.1671 | 97.1436 |
| | 40 | 97.7945 | 97.7645 |
| SVD [74] | 10 | 97.6309 | 97.6092 |
| | 20 | 98.1880 | 98.1576 |
| | 30 | 98.4924 | 98.4754 |
| | 40 | 98.8730 | 98.8311 |
| DCT [55] | 10 | 97.8672 | 97.2254 |
| | 20 | 97.4396 | 97.4123 |
| | 30 | 97.6434 | 97.5978 |
| | 40 | 98.0624 | 98.0232 |
| Improved DCT [58] | 10 | 97.8670 | 97.8521 |
| | 20 | 98.1810 | 97.1643 |
| | 30 | 98.2383 | 97.2199 |
| | 40 | 98.5882 | 98.5665 |
| DWT [66] | 10 | 98.0857 | 98.0838 |
| | 20 | 98.1490 | 98.1464 |
| | 30 | 98.2210 | 98.2171 |
| | 40 | 98.2840 | 98.2780 |
| DyWT [41] | 10 | 98.0027 | 97.9892 |
| | 20 | 98.3641 | 98.3471 |
| | 30 | 98.5950 | 98.5455 |
| | 40 | 98.7889 | 98.7091 |
| Zernike [56] | 10 | 98.8179 | 98.8015 |
| | 20 | 98.9674 | 98.9372 |
| | 30 | 99.4017 | 99.3908 |
| | 40 | 99.4398 | 99.4199 |
| SWT-SVD [90] | 10 | 99.0626 | 99.0362 |
| | 20 | 99.1391 | 99.1316 |
| | 30 | 99.4366 | 99.4204 |
| | 40 | 99.4492 | 99.4307 |

**Table 4:** False Positive Rate (FPR) before and after the application of 8–connected neighborhood check for images without blurring.

| *Forgery Size (%)* | *Initial FPR (%)* | *Improved FPR (%)* |
|---|---|---|
| 10 | 4.6369 | 2.1602 |
| 20 | 2.3692 | 1.2396 |
| 30 | 1.8104 | 0.6072 |
| 40 | 1.1709 | 0.4386 |

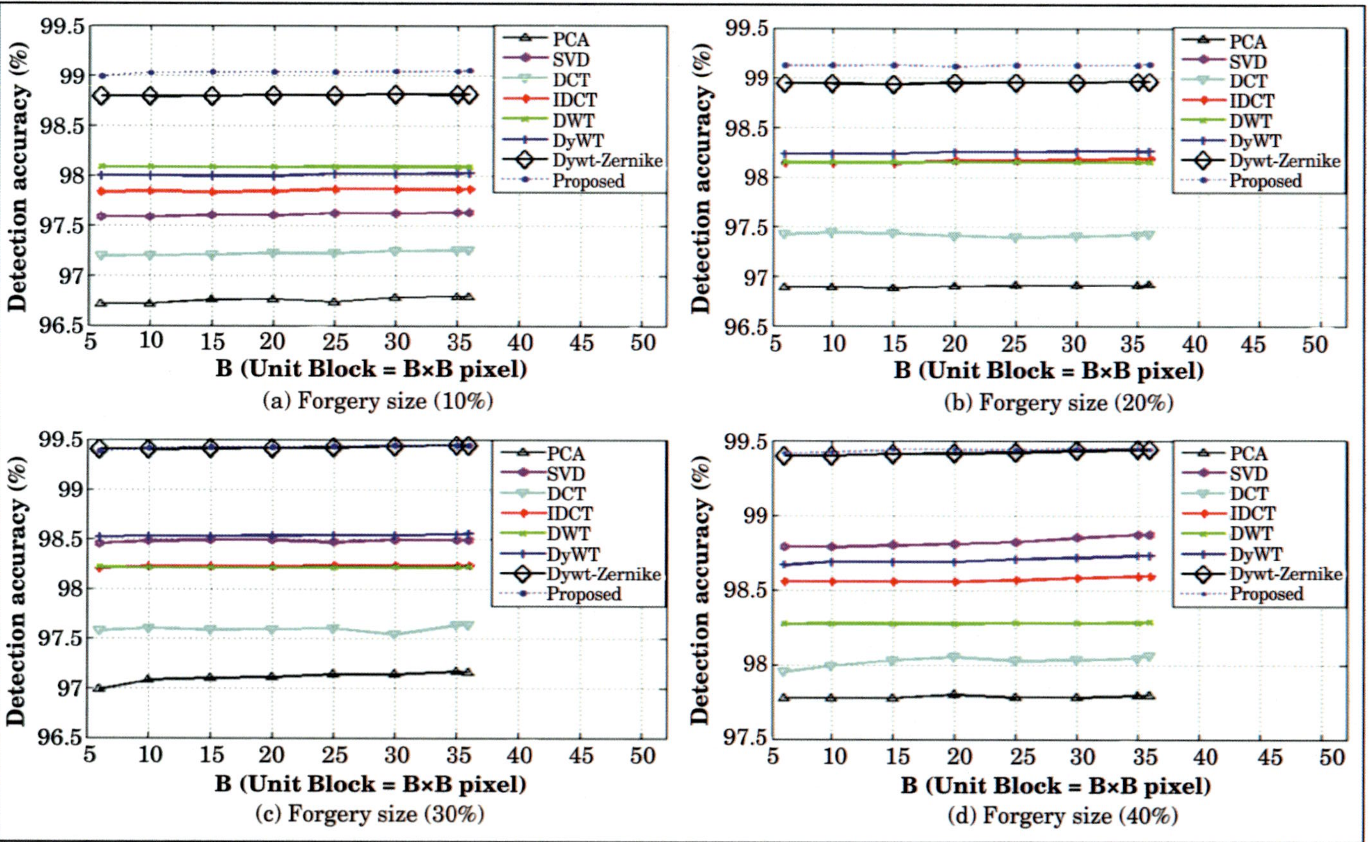


**Fig. 14:** Performance Comparison: Variation of Detection Accuracy with Unit Block Size.

**Table 5:** False Positive Rate (FPR) before and after the application of 8–connected neighborhood check for images with blurring.

| *Forgery Size (%)* | *Initial FPR (%)* | *Improved FPR (%)* |
|---|---|---|
| 10 | 14.1639 | 11.1879 |
| 20 | 13.2843 | 10.7013 |
| 30 | 9.9435 | 7.1284 |
| 40 | 7.8386 | 6.5492 |

## 5. CONCLUSIONS

In this chapter, we present a technique to address post-processing based attacks in copy-move forgery detection; specifically, we deal with blur invariance in region duplication forgery. The method is block–based copy–move forgery detection method for digital images, based on SWT with SVD, that is robust to blurring. We introduced the concept of automatic threshold fitting to minimize manual effort and computation time. We carried out color–based segmentation to achieve blur–invariance and 8–connected neighbourhood checking to optimize the number of false positives. The method is evaluated for two types of forgeries: plain copy–move forgery (a) without blurring, and (b) copy-move forgery with blurring. The results prove that the method presented, provides higher forgery detection accuracy as compared to the state–of–the–art.

In the next chapter, we shall present a technique to address such kind of post-processing based attacks in region duplication detection, combined with the detection of other forms of attacks, such a rotation, rescale, noise addition etc.

# 12

# Combining Geometric and Post-Processing Attacks in Copy–Move Forgery

## 1. INTRODUCTION

As we know from the previous chapters, regions within an image containing extensive uniform texture/patterns (for example, sky, grass, water, sand etc.), makes the image highly vulnerable to copy-move forgery. Since a forged region is copied from and relocated within the same image, detection of this form of forgery becomes difficult and challenging, by using conventional forensic techniques which look for dissimilarities in image statistical characteristics. An instance of copy-move forgery in digital images is presented in Fig. 1, where Fig. 1(a) shows the original image depicting a group of zebras. The image of a zebra has been duplicated in the image (by region duplication), as shown in Fig. 1(b).

This form of image forgery becomes all the more difficult to be detected when the adversary performs intermediate or post–processing based operations on the forged regions, before duplicating it. We have already seen one form of post-processing based attack in copy-move forgery, which has been addressed in the last chapter. Her in this example we can see, in Fig. 1(c) and Fig. 1(d), there are instances where the forged (duplicated) region has been made to undergo rotation and rescale operations respectively, before being moved.

(a) Original image (b) Plain copy-move attack (c) Copy-rotate-move attack (d) Copy-scale move attack

**Fig. 1:** Examples of region duplication attack.

The state–of–the–art copy–move forgery detection techniques adopt diverse approaches, all aimed towards recognizing duplicate pixel groups in an image. Detection of the duplicate image regions becomes particularly challenging when the forger performs some post–processing operations, such as scaling, filtering, JPEG compression, rotation, blurring or adding noise, to duplicated region before the paste.

In this chapter, we address the problem of copy-move forgery detection, as well as the detection of additional intermediate and post-processing based attacks in digital images. These include geometric transforms such as rotation and re-scale operations, and post–processing attacks including blur, noise addition and brightness modification. Detection of region duplication, following conventional techniques, becomes more challenging when an intelligent adversary brings about such additional transforms on the duplicated regions. Here in this chapter, our aim is to demonstrate a method to detect multiple forms of such post-processing and geometric attacks in addition to copy-move forgery, and all these by applying a single detection technique. Also, the technique demonstrated here is capable of detecting multiple duplicate regions in a single image.

In the recent literature, Hung *et al.*[4] developed a method using Scale Invariant Feature Transform (SIFT) for copy–move forgery detection, which was scale and rotation invariant, but sensitive to simple noise and blurring which resulted in poor performance for images with small areas of forgery. Another efficient region duplication detection algorithm was proposed by Bo *et al.*[94] which is based on Speeded Up Robust Features (SURF), and is invariant to re-scale, rotation and additive noise. Muhammad *et al.*[41] proposed an undecimated Dyadic Wavelet Transform (DyWT) based copy–move forgery detection scheme, in which the forged image is de- composed into four DyWT sub-bands, and the LL and HH sub-bands are used for computation of similarity and dissimilarity, respectively, between image blocks. This method achieves robustness to re-scale attack due to the inherent scale-invariant property of DyWT. Li *et al.*[95] exploited Local Binary Pattern (LBP) for feature extraction from image blocks for copy-move forgery detection. Due to the inherent rotation invariant property of LBP, the scheme performs efficiently in detection of copy-rotate-move forgery. However, this method fails to detect copy-scale-move attack. Thajeel and Sulong[93] proposed another copy-move forgery detection scheme based on LBP, which is highly computationally intensive when applied to high-resolution images. The scheme performs efficiently even in the presence of image distortions such as rotation, additive noise, blurring and compression.

Among the recent works, Ardizzone *et al.*[96] proposed a region duplication detection technique, utilizing image key–points, and forming triangles from those. The duplicate image regions are detected based on the triangles' shape. This algorithm fails if flat image regions are used to hide objects. Li *et al.*[97] segmented an image into small patches using Simple Linear Iterative Clustering (SLIC) algorithm, extracted segmentwise key–point features using V. Feat software and finally, detected the forged regions using expectation maximization (EM) algorithm. The computational complexity of this technqiue is comparatively higher, due to the use of segmentation. Tralic *et al.*[98] proposed a methodology which is based on Cellular Automata (CA) and LBP, the major advantage of which lies in the description of local changes of pixel luminance values, defined using LBP, so as to make it robust against image post–processing. Zhu *et al.*[99] used Oriented FAST and Rotated BRIEF (ORB) image features for copy–move forgery detection, which optimizes the number of false alarms, even when an image contains lot of flat regions. Wu *et al.*[100] exploited Log–polar Fourier transform for feature extraction from image blocks, for detection of region duplication. This method performs efficiently in detection of geometric attacks. However, this method does not perform well to detect copy-move forgery with post-processing attacks. Cozzolino *et al.*[101] proposed a copy-move forgery detection technique based on Dense-field algorithm, the complexity of which is low, due to the use of a Patch Match algorithm. This method achieves high robustness to various types of geometric attacks. Bayram *et al.*[57] proposed another algorithm based on Fourier Mellin Transform (FMT), which is able to detect highly compressed and rotated (with less than 10 degrees) copied regions of an image. Also, Park *et al.*[46] developed an algorithm utilizing up-sampled Log-polar Fourier descriptors for copy–move forgery detection. This method performs efficiently even in the presence of image distortions such as scaling, rotation and JPEG compression. However, this technique is less sensitive to additive noise. Li and Yu [102] proposed another FMT based copy-move forgery detection technique, which achieves rotation, re-scale and JPEG compression invariance. Here, the authors optimize the computational complexity by utilizing counting bloom filters.

In this chapter, we present a recent state-of-the-art technique proposed in[48], which succeeds to achieve invariance to the all above forms of attacks in copy-move forgery detection of digital images. Specifically, the scheme detects the following forms of attacks in addition to copy-move forgery:

A. Geometric Attacks (Rotation And Rscale)

B. Post-Processing Attacks (Edge Blurring, Noise Addition, Brightness Adjustment)

This scheme utilizes Fourier Mellin Transform with Log-polar mapping, and a novel color based segmentation technique using K-means clustering, which help us to achieve invariance against the above forms of attacks.

The rest of the chapter is organized as follows. In Section 2, we present the FMT Log Polar based technique for image region duplication detection, combining geometric and post-processing attacks, and their detection. The performance evaluation and results for this scheme, are presented in in Section 4. Finally, we conclude the chapter in Section 5.

## 2. ADDRESSING REGION DUPLICATION ATTACK ALONG WITH GEOMETRIC AND POST-PROCESSING ATTACKS

In this chapter, we present a technique to detect copy-move forgery in digital images, even after the forged image has undergone geometric and post-processing attacks in addition. Log-polar based Fourier Mellin Transform (FMT) are used in this work, proposed in[48], for this purpose, since Log-polar based Fourier Transforms are proved to achieve rotation, re-scale and translation invariance according to the state-of-the-art. However, the challenges of copy-move forgery detection based on Fourier Log-polar Transforms, are detection of post-processing based attacks, and generation of high false positives in region duplication detection. For detection of post–processing based attacks, the authors adopt a novel color–based segmentation technique using K-means clustering, which succeeds to achieve over 90% invariance to post–processing based attacks. For reduction of false positives, the Hue Saturation Value (HSV)[48] image color space has been used, which helps to optimize false positives, due to its high efficiency in capturing minor deviations among image pixels.

In this scheme[48], an image is converted from RGB to HSV color space, and then using DWT, it is decomposed into four sub-bands, *viz.,* approximation (LL), horizontal (HL), vertical (LH) and diagonal (HH). Among the four sub-bands, the approximation (LL) sub and is the low frequency component of the input image, which carries maximum information about the image. We use the LL sub-band for further processing in this method.

Next, a color based segmentation is applied to the LL sub-band of the image, and the individual segments are divided into fixed sized overlapping (pixel) blocks. Block features from each individual block are extracted using FMT[49], implemented by performing a Log-polar mapping[50] followed by Fourier transform[51], to achieve geometric transform invariance. The individual block features are stored into a feature matrix row-wise. Finally, similar block-pairs are detected by computing the Euclidian distances between all block-pairs. To optimize the detection accuracy, the similar block-pair search is refined further, by adopting an automatic threshold fitting.

This method consists of the following broad steps, which are described in detail, next: (1) Pre-processing; (2) Color-based segmentation using K-means clustering; (3) Feature Extraction using FMT Log-polar method; (4) Computing similarity between individual block–pairs; (5) Block matching using automatic threshold fitting; (6) Detection of forged region(s). Fig. 2 shows the operational flowchart of the technique.

## 2.1 Pre-Processing

In general, copy-move forgery detection techniques suffer from high false matches. This is due to the inherent presence of extensive

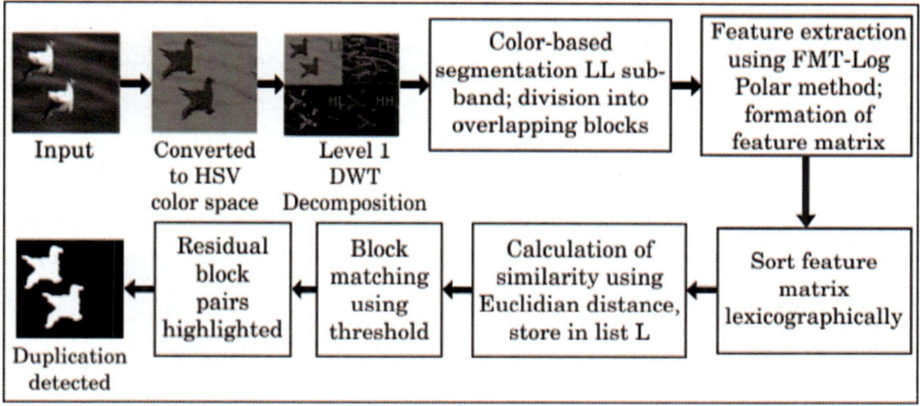


**Fig. 2:** Operational Flowchart.

homogeneous regions in natural images. The HSV color space is efficient in capturing minor deviations among pixels, in naturally similar regions of an image. Hence, in this work, the operations are performed in the HSV color space. This pre–processing step involves conversion of the image from RGB to HSV color space. The region duplication output with RGB *vis-à-vis* HSV color spaces are shown in Fig. 3, which proves that the false positive rate is indeed reduced by the use of HSV space.

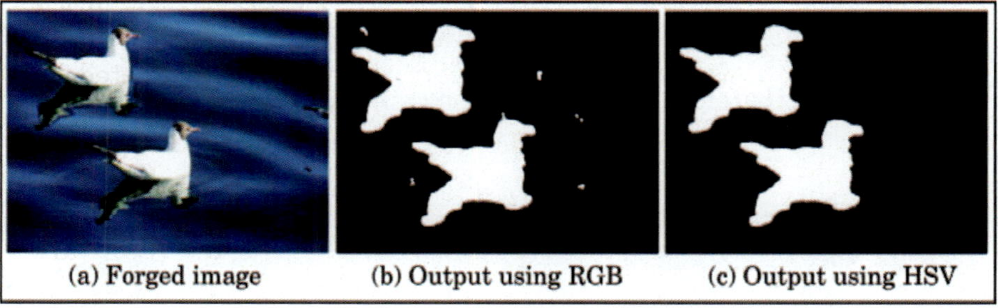

(a) Forged image (b) Output using RGB (c) Output using HSV

**Fig. 3:** Output in RGB and HSV color spaces.

The comparison between the two color spaces is also presented in Fig. 4 below:

Next, Discrete Wavelet Transform (DWT) is used to decompose the image into four subbands: LL, HL, LH, and HH. Let the image be of dimension W × H pixels. By DWT decomposition, size of each

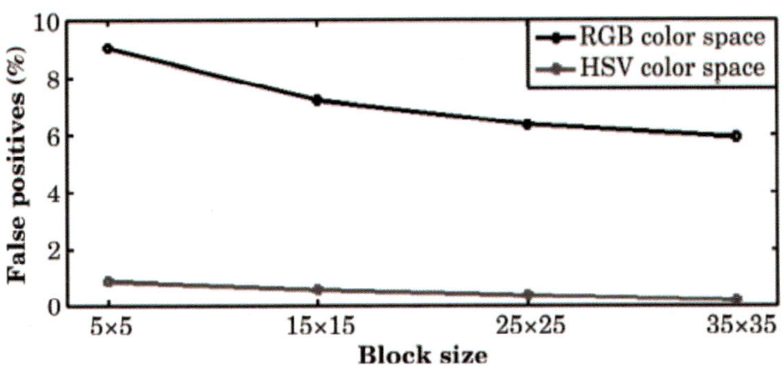


**Fig. 4:** Comparison of false positives for HSV and RGB color spaces.

subband obtained is (W×H)/4 pixels. The LL subband is used in the next steps.

## 2.2. Color–based Segmentation

In copy-move forgery detection, when an image consists of extensive regular textured regions, such as blue sky, green grass, a sandy desert or beach etc., conventional copy–move forgery detection algorithms tend to produce huge false positives. Especially, when an intelligent adversary blurs the edges of forged regions in an image, the forgery becomes difficult to be detected by conventional schemes, also leading to a high false positive rate. To optimize the number of false matches here a color-based segmentation using K-means clustering[52] has been applied.

K-means clustering involves two parameters, *viz.,* the number of clusters to be formed, and a distance metric to quantify the degree of

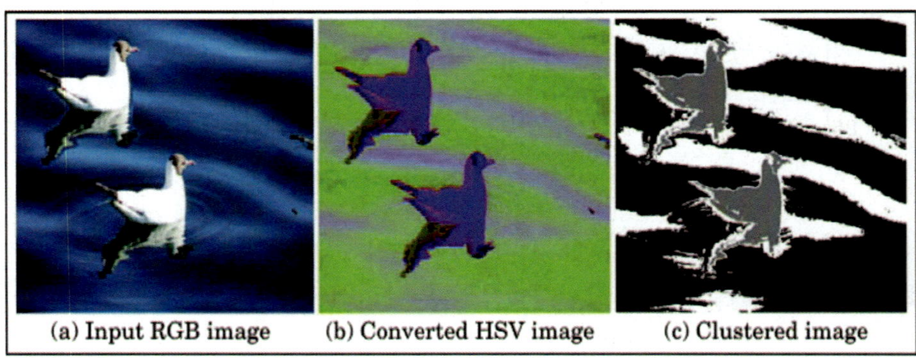


**Fig. 5:** K–means clustering results.

closeness of two objects. Here, objects are nothing but the pixels represented by their 'Hue' and 'Values' (intensity). The result of K-means clustering is used to label the pixels, where every cluster gets an index as returned by the K-means clustering algorithm, and every pixel in the image is labelled with its cluster index distinguished by different grayscale values. Fig. 5 shows the output of K-means clustering applied to one of our test images, taken from the Ardizzone database[96].

To decide upon the value of K (number of clusters) in this scheme, the Elbow method[103] has been used. The computational complexity of the technique increases with increase of K. Hence, we decide upon that value of K which when increased further, causes negligible improvement in performance of the method. Fig. 6 presents the variations in Detection Accuracy (DA), with increase in K, for one of our test images. We can observe from Fig. 6, that in this example, K = 7 onwards the improvement in DA is negligible. Hence for this test image we select K = 7.

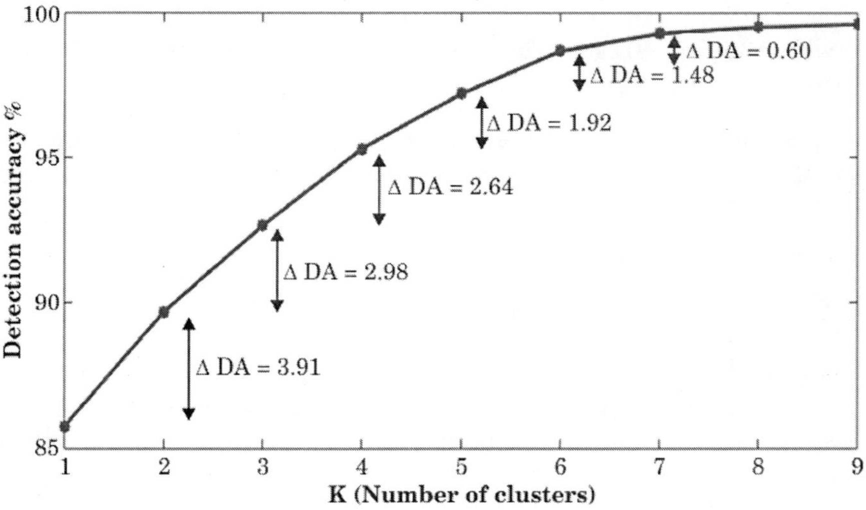


**Fig. 6:** Variation of Detection accuracy vs. K.

## 2.3 Feature Extraction using FMT Log–polar Method

The segmented $\frac{W}{2} \times \frac{H}{2}$ L sub-band obtained in the previous step, is now divided into fixed sized overlapping blocks of size B × B pixels, producing $\left(\frac{W}{2}-B+1\right)\times\left(\frac{H}{2}-B+1\right)$ blocks.

Fourier–Mellin Transform (FMT) is used for block–wise feature extraction in this method. The FMT Log–polar coefficients of an image block, are computed as follows:

$$F(i,j)=\sum_{(x,y)\in B^2} I(x,y)k_{i,j}(\rho(x,y),\theta(x,y)) \tag{1}$$

where (i, j) represents the (i, j)–th coefficient of the block, with i, j = 0, 1, 2 · · · B – 1, I (x, y) represents the (x, y)$^{th}$ pixel intensity of the block, ki,j is the basis function of the transformation, $\rho(x,y)=\sqrt{(x^2+y^2)}$ and $\theta\left(x,y\right)=\tan^{-1}\frac{y}{x}$ is the representation in polar co–ordinate system with $\rho \in [0,\infty]$ and $\theta \in [0,2\pi]$.

Hence, we can write Eq. 1 as:

$$F'\left(i,j\right)=\sum_{(\rho,\theta)\in B^2} I(x(\rho,\theta),y(\rho,\theta))k_{i,j}(\rho,\theta)\rho^2 \tag{2}$$

where ki,j (ρ, θ) is the basis function of Fourier Mellin Transform on the grid point (ρ, θ).

Next, each image block is represented by corresponding FMT coefficient features, which are stored into a feature matrix row–wise. Each row of the feature matrix represents a vector of features for one block.

## 2.4 Calculation of Similarity

Each row of the final feature matrix (consisting of all block features), is sorted lexicographically. In order to measure the similarity between a pair of blocks (rows), say R and R', we compute their Euclidean distance as:

$$D(R,R')=\left(\sum_{i=1}^{B\times B}(R_i-R_i')^2\right)^{\frac{1}{2}} \tag{3}$$

where Ri and R' are the i$^{th}$ entries of blocks/rows R and R', respectively. The calculated Euclidean distances, along with the corresponding block pairs, are stored into a list L.

## 2.5. Block Matching by Automatic Threshold Fitting

Here we use a threshold to distinguish between authentic and forged regions of an image. We carried out empirical studies to find a threshold for L, to distinguish between similar and dissimilar block pairs, for a varied set of test images. The key finding in this work is that, 0.1–0.3% of the entire list L, satisfies the threshold condition, hence consists of similar block pairs. This has been used here to obtain the approximate threshold fit automatically, hence reducing manual effort for every test image, drastically.

The list L is sorted in ascending order (with respect to the Euclidean distances), and then the threshold is chosen to be the distance located somewhere between 0.001th –0.003rd position of the sorted list Lsort. An instance of such a sorted list, consisting of 36229 entries (block–pair distances) is: Lsort = [0.2193, 0.2484, 0.3052, 0.3502, 0.4219, · · · ], where the thresholds can be computed as:

$$T_D = \begin{bmatrix} 0.001 \;\; 36229 \;\; 0.2193 = 7.95 \\ 0.001 \times 36229 \times 0.2484 = 9.00 \\ 0.001 \times 36229 \times 0.3052 = 11.05 \\ 0.001 \times 36229 \times 0.3502 = 12.68 \\ 0.001 \times 36229 \times 0.4219 = 15.28 \\ \vdots \end{bmatrix} \tag{4}$$

It is observed that one out of the first to third threshold values (refer to the above list), gives the optimal detection accuracy results. The ROC curve for the first to fifth entries in the above $T_D$ list is shown in Fig. 7(a). It can be observed from Fig. 7(a), that the first threshold $T_D$ = 7.95 performs best. Hence, in the method, threshold $T_D$ is calculated as:

$$T_D = 0.001 \times \text{length}(L) \times \text{Dmin} \tag{5}$$

where Dmin represents the Euclidean distance of the topmost block–pair in the sorted list.

In the next step, detection of duplicate image regions, we consider only those block pairs (R, R'), for which $D(R, R') \leq T_D$. The remaining block pairs are discarded.

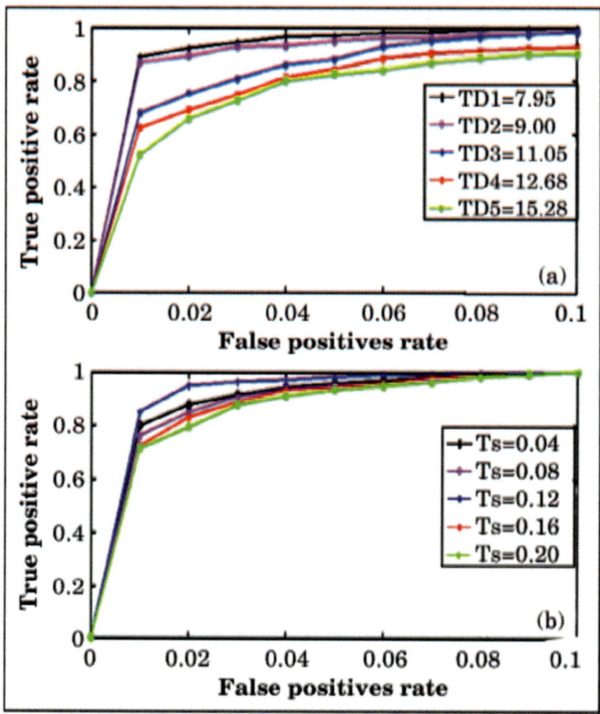


**Fig . 7:** ROC curves for (a) threshold $T_D$ and, (b) threshold TS.

## 2.6 Detection of Duplicate Regions

In an image, for each block pair (A,B) with D(A,B) ≤ $T_D$, we compute their offset as:

$$C_{AB} = \max [\, abs(i-k), abs(j-l)\, ] \quad (6)$$

where (i,j) and (k,l) are the block co–ordinates of A and B respectively, in the entire image.

To address the fact that (pixel intensities of) neighbouring regions of a natural image are highly correlated, which may lead to false positives in region duplication detection, we use an empirically selected minimum separation threshold $T_S$. If the separation between locations of two blocks in an image is less than $T_S$, they are inferred to be similar due to the inherent properties of natural images, and not due to duplication.

Similar to threshold $T_D$ calculation, here also, we compute different values of $T_S$ in an ascending order, depending on the sorted block–pair distances in list Lsort. For Lsort = [0.2193, 0.2484, 0.3052, 0.3502, 0.4219, · · ·], the $T_S$ values computed are: $T_S$ = [0.04, 0.08, 0.12,0.16, 0.20, · · ·]. The ROC curves for these first five $T_S$ values are presented in Fig. 7(b). From Fig. 7(b), it can be observed that the best result is obtained with the third value, $T_S$ = 0.12, which is adopted in the method.

Here, if $C_{AB}$ is greater than the selected minimum separation threshold $T_S$, then blocks A and B ae labelled as duplicate blocks. All block pairs satisfying the above condition are detected to be duplicates.

## 3. PERFORMANCE EVALUATION

The performance of the above technique has been evaluated here in terms of two evaluation metrics,

Precision (P) and Recall (R), which are defined as follows:

$$\text{Precision (P)} = \frac{T_P}{T_P + F_P} \times 100\%$$
$$\text{Recall (R)} = \frac{T_p}{T_p + F_N} \times 100\% \tag{7}$$

where $T_P$, $F_P$, $T_N$, $F_N$ are explained as follows:

Given a copy–move forgery detection algorithm, for every image pixel four outcomes are possible. If the pixel is actually forged and is predicted as forged, it is treated as a true positive ($T_P$). If the pixel is actually forged but is predicted as authentic, it is treated as a false negative ($F_N$). If the pixel is actually authentic but is predicted as forged, it is treated as a false positive ($F_P$). If the pixel is actually authentic and is predicted as authentic, it is treated as a true negative ($T_N$).

In the next subsections, we present the performance evaluation results of the above method with respect to the above parameters. In this chapter, we present the results for 150 512 × 512 color test images, collected from two public databases widely used in forensic research, the CoMoFoD [104] and Ardizzone[96] image databases, and the widely–adopted standard image processing test database: USC SIPI[77].

## 3.1 Plain Copy-Move Forgery Detection

Here, we analyze the precision and recall rates of above technique for plain copy– move forgery detection. The results presented here, are average over all our 150 test images. The performance of the method is presented in Table 1, for varying block sizes (5 × 5 to 35 × 35 pixels). Table 1 shows that the precision and recall of the above algorithm varies from 99.08% to 99.72% and 94.48% to 96.11%, respectively. As evident from Table 1, with small blocks, the naturally similar regions of an image are falsely detected to be forged, hence leading to high false positives and low precision. On the other hand, larger block size helps to reduce false positives, but leads to an increase in false negatives; thus lowering recall.

**Table 1:** Performance evaluation of plain-copy-move forgery.

| | ***Block size (pixels)*** | | | |
|---|---|---|---|---|
| ***Parameter*** | 5×5 | 15×15 | 25×25 | 35×35 |
| Precision (%) | 99.02 | 99.18 | 99.58 | 99.72 |
| Recall (%) | 96.09 | 95.87 | 95.29 | 94.63 |

## 3.2 Detection of Geometric Transforms

Here, we evaluate the above technique for detection of geometric transforms of rotation and re–scaling on forged regions. First, we checked the performance of the technique in detection of rotated (copied) regions at different angles: (60°, 120°, 180°, 240°, 300°), before pasting them. Table 2 shows the performance results with varying block sizes. As we increase the angle of rotation, performance of the algorithm decreases, as evident from Table 2. When the angle of rotation is 180°, precision and recall are equal.

**Table 2:** Performance evaluation of copy–rotate–move forgery detection results.

| | ***Angle*** | ***Block size (pixels)*** | | | |
|---|---|---|---|---|---|
| ***Parameter*** | ***(θ)*** | ***5×5*** | ***15×15*** | ***25×25*** | ***35×35*** |
| Precision (%) | 60% | 98.98 | 99.12 | 99.26 | 99.39 |
| | 120 | 98.66 | 98.99 | 99.12 | 99.18 |
| | 180 | 99.02 | 99.20 | 99.44 | 99.61 |
| | 240 | 97.38 | 97.52 | 97.68 | 97.82 |
| | 300 | 96.98 | 97.12 | 97.26 | 97.38 |
| Recall (%) | 60% | 95.68 | 95.52 | 95.32 | 95.20 |
| | 120 | 95.06 | 94.83 | 94.32 | 94.18 |
| | 180 | 96.02 | 95.82 | 95.28 | 94.52 |
| | 240 | 94.28 | 94.02 | 93.80 | 93.46 |
| | 300 | 93.22 | 93.06 | 92.61 | 92.28 |

Next, we rescaled the copied region with scale factors in [0.75, 1.25], in step of 0.10, before moving it. Table 3 presents the copy–scale–move forgery detection results for varying block sizes. When scale factor is 1.05, both precision and recall are high.

**Table 3:** Performance evaluation of copy-scale-move forgery detection.

| | ***Scale Factor*** | ***Block size (pixels)*** | | | |
|---|---|---|---|---|---|
| ***Parameter*** | | ***5×5*** | ***15×15*** | ***25×25*** | ***35×35*** |
| Precision (%) | 0.75 | 88.09 | 88.91 | 89.06 | 89.90 |
| | 0.85 | 89.92 | 90.53 | 91.07 | 91.97 |
| | 0.95 | 92.82 | 93.08 | 93.89 | 94.27 |
| | 1.05 | 93.78 | 94.62 | 95.23 | 96.44 |
| | 1.15 | 91.02 | 92.12 | 92.96 | 93.09 |
| | 1.25 | 88.18 | 89.02 | 89.98 | 91.68 |
| Recall (%) | 0.75 | 89.74 | 89.02 | 88.19 | 87.82 |
| | 0.85 | 90.26 | 89.09 | 88.12 | 87.80 |
| | 0.95 | 92.59 | 92.23 | 91.74 | 91.11 |
| | 1.05 | 93.64 | 93.14 | 92.80 | 91.98 |
| | 1.15 | 91.52 | 90.86 | 90.06 | 89.74 |
| | 1.25 | 89.78 | 88.62 | 87.96 | 86.88 |

Copy–move forgery detection results, with geometric transformations detection, have been presented in Fig. 8, where we present six test images (two for each attack, *i.e.,* plain–copy–move forgery, copy–rotate–move forgery and copy–scale–move forgery).

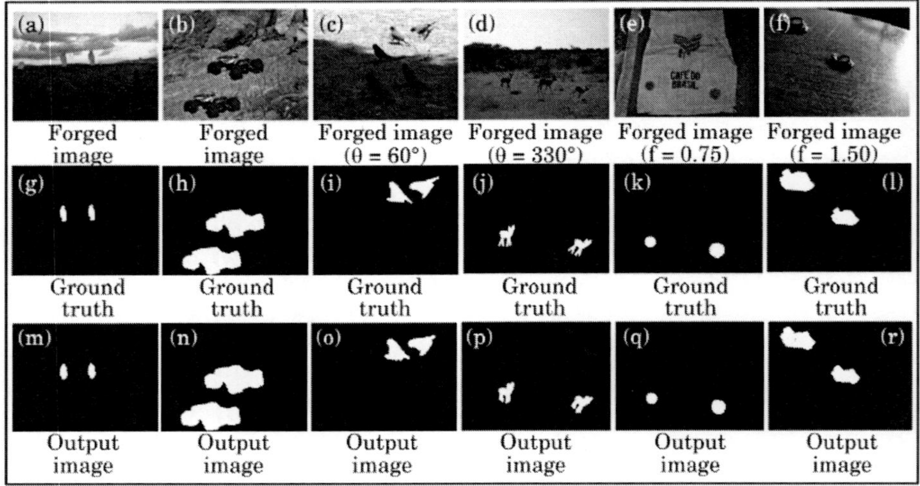


**Fig. 8:** Copy–move forgery detection with rotation (rotational angle θ) and re–scale (scale factor f) detection. (a)–(f) Forged images. (g)–(l) Ground truth results. (m)–(r) Results obtained.

## 3.3 Robustness to Post–Processing Attacks

In addition to geometric attacks, we evaluate the efficiency of the above technique in terms of detection of post-processing based attacks, *viz.*, addition of Gaussian noise, adjustment of brightness and distortion due to blurring of forged regions edges.

***Robustness to additive Gaussian Noise*:** For the sake of experimentation, we add Gaussian noise to the forged image with standard deviations of 0.02, 0.04, 0.06, 0.08 and 0.10. We present performance evaluation results of the method in detection of Gaussian noise added copy–move forged image in Table 4.

From Table 4, it can be observed that with increase in standard deviation (SD), the precision as well as recall of the technique decreases. This is due to the fact that with increase in Gaussian noise, the false negative rate increases for copy–move forgery detection. On the other hand, with increase of block size, precision increases but recall decreases.

In Fig. 9(a)–(b) and Fig. 9(g)–(h), we demonstrate the forgery detection results with additive Gaussian noise having standard deviations of 0.02 and 0.10.

**Table 4:** Performance evaluation results for forged images induced with Additive Gaussian noise.

| | ***Standard deviation*** | ***Block size (pixels)*** | | | |
|---|---|---|---|---|---|
| ***Parameter*** | | ***5×5*** | ***15×15*** | ***25×25*** | ***35×35*** |
| Precision (%) | 0.02 | 87.82 | 88.19 | 88.92 | 89.12 |
| | 0.04 | 86.92 | 87.41 | 87.97 | 88.19 |
| | 0.06 | 86.02 | 86.82 | 87.29 | 87.99 |
| | 0.08 | 84.68 | 85.13 | 85.80 | 86.24 |
| | 0.10 | 83.07 | 83.98 | 84.56 | 85.29 |
| Recall (%) | 0.02 | 75.26 | 74.99 | 74.12 | 73.78 |
| | 0.04 | 74.06 | 73.92 | 73.09 | 72.82 |
| | 0.06 | 72.59 | 72.23 | 71.74 | 71.11 |
| | 0.08 | 71.34 | 72.90 | 72.26 | 71.82 |
| | 0.10 | 72.09 | 71.76 | 71.06 | 70.77 |

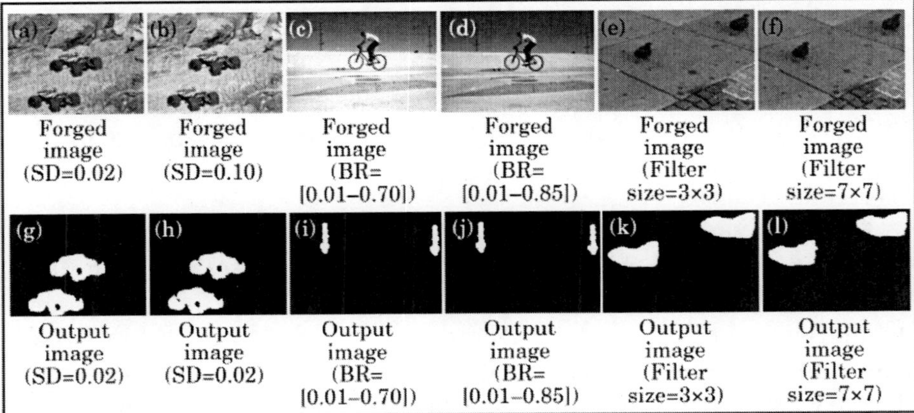


**Fig. 9:** Forgery detection results for post–processing attacks: (a), (g) Additive Gaussian Noise with Standard Deviation (SD) = 0.02. (b), (h) Additive Gaussian Noise with Standard Deviation (SD) = 0.10. (c), (i) Brightness adjustment in range BR = [0.01–0.70]. (d), (j) Brightness adjustment in range BR = [0.01–0.85]. (e), (k) Blurring with filter size 3 × 3. (f), (l) Blurring with filter size 7 × 7.

***Robustness to Brightness Adjustment:*** To test the performance of the above method in detection of copy–move forgery in brightness adjusted forged images, we have manually altered the brightness of our forged test image in the range [0.01–0.70] to [0.01–0.95], in steps of 0.05. In Table 5 we present our experimental results pertaining to robustness of the above method against brightness adjustment. Table 5 shows that increase in brightness also increases the precision and recall. With increase in block size, the performance degrades.

**Table 5:** Performance evaluation results for brightness adjustment in forged images.

| | ***Brightness Range*** | ***Block size (pixels)*** | | | |
|---|---|---|---|---|---|
| ***Parameter*** | | ***5×5*** | ***15×15*** | ***25×25*** | ***35×35*** |
| Precision (%) | [0.01–0.70] | 92.90 | 91.09 | 89.37 | 88.63 |
| | [0.01–0.75] | 93.17 | 91.26 | 89.54 | 88.82 |
| | [0.01–0.80] | 93.90 | 92.09 | 91.72 | 89.90 |
| | [0.01–0.85] | 94.01 | 93.27 | 92.12 | 90.38 |
| | [0.01–0.90] | 94.16 | 93.38 | 92.83 | 91.96 |
| | [0.01–0.95] | 94.46 | 93.87 | 93.06 | 92.82 |
| Recall (%) | [0.01–0.70] | 89.13 | 87.83 | 86.27 | 84.90 |
| | [0.01–0.75] | 91.11 | 90.27 | 88.11 | 86.52 |
| | [0.01–0.80] | 93.62 | 92.12 | 90.61 | 88.82 |
| | [0.01–0.85] | 94.23 | 93.76 | 91.72 | 90.87 |
| | [0.01–0.90] | 95.16 | 94.68 | 93.82 | 92.96 |
| | [0.01–0.95] | 96.22 | 95.27 | 94.76 | 93.01 |

In Fig. 9(c)–(d) and Fig. 9(i)–(j), we demonstrate the forgery detection results with brightness adjustment.

***Robustness to Blurring*:** For this experiment, we performed blurring of the copy–move forged test images, by average filtering, with filters of sizes 3 × 3, 5 × 5, 7 × 7 and 9 × 9. Table 6 shows the performance evaluation results in terms of robustness to blur attack. From Table 6 it is evident that with increase in filter size, both precision and recall decrease; and as we increase the block size the rate of decrease of precision is found to be more as compared to recall.

**Table 6:** Evaluation of robustness to blurring of edges in forged images.

| | ***Filter Size*** | ***Block size (pixels)*** | | | |
|---|---|---|---|---|---|
| ***Parameter*** | | ***5×5*** | ***15×15*** | ***25×25*** | ***35×35*** |
| Precision (%) | 3 × 3 | 99.48 | 98.60 | 96.69 | 95.82 |
| | 5 × 5 | 98.92 | 97.23 | 95.82 | 94.19 |
| | 7 × 7 | 97.02 | 96.43 | 94.17 | 93.82 |
| | 9 × 9 | 95.22 | 94.18 | 93.06 | 92.87 |
| Recall (%) | 3 × 3 | 95.82 | 95.14 | 94.68 | 94.09 |
| | 5 × 5 | 94.72 | 93.92 | 93.02 | 92.76 |
| | 7 × 7 | 93.12 | 92.68 | 91.22 | 90.56 |
| | 9 × 9 | 91.60 | 90.02 | 89.17 | 88.52 |

In Fig. 9(e)–(f) and Fig. 9(k)–(l), we present the forgery detection results of the method for blurred images, with 3 × 3 and 7 × 7 filters.

### 3.4 Robustness to Miscellaneous Attacks

In this section we evaluate the robustness of the above scheme against various miscellaneous attacks. For example,

- The copied region of an image undergoes both rotation and re–scaling before being moved, hence encompassing a two–fold geometric attack.
- Objects (or regions) of an image, duplicated multiple times, at different locations within the same image.
- Different duplicated objects (or regions), having undergone different forms of intermediate attacks.

The results for the above three cases are presented in Fig. 10. First row of Fig. 10 presents the original images, second row, the forged images, and the third row, the output. Fig. 10(d) shows an image having undergone the following miscellaneous attack: the tree at the top right corner is copied, rotated, scaled, and then pasted. In Fig. 10(e), objects (tree, car and steamer) are duplicated multiple times within the same image. In Fig. 10(f), multiple duplicated objects (building and boat) underwent different forms of geometric transforms, in a single image. Here the building object is re–scaled by a factor of 1.2, and the boat object is rotated by 15 degrees.

### 3.5 Comparison with State–of–the–Art

Here we compare the performance of the presented technique with five state–of–the–art copy– move forgery detection schemes, which are capable of detecting geometric region transformations and image distortion with Additive Gaussian Noise. Those are:

1. Log–polar based copy-move forgery detection proposed by Wu *et al.*[100] (LP).
2. SURF–vertex based copy-move forgery detection technique proposed by Ardizzone *et al.*[96] (SURF)
3. Segmentation–based copy–move forgery detection scheme proposed by Li *et al.*[98] (Segmentation).

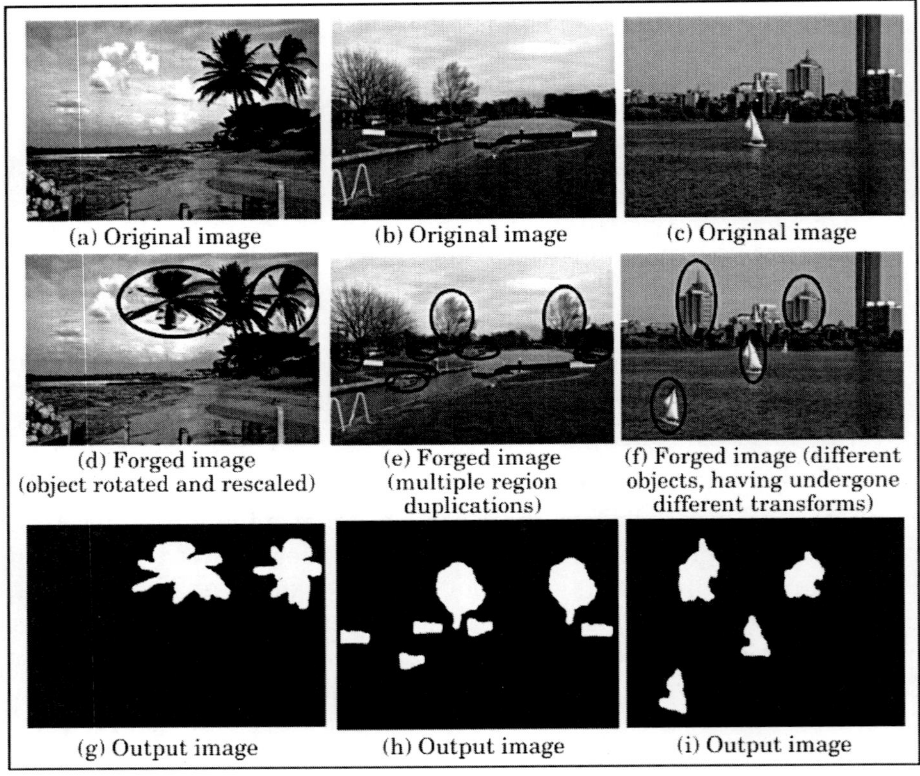


**Fig. 10:** Copy–move forgery detection results for miscellaneous attacks.

4. Modified SIFT–based copy–move forgery detection scheme proposed by Yang *et al.*[97] (SIFT).
5. Unsampled Log–polar based copy–move forgery detection scheme proposed by Park *et al.*[46] (ULP).

We present the comparison results in Fig. 11, in terms of precision and recall. Fig. 11 (a) to Fig. 11 (d), show that the scheme presented in this chapter achieved the highest precision as well as recall values (greater than 90%), in copy–rotate–move and copy–scale–move forgery detection, as compared to the other schemes. From Fig. 11(f), it is evident that as we add Gaussian noise with standard deviations of 0.02 through 0.10 in steps of 0.02, the false negatives increase; hence, recall rate of presented method decreases. From Fig. 11 (f), it can be observed that, the segmentation–based method[32] exhibits a remarkably

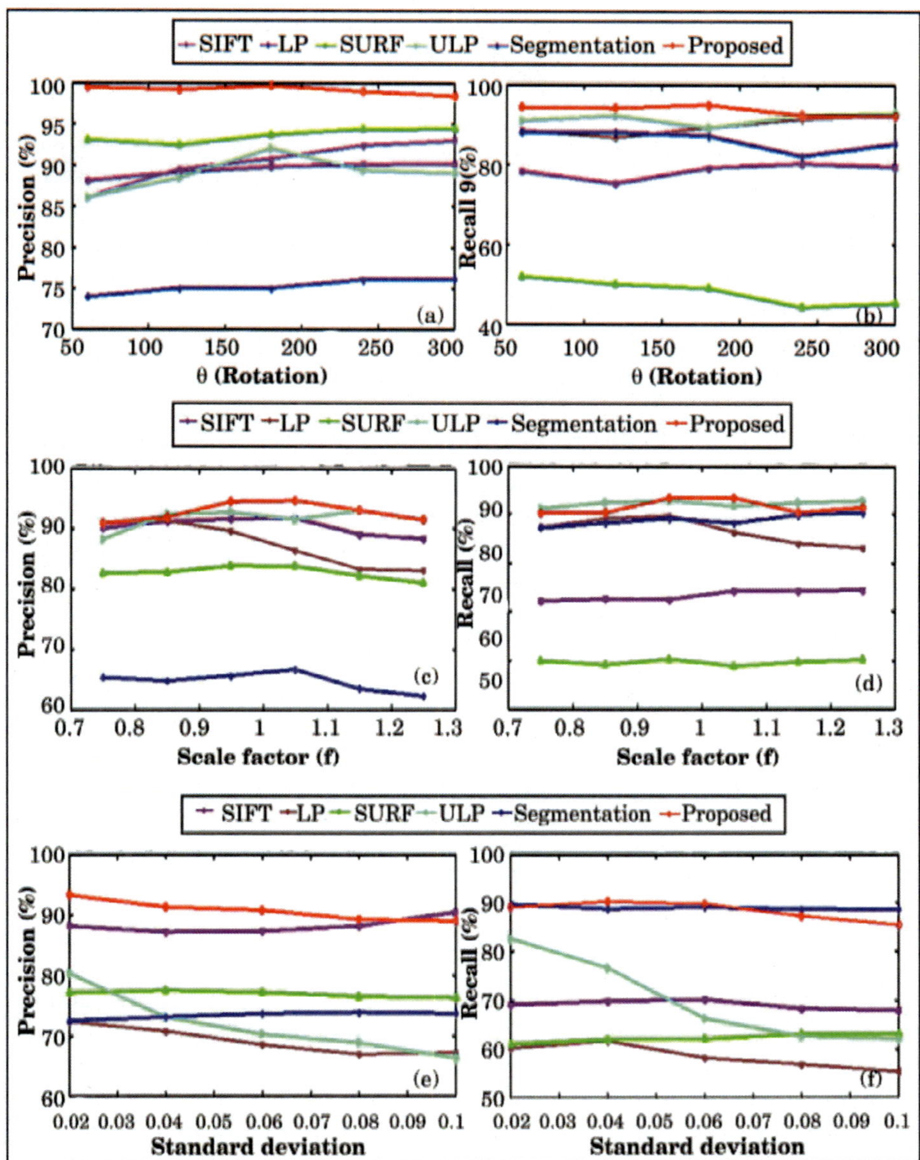


**Fig. 11:** Performance comparison results. (a)–(b) Copy–rotate–move forgery detection results. (c)–(d) Copy–scale–move forgery detection results. (e)–(f) Copy–move forgery detection results for image distortion with Additive Gaussian Noise.

high recall, close to that of the presented method. As compared to the other Log-polar based methods, LP[100] and ULP[46], the presented scheme exhibits better performance on an average.

We also compare the false positive rate of the above method with traditional copy–move forgery detection algorithms, without adoption of any additional approach to reduce false positives. The false positives comparison results have been presented in Table 7. The false positive rate of the proposed method is much reduced as compared to these traditional schemes.

**Table 7:** Comparison of False Positive Rate.

| *Method* | *Principle of Operation* | *False Positive Rate (%)* |
|---|---|---|
| DCT [55] | Discrete Cosine Transform | 8.02 |
| PCA [2] | Principle Component Analysis | 8.16 |
| Improved DCT [58] | Discrete Cosine Transform | 6.23 |
| SVD [74] | Singular Value Decomposition | 6.17 |
| DyWT [41] | Dyadic Wavelet Transform | 19.51 |
| DyWT–Zernike [56] | Dyadic Wavelet Transform with Zernike Moment | 14.19 |
| Efficient DCT [68] | Discrete Cosine Transform | 4.50 |
| DCT–PCA [67] | Discrete Cosine Transform with Principal Component Analysis | 6.06 |
| CWT [45] | Complex Wavelet Transform | 2.99 |
| FMT Log Polar [48] | Fourier Mellin Transform with Log–polar Mapping | 0.93 |

### 3.6 Resistance to Different Forms of Attacks

To summarize the results of our analysis, the results presented above prove that the technique is considerably efficient in detecting geometric transforms (rotation and rescale) and post–processing based operations (additive noise, blur and brightness adjustment) in copy–move forgery. The resistance of the method to the different forms of attacks are summarized in this section.

The experimental results prove that the presented scheme is capable of detecting any arbitrary degree of rotation in copy–move forgery; whereas, the minimum and maximum scale factors that it is capable of handling are 0.75 (down–sampling) and 1.25 (up–sampling), respectively. Similarly, the limits of resistance of the method to different forms of post–processing based attacks in copy–move forgery, have been presented in Table 8. It is evident from Table 8, that the scheme is considerably versatile, with respect to resistance against different forms of attacks, in addition to plain copy–move forgery.

**Table 8:** Resistance against Geometric and Post–processing Based Attacks.

| ***Attack Type*** | ***Resistance Limits*** |
|---|---|
| Copy–rotate–move | Angle of Rotation ∈ [0, 360] degrees |
| Copy–scale–move | Scaling Factor ∈ [0.75, 1.25] |
| Copy–move forgery adding noise | Standard Deviation ∈ [0.02, 0.10] |
| Copy–move–forgery with blurring | Filter Size ∈ [3×3, 9×9] |
| Copy–move–forgery with brightness adjustment | Brightness ∈ [0.70, 0.95] |

## 4. CONCLUSIONS

Copy-move forgery, though one of the most primitive forms of attacks on digital images, is considerably challenging to be detected, since it leaves the natural statistical properties of the image undisturbed. The challenge becomes more difficult, as this form of attack is combined with additional intelligent adversarial modifications to the image, such as rotation, re–scale, brightness adjustment of the forged region, blurring of its edges, addition of Gaussian noise, etc. In this chapter, we present a recent state-of-the-art copy-move forgery detection method for digital images, which utilizes Fourier Mellin Transform with Log–polar mapping. The method helps us achieve efficient copy-move forgery detection, along with invariance to geometric and post–processing based attacks. The color based segmentation scheme and the use of HSV color space, in this work, help us achieve high robustness to the above forms of forgeries. We also present experimental results to prove the efficiency of the above method in terms of forgery detection accuracy as compared to the state-of-the-art, as well as robustness to additional post-processing attacks.

In the next chapter, we shall discuss about key-point based region duplication detection in digital images.

# 13

# Region Duplication Detection Using Image Keypoints

## 1. INTRODUCTION

Traditional block-based copy-move forgery detection schemes are highly computationally intensive, since each and every block of the image needs to be processed by such techniques. Image keypoint based copy-move forgery detection techniques look for high energy pixels in an image, which are the only points processed in such algorithms; hence reducing their computational complexity greatly.

In this chapter, we introduce a keypoint based concept for this purpose. The method presented here is targeted to achieve invariance against geometric based attacks (rotation, rescaling, as well as a combination of both) in digital images, in addition to plain copy–move forgery detection. In this chapter, we present a technique to detect geometrically transformed copy-moved image regions. We use Scale Invariant Feature Transform (SIFT) algorithm for this purpose.

In the recent state–of–the–art, a number of key–point based methods have been proposed for copy–move forgery detection in digital images. Though the problems of re–scaling and rotation in region duplication, have been sufficiently investigated using key–point based methods, post-processing based attacks such as flip, blur, brightness and noise, remain an open challenge in this field. Pan and Lyu[3] propose using SIFT to identify geometric transformations in duplicated regions, because SIFT is not a global vector but it gives local feature property of an image. The key points extracted by SIFT are invariant to different scales. Each key point is associated with 128-dimension feature vector, which makes the key points distinctive. In[3], matching and pruning of the SIFT key points are carried out to estimate duplicated image regions. In [105] also the authors have proposed image region duplication detection based on SIFT features extraction. For block matching in[105], the authors have used kd-tree and Best Bin First (BBF) algorithm. The detection method proposed in[105] identifies the forged regions involving some post operations like Gaussian blurring, lossy compression, rotation, scaling etc. Hashmia *et al.*[106] use a combined approach of Dyadic Wavelet Transform (DyWT) and SIFT, for copy-move forgery detection. The algorithm proposed in [106] has considerably high block matching rate and is the most robust to image pre-processing operations. However it is not appropriate for down-sampling of copied blocks in images. Kang *et al.*[39] proposed a region-duplication detection method based on Singular Value Decomposition (SVD) and passive blind detection techniques. The proposed method [39] obtains singular value block matrix, and correlation coefficients which helps to improve matching capabilities.

As evident from the above discussion, the existing literature contains a number of schemes which are capable of detecting copy-move forgery involving various forms of processing on the copied-moved blocks. The common steps in any image keypoint based region duplication detection scheme in general, is presented in Fig. 1.

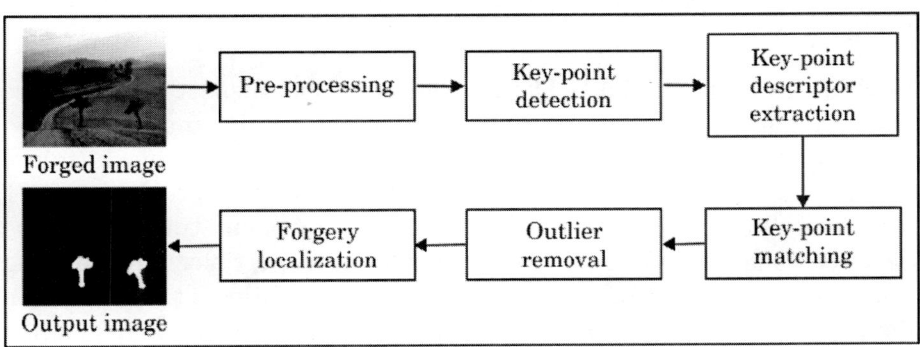


**Fig. 1:** Common steps of image keypoint based region duplication detection

In this chapter we aim to present a technique to detect specifically *rotation* and *rescale* operations, as well as a combination of the two, on copy-moved image regions using image keypoints. We present a method for detecting copy-move forgery with geometric transformations, specifically *rotation* and *rescaling*. We use *Scale Invariant Feature Transform* (SIFT)[107] to carry out detection of region duplication in our test images. The key- points extracted from and image using SIFT are invariant to scaling and rotation.

Rest of the chapter is organized as follows. In Section 2, we present the method for identifying copy-move forgery with rescale and rotation transformations, utilizing SIFT image keypoints. In Section 3, we evaluate the presented technique and assess its performance efficiency. Finally we conclude the chapter in Section 4.

## 2. COPY-MOVE FORGERY DETECTION INCLUDING GEOMETRIC ATTACKS BASED ON IMAGE KEYPOINTS UTILIZATION

In this section we propose utilization of SIFT for rotation and scale invariant copy-move forgery detection. SIFT is local feature aspect of image, and it stands for Scale Invariant Feature Transform. The key-points extracted using SIFT are insensitive to any geometric modification to an image, so that it makes the matching procedure easier.

Fig. 2, presents a flow chart representing the different steps of the technique to be presented. Next, we discuss all the steps shown in Fig. 2 one-by-one.

We first extract the SIFT key-points of the suspect image. Once the key-points are extracted we divide the whole image into non overlapping inspect blocks or segments. For each inspect block we are finding nearest match of that block into the image. For all the SIFT key-points present in the inspect block, we are calculating D-distance between each key-points which are present in inspect block. For finding D-distance we use Euclidean distance algorithm. The Euclidean distance is calculated for 128 dimensional vectors of each keypoints. And then we also find nearest neighbour of each key-points. With the help of matched keypoints we can find the moved region, which is geometrically transformed by applying scaling and rotation. The overall detection method consists of the following steps:

(1) SIFT Features Extraction

(2) Key-points Matching and Pruning

(3) Identifying Region Transformation
(4) Display the original and forged region

We discuss the above mentioned steps in details next.

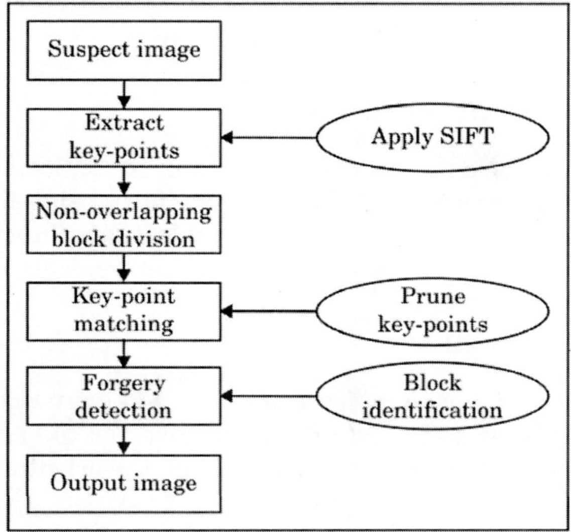


**Fig. 2:** Operational Flowchart

## 2.1 Extraction of SIFT features

In the following we discuss the procedure of extraction of SIFT key-points of an image[107]. In the subsequent subsections we present the utilization of the extracted keypoints for copy-move forgery detection, as well as for addressing the problem of geometric transformations in copy-move forgery.

### *a) Scale space extrema detection*

The first step identifies the location and the scale of the SIFT key-points. The points which are same for different scales or in different views of the suspected image are selected. Those points are invariant and more stable than the other key-points. The input image is convolve with the Gaussian function and gives scale space function (octaves). After that Difference of Gaussian is applied on scale spaces.

### *b) Detection of local extrema*

In order to find maximum and minimum points every point is compared with its own 8 neighbors from 3×3 grid and 18 neighbors from upper and lower DOG's 3×3 grid. In this process some noisy point are also extracted as a selective point. So that elimination of noisy point and edges are required.

### *c) Orientation assignment*

In this step local orientation are assign to each key-point. It provides local features to key-points. The orientation assignment provides rotation invariance to SIFT. For each scale space function gradient orientation g (x, y) and magnitude m (x, y) are calculated.

### *d) Key-point descriptor*

The purpose behind key-point descriptor is to add more local information to the key-points. It adds 128 dimensional vector to each key-points. This 128 dimensional vector is created from all the orientation histogram and magnitude of the key-points.

## 2.2 Key-points Matching and Pruning

We are having two images original image and forged image. Let us take K1 and K2 such that:

- K1 = The key-points present in the inspect block in the original region and
- K2 = The key-points present in the moved block.

In this step for each SIFT feature points present in the original region, we are calculating the D-distance between the rest of the 128 dimensional vectors of the key-points presents in the inspect block. When we reach to the forged region by sliding the inspect block in non-overlapping manner, the same D-distance is calculated for that region. The matching concept is that the key-points extracted in the original image must be extracted into the forged image. Only the duplicated region gives the difference in number of key-point which are extracted. The key-points of copied region and the moved region have some correlation, which helps to identify the forged portion. The key-points comes with SIFT are noisy so we have to prune them. The pruning removes all the false points so that false matches are removed and only correct matched will remains.

### 2.3 Identifying Region Transforms

Now we are finding the potential transformation between the original and forged block. In this work we are considering only copy-move forgery, re-scaling, rotation and both rotation and scaling forgery.

#### *a) Copy-move forgery detection*

If the copied region is directly moved to any other location within the same image then key-points extracted in the original region and the key-points extracted in the moved region are must be same. The SIFT 128 feature vectors of each keypoints are also same in both of the regions. And the distance D which we were calculated are also same for both original region as well as moved region. So that the forged region is easily be detected if there is no distortion has done.

#### *b) Scaling detection*

If attacker re-scaled the duplicated region, then D-distance plays most important role to identify the forgery. The number of keypoints available on original portion are differ from number of the key- points available on the forged region. All the SIFT key-points which are present at original region are not extracted into the forged portion due to scaling distortion. All the key points are not available so that the D-distance between pair of few key-points in the forged region must be multiple of their replicate presents in the original region.

Let us assume that we have two key-point pair present in both copied and moved part. These pairs are $(\vec{a},\vec{b}) \in$ K1 and $(\vec{a'},\vec{b'}) \in$ K2 and d1, d1' are D-distances between above pairs.

$$\begin{aligned} D(\vec{a},\vec{b}) &= d1 \\ D(\vec{a'},\vec{b'}) &= d1' \end{aligned} \tag{1}$$

such that $(\vec{a},\vec{b}) \in K1$ and $(\vec{a'},\vec{b'}) \in K2$ where D is the Euclidean distance between 128 feature vectors of the key-points. And

$$\frac{||d1||}{||d1'||} = \text{constant} \tag{2}$$

We plot histogram of the ratios of D-distances coming from pairs of SIFT key-points in K1 and K2. The maximum frequency of the histogram gives the scaling factor of the forged region.

### *c) Rotation detection*

If the attacker rotates the copied portion and then pasted it into somewhere else in the image, then it is quite difficult to detect the forgery. The number of keypoints detected in the inspect block of the original region are almost same with the number of keypoints detected into the inspect block of forged region. The only difference between both regions is the keypoints occur in rotated position. The D-distance and relative position of the SIFT keypoints with respect to each other are constant. So we are taking D-distance between each key points presents in the inspect block. Let us take one key-point$(\vec{a})$ in the original region, and suppose we have three other key-points $(\vec{b})$, $(\vec{c})$ and $(\vec{d})$ so the D-distances $D(\vec{a},\vec{b})$, $D(\vec{a},\vec{c})$, $D(\vec{a},\vec{d})$ and the relative position of with respect to the other keypoints will not change in the forged region.

$$\begin{aligned} &D(\vec{a},\vec{b}) = d1 \\ &D\left(\vec{a'},\vec{b'}\right) = d1' \\ &d1 = d1' \end{aligned} \tag{3}$$

### *d) Rotation and rescaling detection*

Here we consider the case where both rotation and scaling are performed in the forged blocks. The order of the forgery does not make any difference. The number of SIFT key-points extracted in the forged region only varies according to the scaling factor, rotation does not change the number of SIFT key-points extracted. Now in both type of geometric distortion the scaling is the dominating one. Rotation just gives angle to the region. So the SIFT key-points of the forged region are having a constant ratio of D-distances same as scaling forgery.

$$\frac{||d1||}{||d1'||} = \text{constant} \tag{4}$$

Due to rotation, the relative distances and the relative positions of the keypoints remain constant. That is,

$$\begin{aligned} &D(\vec{a},\vec{b}) = d1 \\ &D(\vec{a'},\vec{b'}) = d1' \\ &d1 = d1 \end{aligned} \qquad (5)$$

Again the maximum frequency of the histogram gives the scaling factor which is drawn from the distance ratios.

### 2.4 Detect authentic and forged regions

In this step the matching results are displayed. All the SIFT key points present in the original image are also present in the forged image except for the moved block, so that we get lots of matched SIFT key-points. But to display only the copied-moved blocks, we have to remove some *inliers*. For this purpose, we use RANSAC method[89]. RANSAC removes the inliers of the image.

## 3. PERFORMANCE EVALUATION AND EXPERIMENTAL RESULTS

In this section we present the performance evaluation results of the above scheme. We take the standard 512 × 512 *Lena* image as our test image. For our experiments we have manually forged the test image. We have manually induced the following types of forgeries in our test image: rotation (degree of rotation È = 90), rescaling (down-scaled by a factor of 75%), copy-move forgery with rotation and scaling both.

The test image has been shown in Fig. 3. Fig. 4 depicts all the SIFT key-points extracted from different scales, in green. All the key-points are invariant to the above mentioned transformations. Similarly we also extract the SIFT key-points for the forged image. Each SIFT keypoint extracted, is associated with 128-dimension feature vector.

Plain copy-move forgery is depicted in Fig. 5. As a part of our manual tampering, a region of the image was duplicated, as is evident from Fig. 5. The colored lines show the matching between the key-points

**Fig. 3:** Test Image

**Fig. 4:** SIFT Key-points mapped into image.

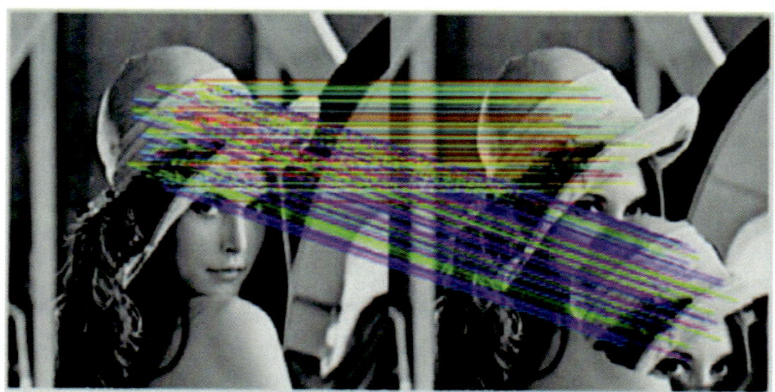

**Fig. 5:** Detection of simple copy-move forgery

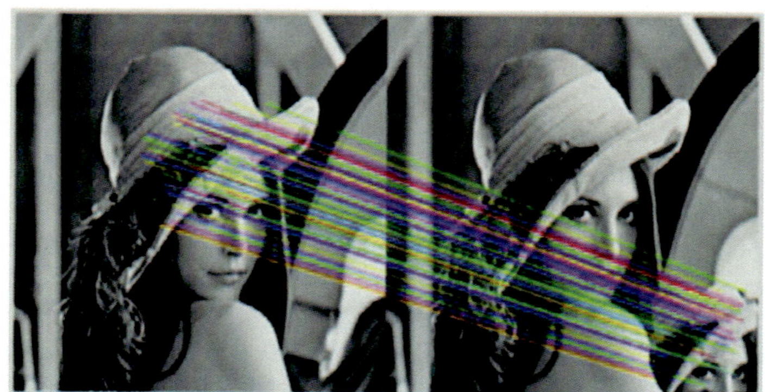

**Fig. 6:** Detection of re-scaled duplicated image region

contained in the copied region and the duplicated region of the image. The 128-dimension feature vectors of the SIFT key-points in both the regions are same, hence they are matched.

Fig. 6 shows a region of the test image been rescaled (by manual intentional tampering). The duplicated rescaled region has been shown in the bottom right corner of Fig. 6. The colored lines depict the matching between the key-points contained in the copied region and the rescaled and pasted region.

Similarly, in Fig. 7 we demonstrate the detection of copied, rotated and moved region in our test image, by the above scheme. The copied and rotated region of the test image has been shown on the bottom

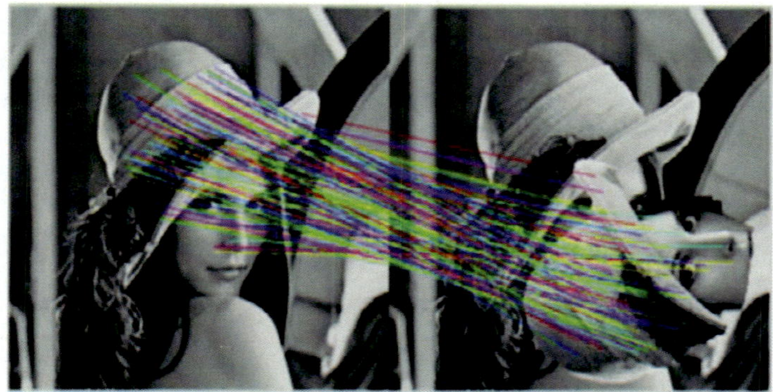

**Fig. 7:** Detection of rotated, duplicated image region.

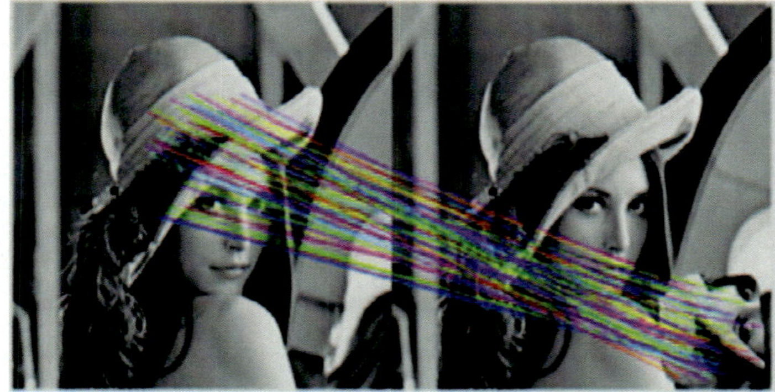

**Fig. 8:** Detection of copy-move forgery with both rotation and re-scaling operations.

right corner of Fig. 7, and the matching between key-points contained in copied and moved regions are shown by colored lines.

Fig. 8 presents the effects of applying a combination of both rotation and rescale operations on the duplicated test image region. In Fig. 8, the duplicated, down-scaled and rotated region has again been shown in the bottom right corner, and the key-points matching between original and duplicated regions has been shown by the colored lines. It is evident from our experimental results that the presented technique is equally capable of detecting rotation, rescale as well as a combination of both, in copy-move forgery of digital images.

## 4. CONCLUSIONS

In this chapter we have presented an efficient method to detect copy-move forgery in digital images, based on SIFT image keypoints extraction. The presented method is also capable of detecting geometric transformations applied on the forged region, with the help of SIFT key-points. Our experimental results prove that the method can detect a region duplication forgery, in which rescaling and rotation attacks are applied together or individually on the duplicated region. The presented method is more effective and gives better performance than the exact block matching techniques, in terms of geometric attacks detection in region duplication.

Due to inherent property of image keypoints and their extraction, the technique presented here, is computationally efficient as compared to the block matching based techniques presented in the previous chapters.

# 14

# Double Compression Based Forgery Detection in Images and Videos

## 1. INTRODUCTION

In present digital age, images and videos play the role of major information carriers, especially with the rapid advancement of digital devices, such as smart phones, laptops, notebooks and digital cameras. However, such form of multimedia data as digital images and videos, are highly prone to illegitimate modification attacks, especially with the advent of large volumes of low-cost and easily available image and video editing software and tools in the present day. Such manipulated images and videos are capable enough to deliver misleading/wrong information. More so, because images and videos act as the prime sources of evidence in the court-of-law, now-a-days. For example, a digital image or a CCTV footage, which is produced as an evidence to a crime scenario in a courtroom, if modified illegitimately before being produced, would mislead the court's decision. This might cause an innocent getting accused with false charges! Hence, integrity and authenticity preservation of digital images and videos, is a critical domain and a crucial requirement in present digital age. Especially, with the wide adoption of Online Social Networks (OSNs), whereby every common man shares/transfers huge volumes of images and videos with the world on a regular basis, the vulnerability of images and videos has risen all the more.

A vast majority of digital images and videos that we deal with in the present day, are in compressed formats. For example, JPEG format for images and MPEG format for videos, are the most widely adopted formats today, all of which are forms of lossy compression. All present day image and video capturing digital devices, store data in such lossy compressed formats, be it general purpose point-and-shoot digital cameras, or high specification Digital Single Lens Reflex (DSLR) cameras, camcorders, video recorders or mobile cameras. All of those record and store images and videos in compressed formats.

Many times it is found that the digital forensic techniques for detection of image/video forgery, in practice in the present day, such as the ones discussed in the previous chapters of this book, are not efficient enough to work with compressed domain images and videos. Here lies the requirement of special digital forensic techniques, specifically designed to work accurately with compressed data, such as JPEG and MPEG files. Techniques designed for uncompressed image/ video forgery detection fail, if produced with compressed files. Hence, in the recent state-of-the-art researchers have started working towards the development of digital forensic techniques, which would work efficiently for compressed images and videos. This chapter and the subsequent chapter, provide an overview of state-of-the-art researches in digital forensics for compressed multimedia.

In the recent years, numerous forensic techniques for forgery detection in compressed images and videos have come up[108-115]. One branch of this research, *i.e.* detection of forged multimedia, is based on *double compression or re-compression detection* in JPEG/MPEG. The problem here may be modelled as follows.

## 1.1 The Problem Model

While dealing with a compressed domain image/video, such as a JPEG or an MPEG, any manipulation, tampering or modification (legitimate or illegitimate) to the file, involves the followings:

(1) Selection of some portion of the compressed file (pixel groups of an image, or frames of a video, or regions within specific frames of a video) for manipulation/editing.

(2) Manipulation/editing to the selected portion of the compressed file.

(3) Replacing the manipulated portion back to the compressed file, at the correct location.

The third step above, that is, re-insertion of the manipulated part back into the original file, leads to the emergence of a second compression factor (also known as quality factor or compression ratio), within the same file. That is, the above form of JPEG/MPEG tampering, leads to a double compression factor in the tampered image/video. In other words, the manipulated image or video gets double or multi-compressed. Therefore, double compression detection constitutes a prime clue to detect this form of tampering in images or videos.

Almost all state-of-the-art digital forensic techniques to detect compressed image/video forgery, are based on detection of double- or re-compression in an image or video. However, it may be noted here that double compression detection is not a sufficient condition to tell whether an image or video is modified *illegitimately*. Because, the double compression occurrence may also be caused due to legitimate modification of the image/video. However, if it is found that some portions of an image or video is double compressed, whereas the rest of it is single compressed, then there is high probability that the regions with double compression, are forged.

**Fig. 1:** An example of simple splicing attack. (a) Authentic image with quality factor *QF1*. (b) Another authentic image with quality factor *QF2*. (c) Spliced image.

Fig. 1 shows an example of splicing attack in images. Here, two authentic images, with two different quality factors, are shown in Fig. 1(a) and Fig. 1(b). Some locations of the image in Fig. 1(b), where two men are present, are cropped out and pasted onto Fig. 1(a), to generate a tampered image, shown in Fig. 1(c). This form of image manipulation constitutes a splicing attack. The spliced image (Fig. 1(c)) depicts two different quality factors, that is, quality factor of forged region is $QF_2$ whereas quality factor of the rest of the (resultant or forged) image is $QF_1$. During the re-compression process, some compression artifacts are generated, like differences in quantization error, rounding error, truncation error[108], intra and inter frame prediction error[109,114,116] etc. Utilizing those compression artifacts, the authors in[110,112,114,116,117] detect double compression based forgery in images and videos.

The rest of the chapter is organized as follows. In Section 2, we present an overview of existing re-compression based JPEG forgery detection techniques, as well as describe a state-of-the-art scheme for JPEG forgery detection. Similarly, in Section 3, we present an overview of re-compression based MPEG forgery detection, and present a state-of-the-art technique for the same. We conclude the chapter in Section 4.

## 2. RE-COMPRESSION BASED JPEG FORGERY DETECTION

### 2.1 JPEG Compression

The framework of JPEG image compression and decompression technique is shown in Fig. 2. First, an image is divided into 8 × 8 non-overlapping pixel blocks, denoted by $B$, followed by 2D Discrete Cosine Transform (DCT) are performed on each block. Hence, obtaining its corresponding DCT coefficient block, denoted by $D^B$. Then, each DCT coefficient block is quantized by an 8×8 quantization matrix, $Q_{QF}$. The quantization matrix is defined by a quality factor $QF$ = [1,100].

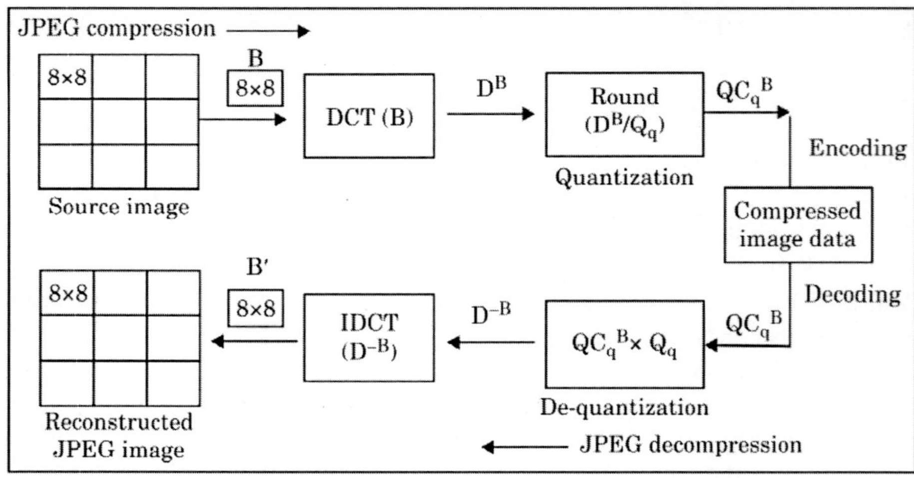


**Fig. 2:** JPEG compression and de-compression.

The JPEG de-compression process is just the reverse of the compression process. First, we de-quantize the quantized DCT coefficient $QC_q^B$ by multiplying the quantized DCT coefficient $QC_q^B$ with the corresponding quantization matrix $Q_{QF}$, to obtain the de-quantized coefficient $D^{-B}$. Then, we recover the image pixel blocks (say $B'$) by applying Inverse-DCT (IDCT) to the de-quantized DCT coefficients, finally followed by a rounding and truncation operation.

The quantization function is a non-invertible operation due to the rounding function. This makes JPEG a lossy compression technique. Due to the quantization step, a quantization error is generated for an image, during the encoding and decoding process in JPEG. The quantization error is defined as:

$$Q_{error} = D^B - \left(\frac{D^B}{Q_{QF}}\right) \times Q_{QF}.$$

Along with the quantization error, a rounding error and a truncation error are also introduced during IDCT. Some float values are generated when performing IDCT on de-quantize DCT coefficients. This is why, a round off, hence truncation are required to make get an integer. This produces the rounding error.

The IDCT operation generates values, which are less than 0 or greater than 255. (Here we are considering an 8-bit grayscale image, where pixel gray-scale values may range between 0-255). Those values are truncated to the range [0, 255] (for 8-bit gray scale image). This leads to generation of the truncation error. Although, the rounding and truncation errors are negligible, they cause JPEG to be a lossy or irreversible compression technique. (For more details of JPEG compression, the readers are requested to refer to[7]).

## 2.2 Double Compression Based JPEG Image Forgery Detection

Double compression detection in images can be done in two ways: (A) Either through statistical analysis of DCT coefficients of the image, or (B) by estimating the optimum quality factor of a JPEG, from the re-compressions detected.

### 2.2.1 *Double compression detection based on statistical analysis of DCT coefficients*

In the following, we present a recently proposed scheme for double compression detection in JPEG images. This was proposed by Li *et al.* in 2018[112]. In this paper, the authors proposed a machine learning based aligned double compression detection in JPEG image. The frequency in DCT blocks of an image, increases from left top corner to right bottom corner during JPEG compression, and the high frequency coefficients represent the details of image, it is almost lost after quantization step. Values in frequency. Since, DCT operation transfer the image into frequency domain from spatial domain, and values in adjacent frequencies in frequency domain are close. So, the correlation between adjacent coefficients of frequency domain in DCT blocks is increased. The authors used this characteristic and extract the intra-block frequency domain features. Also, the pixel difference between DCT blocks at same locations is linearly depended with the difference between DCT coefficients of adjacent DCT blocks at same locations. As we know, inverse-quantization is lossy method, quantization loss influence the dependency. So, the correlation between adjacent DCT blocks at same location reflects the dependency and quantization loss. The authors exploited this characteristic and based on that extract inter-block frequency domain features. Both intra and inter DCT block features combined and fed to ensemble classifier to detect the single and double compressed block in JPEG image.

The overview of method proposed in[112] is shown in Fig. 3. First the RGB JPEG image is converted to YCbCr color space. We select only the Y channel JPEG image coefficients, since the Cb and Cr channels are used for down sampling in JPEG compression process, which lowers the DCT correlation coefficients[118]. In Fig. 3, $|\,.\,|$ denotes the absolute value of JPEG coefficient matrix. The absolute value of JPEG coefficients in frequency spectrum reflects the magnitude of energy content of the image. On the other hand, sign of JPEG coefficients reflects the direction. During the quantization process, magnitude of energy in frequency spectrum is lost (denoted as *quantization loss*). The authors used this difference of quantization loss between single compressed and double compressed JPEG images, to detect the double compression based forgery here.

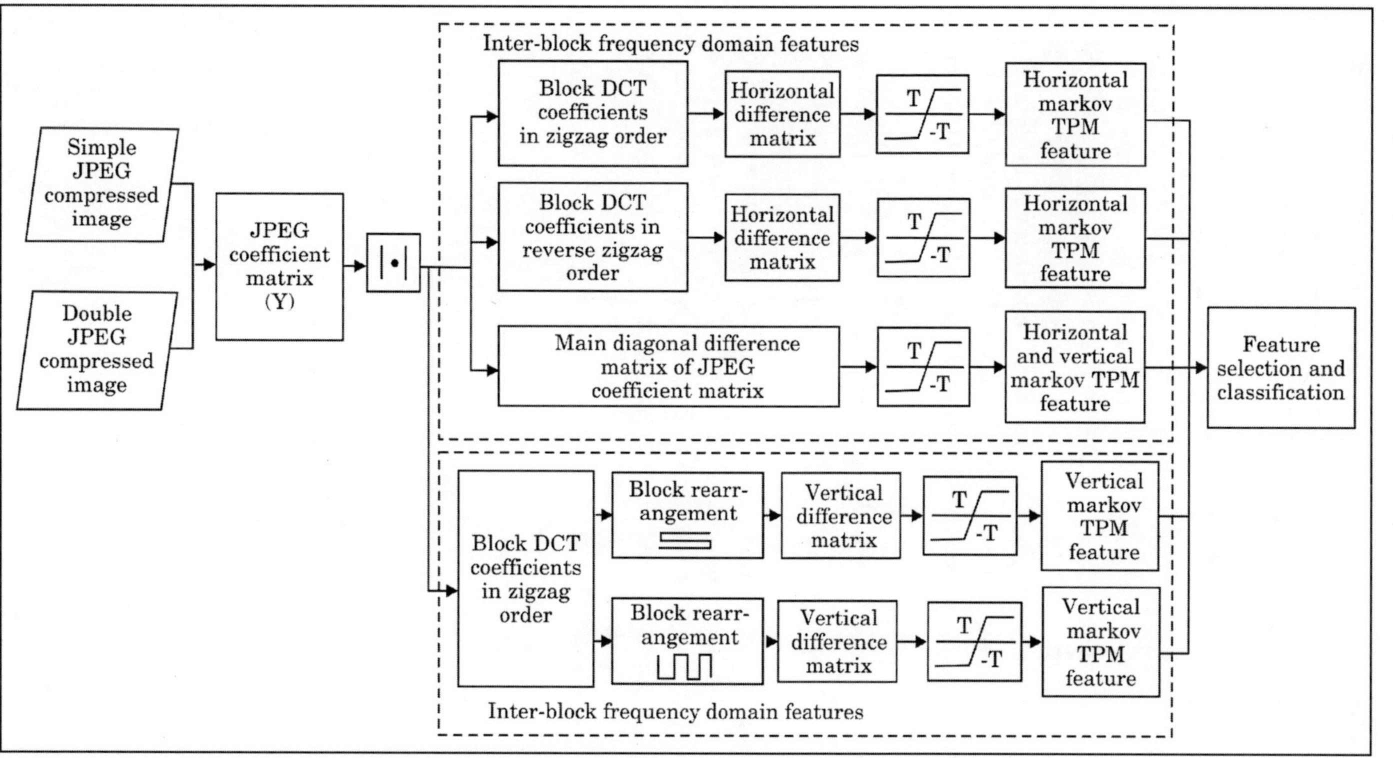


**Fig. 3:** The framework of JPEG image double compression detection.

As shown in *Fig. 3*, two types of features are extracted for classification in [112]. Those are, intra-block frequency domain features and inter-block frequency domain features.

### *Intra-block frequency domain features*

As shown in Fig. 3, the intra-block frequency domain features extraction process involves three methods. First, the JPEG coefficients in 8 × 8 DCT block are arranged in zigzag order from left to right and top to bottom and stored in a row vector of size N × 64, as shown in Fig. 4, where N is total number of DCT blocks JPEG coefficients matrix. From this re-arranged row vector, we calculate the 1st and 2nd order horizontal difference matrices, denoted as $D_h$ and $D2_h$ respectively, as follows:

$$D_h = (u,v) - \mathrm{c}\,(u,\ v + 1) \tag{1}$$

$$D2_h = D_h\,(u,v) - D_h\,(u,\ v + 1) \tag{2}$$

where C$(u,v)$ denotes the $(u,v)th$ DCT coefficient in the re-arranged row vector, denoted by $C$, matrix. A Threshold $T$ is computed empirically to reduce computational complexity. If the value of $D_h$ and $D2_h$ are less than $-T$ or greater than T, the value is replaced by $-T$ and $T$ correspondingly. Then, the 1st, 2nd and 3rd order *Markov Transition Probability Matrix* (TPM) [119] are calculated using the following equations:

$$M1_h(i,j) = \frac{\sum_{u=1}^{r}\sum_{v=1}^{c-1}\delta(D(u,u) = i, D(u,v+1) = j)}{\sum_{u=1}^{r}\delta(D(u,v) = i)} \tag{3}$$

$$M2_h(i,j,x) = \frac{\sum_{u=1}^{r}\sum_{v=1}^{c-2}\delta(D(u,v) = i, D(u,v+1) = j, D(u,v+2) = x)}{\sum_{u=i}^{r}\sum_{v=1}^{c-1}\delta(D(u,v) = i, D(u,v+1) = j)} \tag{4}$$

$$M3_h(i,j,x,y) =$$

$$\frac{\sum_{u=1}^{r}\sum_{v=1}^{c-3}\delta(D(u,v) = i, D(u,v+1) = j, D(u,v+2) = x, D(u,v+3) = y)}{\sum_{u=i}^{r}\sum_{v=1}^{c-2}\delta(D(u,v) = i, D(u,v+1) = j, D(u,v+2) = x)} \tag{5}$$

where,

$$\delta(A = p, B = q) = \begin{cases} 1 & A = p \text{ and } B = q \\ 0 & otherwise \end{cases}$$

$D$ denotes the difference matrix; and matrices are taken one at a time. $r$ and $c$ represent the row and column of $D$, respectively. $i, j, x, y \in \{-T, -T+1, \dots \dots T-1, T\}$ which represent the possible values in $D$.

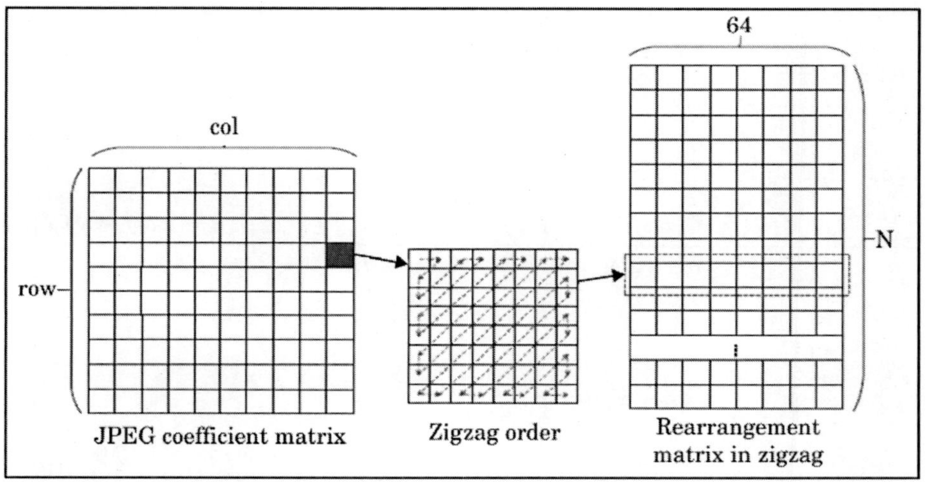


**Fig. 4:** Block DCT coefficient rearrangement process.

Second, the JPEG coefficients in 8 × 8 DCT block are arranged by reverse zigzag order from bottom to top and right to left and store a row vector of size $N \times 64$, where $N$ is the number of DCT blocks in JPEG coefficients matrix. Then, we calculate the 1st and 2nd order horizontal difference matrices using Eq. (1) and (2), respectively. From horizontal difference matrix, we extract the 1st, 2nd and 3rd order Markov TPMs using the Eq. (3), (4) and (5), respectively.

Third, since, the frequency in JPEG coefficient matrix increases from top left to bottom right, hence, the main diagonal difference of DCT JPEG coefficient matrix, directly reflects the static features in the direction of increase of frequency. So, we compute the 1st and 2nd order diagonal difference matrices from the DCT coefficient matrix, using Eq. (6) and (7), respectively. We extract the 1st, 2nd and 3rd order horizontal Markov TPMs using the Eq. (3), (4) and (5) and vertical Markov TPMs using the Eq. (8), (9) and (10), respectively.

$$D_d(u, v) = C(u, v) - C(u+1, v+1) \tag{6}$$

$$D2_d(u,v) = D_d(u,v) - D_d(u+1,v+1) \quad (7)$$

$$M1_v(i,j) = \frac{\sum_{u=1}^{r-1}\sum_{v=1}^{c}\delta(D(u,v)=i, D(u+1,v)=j)}{\sum_{u=1}^{r}\delta(D(u,v)=i)} \quad (8)$$

$$M2_v(i,j,x) = \frac{\sum_{u=1}^{r-2}\sum_{v=1}^{c}\delta(D(u,v)=i, D(u+1,v)=j, D(u+2,v)=x)}{\sum_{u=1}^{r-1}\sum_{v=1}^{c}\delta(D(u,v)=i, D(u+1,v)=j)} \quad (9)$$

$$M2_v(i,j,x,y) = \frac{\sum_{u=1}^{r-3}\sum_{v=1}^{c}\delta(D(u,v)=i, D(u+1,v)=j, D(u+2,v)=x, D(u+3,v)=y)}{\sum_{u=1}^{r-2}\sum_{v=1}^{c}\delta(D(u,v)=i, D(u+1,v)=j, D(u+2,v)=x)} \quad (10)$$

where:

$$\delta(A=p, B=q) = \begin{cases} 1 & A=p \; and \; B=q \\ 0 & otherwise \end{cases}$$

*C* is the rearrangement matrix, $D_d$ and $D2_d$ are the 1st and 2nd order diagonal difference matrices respectively. $D \in \{D_d \text{ and } D2_d\}$, *C(u,v)* is the value of matric *C* at location *(u,v)*. $M1_v$, $M2_v$, and $M3_v$ are the 1st, 2nd and 3rd order vertical Markov TPMs, respectively.

### ***Inter-block frequency domain features***

The inter block frequency domain features extraction process is similar to intra block feature extraction. The only difference lies in the DCT blocks rearrangement, in JPEG coefficient matrix. In order to compute the coefficient between adjacent DCT blocks at the same location, Li *et al.*[112] used a spatial shape S, as shown in Fig. 5.

As shown in Fig. 5(a), one rearrangement matrix is obtained with adjacent DCT block rows, next to each other. Another rearrangement matrix is obtained with adjacent DCT block columns next to each other, as shown in Fig. 5(b). All the DCT coefficients are rearranged by zigzag order and stores in a row vector as shown in Fig. 4. It is ensured that coefficients belonging to the same location, are vertically adjacent in the rearrangement matrix. From this rearranged row vector matrix, we calculate the 1st and 2nd order vertical difference matrices using Eq. (11) and (12) respectively. 1st, 2nd and 3rd order Markov TPMs are

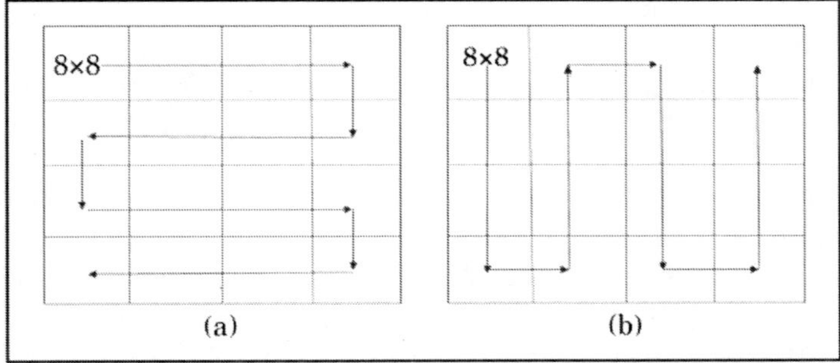


**Fig. 5:** Special S shape of adjacent DCT block. (a) Row wise scanning. (b) Column wise scanning.

extracted from vertical difference matrix using Eq. (8), (9) and (10) respectively. Eq. (11) and (12) are as follows.

$$(D_v(u,v) = C(u, v) - C(u + 1, v) \tag{11}$$

$$D2_v(u, v) = D_v(u, v) - D_v(u + 1, v) \tag{12}$$

where $D_v$ and $D2_v$ are the 1st and 2nd order vertical difference matrices, respectively. $(u,v)$ denotes the location of row vector matrix $C$.

The 1st and 2nd order Markov TPMs are computed from the 1st order difference matrix, and 1st, 2nd and 3rd order Markov TPMs are computed from the 2nd order difference matrix. These extracted Markov TPMs are used as features and fed as input of the ensemble classifier and Support Vector Machine (SVM) to detect the double compressed image.

### 2.2.2 *Double compression detection and localization based on estimated optimum quality factor*

Tariang *et al.*[113] proposed a method to identify double compressed JPEG image based on the quality factor of first compression. Let, $QF_1$ and $QF_2$ denote the first and second compression quality factors respectively. If the first and second compression quality factors are same, *i.e.* $QF_1 = QF_2$, then the resultant error matrix, which is generated during the compression and re-compression process, has $S(i,j) = 0\ \forall(i,j)$ (neglecting the rounding and truncation errors), where $S(i,j)$ represents the $(i,j)$-th element of the error matrix $S$.

If a tampered image re-compressed with $QF_1 = QF_2$, the error matrix would have $S(i,j) = 0 \ \forall(i,j)$ for authentic image region and $S(i,j) \neq 0 \ \forall(i,j)$ for most forged image region. Using this phenomena, Tariang *et al.*[113] detect re-compression forgery in JPEG images.

At first, they estimate the quality factor at varied regions of an image using re-compression quality factor. When most of the regions depict quality factor equal to $QF_1$, then the corresponding is selected as the optimal one. This optimal error matrix is used to detect the location of forgery in a tampered JPEG image. An automated quality factor estimation from a double-compressed image is described below:

1) Initialize recompressed JPEG quality factor, $QF_2 = 40$.
2) Tampered image ($I$ with size $N \times N$) is re-compressed with JPEG quality factor $QF_2$ $I_{QF2}$ Let, denote the re-compressed tampered image.
3) The error matrix $S$ corresponding to $I_{QF2}$, is calculated using following equation:

$$S(i,j) = [I(i,j) - I_{QF_2}(i,j)]^{10} \ \ \forall(i,j) \leq N \qquad (13)$$

4) The error matrix, $S$ is divided into $8 \times 8$ non-overlapping block $B(r,s)$ row wise. To estimate the quality factor of each block, $QF_2(r,s)$ steps (5) to (7) are performed.
5) If $B_{(r,s)}(i,j) = 0, \forall(i,j), 1 \leq i,j \leq 8,$ then
6) $QF_2(r,s) \leftarrow QF_2$ where r,s = 1,2,3, ... ... ..., $^N/_8$
7) End if
8) A counter, denoted by , is introduced, which contains the number of blocks having $QF_2(r,s) = QF_2$.
9) The steps (2) to (8) are repeated for $QF_2 = 41,42,$ ... ... ..., 90.
10) The quality factor ($QF_o$) at which the optimal error matrix is generated, would correspond to the maximum of:

$$C_{40}, C_{41}, \ldots \ldots \ldots \ldots \ldots, C_{90} \text{ i.e., a. } QF_o \leftarrow QF_x$$

$$\text{such that } C_{QFx} = \max\,(C_{40}, C_{41}, \ldots \ldots \ldots \ldots \ldots, C_{90})$$

After estimating the optimum quality factor ($QF_o$), localization of forgery is performed utilizing the ($QF_o$), The correlation between corresponding image pixels of the original and re-compressed images, is high, if the re-compression quality factor and previous compression quality factors, are close. Therefore, we compute the correlation coefficients between the corresponding 8 × 8 blocks of the tampered image, and re-compressed version $I_{QF_0}$ to localize the forged region within the tampered image.

To localize the forged region in a JPEG, the following steps are performed in[113]:

1) The tampered image ($I$) is re-compressed with the estimated optimum quality factor ($QF_o$), producing a re-compressed tampered image $I_{QF_0}$.
2) Both the tampered image $I$ and re-compressed tampered image $I_{QF_0}$ are divided into 8×8 non-overlapping blocks, denoted by $B_{(r,s)}$ and $B'_{(r,s)}$ respectively where $r, s = 1, 2, \ldots {}^{N}/_{8}$.
3) Perform steps (4) to (16) to compute the correlation matrix for each pair of corresponding blocks, $B_{(r,s)}$ and $B'_{(r,s)}$
4) *Count=0*
5) for *i=1 to 8* do
6) For *j=1 to 8* do
7) If $B_{(r,s)}(i,j) \neq B'_{(r,s)}(i,j)$ then
8) *Count=count+1*
9) End if
10) End for
11) End for
12) If *Count* > *Threshold* then
13) $RR_{(r,s)} = 0$ where $R_{(r,s)}$ is the correlation matrix of two correspo-nding blocks.
14) Else
15) $R_{(r,s)} = 1$
16) End if
17) For $r = 1$ *to* ${}^{N}/_{8}$ do
18) For do
19) If $R_{(r,s)} \neq 1$ then
20) Mark $B_{(r,s)}$ as forged block

21) Else
22) $B_{(r,s)}$ is unforged block
23) End if
24) End for
25) End for

In another work by Chao *et al.*[120], the authors present a visual depiction of this forgery detection and localization technique, which is presented in Fig. 6. Fig. 6(a) shows a tampered image, and Fig. 6(b) shows the resultant optimum error matrix image, obtained using Eq. (13) from the image re-compressed with quality factor $QF_o$. Fig. 6(c) shows the $B_{(r,s)}$ vs. $R$ plot for the tampered image in Fig. 6(a). From Fig. 6(c), it can be observed that the correlation coefficients with $R \neq 1$ is changed significantly for some blocks. Those are the blocks detected to be forged.

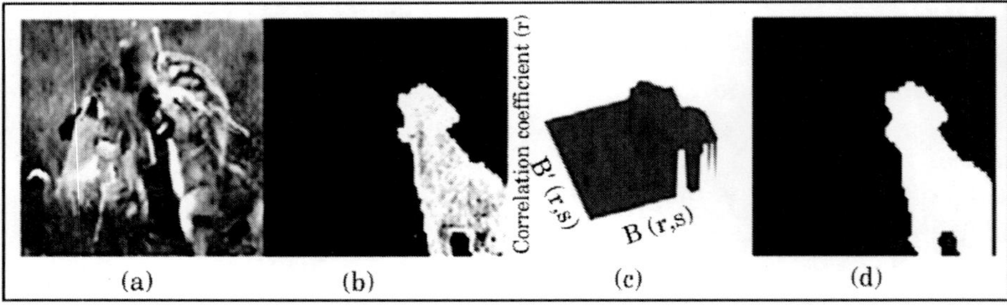


**Fig. 6:** (a) Authentic image. (b) Optimal error image. (c) B(r,s) *vs.* R plot (d) Localized forged region.

### *Eliminating false positives and false negatives in[113]*

To improve the performance of the technique proposed by Tariang *et al.* in[113], the resultant false positives and false negatives need to be minimized. To reduce the rate of false positives and negatives, the following refinement procedure, originally proposed in[121], is adopted here.

The connected regions are identified from the resulting binary image, which obtained by forged localization algorithm, using the 8-connected component labeling algorithm [122]. In the resulting binary image, black pixels denotes the authentic region, and white pixels denotes the forged region. Small connected forged regions or authentic regions, whose enclosing rectangles are smaller than 72 × 72 pixels, are expanded by considering their 8-connected neighborhood. The block is detected as forged if the fraction of the forged blocks in the expanded region, is greater than 0.6. Otherwise, the block is detected as authentic.

After performing the above refinement algorithm, the localization results obtained, are presented in Fig. 6(d).

## 3. RE-COMPRESSION BASED MPEG FORGERY DETECTION

### 3.1 Overview of MPEG-x Video Compression

A video consists of a sequence of frames, which move at a predefined rate of time, to create the illusion of motion, exploiting the persistence of human visual system. The audio related to the scene recorded, forms the other constituent of a video file. In this chapter, we focus on the visual component of a video, and forgery detection in it, following digital forensic approaches.

In general, raw video sequences require a lot of storage space. So, most of the video capturing devices store video in compressed formats, as discussed at the beginning of this chapter. Various types of video codec techniques are used to compress a raw video sequence, and hence to reduce the storage space requirement, such as MPEG-1, MPEG-2[123], MPEG-4, H.264[124], H.265[125] etc. In this chapter, we take up MPEG video compression format, and present the rest of the chapter in relation to forensic investigation of MPEG files.

A video can be represented in three dimensions: one temporal and two spatial dimensions, as shown in Fig. 7. The video compression techniques reduce the spatial and as well as temporal redundancies. Also, the different between consecutives frames in a video is very small, given natural scenes. So, instead of storing all the frames, it is sufficient to store only the reference frames, and predict groups of next frames from those. In this form of video compression, the video frames are divided into three categories: I-frame (Intra frame), P-frame (Predicted frame) and B-frame (Bi-directional predicted frame). I-frames are encoded in transform domain similar to JPEG image compression[126], which reduces the spatial redundancy. P-frames are predicted from its reference I/P-frame. So, efficiency of P-frames to represent a video, is more as compared to I- frames. However, since those are predicted frames, their quality is low. B-frames are predicted from its backward and forward reference frames. The quality of B-frames is lowest compared to the other frame types.

It is not always possible to predict all the frames from one reference I-frame. So, I-frames are inserted at regular intervals, based on the required quality of the video. The frame sequences are divided into groups, called *Group of Pictures* (GOP)[127] of a video. Each GOP has only one I-frame and a particular pattern as shown in Fig. 7. In Fig. 7, the GOP sequence is IBPBPB, and the GOP length is six. Most of the video encoders use fixed GOP size, but it affects the visual quality of the video. So, recently, some encoding techniques like H.264, H.265 etc. have started using *adaptive* GOP size, depending on the content of the video.

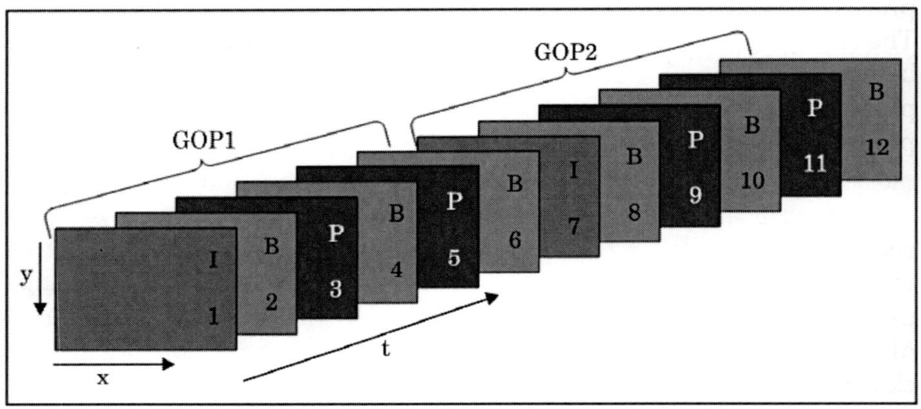


**Fig. 7:** Video sequence.

Each frame is segmented into 16×16 blocks, known as macro-blocks (MB). Each MB of I-frame is encoded as a JPEG. To encode a MB of P/B-frame, the best matching MB in the reference frame is found out and its location along with displacement (motion) vector is stored, to create the reference frame. The predicted frame is compared with the original frame, and the prediction error is computed hence. This prediction error and the motion vector (MV) are also saved. Generally, there are three types of MBs: intra MB (those MB which are encoded from itself), inter MB (those which are predicted from its reference) and skipped MB (no encoding required).

Since, P- and B-frames are predicted frames, an inter-frame prediction error is generated for every GOP. Along with, the inter-frame prediction error, an intra-frame prediction error is also introduced, which are generated during I-frame compression in modern compression techniques [154]. This is because, within an I-frame some macro-blocks (MB) are predicted from its top and left neighbors.

Many researchers such as those in[109,114,116,128], use this intra and inter frame prediction error in video forgery detection. Next, we move on video tampering investigation based on double compression detection in videos.

## 3.2 Double Compression Based Video Forgery Detection

Zhang *et al.*[114] exploited the compression artifacts of I-frames to detect double and multi compression in H.264/AVC videos. The encoding process of I-frames in H.264 videos is similar to JPEG compression. The only difference is that in H.264/AVC, a prediction error is introduced before DCT operation as shown in Fig. 8. Some MBs of I-frames are predicted from their nearest neighbors, and this is called intra-frame prediction. Let, $X_{k,n}$ be the $k^{th}$ MB of the $n^{th}$ I-frame.

Its predicted MB, denoted by $X^{'}_{k,n}$ can be obtained from the reconstruction process of its upper and left neighbors. The H.264/AVC videos have 13 prediction modes for luma intra-prediction and four prediction modes for chroma intra prediction [129]. Using the rate-distortion function to every prediction mode, H.264/AVC codec would choose the best prediction mode. Therefore, for one MB, it may generate different predicted MBs during sequential compression, even with same quantization parameter (QP). This would lead to a change of quantized DCT coefficients.

The reconstructed $X^{'}_{k,n}$ MB can be used as a candidate MB to predict other MBs. In the reconstruction step, de-quantization and inverse discrete cosine transform (IDCT) are performed on the quantized DCT coefficients, denoted by $C_{k,n}$, and generates prediction residual errors, denoted by $R^{'}_{k,n}$. These $R^{'}_{k,n}$ are added with the predicted MB. Also during IDCT, rounding and truncating errors get introduced. These prediction errors, rounding errors and truncation errors would lead to the change of quantized DCT coefficients during sequential compressions, even with the same QP.

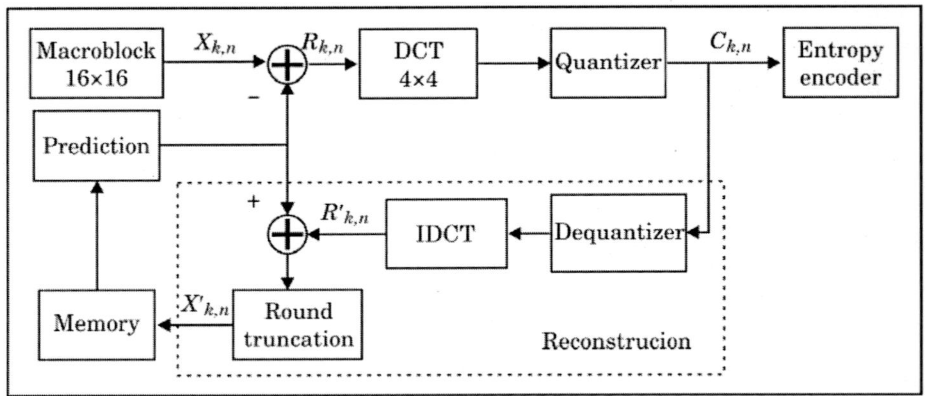


**Fig. 8:** Encoding process of I-frames in H.264.

It should also be noted here that, the DCT and quantization steps are performed on the prediction residuals of current MB, denoted by $R_{k,n}$. So the influence of video content over quantized DCT coefficients is greatly reduced by prediction. Therefore, Zhang *et al.*[114] analyzed the quantized DCT coefficients to detect multiple video compressions with same QPs. Quantized DCT coefficients, whose values are changed after re-compression, are used to extract ratio difference set (RDS) following Eq. (14) below. The extracted RDS are used to generate five statistical features and use Support Vector Machine (SVM) to classify the single and multiple compressed H.264/AVC videos. The RDS extraction process[114] is described in the following:

1) First, entropy decoding is performed on a H.264/AVC video $V$ to get the set of quantized DCT coefficients in every I-frame, $C_n(n = 1,2, \ldots N)$ where n is the index of I-frame and N is the total number of I-frames in $V$.
2) Continue to decode $V$ and then recompress it with the same QP to generate double compressed video $V'$. Then extract the double quantized DCT coefficients, denoted by $C_n' = (n = 1,2, \ldots N)$.
3) Again decode $V'$ and recompress it with same QP to generate triple compressed video $V''$. Then extract the set of triple quantized DCT coefficients, denoted by $C_n'' = (n = 1,2, \ldots N)$.

4) Count the number of quantized DCT coefficients, denoted by $c_n^1$, whose values are different between $C_n$ and $C_n^{''}$, where $n = 1,2, \dots N$. Also, count the number of quantized DCT coefficients, denoted by , whose values are different between $C_n^{'}$ and $C_n^{''}$, where $n = 1,2, \dots N$.

5) Calculate the RDS using the following equation:

$$h_n = \frac{(c_n^1 - c_n^2)}{T_n} \tag{14}$$

where $h_n$ is the RDS of $n^{th}$ I frame and $T_n$ is the total number of quantized DCT coefficients in the I frame and does not change in further compressions.

The obtaining RDS, $H = \{h_1, h_2, \dots \dots \dots, h_N\}$, cannot be used as features directly; because, the number of RDS is dependent on the number of I-frames in a video, and the number of I-frame varies from video to video. Therefore, to maintain a fixed dimension of feature set for all videos, five statistical features are extracted from RDS of each video, as follows:

1) Sort $H$ in ascending order and denote the newly sorted RDS as $H^{'}$
2) Calculate three locations, denoted by $L_1$, $L_2$ and $L_3$, in $H^{'}$, as follows:

$$\begin{aligned} L_1 &= [0.25 \times (N + 1)] \\ L_2 &= [0.50 \times (N + 1)] \\ L_3 &= [0.75 \times (N + 1)] \end{aligned} \tag{15}$$

where function [Y] rounds Y up to its nearest integer and $N$ is the number of I-frame in a video.

3) Extract the five features, denoted by and, as follows:

$$\begin{aligned} F_1 &= H_1^{'} \\ F_2 &= H_{L_1}^{'} \\ F_3 &= H_{L_2}^{'} \\ F_4 &= H_{L_3}^{'} \\ F_5 &= \overline{H^{'}} \end{aligned} \tag{16}$$

where $H_i^{'}$ denotes the $i^{th}$ element of $H^{'}$. $\overline{H^{'}}$ is the mean of, defined as:

$$\overline{H^{'}} = \sum_{i=1}^{N} H_i^{'}/_N$$

Based on the extracted features, an SVM classifier is trained to distinguish between single and multiple compressed videos.

## 4. CONCLUSIONS

In this chapter, we present a detailed overview of present day digital forensic techniques for re-compression based forgery detection images and videos. We have seen that due to this form of forgery, a different compression factor gets introduced into JPEG or MPEG files, which have been exploited by numerous researchers in the recent days to detect such forgeries or illegitimate modifications.

We have presented two schemes for re-compression based JPEG forgery detection, one of which is based on statistical analysis of DCT coefficients in a JPEG, and the other is based on an estimated optimum quality factor from the forged image. We have also presented a technique for re-compression based forgery localization in a JPEG image.

We have also presented an overview of the basic JPEG and MPEG compression algorithms. Finally, we have described a very recent technique for re-compression based MPEG forgery detection, which exploits the video frame prediction errors, inherent in MPEGs.

The next research step in this domain is to devise mechanisms for detection of triple or higher degrees of compression in JPEG and MPEG files.

# 15

# Intra and Inter Frame Video Forgery Detection: State-of-the-Art Problems and Solutions

## 1. INTRODUCTION

From the past couple of decades, the importance of digital videos and protection of their authenticity has been ever-increasing, because of the fact that videos act as major sources of evidence in the court-of-law. For example, CCTV footages submitted in courtrooms as evidence of crimes scenarios.

Now-a-days, cheap video editing tools are widely available to the common mass, by which any adversary can tamper a video at his own free will. So, we need to check the authenticity of the videos, before being considered as a trust-worthy evidence.

Broadly, video forgery can be categorized into two classes based on the domain of forgery in videos:

***a) Temporal forgery*:** The attacker manipulates the video in temporal domain. That is, this form of attack only affects the time sequence of visual information captured by video recording devices. The most common of this type of forgery are frame deletion, frame insertion, frame duplication and fame reshuffling attacks.

***b) Spatio-temporal forgery*:** This modification occurs within specific targeted frames. Basically, this type of forgery is performed to remove object(s) from some frames, or adding object(s) to some frames or modifying object(s) within some frames, illegitimately.

According to the state-of-the-art, video forgery is classified in two categories based on the forgery detection approach:

a) Intra-frame forgery detection (or region tampering detection)

b) Inter-frame forgery detection.

Intra-frame forgery in a video is a spatio-temporal domain forgery. In an intra-frame forgery, some regions within subsequent frames are modified to change the content of the video. Intra-frame forgery includes region duplication, also known as copy-move, and upscale-crop forgery.

Region duplication (copy-move) is a most common intra-frame forgery. In practical scenario, region duplication operation is performed to hide some object in a video or show some false information in a video.

An example of region duplication is shown in Fig. 1, where we performed the following operations:

I. At first we extracted all the frame from the video.

II. Then we copied target objects from the frames (two cars here).

III. We paste those object at different locations within the same frames, and save it.

IV. We performed step II and step III on the next target frames.

V. We encoded all the frames and hence made a forged video.

Upscale-crop operation is performed to eliminate objects from the frames, which are present in the outer-most parts of targeted frames of a video, and then enlarging the affected frames through resampling

**Fig. 1:** An example of region duplication intra-frame forgery. Authentic video sequence (top) and Forged video sequence (bottom).

operation to maintain consistent resolution across the entire video. Example of upscale-crop is shown in Fig. 2.

**Fig. 2:** Example of upscale-crop forgery. (a) and (c) authentic frames from SULFA dataset. (b) and (d) tampered frames obtained by crop and upscale operation in frames (a) and (c) respectively.

Inter-frame forgery is a purely temporal domain forgery in videos. Inter-frame video forgery includes frame insertion (inserting frame(s) from a different video to a target video), frame deletion (deleting frame(s) from the target video to obscure some object), and frame duplication (duplicating a sequence of frames within a video, at some other location, to alter the semantics of the video illegitimately). These type of forgeries have been shown in a schematic diagram in Fig. 3. Besides the above forgeries, frame reshuffling forgery (some frame are cut from video sequence and paste into another location in the same video sequence) is another form. Frame reshuffling is nothing but a combination of frame deletion and insertion.

The rest of this chapter is organized as follows. In Section 2, we present state-of-the-art intra frame video forensic techniques with pros and cons. In Section 3, we present state-of-the-art inter frame video forensic techniques and also discuss the advantages and limitations of those. We conclude the chapter with a discussion on open problems in the domain of video forensics, in Section 4.

## 2. INTRA-FRAME VIDEO FORGERY DETECTION

In the following section, we present a survey of recent intra-frame video forgery detection techniques.

### 2.1 Region Duplication Forgery Detection

In region duplication intra-frame forgery, the source regions and target regions similarity are very high. However in practical scenario, the

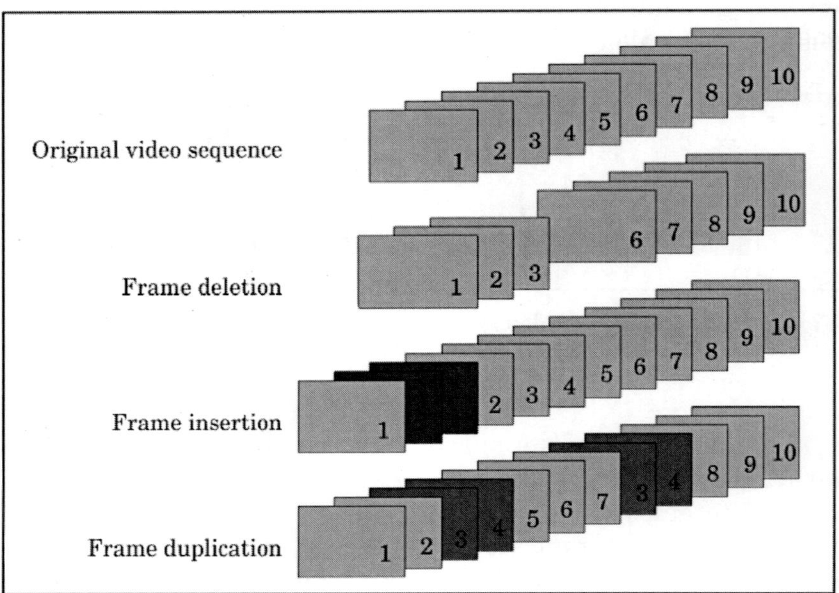


**Fig. 3:** Inter-frame video tampering.

attacker do not simply copy and paste into different location. Because, it has chances to detect through human eyes. So, after coping the target regions, the attacker perform some geometrical operations, like rotation, upscaling, down scaling, mirroring etc , on the copied regions and then past it into target regions. So, there are many challenges to detect region duplication intra-frame forgery. Based on the State-of-the-art techniques, region duplication intra-frame forgery detection can be divided into three categories: (a) Pixel similarity analysis based method, (b) Motion features based method. In, next subsequent section we will discuss about each type region duplication intra-frame forgery detection techniques.

### 2.1.1 *Pixel Similarity and Correlation based Region Duplication Detection*

The techniques that detect region duplication forgery in videos, generally proceed by looking for similarities or correlations between regions of successive video frames or regions of the same frame, which in theory should not have anything in common (primarily because they have different origins or have different time/place associated with their lineage).

To detect region duplication forgery in video many researcher used SIFT/ SURF [130,131], HOG [115,132,133] as features in their proposed algorithm. These is not sufficiently capable to detect region duplication forgery in videos for the following cases:

(a) These algorithm cannot detect the region duplication forgery when attacker perform minoring operation in forged region before pasting.
(b) SIFT or SURF has high dimensionality. So need high computational cost, especially analysis in high resolution videos.

To address these limitation, Su *et al.*[134] proposed MISIFT[135] features based algorithm, which is minoring invariant along with rotation and scaling invariant and also reduce the dimension of the features. The authors perform the following operation to detect the region duplication forgery in videos:

1) Extract all the frames from the video
2) Select one frame, denoted as $I_{current}$.
(3) Extracted MISIFT features set $X$, of $I_{current.}$ The features of current frame are described as follows:

$$X = \begin{Bmatrix} x_1 \\ x_2 \\ \cdot \\ \cdot \\ x_n \end{Bmatrix} = \begin{Bmatrix} f_{11}, f_{12} \dots\dots\dots\dots f_{1m} \\ f_{21}, f_{22}, \dots\dots\dots\dots f_{2m} \\ \cdot\cdot \\ \cdot\cdot \\ \cdot\cdot \\ f_{n1}, f_{n2}, \dots\dots\dots\dots f_{nm} \end{Bmatrix} \tag{1}$$

where $n$ is the number of features of $I_{current}$ and each feature represented by $m(=128)D$ vector. $f_{nm}$ is the $m_{th}$ component of the $n^{th}$ feature point $x_n$.

4) Apply Principle Component Analysis (PCA) [136] on features set $X$ to reduce the dimension. Let, dimension of each feature after PCA used is $\acute{m}$.
5) Compute a similarity vector using Euclidian distance with respect to other descriptors:

$$D_n = \{d_{n1}, d_{n2}, d_{n3}, \dots\dots d_{ni}, \dots\dots\dots\} \; 0 < \text{n} < \acute{m}, 1 < i < \acute{m} \tag{2}$$

where $D_n$ is sorted in ascending order and $dni$ is the distance of $xn$ to a certain feature point. It is assumed that $d_{n1}$, is the distance of the $n^{th}$ feature point to the feature point.

6) The $n^{th}$ feature point $k^{th}$ feature point are matched only if the following constraintis satisfied:

$$d_{n1}/d_{n2} < T_r \;\; T_r \in (0,1) \tag{3}$$

where $d_{n2}$ is the distance of $n^{th}$ feature point from the $t^{th}$ feature point and $T_r$ is the threshold, (here, $T_r = 0.6$).

7) Repeat steps 5 and 6 until equation (2) and (3) traverse for all feature points.

After completing the above steps, two matching point set $Q$ and $W$ will be obtained of $I_{current}$. $Q$ and $W$ have the same number of elements, and $q_i$ and $w_i$ are a pair of matching points. However, experimentally proof that still $Q$ and $W$ contain some mismatched points. In practical, the source and tampered areas must have some distance. So, Su *et al.*[134] used this distance and perform the following operation to reduce the mismatched point and improves the peformance:

For a pair of mismatching features points $q_i$ and $w_i$ and their corresponding coordinates Loc $(q_i)$ and Loc $(w_i)$ on the frame.

8) $q_i$ and $w_i$ point will be retain if satisfied equation (4), otherwise removed from $Q$ and $W$.

$$dis = \sqrt{Loc^2(q_1) - Loc^2(w)} > T_{dis} \tag{4}$$

where $T_{dis}$ threshold.

9) The source and tempered matching points should be concentrate in region, while mismatched points $m_i$ ($m_i \in Q \cup W$) are generally scattered. So if, for a mismatched point , there are must be at least three other matching points fall in with in radius $T_{nei}$ *(Threshold)*, then $m_i$ and its corresponding matching point will retain. Otherwise removed.

10) *K*-means clustering algorithm used to classify the matching points into two categories *i.e,* source region ($\acute{Q}$) and tampered region($\acute{W}$).

11) Any pair of matching feature points will be removed if satisfy the either of the following two conditions:

$$\begin{Bmatrix} q_1 \in \acute{Q} & and & w_1 \in \acute{Q} \\ & or & \\ q_1 \in \acute{W} & and & w_1 \in \acute{W} \end{Bmatrix} \quad (5)$$

12) After removal all the mismatch point, if number of retain matching pair point is greater than 5, then that frame is considered as forged. Otherwise, that frame is authentic.

If current frame forged by region duplication operation, then some subsequent frames also be forged. The changes in tampered region in adjacent of current forged frame is very less. So, to reduce the computational cost, a spatio-temporal context learning algorithm was used to locate the region duplication intra-frame forgery in subsequent frames instead of extract the features for every frames. The spatio-temporal context learning algorithm include the following steps:

13) The obtained points set *Q* from previous step in $k^{th}$ frame is set as initial position of the target. Then spatial context model of $k^{th}$ frame is calculated using following equation:

$$h_k^{sc}(x) = F^{-1}\left(\frac{F(be^{-|\frac{x-x^*}{\alpha}|^{\beta}})}{F(I(x)\omega_\sigma(x-x^*))}\right) \quad (6)$$

where $F^{-1}$ = Inverse Fast Fourier Transform, *F*= Fast Fourier Transform, *b*= normalized constant, *x*= context location, $x^*$ = current tracked target location, $\beta$ shape parameter, $a$ = scale parameter, *I(x)*= image pixel intensity value at location *x* and $\omega$ is the Gaussian weighted function defined as follows:

$$\omega_\sigma(x-x^*) = ae\frac{-|x-x^*|^2}{\sigma^2} \quad (7)$$

14) Compute the spatio-temporal context model for $k^{th}$ frame using following equation:

$$H_{k+1}^{stc} = (1-\rho)H_k^{stc} + \rho h_k^{sc} \quad (8)$$

where $\rho$ is learning parameter, $h_k^{sc}$ is spatial context for $k^{th}$ frame and initialize the spatio-temporal context

15) Compute a confidence map using following equation:

$$C_{k+1}(x) = F^{-1}(F(H^{stc}_{k+1}(x)) \otimes F(I_{k+1}(x)\omega_\sigma(x - x^*))) \quad (9)$$

16) Obtain the maximum value, which is the location of the object; that is,

$$x^*_{k+1} = \underset{x \in \Omega_C(x^*_k)}{argmax C_{k+1}(x)} \quad (10)$$

where $\Omega_C(x^*_k)$ is the local context region based on the tracked location $x^*_k$ in the $k^{th}$ frame.

17) The steps 13 to 16 will stop when it encounters one of the following condition:
    a) The areas obtained go beyond the frames;
    b) The size of the region is less than $T_{nei}$;
    c) The minimum distance between two regions is less than $T_{dis}$;
    d) It is the last frame of the video.

After the above process, we get two suspicious areas in the $i^{th}$ frame, let us say $a_1$(i) and $a_2$(i). If the number of pair matching point more than 5 in $i^{th}$ frame, then $i^{th}$ frame detect as forged. Otherwise detect as authentic.

This technique is able to detect region duplication forgery in video efficiently irrespective of rotation, scaling or minoring operation performed on tampered region. First time, a spatio-temporal context learning proposed in this technique to avoid the frame by frame features extraction and matching. However, this technique suffers when high movement velocity occur in tampered region in the test video.

### 2.1.2 *Motion Feature based Region Duplication Detection*

As we discussed earlier, each video has two classes of statistical properties: (a) intra-frame inherent properties, describes its spatial characteristic and (b) inter-frame inherent properties that describes its temporal characteristics. Each frame in a local temporal window in video comprises two parts: (a) motion part and (b) static part. The statistical part is identical to the reference frame. While motion part is the displacement vectors (also known as motion residual vectors) of motion objects from reference frame to current frame. This motion residual for each frame in a video is an important part of the visual information presented by that frame, contains a substantial portion of the intra-frame properties of that frame. In addition, motion residual vectors also contains the inter-frame inherent properties of the corresponding frame since it represent the temporal changes between current frames to its reference frame. So, motion residual contains the intra-frame as well as inter-frame inherent properties of the frames.

Chen *et al.*[137] exploited this motion residual to detect the intra-frame forgery in a video. Generally, each GOP in encoded video represent as local temporal window. Many researchers [138,139] works with fixed GOP size in a forged encoded video. However, those techniques not suitable flexible GOP size in advanced video framework. So, overcome fixed GOP size limitation, Chen *et al.* [137] adopted collusion operators in the extraction of motion residual in their proposed work. To detect the intra-frame video forgery, at first, Chen *et al.* [137] compute the motion residual using the collusion operation as follows:

a) A collusion operation inside a temporal window of the target video frame sequence, which centered at frame *F(k)* with the window size of $L = 2 \times L_h + 1$ ( $L_h$ is the number of left and right neighbor frames of *F(k)*) , is defined as:

$$C^k = C_{i,j}^k = \mathfrak{C}[F_{i,j}^{(k-L_h)}, \dots\dots\dots F_{i,j}^k, \dots\dots\dots F_{i,j}^{(k+L_h)}] \qquad (11)$$

where $C^k$ is the colluded result for frame *F(k)*. The collusion operator $\mathfrak{C}$ is an aggregated function that groups the pixels in the corresponding position of every frames in the temporal window to generate $C_{i,j}^k$ .

b) The motion residual for $k^{th}$ frame is calculated as follows:

$$R^k = |F^k - C^k| \qquad (12)$$

Since, the motion residual, $R^k$ do not rely on the GOP size and therefore it is very useful in advanced video, where flexible GOP size use.

An authentic video sequence, recorded by a surveillance camera, is shown in Fig. 4(a) and their corresponding forged video sequence, where two men (marked with white circular dotted line) were erased, is shown in Fig. 4(b). The authors[137] extract the motion residual of frame number 40 in the authentic video and its corresponding forged frame, which

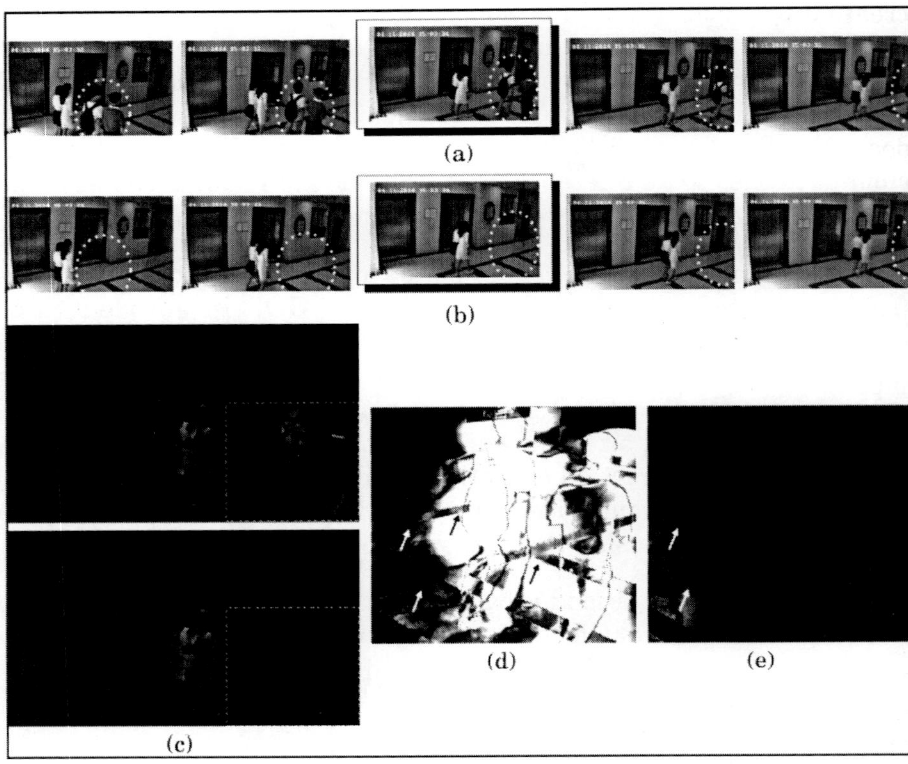


**Fig. 4:** (a) Authentic video sequence from frame number 1 to 80 with step size 20. (b) Corresponding Forged video sequence, where two men are eliminate. (c) Top and bottom: $R^{40}$, namely motion residual of frame 40 of authentic video sequence and forged video sequence respectively. (d) and (e) are enlargement of the rectangle region surrounded by dashed lines in the top and bottom figure of c, respectively. The data values in (e) are remapped to fill the entire intensity range [0, 255] so that its contrast can be increased. To facilitate the comprarison between (d) and (e), the data values in (d) which are less than or equal to the maximum value in (e) are also remapped to [0, 255], while the values higher than the maximum are mapped to the rightmost intensity.

are present in Fig. 4(c). For visual understanding, the zoom in version of authentic region (which is tampered later) and forged region are shown in Fig. 4(d) and Fig. 4(e) respectively[137]. In Fig. 4(d), the arrows indicate a layer of light gray shadow corresponding to the variety of luminance roughs out the floor tile pattern. However, it can observe from *Fig.* 4(e), in the same corresponding forged region of the contrast-increased $R^{40}$ of the forged video, the floor tile pattern rendered by the light gray shadow disappears abruptly around the region where the two walking men erased from. Exploiting this abrupt changes of motion residual Chen *et al.*[137] detect the object based intra-frame forgery in videos. The authors used ensemble classifier, whose decision is based on majority voting, to detect whether a video is single compressed, double compressed without forged and double compressed with forged. Seven image steganalytic features, CC-PEV[140], SPAM[141], CDF[142], CF*[143], SRM[144], CC-JRM[145] and J+SRM[145], are extracted from motion residuals and fed an input of ensemble classifier. At the first step, the authors detect the tested video is single compressed or double compressed through ensemble classifier. At second step, classified the double compressed video with forged and not forged. If the tested video found forged, then perform the localization operation to locate the forged region within the frames in a video. This technique works efficiently to detect the intra-frame forgery for variable GOP structure. But the performance of localization of forged region is very poor.

## 2.2 Upscale-crop Forgery Detection

The earliest work done by[146], to detect spatial as well as temporal forgery in both interlaced and de-interlaced videos. For de-interlaced video, the authors observed that the correlation distribution, introduced by the camera or de-interlacing algorithm, is disturb for tampering video. For interlaced video, the authors show that resampling operation introduces inequality in the motion between fields of a single frame and across field of neighboring frames, which are equal for authentic interlaced video. This technique works effectively only for uncompressed and low compressed video. For heavy compressed de-interlaced video, it is very difficult to estimate the de-interlacing correlation due to compression artifacts. So, performance degrades for high compressed video.

Another upscale-crop and partial manipulation detection technique was presented in[147]. The authors extracted Sensor Pattern Noise (SPN) from reference source camera and designed two minimum average correlation energy Mellin radial harmonic (MACE-MRH) correlation filters from the corresponding reference SPN. The first filter is designed for suspicious video is not scaled and have a very large correlation value. On the other hand, the second filter is designed to maintain a high correlation value even if the suspicious video is upscaled. Based on the two cross-correlation values between the different MACE-MRH correlation filters and the test video SPN, the authors judge whether the test video forged or not. However, this technique found to be dependent on a large number of content dependent parameters and thresholds that required extremely careful empirical setting. To increase the efficiency to detect the upscale-crop forgery in digital video, Singh *et al.*[111] used two artifacts, pixel correlations and noise variations.

## 3. INTER-FRAME VIDEO FORGERY DETECTION

According to the existing literature, there exist broadly two approaches to detect compressed video forgery. These are scene dependency based, and compression artifacts exploitation based approaches. Scene dependency based video forgery detection techniques[96,120,148,149,150] rely on the visual contents of each frame in a video. On the other hand, compression artifacts based video forgery detection techniques such as[109,116,128,151] exploit different types of artifacts, produced during the video encoding and decoding processes. Next, we present an overview of related literature in both these directions.

### 3.1. Compression Artifact Based Inter-Frame Video Forgery Detection

Wang *et al.*[152] proposed a double compression detection based inter-frame video forgery in MPEG-1 video. We know, in a GOP of a video sequence, P and B frames are predicted from directly or indirectly from I frame. When some frames are deleted or inserted in the video sequence and re-encoded the forged video sequence to create the forged video. During this re-encoded process, the type of subsequent frames after location of forgery operation will be changed. The details process of re-encoding forged video sequence after some frames deletion is shown in Fig. 5. In Fig. 5, first row shows the original video sequence, second row shows the video sequence after 3 frames deletion and last row is the re-encoded forged video sequence. If we look on the third row, we can see first two P-frame come from first original GOP, but third P-frame generated from I-frame of second GOP. So, the similarity between second and third P-frames of forged video sequence decreases due to the three frames deletion. So that, the motion compensated error increases. The authors used this motion compensated error to detect the inter-frame video forgery detection. However, this method is very

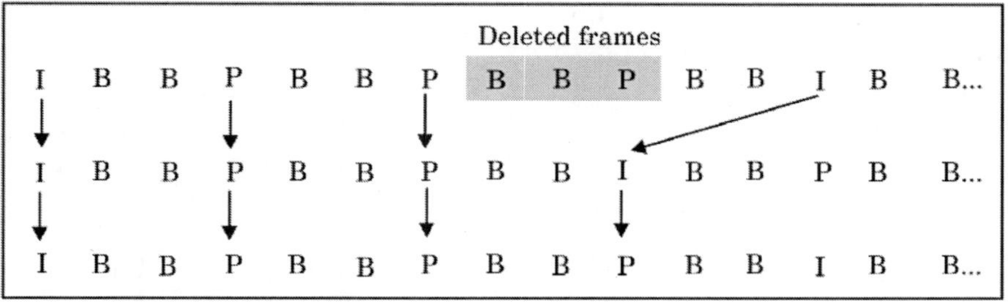


**Fig. 5:** Deletion of three frames in a video sequence.

sensitive to noise and change of GOP. Also, it is unable to detection the forgery when the number of deleted frames is an integral multiple of the GOP.

To increase the performance of forgery detector, Su *et al.*[109] used Motion Compensated Edge Artifact (MCEA) as feature to detect the frame deletion type of forgery detection in MPEG-2 videos. MPEG-2 video use block based motion compensated prediction. So, MCEA generated due to the blocking impairment and motion compensated prediction. When coarse quantization is combined with motion-compensated prediction, blocking artifacts propagate from I-frames into subsequent frames and accumulate, causing structured high frequency noise that is no longer located at block boundaries. MCEA energy has a deep relation with temporal correlation between two subsequent P-frames in a GOP. If frame deletion is performed in a video sequence, then the changes of MCEA energy used as a suitable feature to detect the frame deletion forgery. When coarse quantization is combined with motion-compensated prediction, blocking artifacts propagate from I-frames into subsequent frames and accumulate, causing structured high frequency noise that is no longer located at block boundaries. MCEA energy has a deep relationship with the temporal correlation between two subsequent P-frames in a GOP. If frame deletion type of forgery perform in a video sequence, then the changes of MCEA energy used a suitable feature to detect the forged video. In this work, the authors define an impact factor $a$, the MCEA value distribution of P-frame in a GOP, as Eq. (13)

$$\alpha = \frac{|MCEA^{i+2} - MCEA^{i+1}|}{|MCEA^{i+1} - MCEA^{i}|} \tag{13}$$

where $MCEA^i$, $MCEA^{i+1}$ and $MCEA^{i+2}$ separately denote the *MCEA* value of the first, second and third P-frame in a GOP. This $\alpha$ value is used as decision threshold to detect the frame deletion type of forgery. The impact factor $a$ changes significantly, if the some frames deletion between I and P frames or Two P frames. But, performance of this method decreases when video sequence with low motion.

In another work[117], the authors detect the frame deletion forgery by exploiting the periodic artifacts of DCT coefficient in P and B frames. By default in weighting matrixes, in high frequency area, AC DCT coefficient values of intra weighting matrix are much greater than inter weighting matrix at the same position. Since, inter-frame residual signal contain more high frequency component compare to intra-frame signal. So, to reduce the block boundary artifacts, low quantization step are used in this high frequency area of inter-frame signal compare to intra-frame signal. Hence, the high frequency component in inter-coded frames more than adjacent intra-coded frames. To, utilize this phenomenon, a detection factor *EH*, sum of energies, for each frame is defined over a subset of zigzag scanned DCT coefficients as follows:

$$EH = \sum_{b=1}^{N} \sum_{i>c} \theta_{i,b} \tag{14}$$

where N is the number of 8 × 8 DCT block in a frame, i is the index of DCT coefficients, c is the index of DCT coefficients from which high frequency started and $\theta_{i,b}$ denotes the $i^{th}$ DCT coefficients of $b^{th}$ DCT block.

The authors in[117] extract the EH value for a video sequence, which are presented in Fig. 6. From Fig. 6, we can see the EH value of inter-coded frames larger then intra-coded frames. As we saw earlier, if some frames are deleted from a video sequences, then the coding type of subsequent frames after the deletion point will be changed due to the double compression. So, when some I-frames transcoded into p or B-frames, their high frequency component could be lower than that of adjacent P or B-frames, which are remain same type coding of first compression.

Also, the authors in[117] calculate EH value of B frames experimentally and shows the EH distribution plot of B frames, which are shown in Fig. 7. Fig. 7(a) and Fig. 7(b) shows a EH value of B-

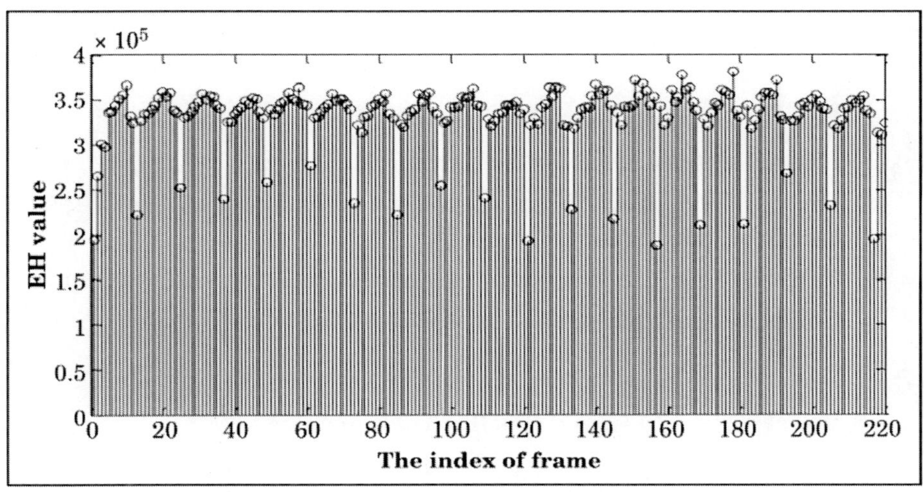


**Fig. 6:** EH of every frame of a video sequence.

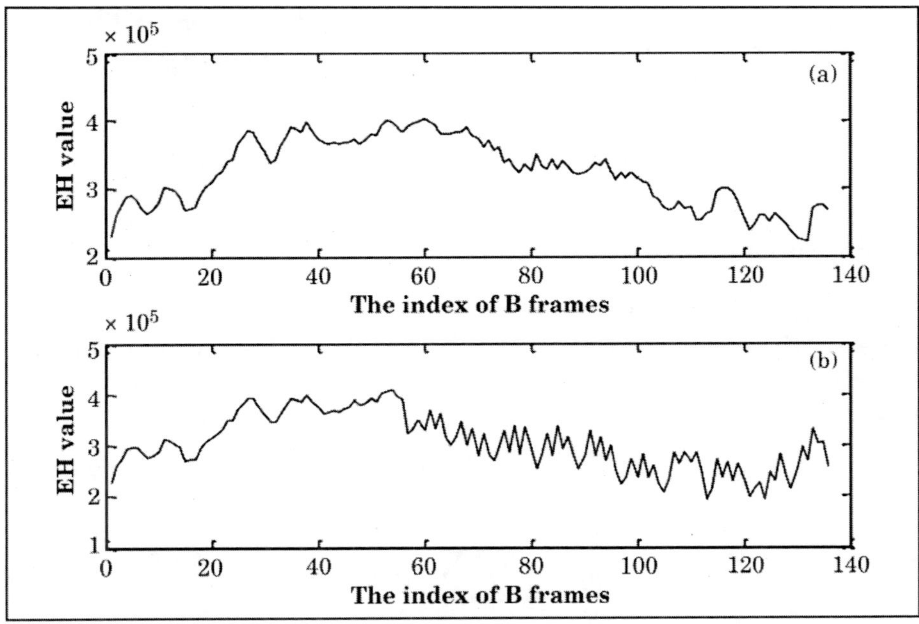


**Fig. 7:** The EH value of B frames, (a) refers to the original sequence, (b) refers to the doctored sequence.

frames of an authentic video and forged video, respectively. From Fig. 7(b), we can found that clear periodic artifact occurs in EH value of forged video after forged location. So, to detect the forged video, Su *et al.*[117] used this phenomenon and proposed the following steps:

1. Decode all the frames from a video.
2. Extract detection factor $EH_B$ from all B-frames
3. Divide $EH_B$ of all B-frames into $n$ overlapping segment; the length of each segment being $m$.
4. Perform Discrete Fourier Transform (DFT) on each segment.
5. Compute a discrimination factor $D$ as follows:

$$D = \frac{\left|3F_n(u) - \left(F_n(u-1) + F_n(u) + F_n(u+1)\right)\right|}{\left(F_n(u-1) + F_n(u) + F_n(u+1)\right)} - \frac{\left|3F_1(u) - \left(F_1(u-1) + F_1(u) + F_1(u+1)\right)\right|}{\left(F_1(u-1) + F_1(u) + F_1(u+1)\right)} \quad (15)$$

   where $n$ denote the index of segment, $Fn(u)$ denote the DFT coefficient of $n^{th}$ segment and $u$ is the two times frequency point corresponding to the periodicity which equals 8.
6. If $D$ > *threshold,* then the tested video is forged.
7. Else, the tested video is authentic.

However, this method also suffers when number of frame deletion is integral multiple of GOP size.

In 2013, Shanableh[116] proposed a machine learning based method to detect the frame deletion type of forgery. Here, the author computed 8 distinct features from every P and B-frames. Those features are follows:

- The mean prediction residual energy of non-intra coded MBs is calculated by equation (16).

$$\mu_E = \frac{1}{N}\sum_i \sum_j P_j(i) \quad (16)$$

  where N is the total number of predicted MBs in a video sequence for a P or B frame and $P_j$ *(i)* is the sum of absolute residual values of $j^{th}$MB of $i^{th}$ frame.
- The standard deviation of prediction residual energy of non-intra coded MBs is calculated by equation (17).

$$\sigma_E = \sqrt{E[(P_j(i) - \mu_E)^2]} \tag{17}$$

where operator E denotes the expectation value and $P_j(i)$ is the sum of absolute residual values of $j^{th}$MB of $i^{th}$ frame.

- The mean and standard deviation of percentage of intra-coded MBs is calculated by equation (18) and (19) respectively.

$$\mu_{intra} = \frac{1}{N}\sum_i I(i) \tag{18}$$

$$\sigma_{intra} = \sqrt{E[(I(i) - \mu_{intra})^2]} \tag{19}$$

where N is the total number of predicted P or B frame in a video sequence, operator E is the expectation value and $I(i)$ is the percentage of intra coded MBs in $i^{th}$ frame.

- The mean and standard deviation of estimated PSNR value is computed by equation (20) and (21) respectively.

$$\mu_{PSNR} = \frac{1}{N}\sum_i \widehat{P(i)} \tag{20}$$

$$\sigma_{PNSR} = \sqrt{E[(\widehat{P(i)} - \mu_{PSNR})^2]} \tag{21}$$

where N is the total number of predicted P or B frame in a video sequence, operator E is the expectation value and $\widehat{P(i)}$ is the estimated PSNR of $i^{th}$ frame.

- The mean and standard deviation of quantization scale values is computed using Eq. (22) and (23) respectively.

$$\mu_q = \frac{1}{N}\sum_i \sum_j Q_j(i) \tag{22}$$

$$\sigma_{PNSR} = \sqrt{E[(Q_j(i) - \mu_q)^2]} \tag{23}$$

where N is the total number of MBs in a video sequence for a P or B frame, operator E is the expectation value and $Q_j(i)$ is the quantization scale of MB of $i^{th}$ frame.

The overview of the proposed method in [116] is shown in Fig. 8. Here, the authors perform the normalize operation on extracted

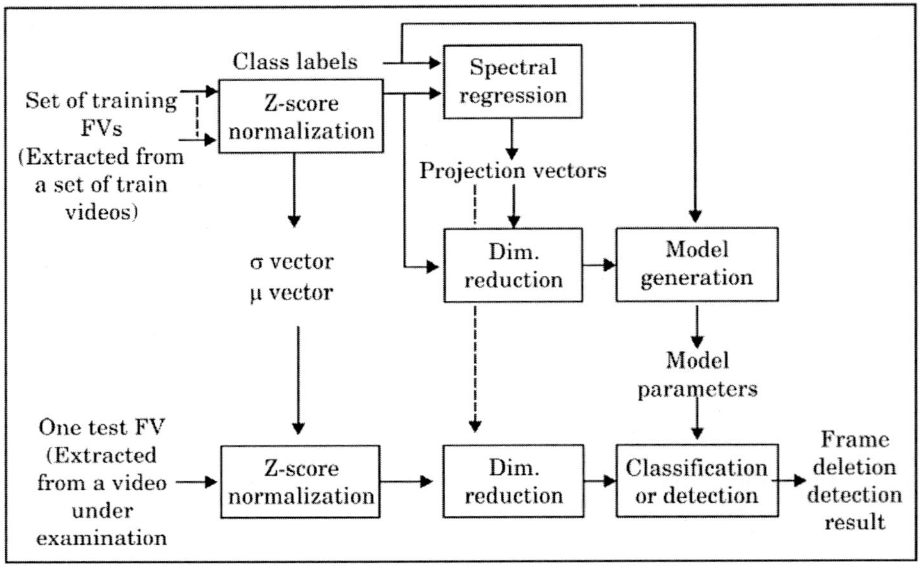


**Fig. 8:** Block diagram of frame deletion forgery detection method.

features and also perform dimension reduction operation using Spectral Regression. These dimension reduced features were used as input to train the classifier. Here, the author used Support Vector Machine (SVM), K- Nearest Neighbour (K-NN) and logistic regression classifier to detect the frame deletion forgery. This technique is effective for both Variable Bit Rate (VBR) and Constant Bit Rate (CBR) video coded. However, this method cannot localize the forged location.

In 2016, Aghamaleki *et al.*[110] proposed a novel method to detect and localize the inter-frame forgery in a video. Their proposed method consist of three modules: Double compression detection, inter-frame forgery detection and decision fusion. As we discuss earlier, to manipulate a video, first need to decompress the single compressed video. Then perform the manipulation operation and recompressed the forged video sequence. So, double compression process involved in video tampering process. Hence, double compression detection is an important clue to detect the tampering video. In double compression detection module, Aghamaleki *et al.*[110] extracted DCT coefficients of all I-frames and first significant digit distribution of extracted DCT coefficients used to identify single compressed and double compressed videos in spatial domain. But, double compression detection is not always imply the existence of manipulation in the double compressed video. Therefore, a second module proposed by Aghamaleki *et al.*[110] to detect the inter-frame forgeries based on the time domain analysis to residual errors of P-frame. Here, the authors employ quantization traces in time domain to find the forgeries location. But, this quantization traces is very sensitive to noise and video motion. To overcome such problem, the authors introduce a spatial mask to extract areas with dominant quantization traces. To achieving this goal, an optimization method is applied on two parameters identifying entropy of frames and motion content. Then, extract the new features for time domain analysis based on the optimized parameters. In third module, output of first module (double compression detection) and output of second module (inter-frame forgeries detection) are fed into decision fusion to classify the tested video into three categories: single compressed video, double compressed video with manipulating and double compressed video without manipulating. Decision module play an important role to minimized the false positive and false negative using the following rules:

- ***Rule 1*:** If a video segment is categorized as a forged video by inter-frame forgeries detection module, it is classified as double compressed video with manipulating by decision fusion module.
- ***Rule 2*:** A video segment that is categorized as a probably forged video by inter-frame forgeries detection module and a doubly compressed video by double compression detection module, is classified as a double compressed video with manipulating by decision fusion module.
- ***Rule 3*:** A video segment that is categorized as a probably tampered video inter-frame forgeries detection module and a single compressed video by double compression detection module, is classified as a single compressed video.
- ***Rule 4*:** A video segment that is categorized as a non-tampered video by inter-frame forgeries detection module and a double compressed video by double compression detection module, is classified as a double compressed video without manipulating by decision fusion module.
- ***Rule 5*:** A video segment that is categorized as a non-tampered video by inter-frame forgeries detection module and a single compressed video by double compression detection module, is classified as a single compressed video by decision fusion module.

This method produce acceptable performance rate for fixed camera and moving content. However, performance of this method degrades for video captured through mobile camera and severe moving content.

## 3.2 Scene Based Inter-Frame Video Forgery Detection

The Lucas Kanade optical flow[153] is proposed by B.D. Lucas and T. Kanade. Fig. 9 and Fig. 10 generated by[120] experimentally. From Fig. 9, we can notice optical flow maintain a consistency for authentic KTH video sequence. But, this consistency is break at forged location in a forged video sequence as shown in Fig. 10 Chao *et al.* [120] used this optical flow to detect the frame insertion and deletion type of video forgeries. The authors used this optical flow in two ways to identify the type of the forgery.

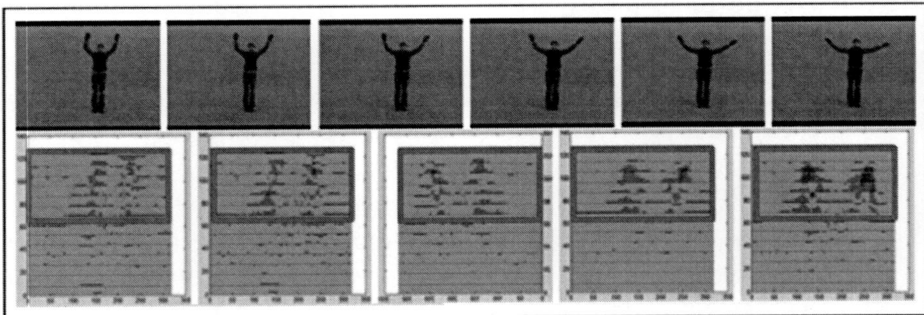

**Fig. 9:** Authentic video sequence (first row) and their optical flows (last row).

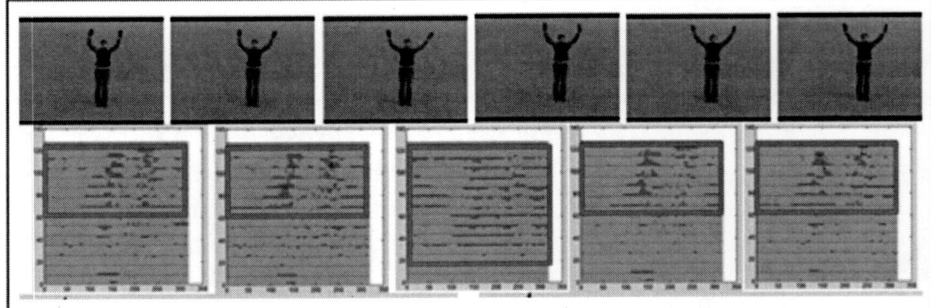

**Fig. 10:** Forged (by frame deletion) video sequence (first row) and their optical flows (last row).

To detect the frame insertion type of forgery detection, Chao *et al.*[120] proposed the following steps:

1) Each video is divided into equal-size windows. Here the window size is 16, because the optimal size for binary search is 2^n, and 16 is less than the frame rate (25Fps), ensuring that there won't be an integrate insertion in a window.
2) Then compute the Lucas Kanade optical flows $S_k(x)$ in $X$ and $S_k(y)$ in $Y$ direction between the first and the last frame in each window.
3) Compute the average optical flow in $X$ and $Y$ directions with below equation (where $X$ can be replaced with $Y$). *NOW* is the number of windows in a video; *AOF(x)* is the average optical flows in the X direction, calculated as :

$$AOF(x) = \frac{1}{NOW} \sum_{k=1}^{NOW} S_k(x) \tag{24}$$

4) When optical flows for windows k, satisfying equation (25) either in X or Y direction, then this window need further investigation and perform steps 4 to 6. Otherwise, that window is authentic.

$$S_k(x) \geq T \times AOF(x) \tag{25}$$

5) Perform binary search within suspected window to locate the forged location. Each suspected window is divided into two equal size sub-window. Compute the optical flows between the first and last frame of sub-window in both X and Y direction.

   If optical flows of left sub-window and right sub-window satisfying the equation (26), where X can be replaced by Y, then forged location may exist in left sub-window. Continue step 5 until window size equal to 1.

$$S_L(x) \geq T \times S_R(x) \tag{26}$$

   Where T is threshold, L for left sub-window and R for right sub-window.

   Else If optical flows of left sub-window and right sub-window satisfying the Eq. (27), where X can be replaced by Y, then forged location may exist in left sub-window. Continue step 5 until window size equal to 1.

$$S_R(x) \geq T \times S_L(x) \tag{27}$$

If a shift point is detected, then frames before and after this point are quite different in their optical flows. If optical flow between frame K and (K+1) and that between frame (K+1) and (K+2) meet equation (26), then (K+1) is a shift point. Else if two optical flows meet equation (27); then (K+2) is a shift point. If the optical flows meet none of the two equations (26) and (27), then it means that there is no shift point in this suspicious window.

6) After the binary research in all suspicious windows, further detection is conducted to identify insertion part. For each point I and J, three optical flows will be computed: optical flow between (I-2) and (I-1), optical flow between (I-1) and (J+1), optical flow between (J+1) and (J+2). If they are similar, it means that the video frames before the shift point I and after the shift point J come from the same video, so frames between these two shift points are inserted.

To detect the frame deletion type of forgery in video, Chao *et al.*[120] performed the following steps:

1) Extract all the frames from the video sequence.
2) Compute optical flow between $I^{th}$ and $(I+1)^{th}$ frame.
3) If equation (28) satisfy in either X or Y direction, where X can be replaced by Y, then it is a suspicious deletion location and perform steps 4 to 6. Otherwise it is authentic location.

$$S_{(k,k+1)}(x) \geq \frac{T_1}{4} \times S_{(k-2,k-1)}(x) \tag{28}$$

where $S_{(k,k+1)}(x)$ is the optical flow between k and (k+1) frames in X direction and $T_1$ is the first threshold. Replace all X by Y to get the average optical flow in Y direction.

4) Compute the average optical flow with equation (29) in both X and Y directions.

$$AOF(x) = \frac{1}{NOF-1} \sum_{k=1}^{NOF-1} S_{(k,k+1)}(x) \tag{29}$$

where *AOF (x)* is the average optical flow in X direction and NOF is number of optical flow figure in a video. Replace all X by Y to get the average optical flow in Y direction.

5) If optical flow of suspicious location in either X or Y direction satisfy the equation (30), then some frames deleted between k and (k+1) frames location.

$$S_{(k,k+1)}(x) \geq T_2 \times AOF(x) \tag{30}$$

where $T_2$ is the second threshold.

6) If none of the optical flow satisfy the equation (30) in neither X direction nor Y direction, then this video hasn't been forged with frame deletion.

In 2015, Zhang *et al.*[148] proposed a consistency of correlation, between subsequent frames, based method to detect the frame insertion and deletion type of video forgeries. As we know, video is consisting of still images and difference between any subsequent adjacent frames are very low. So, the correlation between any subsequent frames is consistence. But, if some frames are inserted into original video sequence or deleted from original video sequence, then consistency of correlation will be low at forged location in the video sequence. Zhang *et al.*[148] used this phenomena and perform the following steps to detect the frame insertion and deletion type of forgeries detection:

1) Extract all the frames from a video.
2) Covert all RGB frames into Gray level frames
3) Compute Local Binary Pattern (LBP) texture feature for every frames.
4) Compute Pearson Correlation Coefficient[154], $r_k$ between $k^{th}$ and $(k+1)^{th}$ LBP coded frames using the following equation:

$$r_k = \frac{\sum_i \sum_j (F_k(i,j) - \overline{F_k}) \times (F_{k+1}(i,j) - \overline{F_{k+1}})}{\sqrt{\sum_i \sum_j (F_k(i,j) - \overline{F_k})^2 \times \sum_i \sum_j (F_{k+1}(i,j) - \overline{F_k + 1})^2}} \tag{31}$$

where k=1,2,3,..........n-1. n is the total number of frames in the test video. $F^k$ $(i, j)$ is the LBP value of $k_{th}$ frame at location (i, j) and $\overline{F_k}$ is the mean LBP value of $k_{th}$ frame.

5) Compute Quotients of consecutive correlation coefficients of local binary pattern (QCCoLBPs), $\Delta r_k$, using the following equation:

$$\Delta r_k = \begin{Bmatrix} r_k/r_{k+1} & if\ r_k \geq r_{k+1} \\ r_{k+1}/r_k & if\ r_k < r_{k+1} \end{Bmatrix} \tag{32}$$

where *k=1,2,3,........n—1*.

6) Calculate mean ($\mu_1$) and standard deviation ($\sigma_1$) of sequence $\Delta r_k$ using the following equations:

$$\mu_1 = \frac{\sum_{k=1}^{n-2} \Delta r_k}{n-2} \tag{33}$$

$$\sigma_1 = \sqrt{\frac{\sum_{k=1}^{n-2} (\Delta r_k - \mu_1)^2}{n-2}} \tag{34}$$

7) Apply Tchebyshev inequality [155] for coarse detection as follows: If equation 21 satisfy, then r the qualified QCCoLBPs as normal points and $\Delta r_k$, marked as $\Delta \acute{r}_k$.

$$|\Delta r_k - \mu_1| < T_1 \times \sigma_1 \tag{35}$$

where $T_1$ represents first threshold.

8) Compute $\mu_2$ and $\sigma_2$ over $\Delta \acute{r}_k$ and apply Tchebyshev inequality[155] to detect forged location as follows:

   If equation 22 satisfy, then $k^{th}$ location detect as forged location in a video sequence.

$$|\Delta r_k - \mu_2| \geq T_2 \times \sigma_2 \tag{36}$$

where $T_2$ represents second threshold.

9) If none of $\Delta r_k$ satisfy equation 22, then the tested video is authentic.

Performance of this method degrades when number of frames deletion is less and also not able to detect forgery for completely silent video.

Another similar kind of word was done by Liu *et al.*[149], to detect the frame insertion, deletion, duplication and replacement type of inter-frame forgeries detection. To detect the inter-frame forgeries, two level of investigation were performed namely, coarse detection and fine detection. In coarse detection, convert the color image from a 3D color space into 2D opposite color space to obtain the chromaticity aberration of the image. Then compute the Zernike Opponent chromaticity moments (ZOCM), in a two dimensional opponent chromaticity space using the Zernike moment correlation. Based on the ZOCM difference between two adjacent frames, detect the outliers. The coarse detection cannot guarantee that all the detected outliers are forged location. So, second level investigation namely fine detection introduced to conform the forged location among the detected outliers of coarse detection. Fine detection performs the following steps:

1) If $l$ is a outlier, extract $k$-nearest RGB frames around point $i$, $Y_l$ contains $(2\times(k+1))$ frames and convert those frames into gray level frames.

$$Y_l = \{I_{l+j}(x,y)|j = 1,2,\ldots..(k+1)\} \cup \{I_{l-j}(x,y)|j = 0,1,\ldots.k\} \quad (37)$$

2) Calculate the texture coarseness of each frame in $Y_l$. Determine the max scope of the pixels by $w_{max}$. For $w$=1,2,....... $w_{max}$ Perform the following steps until $w= w_{max}$.

*Step 1:* Calculate the average over the neighborhood of size $2^w \times 2^w$ at the point *(x,y)* according to equation (38).

$$A_w(x,y) = \sum_{i=x-2^{w-1}}^{x+2^{w-1}-1} \sum_{j=y-2^{w-1}}^{y+2^{w-1}-1} {I(i,j)}/{2^{2w}} \quad (38)$$

where I $(i, j)$ represent a pixel intensity in selected cell.

*Step 2:* for each point compute the averages of non-overlapping neighbor on the active window of the point in horizontal and vertical direction separately according to equation (39) and (40).

$$E_{w,h} = |A_w(x+2^{w-1},y) - A_w(x-2^{w-1},y) \quad (39)$$

$$E_{w,h} = |A_w(x,y+2^{w-1}) - A_w(x,y-2^{w-1})|| \quad (40)$$

*Step 3:* Find the $w_{best}$ among 1 to $w_{max}$ which maximize E in either direction, pick the best size $S_{best}(x,y) = 2^{w_{best}}$ which gives the highest output value $E_{max}$ shown in equation (41) and (42).

$$S_{best}(x,y) = 2^{w_{best}} \tag{41}$$

$$E_{w_{best}} = E_{max} \tag{42}$$

*Step 4:* Finally, compute the average of $S_{best}(x, y)$ according to equation (43), over the image, which is the coarseness feature for $F_{crs}$ the input image.

$$F_{crs} = \frac{1}{m \times n}\sum_{i=1}^{m}\sum_{j=1}^{n} S_{best}(i,j) \tag{44}$$

where m = height of the frame and n = width of the frame.

3) Calculate the difference between two adjacent frames using equation (45) based on the coarseness $F_{crs}$.

$$SF_t = |F_{crs}^{t+1} - F_{crs}^{t}| \tag{45}$$

$$t\epsilon l-k, l-k+1, \dots\dots. l, l+1, \dots\dots. l+k$$

4) Find $S_l$ using equation (46)

$$S_l = \max\{S_{l-k}, S_{l-k+1}, \dots\dots\dots S_{l+k}\}. \tag{46}$$

5) If $, S_l \geq$ *Threshold* then location l in the tested video is forged Else if none such l are found, the tested video is authentic. Experimental results produced the satisfaction results for slow motion video. But, this method also suffer for fast moving contain video.

Recently, Zhao *et al.*[156] proposed two step verification method to detect the frame insertion, deletion and duplication forgeries in a single video shot. At the first step, extract all the frames from the video and convert all RGB frames into HSV (Hue-Saturation-Value) color space. Compute H-S and S-V color histogram of every frame. Here, H-V color histogram was not considered because H-S and H-V color histogram looks like same. Then calculating the histogram similarity between two adjacent frames using the Pearson correlation as shown in equation (47). Let $h_i = \{h_{i1}, h_{i2}, \dots\dots\dots. h_{iN}\}$ denote histogram of $i^{th}$ frame.

$$S(h_i, h_{i+1}) = \frac{\sum_{k=1}^{N}(h_{ik} - \overline{H_i})(h_{(i+1)k} - \overline{H_{(i+1)}})}{\sqrt{\sum_{k=1}^{N}(h_{ik} - \overline{H_i})^2 \sum_{k=1}^{N}(h_{(i+1)k} - \overline{H_{(i+1)}})^2}} \quad (47)$$

where $\overline{H_i} = \frac{1}{N}\sum_{j=1}^{N} h_{ij}$ *i=1,2,3... ...t. t*= total frames in avideo. $S(h_i, h_{i+1})$ is the histogram similarity between $i^{th}$ and $(i+1)^{th}$ frames. $N$ is the number of bins in a histogram. Then draw a distribution plot over the histogram similarity. If consistency of this distribution plot is break, means falling peak found, in any location then that location might be forged by frame insertion or deletion. For frame duplication forgery, the similarity distribution will be exactly same between copy original and duplicate frames. But some cases for authentic video, falling peak may found due to the fast moving content. So, Zhao *et al.*[156] perform second level investigation based on feature matching between two adjacent frames of falling peak location for frame insertion and deletion forgery. So, to conform the forgeries, Speed Up Robust Features (SURF) are extracted and then matching the doubtful SURF coded frames using Fast Library for Approximation Nearest Neighbor (FLANN) algorithm. If no match features found in between two adjacent frames at falling peak location, then that location detect as forged by frame insertion or deletion operation. But, when SURF features of two frames are same, then those two frame are duplicate of each other.

## 4. CONCLUSIONS

In this chapter, we have discussed about intra-frame and inter-frame video forgeries and also presented state-of-the-art techniques to detect these forms of forgeries. The performance of the existing video forensic techniques depends on the video codec used for compressing the video sequence. Specially, most of the forensic methods consider fixed GOP size. But, modern video compression standards, like H.264, H.265, use adaptive GOP and length of the GOP can be up to 250 (depends on the motion of content in the video). In such a situation, fixed GOP size based techniques fail completely.

Also, we showed that some methods detect video forgery based on the I-frame relocation. However, such techniques are unable to detect forgery in videos when the number of forged frames is an integral multiple of GOP. The state-of-the-art techniques suffer when the videos are captured with moving camera or the video contents have fast moving background.

Another problem in the domain of video forensic, especially for inter-frame video forgery, is that there is no standard dataset of realistic tampered videos with ground truths. Researchers in this domain have used self-created forged video datasets, which is a highly time consuming process. So, some standard benchmark dataset of realistic tampered videos are required in the domain of video forensics, to validate the video forensic researches conveniently.

# 16

# Counter Forensics: Major Threat to Forensic Technology

## 1. INTRODUCTION

In the earlier stages of image forensics, the tools and techniques were developed to solve existing forensic problems. The same thing happened in the domain of source camera identification too, where in the early stages of the evolution, different solutions were proposed and evaluated from different aspects. Later, the image source anonymization evolved, to counter the source camera identification. The main objective of image source anonymization is to protect the identity of the photographer against any attempts to identify the source camera device through PRNU noise analysis. From an image forensic point of view any attempt to perform image source anonymization is a way of impeding image source identification. A counter-forensic technique is a strategy used to defeat an existing forensic investigation technique. In counter-forensics, the goal of the adversary is to bypass the analysis of one or more forensic tools. Hence any technique serving such purpose is called attack or counter-forensic scheme. The principle of operation is majorly based on image anonymization, so as to prevent mapping back of an image to its correct source, being inspired by image anonymization techniques used in the literature for privacy protection of online users. Studying different counter forensic technique is extremely useful to plug the security leaks in source camera identification technique and further strengthen the robustness.

As shown in Fig. 1, source camera identification is the procedure of identifying the source camera of an image I. On the other hand, the

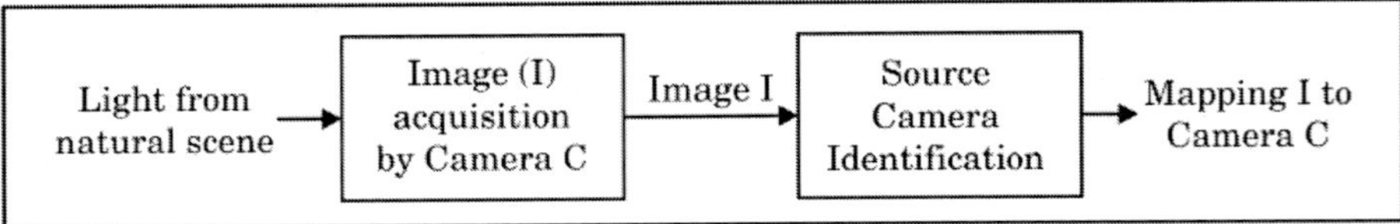


**Fig. 1:** Source Camera Identification Process

counter forensic procedure is shown in Fig. 2. The counter forensic techniques make the mapping of original source of a given image not possible through source camera identification methods.

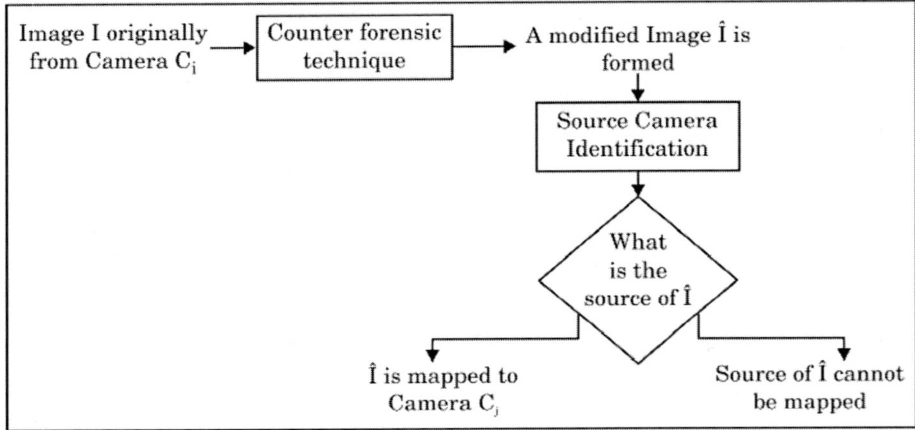


**Fig. 2:** Counter Forensics

In the literature, we can find different counter—forensic attacks which defeat the existing state-of-the-art camera model identification techniques. It is interesting to note that all the counter forensic techniques target the fingerprint based schemes by either removing the Photo Response Non-Uniformity (PRNU) content in an image or by weakening the underlying correlation mechanism. The major classes of counter—forensic attacks on camera model identification are Fingerprint Copy Attack[13], Adaptive PRNU Denoising[12], Seam Carving[14], and Inpainting[157].

The existing counter forensic technique fall into two categories. A counter forensic technique may cause the original source to be misclassified as another camera or it can just make the identification process less reliable. In the first category, if an authentic image I which originally belongs to camera $C_i$ is counter forensically modified to produce counter forensic image I and after applying the state-of-the-art source identification techniques on I, the source camera is found to be $C_j$. Fingerprint Copy Attack[13] falls under the first category. In the second category, when the source identification techniques are applied on I, the decision to map it to $C_{-i}$ becomes less reliable and hence the source mapping cannot be accomplished. Adaptive PRNU Denoising[12], Seam Carving[14], and Inpainting[157] come under the second category.

The rest of the chapter is organized as follows. Section 2 discusses the adaptive PRNU denoising attack, Section 3 discusses the fingerprint copy attack, Section 4 discusses the seam carving attack, Section 5 discusses the inpainting attack. In Section 6, experimental evaluation of all the attacks is presented. We conclude the chapter in Section 7.

## 2. ADAPTIVE PRNU DENOISING (APD)

One way of impeding image source attribution is to suppress the PRNU noise as much as possible. Image PRNU is resilient to various geometric and compression manipulations. Hence, to make an image untraceable to its source camera, different attacks started targeting the PRNU content of an image, a major identifier of the underlying sensor. Adaptive PRNU Denoising (APD) is one such counter-forensic attack which denoises an image, repetitively, until it has sufficiently suppressed the image PRNU to prevent its source mapping. In the following equation, a Denoising Filter (DF) is applied $m$ times to suppress the noise residual of an image I.

$$I = DF\left( DF\left( Df \ldots m\ times\ \ (I)\right)\right) = DF^{m}(I) \tag{1}$$

The procedural flow is shown in Fig. 3. The sensor pattern noise of the camera which has captured the image which needs to be anonymised is calculated as discussed in chapter 4. The APD process then applies a denoise filter many times until the correlation of the noise residual of the image and the sensor pattern noise comes to less than zero. A PCE correlation metric is used as the test statistic and the final image is then used to transmit over a network with its source fingerprint being removed.

The objective is to obtain an image which would correlate very poorly with its own PRNU noise pattern. In order to achieve this, the

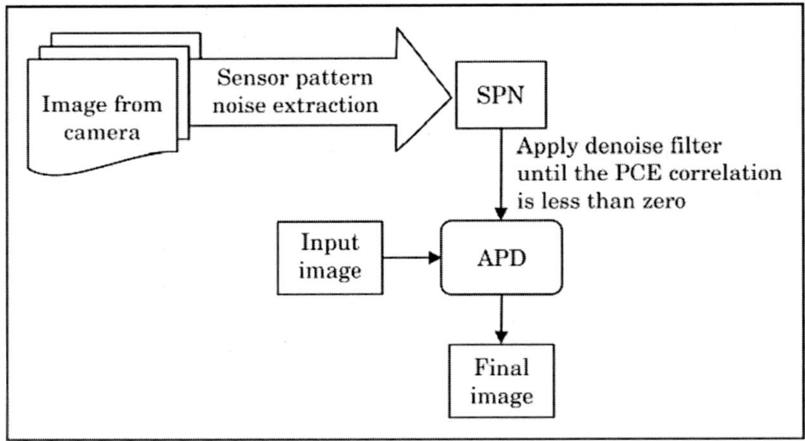


**Fig. 3:** APD Process

PRNU estimate of the image I (NR_I) is computed as in, and a magnitude adjustment factor β is estimated according to the equation below.

$$Corr\ ((I - \ \beta\, X\, NR_I), NR_I)\ \approx 0 \tag{2}$$

APD lowers the correlation of an image to its source efficiently, without affecting any visual artifact. Since no additional artifacts are introduced due to repeated denoising, to detect whether an image has undergone this process, is difficult.

## 3. FINGERPRINT COPY (FP COPY) ATTACK

Fingerprint copy, as the name suggests, is the technique of masking one camera's reference pattern with another. The adversary masks his own camera pattern with another innocent's camera pattern, thus resulting into high rate of false positives in camera model identification.

In a sensitive forensic application as camera model identification, it is of paramount importance to keep the false positive alarms minimal. Hence, fingerprint copy attack poses as an imminent threat to the credibility of forensic source identification systems, by leading an innocent to be detected wrongly as culprit.

Fingerprint copy attack is delivered as follows. Let image *I* be having originating from camera *A*, possessed by an adversary. Let us assume

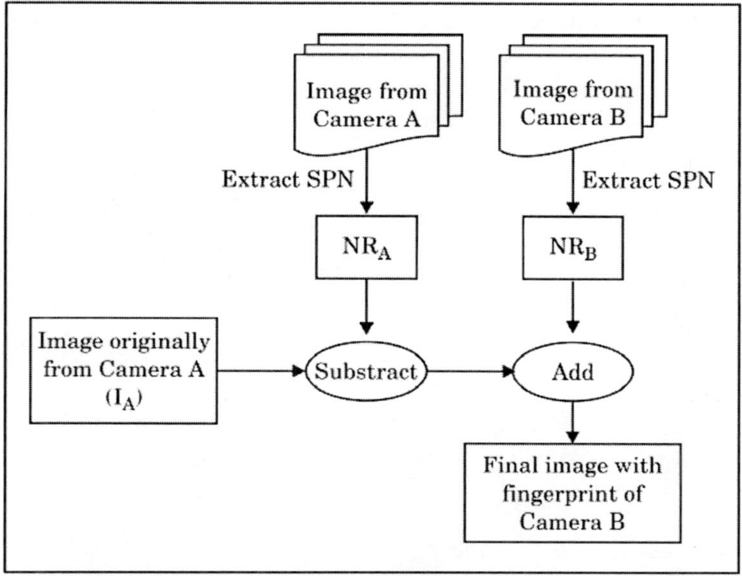


**Fig. 4:** Fingerprint Copy Attack

that the adversary additionally gets access to some images captured by some other person's camera *B*, and estimates the noise residuals of both cameras *A* and *B*, $NR_A$ and $NR_B$, respectively, from the available images. As shown in Fig. 4, now, he removes his camera's fingerprint from *I*, and adds the fingerprint of *B* to *I*, by the following:

$$I = I - \alpha X NR_A + \beta X NR_B \tag{3}$$

Where $NR_A$ and $NR_B$ are the noise residuals of cameras *A* and *B* respectively, and α and β are the camera substitution parameters that determine the strength of the fingerprint copy. As a result, the forensic analyst is fooled to believe that image *I* is originated from camera *B*, and not from *A*, after his investigations. This renders the owner of camera *B* to be falsely detected as the culprit, instead of that of camera *A*.

## 4. SEAM CARVING ATTACK

Seam Carving is a content aware image resizing approach which finds wide use in counter—forensics. Seam carving technique is used to disturb an image's reference noise pattern, so as to defeat PRNU based image source attribution, which operates by correlating image noise pattern with (possible) camera reference patterns. Specifically, seam carving disturbs the PRNU content of an image through image resizing, thus removes seams (connected paths of pixels with least variation from surrounding pixels) of an image.

An example for seam carving image is shown in Fig. 5. Part a of the Fig. shows the vertical seams superimposed. It can be observed that the vertical seams do not attempt to cross the edges of the coins which are the main objects in the picture. After the seams are removed as shown in part b of the Fig. 5, there are no visual distortions introduced.

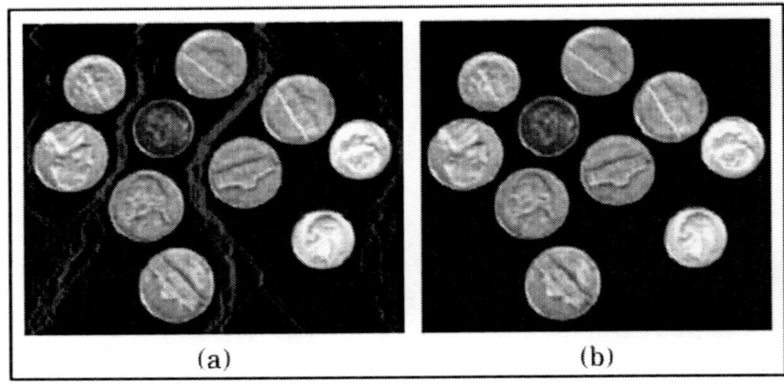


**Fig. 5:** Seam Carving example. (a) Coins image with 50 vertical seams superimposed, (b) Coins image after seam carving

For an image with *m* rows and *n* columns, a vertical seam *s* is nothing but a path connecting pixels from top to bottom with horizontal offsets (between adjacent rows) not more than one pixel, and is represented mathematically as,

$$s = \{s_i\}_{i=1}^{n-1} = \{(col(i), i)\}_{i=1}^{n-1}, where\ |col(i+1) - col\ (i)| \leq 1, \quad (4)$$

Where *i* represents an image column and *col(i)* is a mapping from [1...n] to [1...m]. The seam is a 8—connected path from top to bottom, with exactly one pixel per row.

An optimal seam s* is the seam with the lowest sum of energy, where the energy function is given by,

$$e(I) = \left|\frac{\partial I}{\partial x}\right| + \left|\frac{\partial I}{\partial y}\right| \quad (5)$$

and, an optimal seam $s^*$ is computed as,

$$s^* = \min_{s} \sum_{i=1}^{n} e(I(s_i)) \tag{6}$$

It is evident from the above equation that the optimal seam is computed using the cumulative minimum energy, for all possible connected seams, from the first to the last column. Such optimal seams are removed from the original image to get a seam carved image. What makes a seam carved image difficult to analyse, is the lack of information about the location or number of its seams removed. This is because the process of seam carving is irreversible, and the PRNU pattern of the seam carved image, will correlate very poorly with noise reference pattern of its source.

## 5. INPAINTING ATTACK

Image Inpainting is an image reconstruction technique used for restoration of damaged paintings or very old photographs. It found its use as a counter forensic attack against camera model identification, for the first time in[157]. Its basic operating principle is to reconstruct a pixel from its neighbourhood pixels, in such a way that, in doing so the underlying noise pattern of the image is disturbed, hence making its source identification impossible. In this section, we briefly describe the process of image inpainting used as counter—forensic attack. As shown in the block diagram (Fig. 6), the first step is to select and delete different blocks in the input image $I$. Then the blocks are reconstructed in parallel, and finally all blocks are spliced together to form the inpainted image.

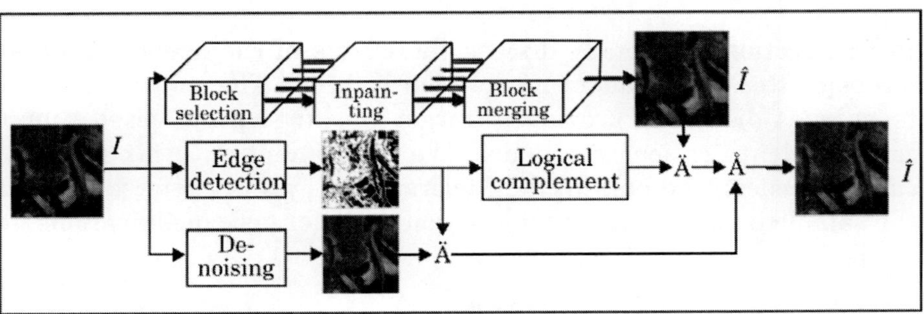


**Fig. 6:** Block diagram for inpainting attack

In the first step, to delete different blocks in an image, a pixel selector $S_s$ is used. ($S_s$ is a matrix with size same as that of the input image and takes a value of either 0 or 1.0 represents deletion of the pixel and 1 represents otherwise). Using $S_s$, the input image $I$ is modified to become $I_s$ where $I_s = S_s I$.

The inpainted image  is given by the following equation:

$$\hat{I}_s = \min_{I_s} \|S_s I_s - I_s\|_F^2 + \lambda \, \|R(I_s)\|_p^p \tag{7}$$

where,

‾ is the inversion operator,

$||\,.\,||_F$ represents the Frobenius norm,

$\lambda$ is the penalty parameter,

*R(.)* is a regularizer operator,

and $||\,.\,||_P$ is the $l_p$ norm.

The final merged image $\hat{I}$ is given by

$$\hat{I} = \sum_{s=1}^{N} (1 - S_s)\hat{I}_s \tag{8}$$

Where $N$ is the number of blocks.

## 6. EFFECT OF COUNTER FORENSICS ON FINGERPRINT BASED CAMERA MODEL IDENTIFICATION TECHNIQUES

In this section, we briefly discuss the effects of the above counter—forensic attacks on camera model identification. The counter forensic techniques discussed previously target the fingerprint based source camera identification techniques. We experiment with six different camera models, and present their average PCE values, before and after the sample images have undergone counter—forensic modifications, in Table 1.

The sensor pattern noise (SPN) of each camera with 100 natural images is calculated. 50 test images (which are not included in SPN calculation) are considered for each camera, and their PCE value against the source is calculated. The average PCE values are displayed in Table 1.

**Table 1:** Average PCE Computed for Six Different Camera Models using Authentic Images *vis-a-vis* Counter Forensically Modified Images

| | Average PCE Value | | | | |
|---|---|---|---|---|---|
| ***Camera model*** | ***With authentic images*** | ***APD*** | ***FP copy*** | ***Inpainting*** | ***Seam carved*** |
| AGFA 505X | 628.1 | –0.31 | 1.05 | 1.42 | 0.28 |
| CANON IXUS70 | 1281.3 | 0.86 | 3.18 | 0.54 | –1.52 |
| KODAK M1063 | 286.4 | 0.15 | 1.71 | 1.35 | 0.59 |
| NIKON D70 | 567.9 | –0.87 | 0.23 | 2.87 | 1.47 |
| OLYMPUS MJU | 663.7 | 1.48 | 2.54 | 0.55 | 0.77 |
| SAMSUNG L74 | 189.2 | 0.59 | 1.88 | 0.61 | 1.25 |

We compare the cases where the images are authentic *vis—a—vis* when various counter—forensic transformations are applied to them. The results show a clear disparity in PCE values, with a high PCE for authentic images and significantly low PCE for counter—forensic images. The results are in agreement with different counter forensic researches such as [12,13,14,157] that target fingerprint based source identification methods, and show that the state—of—the—art methods are highly risked by the presence of counter—forensics.

The counter—forensic attacks discussed above, pose a serious threat to the state—of—the—art camera model identification techniques. If left unattended, these could easily compromise crucial evidences in a court of law. In the following section, we study such properties of counter—forensically modified images, which enable their mapping to the original sources. We analyse the texture properties in counter—forensic images, and propose the adoption of texture based features, as the anti counter—forensic measure in camera model identification.

The source detection accuracy of authentic images *vis-à-vis* counter forensic images is shown in Table 2. In the experiment, 100 images from 10 camera models of Dresden image dataset are considered. Sensor pattern noise is extracted from 50 flat field images, and PCE correlation is calculated for all the authentic images. The same is repeated for the

APD images, FP Copy images, Inpainted images, Seam carved images of the 100 authentic images. It can be clearly observed that the counter forensic image pose a serious problem to PRNU based fingerprint technique of source camera identification.

**Table 2:** Source Detection Accuracy of Authentic images *vis-a-vis* counter forensic images

| | ***With authentic carved images*** | ***APD*** | ***FP Copy*** | ***Inpain-ting*** | ***Seam*** |
|---|---|---|---|---|---|
| Detection Accuracy | 99.5% | 1% | 2.4% | 0.9% | 0% |

## 7. CONCLUSIONS

The counter forensics poses a serious threat to the digital forensic technologies. In this chapter, counter forensics to PRNU based source camera identification technique is discussed. The four major threats of counter forensics, Adaptive PRNU denoising (APD), Fingerprint Copy, Inpainting, and Seam Carving are discussed. An experiment with authentic images and the corresponding counter forensic images is conducted and the results clearly show that the counter forensic images does a severe damage to PRNU based source camera identification. It is imperative in current day and age with so many image processing and editing tools readily available, the counter forensic techniques needs to be studied and analysed to further strengthen the digital forensic techniques.

# 17

# Deep Learning Based Counter Forensics

## 1. INTRODUCTION

Digital forensic techniques for source investigation and identification enable forensic analysts to map an image under question to its source device, in a completely blind way, with no *a-priori* information about the storage and processing. Such techniques operate based on blind image fingerprinting or machine learning based modelling using appropriate image features. Although researchers till date have succeeded to achieve extremely high accuracy (more than 99% on Dresden image dataset) as far as source device prediction is concerned, the practical application of the existing techniques is still doubtful. This is due to the existence of a critical open challenge known as counter forensics (discussed in chapter 7).

Counter-forensics with respect to camera model identification[12,13,14,157] are aimed towards defeating state-of-the-art camera model identification techniques by fooling the forensic analysis process. Counter-forensic attacks against camera model identification are majorly comprised of source anonymization techniques. Source anonymization is a form of intelligent adversarial attack, which hinders source attribution of images through illegitimate image modifications. Such attacks are motivated by image anonymization works that aim at user anonymity, which are of relevance in protecting the privacy of online users. However, image anonymity acts as a hindrance to forensic image source identification. Recent counter-forensic techniques have proved to be quite effective in battling state-of-the-art camera model identification. Hence, it is imperative that the state-of-the-art camera model identification techniques be made capable enough to resist counter-forensic attacks. In this context, here a deep learning based classification model using Convolutional Neural Networks (CNN) is proposed to detect whether an image (to be analysed forensically) is authentic, or it has undergone counter-forensic modifications which would result in invalidation of the forensic analysis results.

The major contribution in this paper is the development of a deep learning based CNN model for classification between authentic and counter-forensically modified images. In addition, the proposed model performs a second level of (multi-class) classification to identify the specific class of counter-forensic attack the (tampered) image has undergone. The performance of a machine learning system largely depends on how effectively features of the concerned dataset are identified and extracted. Many artificial intelligence problems are solved through machine learning, only when the appropriate features are successfully identified and extracted. It is this dependency of machine learning based models on the representation (features) of the data that many times makes such systems ineffective; specifically, when the features are difficult to be identified. Deep Learning is a fast emerging trend, where feature identification and extraction is taken care of by the underlying neural network, *i.e.,* the deep learning network does a representation learning for the given data. This ability of a deep neural network is utilized to perform a representation learning of counter-forensic images and hence to develop a classification model for those. A Convolutional Neural Network (CNN), used to build the proposed model in this work, is a special type of deep neural network which is based on linear mathematical convolution.

Rest of this chapter is organized as follows. In Section 2, we present a deep learning neural network architecture for source identification of counter forensic images, recently proposed by Sameer *et al.* in[158]. We present the Convolution Neural Network architecture of[158] in detail in Section 3. The experimental evaluation settings are described in Section 4. Section 5 presents the evaluation results. We conclude the chapter in Section 6.

## 2. AN ARCHITECTURE FOR COUNTER FORENSIC IMAGE SOURCE IDENTIFICATION

In Fig. 1, the operational flowchart of the proposed two-level classification system is presented. It shows that proposed model primarily consists of a counter-forensic detection module, which is a deep learning network (CNN) that detects whether the image is authentic or counter-forensically modified. If an image is detected to be authentic, it is taken up for forensic investigations. Else, if the image is detected to be counter-forensically modified, the proposed model tries to identify the class of source anonymization performed on it, so as to assist the forensic analyst to adopt possible measures for retrieving the image back to its original form. This is done by a multi-class classification among the major classes of state-of-the-art source anonymization techniques, using deep learning.

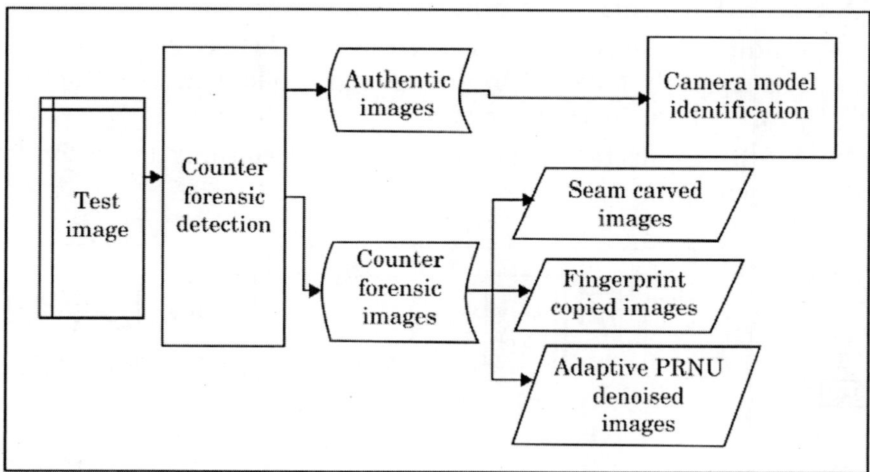


**Fig. 1:** The Operational Flowchart

In a machine learning based classification system, the feature representations have to be accurately defined. However, in scenarios where it is impossible or difficult to predefine a feature representation of given dataset, machine learning techniques are bound to fail. Deep learning techniques, having the ability to acquire knowledge through the inherent characteristics of training data where the knowledge acquired is stored as the weights of the network, overcomes this limitation of machine learning models. Regular neural networks do perform well in image classification, but due to high computational complexity and as the weights in successive layers keep on increasing, having a full connectivity in every layer, would involve huge number of parameters, and quickly lead to overfitting.

## 3. CNN ARCHITECTURE

The CNN architecture for performing the classification is shown in Fig. 2. The architecture indicates the following:

- The first convolution layer (Conv1) with a 3 × 3 kernel and 32 filters, followed by a Rectifier Linear Unit (ReLU).
- The second convolution layer (Conv2) with a 3 × 3 kernel and 32 filters, followed by another ReLU.
- Max Pooling with a 2 × 2 window, followed by the first dropout layer (DropOut1) with drop out parameter 0.2.
- A fully connected layer, followed by a ReLU activation, which is subsequently followed by the second dropout layer (DropOut2) with drop out parameter of 0.5.
- A fully connected layer, followed by a softmax layer for loss computation.

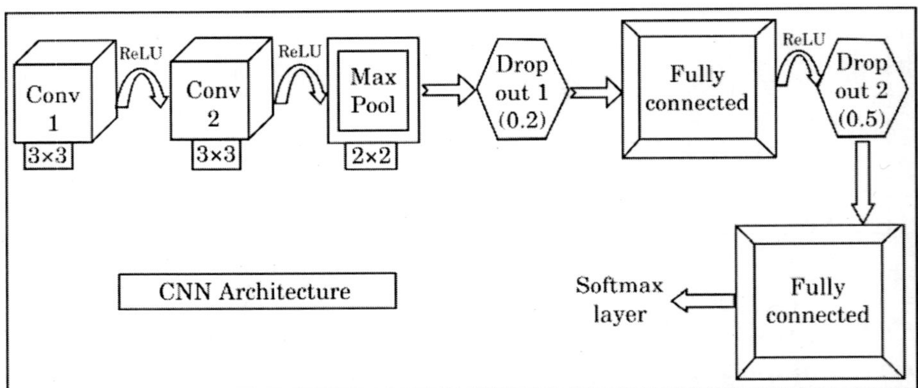


**Fig. 2:** CNN Architecture

## 4. EXPERIMENTAL SETTING

The experiments are conducted on the Dresden Image Database[91], which is a benchmark dataset, available publicly for image forensic research. In this work, a total of 12,500 natural images of the Dresden database are used, out of which 5,000 are authentic and the rest 7,500 are counter-forensically modified. The 7,500 counter-forensic images, consist of three sets of 2,500 images, modified manually through seam carving, fingerprint copy attack and Adaptive PRNU Denoising, respectively.

The proposed CNN takes input on varied batches as 64, 128 and 256 for 32 × 32, 64 × 64 and 128 × 128 image blocks. The proposed network architecture is presented in Fig. 2. A 3 × 3 kernel is used in convolution and a 2 × 2 window in max pooling layer. The convolution layers are followed by a ReLU activation to introduce non-linearity. All the different batches are trained using Stochastic Gradient Descent (SGD) with a momentum fixed at 0.9, learning rate of 0.01 and decay of 0.005. Two dropout layers are used to fight overfitting with dropout probabilities 0.2 and 0.5 respectively. The last layer is a softmax layer that computes the loss function. The CNN training is carried out using the keras framework developed for deep learning. We have used a workstation with an Intel Xeon CPU (E3-1225 v5, 3.3GHz), 16GB RAM and a GPU (Geforce GTX 970) with 1664 CUDA cores.

## 5. EXPERIMENTAL RESULTS

The first step in the proposed methodology is to perform a binary classification between authentic and counter-forensic images. The training samples are labelled with two classes: authentic (5000 samples) or counter-forensic (7500 samples). The confusion matrix representing the binary classification results is shown in Table 1. The overall classification accuracy achieved is 93.4%.

**Table 1:** Confusion matrix representing the binary classification results

| ***Actual*** | ***Predicted*** | |
|---|---|---|
| | ***Authentic*** | ***Counter Forensic*** |
| Authentic | 94.72% | 5.28% |
| Counter Forensic | 7.48% | 92.52% |

In the second step, the counter-forensic images are further classified according to the class of source anonymization attack that they have undergone (seam carved, fingerprint copied, or APD). 2500 labelled training samples are used from each type of counter-forensic class. In Table 2, the second level classification accuracy results are presented between seam carved, fingerprint copied, and PRNU denoised images, with varied image sizes (32 × 32, 64 × 64 and 128 × 128) and batch sizes (64; 128; 256). The maximum classification accuracy of 85.7% is reached for image size 64 × 64, and batch size 128, using a stochastic gradient descent optimizer with learning rate of 0.01 and momentum of 0.9. As evident from Table 2, the classification accuracy varies with image (crop-out) size. The best performance is observed with 64 × 64 sized images.

**Table 2:** Experimental results

| *Image Size* | *32 × 32* | | | *64 × 64* | | | *128 × 128* | | |
|---|---|---|---|---|---|---|---|---|---|
| Batch Size | 64 | 128 | 256 | 64 | 128 | 256 | 64 | 128 | 256 |
| 100 epochs | 33.3 | 48.7 | 48.4 | 73.1 | 72.6 | 75.1 | 36.7 | 34.3 | 33.3 |
| 200 epochs | 42.7 | 50.1 | 53.6 | 76.4 | 78.1 | 76.2 | 42.2 | 40.2 | 38.3 |
| 300 epochs | 48.1 | 52.6 | 56.2 | 77.3 | 81.2 | 77.9 | 50.4 | 52.6 | 42.4 |
| 500 epochs | 52.3 | 59.3 | 59.1 | 81.5 | 84.2 | 82.6 | 55.2 | 57.3 | 51.3 |
| 1000 epochs | 55.7 | 61.2 | 60.2 | 84.6 | 85.7 | 84.1 | 59.2 | 61.2 | 56.4 |

## 6. CONCLUSIONS

In image source identification, the presence of counter-forensic images posess serious threat to a forensic analyst, with respect to the credibility of the investigation results. Thus it is of paramount importance to identify whether an image is counter-forensically modified, and hence to remove those from the source identification module. In this work, a counter-forensic image classification has been performed, by adopting a two-level classification mechanism. At level one the proposed system distinguishes between authentic and counter-forensically modified images. At level two, the counter-forensic images are further classified according to the source anonymization attack that they have undergone. Future research in this direction would involve formulation of anti-counter-forensic measures to combat the existing counter-forensic attacks, and hence to achieve highly accurate source identification, even with counter-forensic images.

# References


[1] Lukas J., J. Fridrich, and M. Goljan, "Digital camera identification from sensor pattern noise," IEEE Transactions on Information Forensics and Security, vol. 1, no. 2, pp. 205–214, 2006.

[2] Farid A.P., A.C. Popescu, "Exposing digital forgeries by detecting duplicated image region", Technical Report, Hanover, Department of Computer Science, Dartmouth College, USA, 2004.

[3] Pan X., and S. Lyu, "Detecting image region duplication using SIFT features," in Proceedings of IEEE International Conference on Acoustics Speech and Signal Processing (ICASSP, pp. 1706-1709), 2010.

[4] Huang H., W. Guo, and Y. Zhang, "Detection of copy-move forgery in digital images using SIFT algorithm," in Proceedings of Pacific-Asia Workshop on Computational Intelligence and Industrial Application (PACIIA), vol. 2, pp. 272–276, 2008.

[5] Farid H., "A Survey of image forgery detection," IEEE Signal Processing Magazine, vol. 26, no. 2, pp. 16-25, 2009.

[6] Zach F., C. Riess, and E. Angelopoulou, "Automated image forgery detection through classification of JPEG ghosts," in Joint DAGM (German Association for Pattern Recognition) and OAGM Symposium. Springer, Berlin, Heidelberg, pp. 185-194, 2012.

[7] Wallace G.K., "The JPEG still picture compression standard," IEEE transactions on consumer electronics, vol. 38, no. 1, pp. xviii—xxxiv, 1992.

[8] Sameer V.U., S. Sugumaran, R. Naskar, "K-unknown models detection through clustering in blind source camera identification," IET Image Processing, vol. 12, no. 7, pp: 1204-13, 2017.

[9] Gloe T., "Feature-based forensic camera model identification," Transactions on Data Hiding and Multimedia Security VIII, pp. 42–62, Springer, 2012.

[10] Huang Y., J. Zhang, H. Huang, "Camera model identification with unknown models," IEEE Transactions on Information Forensics and Security, vol. 10, no. 12, pp. 2692-2704, 2015.

[11] Costa F.D., E. Silva, M. Eckmann, WJ. Scheirer, and A. Rocha, "Open set source camera attribution and device linking," Pattern Recognition Letters, vol. 39, pp. 92-101, 2014.

[12] Karakucuk A. and A. E. Dirik, "Adaptive photo-response non-uniformity noise removal against image source attribution," Digital Investigation, vol. 12, pp. 66–76, 2015.

[13] Quiring E. and M. Kirchner, "Fragile sensor fingerprint camera identification," in Proceedings of IEEE International Workshop on Information Forensics and Security (WIFS), pp. 1–6, 2015.

[14] Dirik A.E., H. T. Sencar, and N. Memon, "Analysis of seam-carving based anonymization of images against PRNU noise pattern-based source attribution," IEEE Transactions on Information Forensics and Security, vol. 9, no. 12, pp. 2277–2290, 2014.

[15] Kharrazi M., H. T. Sencar, and N. Memon, "Blind source camera identification," in Proceedings of IEEE International Conference on Image Processing, vol. 1, pp. 709–712, 2004.

[16] Celiktutan O., and B. Sankur, "Blind identification of source cell-phone model," IEEE Transactions on Information Forensics and Security, vol. 3, no. 3, pp. 553–566, 2008.

[17] Tsai M.J., CS. Wang, J. Liu, and JS. Yin, "Using decision fusion of feature selection in digital forensics for camera source model identification," Computer Standards & Interfaces, vol. 34(3), pp. 292-304, 2012.

[18] Marra F., G. Poggi, C. Sansone, and L. Verdoliva, "Evaluation of residual-based local features for camera model identification," *In* Proceedings of International Conference on Image Analysis and Processing, pp. 11–18, Springer, 2015.

[19] Akshatha K., A. Karunakar, H. Anitha, U. Raghavendra, and D. Shetty, "Digital camera identification using PRNU: A feature based approach," Digital Investigation, vol. 19, pp. 69–77, 2016.

[20] Roy A., R.S. Chakraborty, V.U. Sameer, R. Naskar, "Camera Source Identification Using Discrete Cosine Transform Residue Features and Ensemble Classifier," in Proceedings of IEEE International workshop on Computer Vision and Pattern Recognition (CVPR, pp. 1848-1854), 2017.

[21] Xu B., X. Wang, X. Zhou, J. Xi, and S. Wang, "Source camera identification from image texture features," Neurocomputing, vol. 207, pp. 131–140, 2016.

[22] Goljan M., J. Fridrich, and T. Filler, "Large scale test of sensor fingerprint camera identification," Media Forensics and Security, vol. 7254. International Society for Optics and Photonics, p. 72540I, 2009.

[23] Gisolf F., A. Malgoezar, T. Baar, and Z. Geradts, "Improving source camera identification using a simplified total variation based noise removal algorithm," Digital Investigation, vol. 10(3), pp. 207-14, 2013.

[24] Bayram S., H. T. Sencar, and N. Memon, "Sensor fingerprint identification through composite fingerprints and group testing," IEEE Transactions on Information Forensics and Security, vol. 10, no. 3, pp. 597-612, 2015.

[25] Lin X., CT. Li, "Preprocessing reference sensor pattern noise via spectrum equalization," IEEE Transactions on Information Forensics and Security, vol. 11, no. 1, pp. 126-40, 2016.

[26] Lawgaly A., and F. Khelifi, "Sensor pattern noise estimation based on improved locally adaptive DCT filtering and weighted averaging for source camera identification and verification," IEEE Transactions on Information Forensics and Security, vol. 12, no, 2, pp. 392-404, 2017.

[27] D. Valsesia, G. Coluccia, T. Bianchi, and E. Magli, "Compressed fingerprint matching and camera identification *via* random projections," IEEE Transactions on Information Forensics and Security, vol. 10, no. 7, pp. 1472-85, 2015.

[28] Tuama A., F.Comby, "Camera model identification with the use of deep convolutional neural networks," *In* Proceedings of IEEE International Workshop on Information Forensics and Security, pp. 6, 2016.

[29] Gloe T. and R. Bohme, "The Dresden image database for benchmarking digital image forensics," Journal of Digital Forensic Practice, vol. 3, no. 2-4, pp. 150–159, 2010.

[30] Krizhevsky A., I. Sutskever, and G. Hinton, "Imagenet classification with deep convolutional neural networks," in Advances in Neural Information Processing Systems, pp. 1097-1105, 2012.

[31] Szegedy C., W. Liu, Y. Jia, P. Sermanet, S. Reed, D. Anguelov, D. Erhan, V. Vanhoucke, A. Rabinovich, "Going deeper with convolutions," *In* Proceedings of IEEE Conference on Computer Vision and Pattern Recognition (CVPR), 2015.

[32] Bondi L., L. Baroffio, D. G¨uera, P. Bestagini, E. J. Delp, and S. Tubaro, "First steps toward camera model identification with convolutional neural networks," IEEE Signal Processing Letters, vol. 24, no. 3, pp. 259–263, 2017.

[33] Chen M., J. Fridrich, M. Goljan, and J. Lukas, "Determining image origin and integrity using sensor noise," IEEE Transactions on Information Forensics and Security, vol. 3, no. 1, pp. 74–90, 2008.

[34] Marra F., D. Gragnaniello, and L. Verdoliva, "On the vulnerability of deep learning to adversarial attacks for camera model identification", Signal Processing: Image Communication, vol 8, pp. 65-240, 2018.

[35] Cox I., M. Miller, J. Bloom, J. Fridrich, and T. Kalker, "Digital watermarking and steganography", Morgan Kaufmann, 2007.

[36] Sencar H.T., and N. Memon, "Overview of state-of-the-art in digital image forensics", Algorithms, Architectures and Information Systems Security, pp. 325–348, 2008.

[37] Redi J.A., W. Taktak, and J. Dugelay, "Digital image forensics: A booklet for beginners," Multimedia Tools and Application, vol. 51, pp. 133–162, 2011.

[38] Britz M.T., Computer Forensics and Cyber Crime: An Introduction, 2/ E. Pearson Education India, 2009.

[39] Kang X., and S. Wei, "Identifying tampered regions using singular value decomposition in digital image forensics," *In* Proceedings of International Conference Computer Science and Software Engineering, vol. 3, pp. 926–930, 2009.

[40] Zhang J., Z. Feng, and Y. Su, "A new approach for detecting copy–move forgery in digital images," In Proceedings of 11th IEEE Singapore International Conference on Communication Systems, pp. 362–366, 2008.

[41] Muhammad G., M. Hussain, G. Bebisi, "Passive copy–move image forgery detection using undecimated dyadic wavelet transform," Digital Investigation, vol. 9, no. 1, pp. 49–57, 2012.

[42] Lynch G., F. Y. Shih, and H.M. Liao, "An efficient expanding block algorithm for image copy–move forgery detection," Information Science, vol. 239, pp. 253–265, 2013.

[43] Caldelli R., I. Amerini, and L. Ballan, "On the effectiveness of local warping against SIFT-based copy–move detection," *In* Proceedings of IEEE Conference on Communications Control and Signal Processing (ISCCSP), pp. 1–5, 2012.

[44] Davarzani R., K. Yaghmaie, and S. Mozaffari, "Copy–move forgery detection using multiresolution local binary patterns," Forensic Science International, vol. 231, no. 1, pp. 61–72, 2013.

[45] Wu Y., Y. Deng, and H. Duan, "Digital dual tree complex wavelet transform approach to copy-rotate-move forgery detection," Journals of Computer Information System, vol. 57, no. 1, pp. 1–12, 2014.

[46] Park C.S., C. Kim, J. Lee, and G. R. Kwon, G, "Rotation and scale invariant upsampled log-polar fourier descriptor for copy-move forgery detection," Multimedia Tools and Applications, vol. 75, no. 23, pp. 16577–16595, 2016.

[47] Zhu Y., X. Shen, and H. Chen, "Copy–move forgery detection based on scaled ORB," Multimedia Tools and Application, vol. 75, no. 6, pp. 3221–3233, 2015.

[48] Dixit R. and R. Naskar, "Copy–move forgery detection utilizing Fourier–Mellin transform log-polar features," Journal of Electronic Imaging, vol. 27, no. 2, pp. 023007, 2018.

[49] Sheng Y. and H. H. Arsenault, "Experiments on pattern recognition using invariant Fourier- Mellin descriptors," Journal of the Optical Society of America, vol. 3, no. 6, pp. 771–776, 1986.

[50] Hotta K., M. Taketoshi, and K. Takio, "Scale invariant face detection and classification method using shift invariant features extracted from log-polar image," IEICE Transactions on Information and Systems, vol. 84, no. 7, pp. 867–878, 2001.

[51] Ruanaidh o., Joseph JK, and T. Pun, "Rotation, scale and translation invariant digital image water- marking," *In* Proceedings of International Conference on Image Processing, vol. 1, pp. 536–539, 1997.

[52] Hartigan J. and M. Wong, "Algorithm as 136: A k-means clustering algorithm," Journal of the Royal Statistical Society. Series C (Applied Statistics), vol. 8, no. 1, pp. 100–108, 1979.

[53] Birajdara G.K., V. H. Mankar, "Digital image forgery detection using passive techniques: a survey", Digital Investigation, pp. 226–245, 2013.

[54] Redi J.A., W. Taktak, and J. Dugelay, "Image splicing detection using 2D phase congruency and statistical moments of characteristic function", *In* Proceedings of Society of Photo-optical Instrumentation Engineers (SPIE) Conference Series, vol. 6505, pp. 26, 2007.

[55] Fridrich A.J., B. D. Soukal, and A. J. Lukáš, "Detection of copy–move forgery in digital images," *In* Proceeding of Digital Forensic Research Workshop, 2003.

[56] Yang J., P. Ran, and J. Tan, "Digital image forgery forensics by using undecimated dyadic wavelet transform and Zernike moments," Journal of Computer Information Systems, vol. 9, no. 16, pp. 6399–6408, 2013.

[57] Bayram S., H.T. Sencar, and T.N. Memon, "An efficient and robust method for detecting copy–move forgery," *In* Proceedings of IEEE International Conference Acoustics, Speech and Signal Processing, pp. 1053–1056, 2009.

[58] Huang Y., W. Lu, W. Sun, and D. Long, "Improved DCT-based detection of copy–move forgery in images," Forensic Science International, vol. 206, no. 1, pp. 178–184, 2011.

[59] Savchenko V., N. Kojekine, and H. Unno, "A practical image retouching method," *In* Proceedings of First International Symposium on Cyber Worlds, pp. 480–487, 2002.

[60] Christlein V., C. Riess, J. Jordan, C. Riess, and E. Angelopoulou, "An evaluation of popular copy– move forgery detection approaches," IEEE Transactions on Information Forensics and Security, vol. 6, pp. 1841–1854, 2012.

[61] Cao Y., T. Gao, and L. Fan, "A robust detection algorithm for copy–move forgery in digital images," Journal of Forensic Science, vol. 214, no. 1, pp. 33–43, 2012.

[62] Lin H.J., C.W. Wang, and Y. T. Kao, "Robust detection of region-duplication forgery in digital image," Pattern Recognition, vol. 4, pp. 746–749, 2006.

[63] Ling H., C. Wang, and Y. Kao, "Fast copy–move forgery detection," WSEAS Transactions, Signal Processing, vol. 5, no. 5, pp. 188–197, 2009.

[64] Lee J., "Digital image enhancement and noise filtering by use of local statistics," IEEE Transactions on Pattern Analysis and Machine Intelligence, vol. 2, pp. 165–168, 1980.

[65] Wallace G., "The JPEG still picture compression standard," IEEE Transactions on Consumer Electronics, vol. 34 (4), pp. 30–44, 1991.

[66] Li G., Q. Wu and D. Tu, "A sorted neighborhood approach for detecting duplicated regions in image forgeries based on DWT and SVD," *In* Proceedings of IEEE International Conference on Multimedia and Expo, pp. 1750–1753, 2007.

[67] Sunil K., D. Jagan, and M. Shaktidev, "DCT-PCA based method for copy–move forgery detection," *In* Proceedings of 48th Annual Convention of Computer Society of India, vol. 2, pp. 577–583, 2014.

[68] Wang H., and C. Shi, "An efficient passive authentication scheme for copy–move forgery based on DCT," in Proceedings of International Conference on Cloud Computing and Security, pp. 417–429, 2016.

[69] Gonzalez R.C., and R. E. Woods, "Digital image processing," Pearson Education India, 2009.

[70] Wang L., Y. Zhang, and J. Feng, "On the Euclidean distance of images," IEEE Transactions on Pattern Analysis and Machine Intelligence, vol. 27, no. 8, pp. 1334–1339, 2005.

[71] Androutsost D., K. N. Plataniotist, and A. N. Venetsanopoulost, "Distance measures for color image retrieval," *In* Proceedings of International Conference on Image Processing, vol. 2, pp. 770–774, 1998.

[72] Yap P.T., and P. Raveendran, "Image focus measure based on Chebyshev moments," Journal of Vision, Image and Signal Processing, vol. 151, no. 2, pp. 128–136, 2004.

[73] V. C. Klema, and A. J. Laub, "The singular value decomposition: Its computation and some applications," Transactions on Automatic Control, vol. 25, no. 2, pp. 164–176, 1980.

[74] Ting Z., and W. R. Ding, "Copy–move forgery detection based on SVD in digital image," *In* Proceedings of Second International Congress on Image and Signal Processing, 2009.

[75] Kingsbury N., "A dual-tree complex wavelet transforms with improved orthogonality and symmetry properties," *In* Proceedings of International Conference on Image Processing, vol. 2, pp. 375–378, 2014.

[76] Computer Vision Group, University of Granada Image Database, Computer Vision Group, University of Granada. [Online]. Available: http://decsai.ugr.es/cvg (accessed on Feb. 16, 2016).

[77] Signal and Image Processing Institute, University of Southern California, Department of Electrical Engineering. [Online]. Available: http://sipi.usc.edu/database/database.php?volume=misc (accessed on Feb. 16, 2016).

[78] Muhammad G., Al-Hammadi, M. Hussain, and G. Bebis, "Image forgery detection using steerable pyramid transform and local binary pattern," Machine Vision and Applications, vol. 25, no. 4, pp. 985–995, 2014.

[79] Ustubioglu B., G. Ulutas, M. Ulutas, V. Nabiyev, and A. Ustubioglu, "LBP-DCT based copy move forgery detection algorithm," Information Sciences and Systems, pp.127–136, Springer, 2016.

[80] Lee J., C. Chang, and W. Chen, "Detection of copy–move image forgery using histogram of orientated gradients," Information Sciences, vol. 321, pp 250–262, 2015.

[81] Huang D.., C. Huang, W. Hu, and C. Chou, "Robustness of copy-move forgery detection under high jpeg compression artifacts," Multimedia Tools and Applications, vol. 76, no. 1, pp. 1509–1530, 2017.

[82] Li L., S. Li, H. Zhu, and X. Wu, "Detecting copy-move forgery under affine transforms for image forensics," Computers and Electrical Engineering, vol. 40, no. 6, pp.1951–1962, 2014.

[83] Li L., S. Li, and J. Wang, "Copy-move forgery detection based on PHT," in Proceedings of World Congress on Information and Communication Technologies (WICT) pp.1061–1065, 2012.

[84] Lin H., C. Wang, and Y. Kao, "Fast copy-move forgery detection," World Scientific and Engineering Academy and Society Transactions on Signal Processing, vol. 5, no. 5, pp. 188–197, 2009.

[85] Sridevi M., C. Mala, S. Sandeep, and N. Meghanathan, "Copy–move image forgery detection in a parallel environment," SIPM, FCST, ITCA, WSE, ACSIT, CS and IT, vol. 6, pp. 19–29, 2012.

[86] B. Mahdian, and S. Saic, "A bibliography on blind methods for identifying image forgery," Signal Processing: Image Communication, vol. 25, pp. 389–399, 2010.

[87] Tralic D., S. Grgic, X. Sun, and P.L. Rosin, "Combining cellular automata and local binary patterns for copy-move forgery detection," Multimedia Tools and Applications, vol. 75, no. 24, pp. 16881–16903, 2016.

[88] Dixit R. and R. Naskar, "Dywt based copy-move forgery detection with improved detection accuracy," *In* Proceedings of 3rd International Conference on Signal Processing and Integrated Networks (SPIN) pp.133–138, 2016.

[89] Amerini I., L. Ballan, and R. Caldelli, "Copy–move forgery detection and localization by means of robust clustering with J-linkage," Signal Processing: Image Communication, vol. 28, no. 6, pp. 659–669, 2013.

[90] Dixit R., R. Naskar, and S. Mishra, "Blur-invariant copy-move forgery detection technique with improved detection accuracy utilising SWT-SVD," IET Image Processing, vol. 11, no. 5, pp. 301-309, 2017.

[91] Lin X. and C.-T. Li, "Large-scale image clustering based on camera fingerprints," IEEE Transactions on Information Forensics and Security, vol. 12, no. 4, pp. 793–808, 2017.

[92] G. Nason and B. Silverman, "The stationary wavelet transforms and some statistical applications," *In* Wavelets and Statistics (Lecture Notes in Statistics, pp. 281–299), Springer, 1995.

[93] Thajeel S. and G. Sulong, "A novel approach for detection of copy move forgery using completed robust local binary pattern," Journal of Information Hiding Multimedia Signal Process, vol. 6, no. 2, pp. 351–364, 2015.

[94] Bo X., W. Junwen, L. Guangjie, and D. Yuewei, "Image copy-move forgery detection based on SURF," *In* Proceedings of International Conference on Multimedia Information Networking and Security, pp. 889–892, 2010.

[95] L. Li, S. Li, H. Zhu, S. Chu, F. Roddick, and J. Pan, "An efficient scheme for detecting copy-move forged images by local binary patterns," Journal of Information Hiding and Multimedia Signal Processing, vol. 4 , no. 1, pp. 46–56, 2013.

[96] Ardizzone E., A. Bruno, and G. Mazzola, "Copy–move forgery detection by matching triangles of key points," IEEE Transactions on Information Forensics and Security, vol. 10, no. 10, pp. 2084-94, 2015.

[97] Yang B., X. Sun, H. Guo, Z. Xia, and X. Chen, "A copy-move forgery detection method based on CMFD–SIFT," Multimedia Tools and Applications, vol. 77, no. 1, pp. 837-855, 2018.

[98] Li J., X. Li, B. Yang, and X. Sun, "Segmentation–based image copy-move forgery detection scheme," IEEE Transactions on Information Forensics and Security, vol. 10 no. 3, pp. 507–518, 2015.

[99] Zhu Y., X. Shen, and H. Chen, "Copy-move forgery detection based on scaled ORB," Multimedia Tools and Applications, vol. 75, no. 6, pp. 3221–3233, 2016.

[100] Wu Q., S. Wang, and X. Zhang, "Log-polar based scheme for revealing duplicated regions in digital images," IEEE Signal Processing Letters, vol. 18, no. 10, pp. 559–562, 2011.

[101] Cozzolino D., G. Poggi, and I. Verdoliva, "Efficient dense-field copy–move forgery detection," IEEE Transactions on Information Forensics and Security, vol. 10, no. 11, pp. 2284–2297, 2015.

[102] Li W., and N. Yu, "Rotation robust detection of copy-move forgery," in Proceedings of 17th IEEE International Conference on Image Processing (ICIP), pp. 32113–2116, 2010.

[103] Goutte C., P. Toft, E. Rostrup, F. Nielsen, and L. K. Hansen, "On clustering fMRI time series," NeuroImage, vol. 9, pp. 298–310, 1999.

[104] Tralic D., I. Zupancic, S. Grgic, and M. Grgic, "CoMoFoD–New database for copy-move forgery detection," *In* Proceedings of 55th International Symposium, pp.49–54, 2013.

[105] Jing L. and C. Shao, "Image copy-move forgery detecting based on local invariant feature," Journal of Multimedia, vol. 7, no. 1, pp. 90-97, 2012.

[106] Hashmi M., V. Anand, and A. Keskar, "Copy-move Image Forgery Detection Using an Efficient and Robust Method Combining Undecimated Wavelet Transform and Scale Invariant Feature Transform," AASRI Procedia, vol. 9, pp.84-91, 2014.

[107] Lowe D., "Distinctive image features from scale in variant keypoints', International Journal of Computer Vision, vol. 60, no. 2, pp. 91-110, 2004.

[108] Bianchi T., A. De Rosa, and A. Piva, "Improved DCT coefficient analysis for forgery localization in JPEG images," *In* Acoustics, Speech and Signal Processing (ICASSP), IEEE International Conference on, pp. 2444–2447, 2011.

[109] Su Y., J. Zhang, and J. Liu, "Exposing Digital Video Forgery by Detecting Motion-Compensated Edge Artifact," *In* International Conference on Computational Intelligence and Software Engineering, pp. 1–4, 2009.

[110] Aghamaleki J.A. and A. Behrad, "Malicious inter-frame video tampering detection in MPEG videos using time and spatial domain analysis of quantization effects," Multimed. Tools and Applations., vol. 76, no. 20, pp. 20691–20717, 2017.

[111] Singh R.D. and N. Aggarwal, "Detection of upscale-crop and splicing for digital video authentication," Digital Investigation., vol. 21, pp. 31–52, 2017.

[112] Li J., W. Lu, J. Weng, Y. Mao, and G. Li, "Double JPEG compression detection based on block statistics," Multimed. Tools and Applications, pp. 1–16, 2018.

[113] Tariang D.B., A. Roy, R. S. Chakraborty, and R. Naskar, “Automated JPEG forgery detection with correlation based localization,” in IEEE International Conference on Multimedia & Expo Workshops (ICMEW), pp. 226–231, 2017.

[114] Zhang Z., J. Hou, Y. Zhang, J. Ye, and Y. Shi, “Detecting multiple H. 264/AVC compressions with the same quantisation parameters,” IET Information Security, vol. 11, no. 3, pp. 152–158, 2016.

[115] Lee J.C., C.P. Chang, and W.K. Chen, “Detection of copy-move image forgery using histogram of orientated gradients,” Information Sciences (Ny)., vol. 321, pp. 250–262, 2015.

[116] Shanableh T., “Detection of frame deletion for digital video forensics,” Digital Investigation, vol. 10, no. 4, pp. 350–360, 2013.

[117] Su Y., W. Nie, and C. Zhang, “A frame tampering detection algorithm for MPEG videos,” in 6th IEEE Joint International Information Technology and Artificial Intelligence Conference, vol. 2, pp. 461–464, 2011.

[118] Chen Y.L. and C.T. Hsu, “Detecting recompression of JPEG images via periodicity analysis of compression artifacts for tampering detection,” IEEE Transactions on Information Forensics and Security, vol. 6, no. 2, pp. 396–406, 2011.

[119] Chen C., Y.Q. Shi, and W. Su, “A machine learning based scheme for double JPEG compression,” *In* 19th IEEE International Conference on Pattern Recognition, pp. 1-4, 2008.

[120] Chao J., X. Jiang, and T. Sun, “A Novel Video Inter-frame Forgery Model Detection Scheme Based on Optical Flow Consistency,” *In* Proceedings of the 11th International Conference on Digital Forensics and Watermaking, pp. 267–281, 2013.

[121] Lin C.S. and J.J. Tsay, “Passive forgery detection for JPEG compressed image based on block size estimation and consistency analysis,” Applied Mathematics & Information Sciences, vol. 9, no. 2, pp. 1015, 2015.

[122] Gonzalez R.C. and R.E. woods, Digital Image Processing. Prentice hall Upper Saddle River, NJ, 2002.

[123] Sikora T., “MPEG digital video-coding standards,” IEEE Signal Processing Magazine, vol. 14, no. 5, pp. 82–100, Sep. 1997.

[124] Richardson I.E., H. 264 and MPEG-4 video compression: video coding for next-generation multimedia. John Wiley & Sons, 2004.

[125] Sullivan G.J., J.-R. Ohm, W.-J. Han, T. Wiegand, and others, “Overview of the high efficiency video coding (HEVC) standard,” IEEE Transactions on circuits and systems for video technology, vol. 22, no. 12, pp. 1649–1668, 2012.

[126] Lin P.Y., “Basic Image Compression Algorithm and Introduction to JPEG Standard,” Natl. Taiwan Univ. Taipei, Taiwan, ROC, 2009.

[127] Sitara K. and B. M. Mehtre, "Digital video tampering detection: An overview of passive techniques," Digital Investigation, vol. 18, no. Supplement C, pp. 8–22, 2016.

[128] Yu L., H. Wang, Q. Han, X. Niu, S.M. Yiu, J. Fang and Z. Wang, "Exposing frame deletion by detecting abrupt changes in video streams," Neurocomputing, vol. 205, pp. 84–91, 2016.

[129] Rec I., "H. 264 advanced video coding for generic audiovisual services," ITU-T Rec. H. 264-ISO/IEC 14496-10 AVC, 2005.

[130] Amerini I., L. Ballan, R. Caldelli, A. Del Bimbo, and G. Serra, "A sift-based forensic method for copy—move attack detection and transformation recovery," IEEE Transactions on Information Forensics and Security, vol. 6, no. 3, pp. 1099–1110, 2011.

[131] Lowe D.G., "Distinctive image features from scale-invariant keypoints," International Journal of Computer Vision, vol. 60, no. 2, pp. 91–110, 2004.

[132] Subramanyam A.V. and S. Emmanuel, "Video forgery detection using HOG features and compression properties.," in MMSP, pp. 89–94, 2012.

[133] Dalal N. and B. Triggs, "Histograms of oriented gradients for human detection," in Proceedings of IEEE Computer Society Conference on Computer Vision and Pattern Recognition (CVPR), vol. 1, pp. 886–893, 2005.

[134] Su L. and C. Li, "A novel passive forgery detection algorithm for video region duplication," Multidimensional Systems and Signal Processing, vol. 29, no. 3, pp. 1173–1190, 2018.

[135] Ma R., J. Chen, and Z. Su, "MI-SIFT: mirror and inversion invariant generalization for SIFT descriptor," *In* Proceedings of the ACM International Conference on Image and Video Retrieval, pp. 228–235, 2010.

[136] Jolliffe I.T. and J. Cadima, "Principal component analysis: a review and recent developments," Phil. Trans. R. Soc. A, vol. 374, no. 2065, p. 20150202, 2016.

[137] Chen S., S. Tan, B. Li, and J. Huang, "Automatic detection of object-based forgery in advanced video," IEEE Trans. Circuits Syst. Video Technol., vol. 26, no. 11, pp. 2138–2151, 2016.

[138] Labartino D., T. Bianchi, A. De Rosa, M. Fontani, D. Vázquez-Padín, A. Piva, M. Barni, "Localization of forgeries in MPEG-2 video through GOP size and DQ analysis," *In* IEEE 15th International Workshop on Multimedia Signal Processing (MMSP), pp. 494–499, 2013.

[139] Bidokhti A. and S. Ghaemmaghami, "Detection of regional copy/move forgery in MPEG videos using optical flow," *In* International Symposium on Artificial Intelligence and Signal Processing (AISP), pp. 13–17, 2015.

[140] Pevny T. and J. Fridrich, “Merging Markov and DCT features for multi-class JPEG steganalysis,” in Security, Steganography, and Watermarking of Multimedia Contents IX, vol. 6505, pp. 650503, 2007.

[141] Pevny T., P. Bas, and J. Fridrich, “Steganalysis by subtractive pixel adjacency matrix,” IEEE Transactions on Inforamtion Forensics and Security, vol. 5, no. 2, pp. 215–224, 2010.

[142] Kodovsky J., T. Pevn\‘y, and J. Fridrich, “Modern steganalysis can detect YASS,” *In* Media Forensics and Security II, vol. 7541, pp. 754102, 2010.

[143] Kodovsky J., J. Fridrich, and V. Holub, “Ensemble classifiers for steganalysis of digital media.,” IEEE Transactions on Inforamtion Forensics and Security, vol. 7, no. 2, pp. 432–444, 2012.

[144] Fridrich J. and J. Kodovsky, “Rich models for steganalysis of digital images,” IEEE IEEE Transactions on Inforamtion Forensics and Security, vol. 7, no. 3, pp. 868–882, 2012.

[145] Kodovsky J. and J. Fridrich, “Steganalysis of JPEG images using rich models,” *In* Media Watermarking, Security, and Forensics, vol. 8303, pp. 83030A, 2012.

[146] Wang W. and H. Farid, “Exposing digital forgeries in interlaced and deinterlaced video,” IEEE Transactions on Inforamtion Forensics and Security, vol. 2, no. 3, pp. 438–449, 2007.

[147] Hyun D. K., S.-J. Ryu, H.-Y. Lee, and H.-K. Lee, “Detection of upscale-crop and partial manipulation in surveillance video based on sensor pattern noise,” Sensors, vol. 13, no. 9, pp. 12605–12631, 2013.

[148] Zhang Z., J. Hou, Q. Ma, and Z. Li, “Efficient video frame insertion and deletion detection based on inconsistency of correlations between local binary pattern coded frames,” Security and Communication Networks, vol. 8, no. 2, pp. 311–320, 2015.

[149] Liu Y. and T. Huang, “Exposing video inter-frame forgery by Zernike opponent chromaticity moments and coarseness analysis,” Multimedia. Systems, vol. 23, no. 2, pp. 223–238, 2017.

[150] Li Z., Z. Zhang, S. Guo, and J. Wang, “Video inter-frame forgery identification based on the consistency of quotient of MSSIM,” Security and Communication Networks, vol. 9, no. 17, pp. 4548–4556, 2016.

[151] Aghamaleki J.A. and A. Behrad, “Inter-frame video forgery detection and localization using intrinsic effects of double compression on quantization errors of video coding,” Signal Processing: Image Communication, vol. 47, pp. 289–302, 2016.

[152] Wang W. and H. Farid, “Exposing digital forgeries in video by detecting double MPEG compression,” *In* Proceedings of the 8th Workshop on Multimedia and Security, pp. 37–47, 2006.

[153] Lucas B.D. and T. Kanade, "An Iterative Image Registration Technique with an Application to Stereo Vision," *In* Proceedings of the 7th International Joint Conference on Artificial Intelligence - Volume 2, pp. 674–679, 1981.

[154] Hall G., "Pearson's correlation coefficient," other words, vol. 1, no. 9, 2015. [Online]. Available: http://www.hep.ph.ic.ac.uk/~hallg/UG_2015/Pearsons.pdf (accessed on June 16, 2018).

[155] Amidan B.G., T. A. Ferryman, and S. K. Cooley, "Data outlier detection using the Chebyshev theorem," *In* IEEE Aerospace Conference, pp. 3814–3819, 2005.

[156] Zhao D.N., R.-K. Wang, and Z.-M. Lu, "Inter-frame passive-blind forgery detection for video shot based on similarity analysis," Multimedia Tools and Applications, pp. 1–20, 2018.

[157] Mandelli S., L. Bondi, S. Lameri, V. Lipari, P. Bestagini, and S. Tubaro, "Inpainting-Based camera anonymization," *In* Proceedings of IEEE International Conference on Image Processing (ICIP), pp. 1522-1526, 2017.

[158] V. U. Sameer, R. Naskar, N. Musthyala, and K. Kokkalla, "Deep learning based counter–forensic image classification for camera model identification," *In* Proceedings of International Workshop on Digital Watermarking, pp. 52–64, Springer, 2017.

# Subject Index

**T**



**U**



**W**